THESE
TURBULENT
TIMES

LIVERPOOL FC'S
SEARCH FOR SUCCESS

A TOMKINS TIMES
ANTHOLOGY
Volume I

PAUL TOMKINS
& VARIOUS AUTHORS

EDITED BY
CHRIS ROWLAND & DANIEL RHODES

Gprf
Publishing
Limited

ISBN 978-0955925344

Published By GPRF Publishing Limited

© **Paul Tomkins**

First edition published 2013.

Printed by Anchor Print Group Limited.

THE BEST OF
THE TOMKINS TIMES

By

Paul Tomkins @paul_tomkins
Daniel Rhodes @AnalyseSport
Chris Rowland @ChrisRowland1
Dan Kennett @DanKennett
Andrew Beasley @BassTunedToRed
Zach Slaton @the_number_game
James Keen @jimtheoracle
Matthew Harrison @mophead_88
Krish Bhautoo @krishaldo21
Simon Steers @sisteers
Paul Grech @paul_grech
Tony McKenna @LFCmarkets
Mihail Vladimirov @mihail_v
Lee Mooney @leejmooney
Daniel Geey @FootballLaw
Ted Knutson @mixedknuts
Ben Stoneman
Aki Pekuri
Martin McClaughlin
Dave Cronin
Graeme Riley
Bob Pearce
Andrew McKay
Neil Dunkin
and Mike Begon

Additional editing by Chris Hadley @cshadley

Cover illustrations by Dan Leydon:
danleydon.tumblr.com
etsy.com/shop/footynews
@danleydon on Twitter.

Tables and graphs by Nate Smith
ohyoubeauty.blogspot.com/
@natefc on Twitter.

All design and typesetting by Paul Tomkins.

For Jeff Reed, our friend and inspiration across the pond.

CONTENTS

6

INTRODUCTION

By Paul Tomkins

June, 2013

An Introduction to 'TTT'

The Tomkins Times was launched in September 2009, just a few months after Liverpool finished 2nd in the league with 86 points, but four weeks into a season which was already dogged by angst and unrest. Before introducing the 300 pages of football that follows, it seems appropriate to briefly discuss the site itself.

TTT has proved unexpectedly successful; perhaps even more surprisingly so given the club's worst run of league finishes for fifty years, coupled with a global recession. Looking back, it doesn't seem the best time to launch a paid subscription website, but to date it's worked very well. TTT exists because necessity is the mother of invention. Having had to rely solely on book sales to make a living (and unless you're JK Rowling, I wouldn't recommend trying it), I reached rock bottom when, with good results a key driver of sales, Liverpool slumped to another defeat and the weekly retail figures flatlined. Unable to work for anyone else due to chronic illness, I was at a loss.

At my wits' end, I invited my mailing list to send me ideas, and Anu Gupta, of Digital Query, was one of three people to suggest a subscription-based website; the difference between him and the other two was that he offered to build such a site for free, and to take a fee only if it took off. I had nothing to lose, but of course, people are very good at offering things only to never be heard from again. However, true to his word, Anu delivered the site, complete with paywall, within seven days. The aim was to get 200 people paying £3.50 a month, which, after PayPal took their cut, would cover my rent. We reached that figure within a couple of days, and by the end of the first month the total number of subscribers was around 500. Now the total is into the thousands.

Since its inception, the site has developed. Rather than remain an output for just my thoughts, I am employing other people to contribute, in terms of editing and writing. This has led to far more varied output than I alone could ever dream of mustering.

At TTT we don't think stats are everything, but we do think they can bolster arguments and provide insights. That said, they are always there to be challenged and debated. They are part of the story; but people need to work out *how much* of the story. We do a lot of work with analytics, given the number of professionals in that field who subscribe to the site, but their work is open to interpretation; a starting point for further investigation, a jumping-off point for further conversation. It's about getting a balance between what we see with our own eyes and what the data tells us, but *both* can be either true or misleading. As long as it's intelligently written and well researched, we are happy to have any type of article on the site. None of us think we know it all.

There have also been some unexpected benefits of the paywall, such as the excellent, mutually respectful nature of the community, with the fee putting off spammers, trolls, time-wasters and immature teens who think that what they see on the rest of the Internet is the normal way to behave. Indeed, in many ways the best part of the site is the village behind the walls, where newcomers are welcome, so long as they don't act like a fearsome idiot.

At times I managed to be in the right place at the right time, with access to the club that I never previously imagined possible. I've never been someone to insert myself into situations: in 2005, the club's website approached me to write for them; in 2009, shortly after the launch of TTT, Rafa Benítez invited me to Melwood to discuss all kinds of issues surrounding the club; and in 2010, John Henry got in touch to invite me to lunch, as part of his desire to get a wide range of opinions on the club he'd just bought.

The one thing I would change, in hindsight, is the name of the site, but as I was expecting it to be a fairly low-key blog featuring only my writing, and as I was eager to trade on the reputation I'd built up over the previous decade, it made sense to use "Tomkins" in the title (in a kind of homage to the Huffington Post). But it has grown into something where I remain only part of the equation.

Before moving onto the football, I'd like to thank all of the subscribers, who have kept the site afloat and thriving, and also those who have contributed over the years, in paid and unpaid capacities. These kind souls have helped add a wonderful breadth to the TTT canon. Thank you!

Four Years of Football

Four managers. Two sets of owners. One Director of Football. One famous court case. Two cup finals. One trophy. One racism scandal. Two Cuban heels. Three £20m+ players. One Serbian bitten in front of the Kop. Zero Champions League qualifications. All in all, a rather mixed bag, albeit a bag from which most of the good things have been removed.

TTT began life under Rafa Benítez, before a succession of managers replaced him in the dugout. Upon the firing of the Spaniard, Dion Fanning of the *Irish Independent* wrote that his tenure would be looked back upon as a golden era. He wasn't wrong. Already, just a few years on, it seems a world away, as the Reds yoyo between 6th and 8th, with a couple of forays into the relegation zone along the way.

By the end, Benítez was tired, and I was tired of defending his record to the fools who could not recognise a good thing when they saw it. His later transfers did not work out so well, and his budget was slashed by Gillett and Hicks going into what would turn out to be his final season; with £20m earmarked for a striker (and the mercurial Stevan Jovetić lined up), the Americans pulled the rug from under the manager.

The season started badly, with two defeats from the opening three games, which led Benítez, in light of criticism of young players like Lucas Leiva, to ask publicly that the senior players step up. This didn't go down too well with some of those in question. From then on the season was a kind of nosedive, in which levelling out was a mere temporary respite before the plunge returned. The Champions League campaign was poor, although the Reds were an away goal away from the final of the Europa League, the rebranded Uefa Cup which the Spaniard had won in 2004 and would win, with Chelsea of all clubs, in 2013. In the end, Liverpool could never quite mount a challenge for the top four, and finished 7th, with 63 points – albeit a total still not matched at the time of writing.

Change was needed. Ideally, Gillett and Hicks, along with their lackeys, would have been the ones heading out that summer, along with a few players. Instead, the manager was the scapegoat. In came Roy Hodgson, he of 35 years' experience and very little meaningful success outside of 1970s Scandinavia. He was expected to steady the ship, and did so in the manner of a lunatic firing a harpoon at its hull.

Hodgson's football was not easy on the eye. Esteemed Daily Show writer and performer (and Liverpool fan) John Oliver, speaking on his brilliant Bugle podcast, said Hodgson's Euro 2012 England side played "a style of football that was not easy on *any* of the five senses". Go back further to Hodgson's Liverpool days, and it wasn't so much about not being easy on the senses – it was frankly abusive to them.

There is Hodgson's famous irate exhortation from the technical area – as reported by those within hearing distance – that Daniel Agger, his cultured Danish centre-back, "Just fucking launch it!" This came after Hodgson's second Premier League game in charge – away at Manchester City – when, admittedly shorn of Javier Mascherano shortly before kick-off, he sent out his team in the seldom seen 4-4-acres-acres-tumbleweed-2, with Fernando Torres and David N'Gog expected to compete for a succession of hopeful punts upfield as the cavalry camped on the edge of their own box. Lucas Leiva was sidelined in favour of the ponderous Christian Poulsen, 30, with the Brazilian midfielder later admitting that Liverpool tried to move him on; and the hugely promising (if erratic) young left-back Emiliano Insúa usurped by the god-awful Paul Konchesky, 29. The short-sightedness of the situation was summed up in January 2013 when, with Hodgson's signing Konchesky now a regular in second-tier football, Insúa – at the age of 24 – was bought by a rampant Atlético Madrid, with the Spanish club paying Sporting Lisbon €10m. To make matters worse, 18-year-old Alex Kačaniklić, now excelling for Fulham and Sweden, was part of the deal that brought Konchesky to Anfield. Lunatics were running the asylum.

In came Joe Cole, 29, who, like Poulsen, used to be a better, fitter player. Although Hodgson consented, the deal was driven by Christian Purslow, a financier who seemed to fancy himself as some kind of football guru. Liverpool were buying the wrong types of players, at the wrong end of their careers, and overpaying in fees and/or wages. In fairness to Hodgson, he was simply a man promoted beyond his capabilities.

In October 2010, the Americans were finally ousted ... by more Americans. Still, at least FSG (or NESV as they then were) were regarded as the polar opposite of Gillett and Hicks in their homeland, having ended almost a century of failure at the Boston Red Sox. They were seen as smart and united, in contrast to those they wrested the club from, who were perceived as dumb and divided.

The new owners instantly installed Damien Comolli as Director of Football, although the Frenchman, despite some clever work at Spurs, didn't go on to cover himself in glory at Liverpool. By January, with the Reds losing too many games in poor style, the owners shocked the football world by bringing back the club's ultimate living legend, Kenny Dalglish. The team shot up the table, rising from below midway to 6th, with form that would have seen a 3rd-place finish if the 18 games were extrapolated to 38. This was achieved after the shock of Fernando Torres moving to Chelsea for £50m, and the even bigger surprise of Liverpool reinvesting £35m of it on Andy Carroll.

Dalglish's initial impact was just what was needed, although his record once made permanent manager (two games before the end of 2010/11 through to the end of 2011/12) did not read so well. The league form fell away markedly, to very poor levels, although he did take the Reds to two cup finals in his one full season back at the helm, winning one of them.

In March 2012, Damien Comolli was dismissed, presumably in relation to the recruitment of players for exorbitant fees. Carroll, his major folly, remains a good player, but the price tag wore away at any extra potential the Geordie may have otherwise possessed. Downing is steadily efficient, and at times fairly effective, but £20m was far too much for a player of his age and ability, particularly as he was pursued ahead of Juan Mata, who was perceived to lack the requisite work-rate. (Of course, this does not mean the Spaniard wouldn't still have gone to Chelsea.)

And the £16m spent on Jordan Henderson was widely derided throughout the Wearsider's debut season, even if, to this writer at least, he played well in central midfield when given the chance. A trio of signings under £10m (José Enrique, Craig Bellamy, Sebastián Coates and Charlie Adam) seemed somewhat inconsequential after the big splurge.

Of course, Luis Suárez was the one big success, and what a success! However, the Uruguayan arrived with a noted flip-side, and Comolli's inexperience when handling the aftermath of the Patrice Evra racism situation was perhaps another nail in his coffin. And strangely, as of June 2013, Liverpool have won 62% of the league games during Suárez's absences, and only 39% when he's played.

Despite racking up just 52 league points, Dalglish's dismissal still came as a shock. FSG wanted a new set-up: an experienced Director of Football (under a different title) working with an exciting young manager. They achieved the latter, although Brendan Rodgers, at a time when the club was said to be still looking to appoint someone like Louis Van Gaal as the technical overlord, made it clear in his inaugural press conference that he wouldn't work under anyone. This showed self-belief, but the club was now managed by a rookie boss who'd never won a trophy or finished in the top half of the Premier League table. He had, however, done a fine job at Swansea, and clearly had promise. But would that be enough?

In terms of results in his first season, it would appear *not quite*, even if there were aspects of the campaign that were pleasing, particularly after the halfway mark. The league form was nine points better, but that was when compared with a season (2011/12) in which there were terrible injuries (it says a lot that Charlie Adam and Jay Spearing were the two most frequent starters in central midfield in the league), two gruelling cup runs (a total of seven games against big rivals, plus games against Stoke) and the absolutely disastrous Suárez/Evra incident, which saw the star striker lose his goal touch amidst the furore, and – when finally banned all those months later – his eligibility to play football for nine matches.

Rodgers had also spent around £40m net in 2012/13, to add to what he inherited, but of course, he didn't have a five-month bedding in period like Dalglish (who also had 13 years before that, and the enormous goodwill of the fans). Also, the new man was expected to lower both the playing age and the wage bill.

However, no matter which way you stretch or spin it, Rodgers' impact – which, in a debut season, is so often a chance to inspire – was negligible across all competitions.

The Reds won 47% of their 51 matches in 2011/12 and 46.3% of their 54 in 2012/13. More goals were scored under Rodgers, and more clean sheets maintained, but the overall win rate was fractionally lower, and for traditionalists, there was nothing to polish for the trophy cabinet. However, optimism can be taken from the second half of the campaign, as new signings Daniel Sturridge and Philippe Coutinho elevated the XI to new heights. As long as they are not flashes in the pan – and their talent suggests that they are the real deal – then the manager and his technical committee are on the right lines.

The question for the future is whether or not Rodgers has helped lay strong foundations, or merely missed a great opportunity to make himself an instant favourite on the Kop with a trophy or a top four finish (or at least going close).

He has been fortunate to inherit what could prove to be best crop of youngsters in the club's history, with Raheem Sterling, Suso, Andre Wisdom, Jordon Ibe, Jerome Sinclair and João Carlos Teixeira all looking capable of becoming future superstars, and possibly even eclipsing the talent pool of the '90s. To his credit, Rodgers handled them well. The difference from the likes of Steve McManaman, Steven Gerrard, Michael Owen, Jamie Carragher and Robbie Fowler is that all six of these teenagers (as of the start of 2012/13) were bought in from other academies. Rather than hold the locals back, they are there to provide stiff competition, and to not limit the outlook of the club to those born in the area, given that, on average, each British city will only tend to produce one great player every few years. Hopefully the next world-class Liverpudlian will also be on Liverpool's books, but some Londoners, Midlanders and even boys from Braga and Cadiz can help spread the bets on future superstardom.

It feels clear to me that Liverpool FC is in a better place than at any time since the end of 2008/09. The club is not tearing itself apart, and the battle Rafa Benítez won to overhaul the youth set-up is bearing fruit. Rather than looking to sell to buy, there has been an investment in talent, even if that talent hasn't always been worth the money paid. A reasonable amount, in net terms, has been invested in the team since January 2011, and while Andy Carroll looks £20m "wasted" (if £15m is recouped), another youngster, Jordan Henderson, looks like a potential future captain. Jamie Carragher's retirement removes one stalwart from the equation, but otherwise the squad, at the time of writing, is almost entirely under 30 years old. Only Steven Gerrard, of the outfield players, is over that age, along with the recently-added Kolo Touré.

Question marks remain over Rodgers, given that he's never won a trophy and, as yet, has failed to show much of a killer instinct in *must-win* games, beyond the play-off final with Swansea. However, unlike Hodgson, his brand of football is suitable for a big club, and ideas like employing the eminent sports psychiatrist Dr Steve Peters could help make big improvements at little financial cost. With any luck, Rodgers will prove to be like Jürgen Klopp, who took his time in making Dortmund a great side. But we cannot be sure of anything yet, and as with Liverpool youth prodigies, it's dangerous to bestow greatness before it's been earned.

The summer of 2013 will give Rodgers the chance to create the team he wants. In a way, it might finally stop feeling like a Rafa Benítez team, with several of the former manager's players still key components up to this point. There are strong rumours of Pepe Reina and Martin Škrtel departing, and of course, Carragher, who was converted back to centre-back and coached to greatness by the Spaniard, has retired. It seems that Glen Johnson, Daniel Agger and Lucas Leiva, plus Steven Gerrard, will be the only first team players to remain from the halcyon days of Champions League runs and top three finishes.

This is clearly a new world for Liverpool FC. Let's hope it's a brave one.

MY LUNCH WITH 'THE QUIET AMERICAN'

By Paul Tomkins

November, 2010 and June 2013

Autumnal rain lashes down at sharp angles on a Liverpool city centre street as, looking smart but not waterproof, I await my first ever meeting with a billionaire. A large black SUV – expensive, but not ostentatious – pulls up to the kerb, and the driver – dressed in jeans – opens the door to allow the dignitary to alight.

In terms of the man's profile, the whole occasion is decidedly low-key. But then again, almost everything about John W Henry – the man who, less than a month earlier, had bought Liverpool Football Club – is understated. His clothes are smart-casual. His voice is little more than a whisper; a *low-talker*, as his compatriot Jerry Seinfeld might say. Softly spoken, but certainly not a *mumbler*.

I know some of the 'SaveLFC' guys who met with him a couple of weeks back, and they said he even carried the drinks. He's that kind of guy. When I emailed him a PDF of my new book in reply to his initial contact, he was genuinely thankful, as if I'd emailed him a new born baby converted into binary code. In person I experienced no obvious ego, but a great belief in winning. If I had to sum him up in two words, I'd say 'quiet confidence'.

First of all, the whole occasion nearly never happened. A *John W Henry* sent me a message more than a week ago asking me to give him a call, but as it was from a Facebook account with almost no activity, I ignored it, as you would. Hoaxers, eh?

It was only when he began to follow me on Twitter a number of days later, coinciding with an email from a 'John W Henry' a couple of minutes later, that I realised it was the man himself. He got in touch as, having tried to find out as much as possible about the club many months ago, he ordered a whole stack of books from Amazon. I don't know what he thought of the others he read, but he liked mine.

He said he wanted my thoughts on NESV's ideas for the club; not to get involved with them, merely to see what my reaction was. Now obviously, it's not my place to explain what those ideas are before NESV are in a position to do so – and some are purely theoretical at this stage – but my reaction was one of great encouragement. They sounded eminently sensible. Nothing flashy, nothing silly, nothing to try and woo the fans; above all else, no false promises. And I'm sure there's lots he didn't tell me, too. But I got the feeling this is now a club that can keep its best players, and add young, hungry, up-and-coming top-class talent to improve the team.

(As I am about to hit Send to publish this piece, Damien Comolli – former Arsenal scout and the man who signed many of Spurs' better players, and who shares NESV's 'Moneyball' vision – has been appointed, presumably as Director of Football. I knew from yesterday that something along these lines was going to happen with regard to overseeing transfers, but only joined the dots earlier today when Comolli quit his post at St Etienne.)

No-one can predict the future, and Henry accepts that a few mistakes may be made along the way – who doesn't make mistakes in football? – but I liked what I heard. Success cannot be guaranteed, but the club will be much better run from now on. Most importantly, the Gillett and Hicks acquisition debt has been cleared, so the club is no longer haemorrhaging money.

The primary aim has to be to undo all the bad work of the previous administration and ousting them means the biggest part is already taken care of. More will follow. But it's about building up again from a base, after the previous owners almost razed the club to the ground. It's clear that NESV don't have the insane kinds of money that some of our rivals possess – those 'super-benefactors' – so it's about being clever; as they were with the Red Sox, in ending 86 years of 'hurt' as we say in this country. But football over here is a more unequal system, and he's still trying to get his head around how differently players' contracts are treated (and honoured) in England.

Let me be clear: I'm not interested in doing his PR. Go and read anyone else's experiences of the man, and you'll find much the same experiences that I had. And he never asked anything of me, beyond my opinion. As loathed as Hicks is in US sporting circles, Henry is admired. You don't need me to tell you that. And I don't want to get involved on that level.

Because, as fans, our experience with Gillett and Hicks tells us that trust has to be *earned*; watch what people do, not what they say. That said, having been told of a couple of things they've already done behind the scenes, I have to say, they seem to mean business.

During our meal, Mr Henry's mobile phone rings two or three times; we are running well beyond our allotted time, and the person at the other end of the line, calling from Melwood, is having to wait for his chance of a tête-à-tête. "Fifteen more minutes, Roy." Finally, it's time for the club's owner to make his way to the training ground. In that initial meeting it was clear to me that Henry was labouring under the misconception that Hodgson won the title with Inter Milan, which was patently untrue; he seemed surprised when I set him straight on the matter. I also got to discover why Christian Purslow left the club, and gained a greater sense of what went on behind the scenes at one of the world's most famous sporting institutions.

Two hours on, as we await the bill, men from the restaurant kitchen queue at our table like nervous alter boys in order to shake his hand and have a scrap of paper signed. Then it's back out into the rain, and for me, back to what passes for normality.

* * *

I was fortunate enough to have further contact with the principal owner, up until March 2012. In November 2010 he asked who I thought could do a better job than Roy Hodgson, given that I felt the former Fulham man wasn't the right man for the club. I asked a respected football thinker, who does this kind of thing for a living, and he came back with a list of five up-and-coming managers, some of whom have gone on to great success and some of whom have failed to push on. I forwarded the list but never heard back. On top of these names, I did make it clear that I agreed with the fans' notion that Kenny Dalglish would make a good interim appointment, to unite a fractured fan-base and provide a better second half to the season (although this was two months before he was appointed). I didn't expect Dalglish's side to do quite so well in his first 16 league games back (with his role made permanent two games before the end of 2010/11, based on his positive impact), nor quite as poorly over the next 40. Henry knew that Hodgson wasn't the right man to take Liverpool forward, but despite asking for ideas on alternatives, he clearly didn't want to replace him until the summer of 2011. However, results under the Englishman continued to disappoint, and when 10,000 fans stayed away from the traditionally well-attended New Year's Day fixture, the writing was on the wall. Around that time, Henry had dinner with Kenny and Marina Dalglish, and also their son, Paul, at which point I knew change was coming.

After that I didn't hear too much from Henry, beyond the occasional email to ask about minor details, such as what I thought certain new signings would bring. He is a great asker of questions, and my assumption at the time was that he wanted, as a neophyte, to be able to ask the people who work for him intelligent football questions. He asked for my help in creating his own *Guardian* chalkboards.

I was invited to lunch again in late 2011, but due to my father's terminal cancer I was unable to attend. Henry sent a very thoughtful gift to my father at his hospice. And in late March 2012 Henry phoned one Sunday evening, out of the blue, following another league defeat, to ask about the best candidates to replace Damien Comolli, if the club went down that route; again, I passed him onto someone with a greater knowledge of European football, as I wouldn't know where to start. Henry did mention that other people had recommended that they speak to Johan Cruyff and Louis van Gaal, and I agreed that you couldn't get much better than those as sounding boards. Managerial performance wasn't discussed, although clearly the owner was worried about the league form.

All ties were broken shortly after that, when I was erroneously blamed by some mouth-frothing fans for Dalglish's dismissal. (Even though I wasn't totally sure where the team was headed under the great man, I would have to possess a death wish to suggest such a thing. I was genuinely shocked when he was sacked – because he is *Kenny Dalglish* – and unhappy at the way it was handled.)

It's fair to say that FSG's stewardship hasn't gone as smoothly as I was anticipating, although they have had to learn a lot in a short space of time, having taken over a club that was on its knees, with no prior experience of "soccer".

Dalglish did brilliantly as an interim coach, but that success left little leeway in terms of finding an alternative in the summer of 2011. He simply *had* to be appointed full-time, based on results. The Suarez/Evra affair worked against both Dalglish and Comolli, although the underwhelming manner in which they spent over £100m can't have gone down too well (although Suárez's increased value is reasonable recompense). And although the cups were important to the fans, it's harder to get back into the top four unless the league is prioritised; and the top four is football's virtuous circle, where greater funds and exposure lead to better players arriving, which helps build the kind of squad that can compete for the ultimate prizes. Funnily enough, the domestic cups are also often won by top four clubs, often with their shadow squads.

From the outset Henry said that NESV/FSG would make mistakes, although possibly a few too many have been made along the way, including, at times, a lack of leadership in Liverpool. However, the club, with its wage bill now under control and a promising young squad, seems set to move forward, if the right calls are made. The new transfer committee, in place too late for the summer of 2012, made an exceptional start by procuring Coutinho and Sturridge for £20m in January 2013, and a number of lucrative financial deals have been signed by the club, even if the new Warrior away kits are fairly ghastly. Progress on the stadium has been slow, but things finally seem to be moving along behind the scenes, with Anfield set to be expanded and refurbished.

In many ways I'm happy to be out of a loop I never asked to enter. While mine was only one of several opinions canvassed, I did feel the pressure of having to proffer something insightful, aware that, if I got it wrong, it might impact in a negative way. But while it lasted, it was fascinating to get some *genuine* insight, the like of which most fans will never experience. And whether or not FSG prove successful at Liverpool, I did get the sense that John Henry is a genuine man, more concerned with sporting success than profit. However, as a whole, the jury is still out, and time will be the ultimate judge of FSG's decisions and their motives.

MOMENTUM: CONFIDENCE OR CONFIDENCE TRICK?

By Mike Begon

April, 2012

"Of course I don't believe in it. But I understand it works whether you believe in it or not." – Physicist Niels Bohr, talking about a 'lucky' horseshoe.

Hardly a *Match of the Day* or a *Five Live 'Kicking Off'* goes by without someone mentioning 'momentum' or 'success breeding success' or something like it. In dark despair, after a long run of defeats, in desperate hope following a big win; everyone believes in momentum.

Everyone knows it must be a fact of sporting life. Most of us have experienced it – or feel we have. But is there actually anything in it? Twenty million people – or whatever it is – can't be wrong. Except that sometimes they can.

Momentum, psychological momentum and the momentum chain

To put it bluntly: for something to be true requires more than people *believing* it to be true. It requires evidence. Serious studies have gone in search of that evidence. Before examining them, though, we should define some terms and draw some distinctions that exist in the more technical literature. Psychological momentum describes 'changes in performance based on success or failure in recent events that change the beliefs or the psychology of athletes'. Clearly, it can be either positive or negative. Sports psychologists also refer to the 'momentum chain', acknowledging that what is being proposed is that the idea of success breeding success can be deconstructed into two separate psychological processes: 'success breeds confidence' and 'confidence breeds success'.

It's also useful to consider what we mean by momentum itself, irrespective of whether it has a psychological component, especially because, as we shall see, it's often difficult to tease out that psychological component. If a team, for example, wins 25 of its matches over the course of a 38 game season, then those 25 wins will come in sequences – some long, some short. The same would be true of a team that wins only ten times, except of course that the sequences, on average, will be shorter. But in either case, you can predict the sorts of sequence-lengths you would expect by chance alone if their wins were distributed at random through the season.

Positive momentum, then, would be demonstrated if there were a greater number of longer sequences than you would expect by chance alone – and you'd need to apply some statistical technique to test for that. Long – even 'surprisingly long' – sequences of wins, are not evidence of momentum. They need to occur at a significantly greater frequency than would be thrown up by chance.

Hot hands and winning streaks

The studies of momentum themselves tend to fall into one of three categories, surveyed in an article by Roger Vergin, in *The Journal of Sport Behaviour* in 2000.

First, they look at the performances of individuals, often in a controlled, experimental setting, with each individual being set tasks to do whilst being monitored. Basketball players and fans, for example, mostly share a belief in the idea of 'hot hands', where a successful basket increases the chances that the player's next attempt will also be successful.

Next, there are studies that seek team momentum within a match: is a team more likely to win if it comes from behind to tie the score?

And finally, there are studies looking at team performance over various sequences of games, including whole seasons. It's mostly done through statistical analysis, measuring the likelihood of those sequences of results arising from pure chance alone. All of these are of some interest no doubt, but for most football supporters, at least, it's the last of these that really interests us.

Success breeds confidence but is the chain complete?

To start with the first link in the momentum chain – there is no doubt from Vergin's survey, that success makes athletes feel more confident in their ability and – crucially – their chances of future success. The difficulty comes in finding evidence for the second link.

Most early studies, including several that claimed to have detected momentum, failed to take account of obvious confounding factors, of which the most obvious is ability. If a team wins because it's a great team, and it remains a great team for the next match, then it's no surprise if it wins that one too. But that tells us nothing about psychological momentum or the existence of a *momentum chain*. Nor would I draw too deep a conclusion from the fact that my basketball shots consistently miss, while for Liverpool FC stakeholder LeBron James, success follows success.

So if we dismiss these flawed studies, it's clear from Roger Vergin's survey of investigations up to 2000 that no actual evidence of a momentum chain had been found.

Evidence, or lack of it

Vergin himself looked at the winning and losing patterns of the 28 Major League Baseball teams over the 1996 season and of the 29 National Basketball Association teams over the '96-97 and '97-98 seasons. Whichever way he looked at it, and with relatively sophisticated statistical tests at his disposal, he could find no evidence whatsoever of psychological momentum.

Studies are continuing. In 2010, Leard and Doyle sought evidence of a momentum effect in National (Ice) Hockey League games (as well as an effect of home advantage and, being ice hockey, whether winning a fight in a game increased your chances of winning the game itself – it didn't).

In their abstract to the article, they say:

"Contrary to previous studies on momentum, the authors find some evidence that game-to-game momentum has a positive effect on winning."

But don't get your hopes up. They found no statistical support for an effect of winning streaks as such. They did find that if a team on a two- or three-match winning streak played a team not on such a streak, then the 'hot' team's chances of winning were increased by 3.5%. However, there was no evidence for an effect when they looked at four match streaks. Nor did they make any apparent attempt to separate psychological momentum from the confounding momentum of simply being a good team (especially when playing a bad team). In 2011, T. L. Urban looked for momentum effects in the end-of-season National Basketball Association play-off series and did attempt to account for differences in apparent team quality. There was an effect. But it was negative.

Winning one game made you more likely to lose the next.

Also in 2011, Yaari and Eisenman returned to idea of 'hot hands' in basketball, examining individual free throws over five full seasons (2005/6–2009/10). They did find evidence for hot hands. But they were also very conscious that this could arise either – simply – because of better and worse periods (players in and out of form etc.), or because of what we're interested in here: the momentum chain with success breeding success. They admit to difficulties in drawing this distinction but did try two methods and concluded:

"These two points suggest that the observed pattern interpreted as 'hot hands' in the analysed data, is in large part a consequence of better and worse periods".

Hot hands exist to an extent, but as far as they could tell, no momentum chain.

Data for English football

And last but really not least, and much closer to home in several senses, author and *Tomkins Times* contributor Graeme Riley has amassed an enormous database of around 180,000 games played in the top four English divisions since 1888.

There's no doubt that sports statistics specialists could do more to exploit this gold mine of an archive, but even preliminary analyses are informative. One needs to take the home and away sequence into account. Teams 'tend' to play home-away-home-away and 'tend' to win at home and lose away, so we should factor that in when looking for a hot (or cold) streak. But if we do so, we find, for example, that if you lose at home and then play away, you are 2.56 times more likely to lose than win, whereas if you win at home and then play away, you're only 2.02 times more likely to lose than win. And if you lose away and then play at home, you're 1.98 times more likely to win than lose, whereas if you win away and then play at home, that goes up to you being 2.47 times more likely to win than lose.

So, once again, we have evidence for success following success, and no doubt to a statistically significant extent. But it is not, and cannot be, evidence for success breeding success (psychologically). In fact, since the effect is small, and it must combine the influence of teams simply being good or in good form with the influence (if any) of confidence, then there doesn't, again, seem to be much room for a confidence effect.

The momentum myth

So what can we conclude from all this? First, evidence for any kind of positive momentum effect at the team level is weak, at best. That evidence suggests, at most a small effect – although nothing close to what most people imagine.

If we assume, further, that any observed effect combines the consequences of simply being good (or bad) with whatever deeper psychological effect that there may be, then the evidence is simply not there for what so many take for granted: psychological momentum and the full momentum chain. So those who doubt the existence of psychological momentum in team sport have every reason to trust their doubts. Whereas those who believe the momentum chain must and does exist will have to file it under 'beliefs without supporting evidence'.

Why the illusion?

We should also conclude, I think, that something odd is going on. How is it that a phenomenon so many of us feel must be true turns out to be an illusion? Especially when the first part of the momentum chain is solid enough: success does indeed breed confidence. We can think of possible answers falling into three categories.

First, success may not only breed confidence but other things too, and these may serve to negate any effects that confidence might have had. Second, success may not be driven by confidence alone, and these other generators of success may arise out of things other than success itself. And third, we may simply be fooling ourselves.

Within the first category, success may breed over-confidence or complacency and hence a diminished – not an improved – performance: so-called positive inhibition. Or success may have been achieved at the expense of an outstanding physical and psychological effort that leaves the team drained for the next game. These effects could even exist alongside the positive effects of psychological momentum, but tend to cancel them out, especially if some players in the team are subject to one effect while their team-mates are most influenced by the other.

Within the second category, failure may make a team more focused or motivated and hence more likely to succeed next time around – so-called negative facilitation. This too could easily exist alongside the negative momentum of undermined confidence. Indeed, these days especially, sports psychologists are employed specifically to encourage negative facilitation and suppress any loss of confidence and so prevent negative momentum. Though of course, good managers and on-field captains have always done this.

Deluding ourselves

But the simplest explanation would be the third: we think we're better and more likely to be successful when we're confident, but we aren't. There may even be a scientific explanation for this – or at least, a bit of science combined with some wild speculation.

Success stimulates dopamine in the brain, and we find elevated dopamine levels pleasurable. Recent studies on monkeys have even associated such neurological effects, arising from rewards given after successful completion of a laboratory task, with increased chances of success in the next (similar) task – success really does appear to be breeding success. But these effects are far too short lived, a matter of seconds, to have any real relevance in linking one football match to the next.

All it requires though (this is the wild speculation) is for success to generate a pleasurable confidence, which we correctly interpret as an indication of future success in the short term, but for the memory of that confidence to be misinterpreted as an indication of success one week down the line.

We're probably fooling ourselves in another way, too. Psychologists have been aware for some time that people are pretty bad at judging what is reasonable to expect from random sequences of effects. We tend to 'see' meaningful patterns when none actually exist. As one example, imagine a team with a 50% chance of winning each game (and for simplicity, ignore the possibility of draws). A sequence of results reading WLWLLWWLL would draw no attention whatsoever. But a sequence reading WWWWWWWWW would escape the attention of nobody. And yet: at the outset, the two sequences were equally likely. The second cries out for an explanation (momentum, obviously); the first does not – quite rightly.

None of which is likely to change the mind of anyone, of course – least of all the pundits. But then, there's nothing new there. Amon Tversky appears to have initiated this research in 1985 with his article 'The Hot Hand in Basketball: on the Misperception of Random Sequences'. This, quoted by Yaari and Eisenman, was his experience:

"I've been in a thousand arguments over this topic, won them all, but convinced no one".

THE PROS AND CONS OF SELLING SUÁREZ

By Paul Tomkins
June, 2013

Before going any further, if Luis Suárez wants to leave Liverpool FC, then the only issue is that of acquiring the best possible transfer fee. Various quotes are appearing in the media, with the player's words being analysed and different meanings construed. As I write, the latest is that he's quoted as saying that he definitely wants to leave.

Above all else, I don't think he's the kind of player, both in terms of ability and personality, to keep hanging about if he's unhappy. He's someone who needs to be smiling. He's been at Liverpool for two and a half seasons, and although the club and its fans have stood by him through difficult times, he hasn't got to play Champions League football. He joined without it being on the table, but presumably the plan was to be in it by now. He turns 27 next season, and by conventional standards that will mean he'll be at his peak.

I've no doubt that Suárez has been his own worst enemy. However, I do agree with him that he's been badly treated by the media and the FA. His bans have been longer than those of English players, for example. For alleged racism and biting, John Terry and Jermain Defoe received a four game ban and a yellow card. Suárez got 18 games. And the whole Evra affair remains based on anecdotal evidence rather than hard facts. He may have been guilty, but the case against him would have been thrown out by a court of law, as word of mouth is not true evidence.

Sensational

Suárez, as an individual player, is *sensational*. And he works hard for the team. But perhaps the team has to work too hard to accommodate him. I've been saying for months, ever since the infamous bite on Branislav Ivanović, that Liverpool fans should not fear the departure of the mercurial talent. If football was a game of one vs one, he'd be up there with Lionel Messi as my pick. But it's not.

Around the time of the bite I made the point that Arsenal, without Robin van Persie, were doing just as well as they did with him the year before (when he scored at an incredible rate), even though the received wisdom was that they were totally reliant on him. Take away his goals, people said, and Arsenal would be mid-table. Well, yes, but so would any team who omitted their best player and took the field with ten men every week.

In reality, Arsenal ended the season with three more points than in 2011/12. Had they kept van Persie, and still added the players that replaced him, then they might have been better still. But the wage bill would not have stood that strain. And the player would have left on a free transfer this summer.

The "mistake" – although Arsenal didn't have a lot of choice due to van Persie's contract expiring in 2013 – was to sell to a rival. Arsenal were no worse without him, once they reinvested the money and the replacement players settled. United, of course, were stronger *with* him.

Another problem Arsenal had was that the player, at 29 and with one year left on his contract, was only worth £24m. They lost a £50m player (based on his performances) for half that due to circumstances. Liverpool don't have to sell Suárez, and they don't have to sell him on the cheap – although his disciplinary issues might take a toll. To me, he's another £50m player, but his disciplinary record could take that down to £40m. He is, after all, a risk.

Sell To Improve

Liverpool want to be in the Champions League. But who has broken into that elite group in recent seasons? Since Liverpool won the trophy in 2005, it's been just two teams: Spurs and Manchester City.

City did it by spending outrageous sums of money courtesy of Arabian riches and a manager who had won three Serie A titles. But Spurs? They broke into the top four with a journeyman manager (more relegations than trophies) who, while not as hapless as his harshest critics make out, is nonetheless far from as talented as his many allies in the press would have you believe. I mean, Harry Redknapp's no *genius*, is he?

So how did Spurs do it? Well, to this outsider, it seems that it was by selling their best players. The key was that they held out for the best possible fees (something at which Daniel Levy is a master), and they reinvested wisely in younger players who would go on to prove even better. This may be easier said than done, but that's why clubs need to get their transfer dealings right.

By my detailed calculations (based on analysing over 3,000 transfers, which I've just done again with new data), just a third of all transfers are undeniably successful. This is when factoring in the purchase price, the amount of games started and the transfer fee recouped. About 10% are very successful, and just 1% are überdeals.

One such überdeal was Kolo Touré's move to Arsenal. He cost a few hundred thousand pounds, played over 200 league games and was sold for about 80 times what was paid. Liverpool may be picking him up at the (wide) arse-end of his career, but he's a sensible free transfer. Arsenal getting him over a decade ago was a masterstroke. It's not easy to be that clever, but Liverpool have to try.

Spurs picked up Dimitar Berbatov for about £10m, and sold him for three times that amount. They made the same kind of mark-up on Robbie Keane. They sold Michael Carrick for about ten times what they paid. And Luka Modric generated a £15m profit.

Selling such players signals a lack of ambition to some. But it led Spurs into the top four, and to achieve seasons in excess of 70 points. Modric was a bargain when purchased, but Moussa Dembele is a great replacement. Gareth Bale was also a bargain, and if he is sold this summer for up to six times what was paid, then Andre Villas-Boas could buy three excellent players with the money. Spurs would suddenly be less reliant on their best player, and may end up with a more even spread of talent throughout the XI.

Borussia Dortmund reached the Champions League Final after selling Nuri Sahin in 2011 and Kagawa in 2012, two of their best players.

The worry for them is that Bayern Munich may have just stolen away their current two best players, and, having little option but to sell to their strongest rivals (Mario Götze's buy-out clause was met), Dortmund are compromised. But three years ago Robert Lewandowski was a little-known 21-year-old picked up for £4.5m. Sahin's replacement, Ilkay Gündogan, was picked up for the same fee a year later, aged 20.

We seem incapable of sensing that players who are just as good, or even better, are out there, their potential as yet undiscovered. Many Liverpool fans think Suárez is the third-best player in the world. But no-one put him in the top 10 when he left Ajax. Similarly, when Fernando Torres joined in 2007, many questioned his ability.

Everyone would have rated Torres more highly in late 2010, and yet while the Spaniard has gone on to win trophies with Chelsea, and regain a modicum of form, he's been far inferior to Suárez since the start of 2011. Liverpool came out of the potential disaster of losing their best striker to a rival by procuring an even better player for half the fee they received.

Of course, the problem was that £35m went on Andy Carroll. Liverpool sold Torres and Babel (original combined cost £34m) for £57m in January 2011, and spent £57m on Suárez and Carroll; and now, two and a half years on, they could sell Suárez and Carroll for … roughly £57m. In a sense, it would be a chance to try and reinvest the money more wisely this time. Liverpool placed two huge bets in 2011, and can now walk out of the casino with the same amount of money as they entered with. It just depends if, as fans, you see it as two years enjoying what that £57m bought, or as time wasted.

The new transfer committee, which came into being after last summer's mixed business, has had two sure-fire hits (based on performances so far, without access to a crystal ball), aged 20 and 23. Combined cost? £20m. With this in mind, it might be wise to trust them; certainly more so than Rodgers, whose own picks have been patchy. The club clearly see the manager as more of a coach than a trader.

To me, it's clear that if you sell your best players overseas, as Liverpool did with Kevin Keegan in 1977 and Ian Rush a decade later, the team as a whole can be improved without its position in the English league being compromised. Improvement happened on both occasions.

Liverpool lost Michael Owen to Real Madrid in 2004 and won the Champions League 12 months later, as they became less one-dimensional. The Reds also won the European Cup the year after Keegan left, and the year after Rush moved to Italy was a record-breaker in terms of virtually wrapping the league up by March, as Barnes, Beardsley, Houghton and Aldridge made every Red forget about Ian Rush for 12 months. Liverpool never reached a cup final with Torres (although the Reds were an excellent side in his first three years), but reached two and won a trophy with Andy Carroll.

With Or Without You

Stats that compare the results of games players miss with those they play are always potentially misleading. All manner of factors are at play, and you may mistake coincidences for facts.

That said, a 39% win rate when Suárez plays in the Premier League, compared with 62% when he is absent, suggests that Liverpool are the opposite of "reliant" on him. To put it into context, 39% is roughly Everton's level, 62% is Manchester City's.

Even allowing for the fact that Suárez may have missed easier games than he's played, and he's played a lot more than he's missed, you'd expect to see some positive reinforcement of his importance in the stats; not the exact opposite.

On top of this, Opta Joe Tweeted: *"Without Luis Suárez's goals this season, Liverpool would still have finished seventh in the Premier League table."*

There's also the fact that he'll have served 19 games of suspension in 18 months. In the eyes of many he has also damaged the reputation of the club, although Eric Cantona was a similar character at United, and their supporters still revere him.

The difference is that Cantona elevated United to new heights; by contrast, Suárez hasn't improved Liverpool's results. Maybe in a better Liverpool side Suárez could have proved the difference, but his style is so unique, so off the cuff, that an argument can be made for him being too unpredictable to be in synch with.

Still, there are clearly times when he links brilliantly with others, with his assist for Daniel Sturridge's goal against Chelsea one of the passes of the season. But it is his wastefulness, when shooting from every possible angle, which is hard to quantify. He will score the occasional world-class goal with an impudent effort, but how many more might have been scored had he not so often tried to do the impossible? It's like trying to score direct from a corner. You may do it once in 100 attempts, but you might have scored five by looking for a near-post flick-on.

In the excellent Mixed kNuts blog, Ted Knutson takes a detailed look at Suárez's stats in order to assess his strengths and weaknesses. It seems that Suárez is a mix of the best and worst attributes in the Premier League, which, one could argue, cancel each other out.

"Let's start with the good. 2nd in the Premier League in goals. 1st in Shots per Game. 3rd in Key Passes per game. 1st in successful dribbles per game. Suárez was a handful and then some."

So far, the stats back up what Liverpool fans think. He's exciting, great to watch.

"Now for the bad. 1st in the league for being dispossessed. 2nd for turning the ball over. 3rd in Offsides per game. Great key pass numbers, but only 5 assists on the season. A 76.6% pass rate. (For comparison, Mata and Hazard were both over 85%, RVP was 80.2%.) A 12.2% conversion rate on total shots."

Therefore, the stats also back up what a lot of fans say: that Suárez can be incredibly wasteful and frustrating.

Based on those stats, Suárez hits the target far more rarely than Europe's other elite strikers. As an example, Dortmund's Lewandowski turns twice as many of his shots into goals.

Look at it like this. Player A takes 500 shots in a season and scores 50 goals. We marvel at the incredible tally – 50 goals! – but by taking 500 shots he's denying team-mates chances. If, without Player A, the team has 400 shots, but scores a greater number of goals by sharing them around, then that's clearly better. The key is to make sure that you can share them around; something Liverpool were not capable of doing in the first half of last season, but were after the January window.

Cristiano Ronaldo is a fine example. He averages almost seven shots per game. The reason Messi is a far better player is because he doesn't spend the entire game shooting in order to break records. On the one hand, you want players who take the responsibility to shoot when the chance is there. On the other, you can't have egotists who think they are bigger than the team, having a pop from all over the pitch.

I don't think Suárez is as egotistical as Ronaldo – he doesn't strut about, correcting that one hair that's out of place – but he does inadvertently make each game about himself. Perhaps the team suffers as a result.

Popular

A problem with selling Suárez is that he's popular with the players and the fans. He's the kind of player others want to play with, rather than against. He's an attractive selling point, when it comes to signing other players. Come and play alongside one of the world's best.

Without a manager of worldwide repute, and also lacking the bait of Champions League football, it could be argued that the club needs all the selling points it can get right now.

The club's name is still a gold standard, but aside from Gerrard, Suárez is the one big name. With Carragher retiring and Reina possibly moving back to Barcelona, Liverpool will have few household names. However, the club is full of potentially great young players, and a young manager whose best days should be ahead of him. This is indeed like the Dortmund way of doing things, with Rodgers fairly similar to Klopp when he took over at the Westfalenstadion; but of course this doesn't mean he'll go on to match the great German's success. After all, after three games, Nigel Clough looked like the new Kenny Dalglish.

The Kop doesn't rock to many songs these days, but Suárez can get the place buzzing. Of course, he also lifts the opposition fans wherever he goes, causing them to unite against him. He also winds up opposition players, and more than anything, he winds up himself.

If Suárez stays – as seems increasingly unlikely – I'd be happy. But I won't be sad if he leaves, providing that it's to an overseas side, for a good fee, and that the money is reinvested in the team. I just can't attach myself to players anymore. They are all passing through, just at different speeds. I enjoy what they give us, and then we all move on.

Not Needed

For all Suárez's brilliant dribbling, one Coutinho through-ball can just as easily get Liverpool in behind teams. As direct as Suárez is, Sturridge's pace arguably makes him an even greater threat through the centre; based on goals per game, Sturridge wins out, albeit from a shorter period of time.

This pair combined seem to elevate Liverpool more than Suárez alone. If three other players can come in for the money recouped from a Suárez sale, then the XI can be a lot better than it has been. Some very exciting young talents have been heavily linked with the club, and as a replacement for Carragher, Kolo Touré brings some much-needed experience.

The biggest problem, however, is that what should have been a season spent moving forward could quickly become yet another transitional campaign. Carragher has gone. Reina might go (though I hope not). Downing and Škrtel will probably go. There's talk that Johnson might be sold (though I'd also oppose that). And at least two or three others will be pruned from the squad. On top of that, Liverpool will need to beat the odds in terms of two-thirds of all transfers making very little mark; although the more each player costs, the greater the chances of him succeeding.

Swapping a £45m player for three £15m players should mean a better Liverpool squad. If done right, it can also improve the XI, but with this in mind I'd be wary of selling the rest of the club's better players unless absolutely necessary.

Too many changes and Liverpool will become a team of strangers. But that's probably better than having players who don't even want to be there.

MY DAY WITH "CRISIS"-HIT BENÍTEZ

By Paul Tomkins

October, 2009

If Anfield is the outer appearance of Liverpool FC – its face, its skin, its very public expressions – then Melwood is its heart, its guts, its nervous system.

When Rafa Benítez personally invites me to meet him for lunch at the legendary training ground, Liverpool have just seen their six-game winning streak come to an end in Italy, but things are still looking good. There is no agenda; just a long overdue chance to say hello, and say thank-you for taking the time to write for the official site for four years.

And it is still only a few months ago that Real Madrid and Manchester United were thrashed, and a genuine title challenge was mounted, despite the 4th-most expensive squad (now 5th) and the 4th-most expensive wage bill (now 5th).

(Anyone who doubts the utterly vital importance of the wages factor, read *Soccernomics 'Why England Lose'*; the biggest payers win the biggest prizes more than nine times out of ten.)

By the time the meeting takes place, the newspapers are full of 'crisis' talk, just months after the best league season that any late-teen Red will have lived through. (The kind of late-teen now spouting off on Internet forums about Rafa's ineptitude, not that many can conjure such words.)

Inadvertently, I am entering the eye of the storm. Or so I expect. The world is chattering about Benítez and his future, and here I am, about to spend part of the morning and almost the entire afternoon with him, chatting one-to-one about the club we both love.

Melwood has clearly come a long way since the days when Bill Shankly turned up to find a glorified flea pit. Space-age facilities, pitches that put the lawns at Hampton Court to shame, and a bold red decor; all fenced off from the world and autograph hunters by the same old breeze block brick wall.

I glance across at the legendary hill, constructed for gruelling trudges up and down, and the target boxes divided into nine squares, each with a number painted, the like of which I recall from pictures of Shankly's time. But otherwise it's from another planet, not just another era.

Having been on the Kop for the visit of Lyon last night, I dread the mood given that the final 20 minutes saw a win turn to defeat, and more players limp off. I half expect Rafa to cancel, and for everyone to be in a foul mood; a time for inquests and recriminations.

However, I encounter no such despair; morale seems okay (if, understandably, no-one is performing cartwheels and dancing on tables like the cast of Fame). Admittedly, I have no prior experience of the place to compare it with, but I am buoyed by the aura. I get to see some of the training, but of course, there aren't a lot of fit senior players out there, and it's only a short, gentle session after the night before.

Around noon, Rafa greets me warmly for the second time that day, only now I will have his full, undivided attention. We head to his office, and within minutes he's sketching formations on scraps of loose paper.

Despite the ever-widening criticism, this is a man who, over the previous four seasons, has seen his team average 78 points in the league; or, the grand total with which Arsène Wenger won his first title. The team Rafa inherited averaged 62.5 points between 2002 and 2004 and did nothing in Europe in Houllier's final two seasons (in other words, the seasons he was sacked for).

Benítez is a man who generated around £100m from repeated Champions League qualification, and reached two finals, despite no wealthy benefactors pumping in unlimited funds, and despite contrasting messages from up on high during the past few years, that leave many people confused.

This is a man who has never had enough money – crucially – *at any one time* to put together a squad to match the expense of his rivals'. More than half of what he's spent, he's recouped, in order to make that overall spend, yet he gets credited with having spent mythical amounts.

This is not the '70s and '80s, when success bred success, as two geniuses held the reins for 24 years, before two other top managers kept things ticking over (and in Dalglish's case, took them to a new level of aesthetic brilliance).

This is also not the '90s, when Graeme Souness, enjoying the last time the club was as relatively rich as its rivals (pre-Premier League boom, pre-United marketing machine, pre-billionaire backers), broke British records on spending, trying to get the Reds back to the top, only to turn them into an awful collection of overweight, disinterested no-hopers, with the odd decent skinny kid thrown in.

Once that money was spent, and the thoroughly decent Roy Evans had been cheated by another record signing, Stan Collymore, who didn't even bother turning up for training some of the time (but who is now an 'expert' on management), Liverpool had become also-rans.

And so I meet Benítez during a bad spell for the club, but a bad three months; not a bad three years, to point to the record of one of his critics this week. The club are still in better shape than when Rafa arrived; that ex-manager (Souness) left things in a total mess.

Some more context: at the end of last season, having shown them their best six months in over a decade, Martin O'Neill was being vilified by the Aston Villa fans. Now, he's great again. Arsène Wenger was being gunned at by Gunners, now he's back on track. Top managers have bad spells. Shit happens. Well-run clubs stick by good men; bad ones end up like Newcastle.

Why Am I Here?

With everyone from the club making me feel incredibly welcome, any nerves about meeting the man himself have ebbed away. In wandering around the canteen area, I see all of the reserve team playing table tennis and pool, ahead of their own light training before the evening's game. Then the manager approaches me, and our meeting begins within the techno-zone that is his plush office.

Rafa makes it clear that I am here so that he can say thank-you for my efforts over the past five years, and to let me know that he's impressed by how much I get right about him and his methods; he finds it unusual that someone takes the time and makes the effort.

Of course, this being Rafa, he points out a couple of things I've got wrong. (I like this: it makes me feel that he is not just bullshitting me; and he's clearly right about what I got wrong.)

He makes it clear that he doesn't want to colour or influence what I write, but of course, is glad that someone takes on his critics upon his behalf with actual facts, rather than spurious conceits. I am not asked to change anything I do, nor to do anything for him. He just wants to make sure that when I talk about things like zonal marking, I am aware of the exact way the team lines up, whose job is what, and so on.

I explain that once I was made aware, from the outset in 2005, that he was a regular reader of my column on the official site, I had to make sure I knew what I was talking about; that my main aim was indeed to understand his methods rather than judge him, and that if I did judge him, I'd better be able to back up what I was saying.

Facts became more important to me than ever before, and when I looked at what kind of budget he was working on (compared with his rivals), or how many games he was winning, and all the other things that go to make up the context, my belief in him grew.

Equanimous

The word I'd use to describe the manager is 'equanimous', which my dictionary notes as "mental calmness, composure, and evenness of temper, esp. in a difficult situation".

If he doesn't punch the air in victory, he also won't punch a player in defeat.

But this is not to say that he is not passionate; on several topics he gets very animated. His love for the club is clear. His desire to succeed is clear. His burning ambition to get the most out of what he has at his disposal is also clear.

I find him a warm, welcoming man – nothing like the ludicrous 'cold' stereotype – and Melwood is the epitome of professionalism. Other staff members point out that they've seen him give lots of encouragement to players, and certainly offer a human touch.

Yes, the conversation is almost exclusively about football, but his office has enough reminders of his family life outside the game to show that he is not some soulless robot, and his humour is clear. And anyway, he didn't invite me there to talk about that week's Strictly Come Dancing, did he?

We spend almost four hours over lunch in his personal meeting room, and afterwards in his office, going through tactics, personnel, and almost anything else you care to mention.

It is such a natural, easy conversation, at times I have to remind myself who I am talking with; and 'with' is the right word. At no point does he talk at me. And in person, his English is easier to understand than it is with a microphone thrust in his face. (For the record, I took no notes, nor made any recordings; it was just two men talking football.)

After several diagrams sketched on A4 sheets, he leads me to the canteen and shows me the day's healthy selection. As I stand trying to decide, Alberto Aquilani taps him on the shoulder to ask about the reserve game later that night. They talk briefly in Italian. The boss turns back, and approves of my choice: paella, which I was pleasantly surprised to find amid the pasta dishes.

Later we discuss the new Italian midfielder: an independent expert had told the club that he would be fit for the end of August, but that date ended up being pushed back and back. It was frustrating, but Rafa was very happy with what he was now seeing in training – the lad has vision and technique – even if he obviously still has to adapt to the pace of the English game.

(Later, as Rafa shows me around the entire complex, I am shown the special new machine, which bears a player's weight, that helped Aquilani train despite the injury.)

The fee is £17m, he tells me, and he points out that John Arne Riise ("a good lad") has just texted him to once again to offer his support, and to say Liverpool have got a real gem in Aquilani.

(I like that a player the manager has sold still texts his old boss; no signs of a lack of affection there, even if Rafa makes it clear that it is obviously not his job to be best mates with his charges, just as Fabio Capello won't be bonding with his players beyond the acceptable bounds.)

It was a difficult summer, Rafa explains, with Alonso determined to leave and Barcelona niggling away at Mascherano.

The manager certainly wanted to do more business in the market himself, but was unable to. His frustrations are evident, and he lists a few players he went in for; in most cases his interest was well known, but one less so. A shame, I think, when I hear the name. I'm also told of one world-class star in the making (Pato) that Liverpool made an early approach for in 2007, but before the deal could be tied up, due to dallying, he was lured elsewhere.

We discuss the Alonso situation at length. Rafa made the decision at the end of the midfielder's fourth season, in 2008; for two years Xabi wasn't quite cutting it – loads of Kopites were even saying as much – and in Gareth Barry, Rafa had in mind a more robust player, with different qualities and, crucially, an English passport for the changing rules. And with Xabi's wife expecting a baby, there had been rumblings of a desire to return to Spain.

A new formation was devised, to take into account Barry's energy and his ability to get up and back, and also to cross with deadly accuracy, but for well-known reasons, the deal fell through.

By then the bridges with Alonso were somewhat burned, and although the Basque player had his best-ever season, he had his heart set on leaving. Nothing new there, I know, but nice to have it explained in depth, in person. According to Rafa, the player wanted out, and Liverpool got £30m.

Time to Go?

We are briefly interrupted at different times by Sammy Lee and Frank McParland, and I am introduced to both: intense, driven men who share Rafa's desire for success, with the trustworthy sign of a firm handshake.

I'm not sure if the meeting is supposed to last as long as it is, and I keep asking the boss if he has something else to be doing; but he's taken training, the physios are doing their jobs, and Rafa isn't about to knock off early. It may have been a few hours, but it's only a small part of his working day.

Even so, I can see how eager he is to have the world understand his ideas, especially when ex-players and the vast majority of the media are clearly hostile and keen to misrepresent him; he knows that unlike some of his rivals, he doesn't have friends in high places, such as Fleet Street, Sky TV, the League Managers' Association and the FA. (These are my assumptions; he gives no specifics. But it's not hard to see which managers work the system to their advantage through old pals' networks, and which clubs have greater influence in certain areas.)

Whenever I think I'd better leave him in peace, we get onto another subject. Zonal marking pops up. So, too, does Rafa – from his seat, demonstrating positioning, who should be where, against the backdrop of his broad office window's glare.

This isn't enough. A DVD from his extensive library is slipped into the machine, he's now showing me how the system Liverpool deploy is actually a mix of both zonal and man-marking. I am shown who should be where, and what each individual's job is; how that job changes depending on which foot the taker is using (inswinger/ outswinger); and how there is as much personal responsibility as the alternative – everyone knows his job.

Then he takes me, beat by beat, through other teams, the gross failings of some man-markers, and also points out several players who, despite being labelled man-markers, are marking zones! (Men on the posts, and others here and there.) We look at a side who are very successful at defending set-pieces (Aston Villa), and he shows me how they defend in a similar way to the Reds (and holy shit, they do!); they just happen to have a lot of tall players.

Unfortunately, tall players who are also technically gifted, as all-rounders, cost more money; you can buy giants who can defend set-pieces, but can't then play the game in the manner you require.

If you want very good footballers like Mascherano, Benayoun and Insúa, then, as with most things in life, there's a flip side. Good footballers who are also imposing physical specimens cost a premium. And even Chelsea, with their giants and noted headers of a ball, have conceded four set-piece goals in their last two away games.

Difficult

I put to Rafa a lot of the 'difficult' questions fans had raised with me, and he answers each without a problem.

Obviously I cannot discuss all of his answers, because they were in the context of a private conversation, and I don't want to betray confidences about certain players. He knows the balance of the team isn't quite right, and he's working hard to make the necessary adjustments; but issues with form and fitness are not helping.

It suddenly occurs to me that if every individual critic of Rafa's could sit down and have a similar conversation, they'd be converted. At the very least, they'd be a lot wiser.

That wouldn't mean they'd suggest mistakes aren't still made: every signing can go bad, every substitution comes with a risk, and so on. You can make the right decisions and get unlucky, or make the wrong decisions and get good fortune.

I sense that a big part of his job is building up the confidence of struggling players, and keeping the egos in check when certain players think they've 'made it'. But then, that's just one of the tough aspects of management.

Stubborn

People inevitably say that Rafa is stubborn, but I don't know one top manager who doesn't have the courage of his convictions. Personally, I don't want a manager who has one set of beliefs one week, but who then changes his mind the next. If you know something works more often than not, you stick with it when it's not working; changing is not the answer.

For example, four years of having either the best – or one of the best – set-piece records (defensively), is to be taken more seriously than a spell of ten games. And anyway, will total man-marking make Insúa or Mascherano 6ft 5? People will criticise his decisions, such as playing three at the back at Sunderland; while ignoring the fact that previous deployments of the system, though infrequent, had proved successful.

We discuss the irony of the boos after removing Benayoun (whom he felt had played well, but run himself to a standstill) when a year earlier, the general consensus was that 'he wasn't fit to wear the shirt'.

And of course, there was the issue of confidence. The night before, Liverpool had at last found some of this precious elixir after taking the lead; but as soon as Lyon equalised, you could see it visibly drain away. That happens when things aren't going your way.

Rafa tells me of Luis Aragonés' saying "You can't buy confidence in Marks & Spencers". There is no magic wand, no secret message, no miraculous injection; you can only keep plugging away, doing the right thing, and hope that it changes.

We've all seen a striker who can't score for love nor money, then one goes in off his arse and he's bubbling again. That same thing can happen with a team; except that on top of individual struggles, that undefinable "wavelength" confidence goes askew as well. Everyone is hesitant, in their passing and in their movement.

The same group of players who were passing-and-moving to near-perfection in the second half of last season (even when Alonso was absent, such as at Old Trafford in the 4-1 win) haven't suddenly forgotten how to play football.

With candour, Benítez admits to some mistakes, particularly in the transfer market, but points out that he had to gamble on cheaper players when his first choices (whom his rivals could afford) were beyond the finances of the club. He knows that he's often had to sell in order to buy; also something that's not true at other major clubs.

He tells various stories of players who, despite big reputations, surprised senior Reds with their lack of understanding of what they were asked to do, those who couldn't adapt, those who couldn't (or wouldn't) learn English, or whose wives wanted away. There are those who demanded guaranteed first-team football or they'd leave; so they left.

Then there are the agents, hangers-on, etc, and you realise that controlling a group of disparate, super-rich and in most cases egotistical men (Everyone's Got One – only some more than others), half of whom are going to be unhappy with you that week when the XI is announced, is a minefield. And for a clear outsider like Benítez, who doesn't have his cliques within the English game, it's certainly no easier.

We discuss who could still be at the club if he could afford to give contracts in line with Chelsea, Man Utd and Man City. He names good squad players at other clubs who are kept happy by handsome salaries. We talk of how nice it would have been to have someone like Peter Crouch still at the club, but he obviously had to be behind Torres in the pecking order for front-line striker, and the manager couldn't offer him big wages to try and make him happier (if not 'happy') on the bench.

We discuss several major players, now at rival clubs, whom he thought had been signed (dating back to 2005), only for the deal to fall through for reasons beyond his control. Again, mostly well-known stuff, but some surprises, and an insight into how he felt his hands were tied. We discuss actual transfer fees, not what the media claims he has spent. And he points out that he often didn't set the fee; after all, the negotiating wasn't his job. He was surprised at how much the club ended up paying for players he had been told in his initial enquiries could have been bought for less.

We discuss how, for example, people accuse him of wasting money on Andrea Dossena ("a top pro", he says, but one who has struggled with the system), yet one reason the Italian isn't in the side is the emergence of Insúa – a very shrewd buy. Whether or not Dossena would eventually come good (if given playing time) almost becomes moot; Insúa, for around £1m, is excelling.

Insúa could now be worth much more than the fee paid for both him *and* Dossena [in 2013, that proved true when the player joined Atlético Madrid], but people will only focus on the negative. Although he doesn't say so, if Insúa had cost £7m and Dossena £1m, there'd be no problem. So ... what's the problem? (And that's before adding Aurelio, a free transfer; three international left-backs, two of whom can also play in midfield, for £8m.)

Rafa is surprisingly candid as we speak about pretty much every first team member, followed by every reserve, and even a number of youth players. He lists their strengths, and talks with admiration about many, but even the best, he wants to improve in certain areas. It's perfectionism that drives a hunger in individuals; there's surely a reason that Steven Gerrard's best form as a footballer has come under Rafael Benítez's stewardship? Who cares if Rafa gives him a cuddle or bakes him a cake?

Later on, as I get the full tour, we pass one lesser known teenage reserve, and Rafa, pulling me to one side so the kid can't hear, makes it clear that this lad has something about him. "Look out for him, good mentality." But sometimes it's better if the kid doesn't get ideas above his station. [It's Victor Pálsson, who now plays regularly for NEC in the Dutch top division.]

Overhaul

One subject that I bring up is the number of players he's accused of buying. He grabs the white A4, and draws out lists of how many first team players he inherited that were just not good enough (roughly half). He does the same with the reserve team (almost every player), and then the youth team (every player bar one). It turns out to be around 50 players in total.

So when he is accused of buying far too many players, he points out that he had little choice; that many were bought because they were better than what was already there, even if, with youngsters, you can never guarantee who will make the grade, or how quickly they will progress. And even a 17-year-old needs a professional contract.

He wonders why there is this obsession with all these signings, when every big club stocks its youth and reserve teams with imports and purchases.

My take is this: if you have 50 players at a club (from top to bottom) who you believe are not good enough – and therefore they need to go – you will not replace them sufficiently with 50 signings.

The law of averages says that some new purchases will get injured, some will not settle, some will turn out to be 'not as advertised' (i.e. they couldn't do what was asked of them, or, though well-scouted, were not as good when seen in your team. Some will have been poorly scouted, hence Benítez's desire to improve that side of things.)

Make 50 signings, and maybe, with a good wind, 25 will be successes of varying degrees, from acceptable to outstanding; far less if you're talking about teenagers, who can fail to develop or lose focus. It might take three years to make those 50 signings, and you may still be very short at every level of the club. So to get the next 25, you might need to buy 50 more, by which time some of the successes have left for varying reasons. So it's a constant process of improvement, hampered by the financial inability to shop for more than the occasional established world-class player.

How can it go wrong?

He talks glowingly about the Spanish youngster Francisco Duran's ability, but after three cruciate injuries, there's a chance the player, who was coveted by Arsène Wenger but chose Liverpool, will never be the same again. Wonderful prospect in 2007, but fate has handicapped his development. He may not have become the next Cesc Fabregas, but then neither would Fabregas, had he had three such horrible injuries.

He mentions young players, now at other clubs, that he thought he had done enough to sign, but was let down when a lack of urgency was shown by those he was asking to do the business. I am invited around to look at his PC monitor, to see his database of the full Melwood cast list, and who he has in mind for each position, from first team through to young prospects. I learn which kids are showing a great attitude, and which ones are disappointing him; the kind of thing you just don't get to see unless you're part of the club. It's great information, but something for him to discuss with the players in question (and not for me to mention in public). Some, it saddens him to see, seem to have entourages already. He dreads good young players losing their focus, or having their heads turned. That's why mentality is so important.

He rates Daniel Pacheco, the fans' darling-in-waiting, but although he doesn't say as much, he is another small, clever player, the like of which is already in abundance in a team lacking height. But Pacheco definitely has a chance, if he can span the great gap that exists from the reserves to the first team.

I mention Krizstian Nemeth, and Rafa clearly likes him; but he needs first-team experience to toughen up. He's definitely not out on loan to be offloaded, but at this stage Andrei Voronin, with his added experience (given that the first team is still very young, on average), was felt to be the better option as back-up second-striker. Peter Gulacsi (whom I earlier watched close up in a one-on-one session with a goalkeeping coach) is another prospect he has high hopes for; but young goalkeepers can get crucified after a mistake, and 20 is young for the bench in that position. Finally, Daniel Ayala is singled out for praise as someone with a great attitude and a very bright future. (Having walked past the 18-year-old, all I can say as I'd have hated him marking me! Jesus Christ, I almost shat myself when he looked my way...).

The difficulty, of course, is in finding loans for promising players that will see them get games; we discuss incentives for those clubs taking these young Reds, such as San José's year in Spain. Send them to rival Premier League clubs, as happened in the past, and it's likely to only be a struggling side who shows an interest (Chelsea aren't going to want your best reserves, are they? – and nor will they get them), only for that club's manager to then panic (or get sacked) and the club jettison them to their own reserves when the going gets tougher. It happened with Neil Mellor and Anthony Le Tallec. So the aim is to find clubs who will definitely develop them.

Finally, we discuss the sell-on clauses that some younger 'flops' (who are now succeeding abroad) have in their contracts. Again, I won't go into details, but it's nice to know that profits will be made on small investments.

Adios

Before I leave, I get the full guided tour by the boss (known simply as 'boss' to every player), and at the front doors, Rafa shakes my hand not once but twice.

He smiles warmly, wishes me well, pats me on the shoulder, and I can't help but think: "Crisis? What crisis?"

CONVERSATIONS WITH A EUROPEAN CHAMPION

By Paul Tomkins

June, 2010

"I was born Spanish, I am no longer as thin (the anxiety doesn't help), and yes, sometimes I help serving the dinner."

This was Rafa Benítez in an email to me after I'd run a piece explaining that senior figures within the media [two high-profile *Sky Sports* presenters at the time] referred to the Liverpool manager as "the fat Spanish waiter". Just another example of a fine sense of self-deprecating humour, from a man portrayed as almost robotic by many critics. Following Rafa's invite to meet him at Melwood last October, I maintained a dialogue with the Liverpool manager. Any help with stats or tactical advice, I was free to ask. And in turn, he'd occasionally drop me a line to thank me for an observation here and there. Now that he is sadly no longer manager, I see no harm in bringing this to light, as a way of paying my respects to a much misunderstood man, and manager.

After that meeting in the autumn, I rushed home and wrote 5,000 words 'My Day With Crisis-Hit Benítez'. The article was circulated widely the day after; *The Tomkins Times* even melted twice from the huge spike in traffic. Word spread via Twitter, and a friend of Benítez's family saw the positive reaction to the article. The next day, I was awoken early as my mobile phone rang. It was Rafa, thanking me for the article; we hadn't met with one in mind, but I had been suitably inspired after four hours of chewing the fat on all things Liverpool. Word had got back to him, via that friend who'd seen it on Twitter, that there was still a lot of positive feeling towards him. Two days later the Reds deservedly beat Manchester United two-nil, although the team never really escaped the pressure brought to bear by two defeats in the first three games. Half asleep that Friday morning, and with Rafa's English harder to discern on an imperfect line, he also wanted to correct me on a small factual error. But he did so in a very polite manner; he just wanted to be clear on the matter. There's no doubt he's a perfectionist, but I saw that as one of those good things that, like almost anything positive in life, also comes with its drawbacks.

Indeed, when people ask me what mistakes he made, or what his faults are, I find it hard to answer, because, as with all managers, attributes are perceived as either strengths or weaknesses depending on recent results.

Too distant with players? Well, isn't that Fabio Capello's style, and wasn't being 'pally' seen as a fault of Steve McLaren? Not a good man manager? Well, Harry Redknapp's famed skills are fine when they work, but overlooked when it comes to insulting his own players (Darren Bent) or leaving expensive stars on the bench (Robbie Keane).

Too negative? Well, was there anything more negative than Jose Mourinho's Inter Milan in Europe this season? Some call it negative, others call it *tactical*. Contrary to what some believed – such as Jamie Carragher, when he phoned to take exception to something I'd written (and which I put him clear on) – Rafa wasn't feeding me criticisms of senior players. Frankly, I didn't want them. That was one shitstorm I didn't want to get in the middle of.

That is not to say that he didn't make observations. He noted how, after the Aston Villa game, he'd had 'problems' with Carragher and Gerrard; but he immediately added that he'd sat down with both and had productive conversations that had pleased him greatly. Of course, this does not automatically mean that he was telling me the full story.

Mostly, when talking of players, he spoke of his charges' strengths and weaknesses; but only stuff he'd have already made them aware of. The only player he expressed dissatisfaction with back in October was Albert Riera, whom he felt had let his Spain call-ups go to his head. Subsequent developments bore this out.

But more than anything, Benítez was keen to pass on tactical insights: the deployment of subtly different midfield formations and roles in different games, when to the untrained eye it looked like the Reds were playing the same system; specific jobs at set-pieces; the united movements of the back four; and so on.

Having said that, at times he did express frustration with how the club was being run (such as when Martin Broughton had been in charge for a week but not been in touch. 'After one week, the new Chairman has not contacted with the Manager, in a Football Club is not normal' said Rafa, via his personal email account). I got the impression he saw the writing on the wall back then.

A lot of the stuff we spoke about in October was along the lines of what he ended up telling The Times' Tony Evans a few weeks later. The problem I had (due to the fact that I'm not a trained journalist) was being unsure of what was confidential and off the record, and not wanting to cause any problems for Rafa – and his ability to get the best results – by divulging anything he'd said that he'd preferred remain private.

In the end, Evans spilled many of those beans. Some of the other stuff Rafa told me I'll continue to keep private (such as his views on certain other managers, some of which were fairly controversial, and one or two other subjects), but certain other things I've managed to gradually feed into my writing, such as transfer targets that got away.

Indeed, even though it was a couple of years on, Rafa was still angry that young players like Walcott, Ramsey and Pato had all been approached well before they ended up moving to other big clubs, and that the two British teenagers had even been in his office for transfer talks. But much to Benítez's chagrin, Rick Parry felt there were better players already at the Academy, and refused to sanction a bid of just £1.5m for Ramsey. A manager is judged on his transfer record, but time and time again Benítez wanted a top player (Simao, Alves), but had to make do with a cheap alternative (Pennant, Arbeloa). Sometimes it worked, sometimes it didn't.

One signing that remains controversial is the acquisition of Alberto Aquilani. In early March, Rafa explained his thinking on the Italian:

"Aquilani wants to improve, but now it is difficult to give him games. Really it depends on him, he has vision for the pass and is dynamic, but still has to adapt to the pace in England, we will see in the next months."

And in the coming months, we did indeed get to see some of that vision and dynamism, but also that the stamina wasn't yet what was required. And so, in the main, Rafa did what he's known for – talking football, obsessively. For me, all the book sales and positive feedback I've had since 2005 pales compared to a double La Liga and European Cup-winning manager telling me that he respects my work, and that I have a good understanding of the game and, in particular, his methods. After all, that was what I saw my role to be: to try and explain the methods of an overseas manager whose English is not perfect, and whose approach to the game is often at odds with the old-fashioned ex-pros in the media. This sums up Benítez's attitude to my work, and how I will continue to approach writing about Liverpool FC:

"For me it is important that you defend your Manager, not Rafa Benítez."

Finally, in the past year I've spoken to a lot of people who know Rafa and his family on a personal level. They all speak very highly of the Benítezes, and of their great work in the community. These were not casual interlopers, but people who threw themselves into the local culture. Perhaps Rafa is not the easiest man to work for – his standards are exacting, and probably draining – but then again, plenty of the Valencia players thought Rafa's successors were more warm and welcoming; unfortunately, none has yet been anywhere near as successful.

Nunca Caminarás Solo, Rafa.

STRIKING IT RICH: DECADES OF FEARSOME FORWARDS

By Paul Tomkins
March, 2013

The last 23 years as a Liverpool fan have been fallow in terms of league titles, although other forms of silverware have arrived at a reasonably regular rate. However, one thing that Liverpool have been blessed with in that time – and indeed, going back many further decades – is outstanding strikers. And few have been better than the current no.7.

Luis Suárez is a genius. That phrase may be overused in football circles, but the Uruguayan deserves the title. He is unique: he does things that no other player dare imagine. And on top of phenomenal skill he has the work-rate of a journeyman whose total *lack* of skill means that all he can do is run and run and run.

Suárez is not a "silky" player. He doesn't necessarily make what he does seem easy, because he's not upright and stationary in the manner of some of the game's geniuses; he's usually hunched over as he chases a pass or a lost cause as if a pack of wolves is in hot pursuit, and he often seems off-balance when he dribbles past countless defenders, even though he still repeatedly dribbles past countless defenders. Suárez is not the sort to stand and admire his own pass. Indeed, most of the time he's trying to get on the end of it.

Liverpool fans have been blessed in terms of witnessing outstanding strikers in all shapes and sizes. In the '40s and '50s, Billy Liddell was an absolute idol; wartime, and the fact that the Reds slipped into the second tier removed the kind of recognition he may otherwise have garnered. He was still a regular in the late '50s, although he did play on until 1961. By 1961/62, Roger Hunt was the main man, scoring 40 goals in 41 league games.

Hunt remained incredibly prolific throughout the '60s, but was perhaps overshadowed nationally and internationally by Jimmy Greaves, who was an extraordinary finisher. That said, Hunt remains Liverpool's record *league* goalscorer, with 245 goals.

As the '70s dawned, Hunt gave way to Kevin Keegan, as Bill Shankly tore up his successful but ageing side. Keegan won plaudits around the world, although it took a move to Hamburg in 1977 to make him the double European Player of the Year, despite having powered the Reds to the European Cup in his final season. Out went the great Keegan, and in came the sublime, godly Kenny Dalglish. How often do teams lose their best player and go out and buy someone even better?

Ian Rush then emerged from the reserves, to partner Dalglish, and broke records until 1987, at which point John Barnes, John Aldridge and Peter Beardsley took over. Barnes was a genius, Beardsley a lock-picker and Aldridge a consummate poacher, with the trio racking up a ton of goals.

Rush returned, and while not as prolific as in his youth, his all-round play was a joy to behold. It was this maturity that helped him usher in the emergence of Robbie Fowler, who was perhaps the most naturally gifted finisher of them all; although Rush himself was still scoring in excess of 25 goals a season in all competitions before the emergence of the Toxteth teenager in 1993.

In 1989 it looked a harsh decision to jettison Aldridge for Rush. But although Aldridge averaged 30 goals a season in all competitions in his two full campaigns, 27% of his goals (16 of 63) were penalties. And while you can only commend a striker who also takes good penalties, it could be that you possess a right-back or central-midfielder who takes even better ones. So while Rush MKII never quite matched Aldridge's tallies, it's fair to say that 26 goals from open play is a better indicator of striking ability than 30, of which only 21 or 22 are from open play. By contrast, Roger Hunt scored only one penalty for the Reds, while Ian Rush managed just three, meaning that over 99% of the goals by Liverpool's two most prolific strikers were not free shots at goal, with the opposition behind a white line.

By 1996, both Rush and Aldridge seemed like distant memories with Robbie Fowler in his pomp. Like Aldridge he too took penalties, although they only accounted for 11% of his goals, as opposed to 27%. (It was actually under 10% first time around, with three of his eight goals as Fowler MKII coming from the spot.)

Fowler wasn't that quick, and he wasn't that tall. He clearly wasn't an athlete. But he had an uncanny ability to work the space for a shot, and have it nestle just within the right part of the side netting. However, injuries took their toll, and within four years he was struggling to find his old form. It says a lot that he's still revered after just four seasons at his peak, although he still contributed 17 goals in the treble season of 2000/01, before his move to Leeds a year later. But by 1997 a younger, much quicker model was rolling off the production line, as the English game became more about pace.

Michael Owen was never quite as prolific for Liverpool as the hype suggested (19 league goals was his best tally, compared with the 28 of Fowler and 32 of Rush), but he did possess an incredible record for England, and was a very important component in Gérard Houllier's counter-attacking side that won four cup competitions. Liverpool have had better strikers before and since, but while Owen never reached 30 goals a season, and never managed 20 in the league, it's also true that he rarely played 30 league games a season, and therefore his strike rate was consistently impressive. Just 8% of his goals were from the spot, although he did have a fairly poor conversion rate.

Like Fowler, injuries started eating into Owen's ability to excel, and in 2004 he left for Real Madrid, three years after being crowned European Footballer of the Year.

Then came the only real break in quality: three years without a genuinely outstanding striker, with Rafa Benítez committed to accepting an inheritance of Djibril Cissé and Milan Baros (who both had their moments, but little else), and whose first big-name purchase, Fernando Morientes, failed to cope with English football. Peter Crouch was a handful, and Fowler even made a brief return, but none was especially prolific.

This three-year period coincided with two Champions League finals and FA Cup success, plus the highest league points tally since 1988, which shows that getting the balance of the team right can make a huge difference, and that it's not all about star strikers. That said, you'd always rather have an outstanding no.7 or no.9 than a mediocre one, so long as the team's game doesn't become one-dimensional as a result.

In 2007, Fernando Torres arrived, and although the trophies dried up, he was regarded as the best centre-forward in the world during his peak at Anfield. Like Owen, he suffered too many muscle injuries, and had the Spaniard played more than 24 league games in 2008/09 (in which he still scored 14 goals), Liverpool might have racked up a few more than 86 points and taken the title. A year later he only managed 22 league games, but still scored 18 times, although he never looked as good once Roy Hodgson took charge.

No sooner had Torres' star started to dim than Luis Suárez arrived. If Torres was more prolific – he certainly needed fewer shots to score his goals – then Suárez has proved to be the superior all-round player.

Torres, like Rush and Owen, relied on pace, whereas Suárez takes the devilish work-rate of Keegan and adds some of the vision and toughness of Dalglish and the impudence of Fowler. And now that Suárez is getting close to replicating his Ajax and Uruguay scoring form, we can feel truly blessed.

Like Hunt, Rush and Torres he hasn't boosted his tally with penalties (not least because he missed a couple last season!), but unlike those greats he has the ability to curl in free-kicks from distance, with five scored already this campaign. And while Suárez is clearly a hugely emotional player, who wears his heart on his sleeve, he never displays the moodiness that affected Torres' later appearances, and which can see some players standing around sulking when things don't go their way. He never gives up, and that can be infectious. If your best player works hard, there's no excuse for the rest of the team.

Suárez is clearly the key factor in Brendan Rodgers' reshaped front line, but he's not on his own, particularly after a successful January transfer window, two years after Suárez himself was a January signing.

Philippe Coutinho has come in and excelled in his first two league starts – a goal and two assists, all achieved as part of individual dribbles – and Stewart Downing appears to have beefed up, physically and psychologically, on the wing. Raheem Sterling had an excellent first half of the season, although having only turned 18 in December, is now enjoying some well-earned downtime (in first-team terms) as his body learns to cope with the demands.

Going forward, Liverpool are a joy to behold right now, and only the best teams in the league appear to be able to do anything about it. The balance isn't yet quite right – although the return to fitness and form of Lucas will help – but it looks a lot better than earlier in the season, when things weren't quite working as hoped. There have been forward steps this season and backwards steps, but now the positive is starting to outweigh the negative, and it's possible to get a sense of a team starting to go places. But having extolled the virtues of Suárez, there is one other striker to get excited about.

After over five decades of almost consistent top-class striking talent adorning the first XI, Liverpool may have procured yet another outstanding striker this year. To my mind, Daniel Sturridge has almost everything necessary to be a phenomenal forward.

Teenage prodigies appear to be the Holy Grail in football, but quite a lot of players only click into gear between the ages of 22 and 25. In a sense, Sturridge fits both categories: he was a fantastic teenager, but his development was clearly arrested.

In around 15 years of following Liverpool's youth football fairly closely, I've probably seen a handful of players who looked so good that it would be a shock if they didn't make the grade. That started with Owen in the '90s, with the most recent example being Sterling. In between, Jack Wilshire wowed in Arsenal's midfield in the 2009 Youth Cup Final, against a Liverpool side including Jack Robinson, Andre Wisdom, Daniel Ayala, Thomas Ince and Alex Kačaniklić.

In that same class I'd put Daniel Sturridge who, in the second leg of the 2006 Youth Cup Final, stood head and shoulders above anyone else on the pitch, despite being just 16 at the time. Liverpool may have won the competition, but Manchester City clearly had the future star. I wrote on many occasions how pleased I'd be if Liverpool could snaffle him away from City, but he went to Chelsea instead.

(As a quick aside, none of Liverpool's players in the successful 2006 and 2007 sides are currently playing Premier League football, while Sturridge, Micah Richards and Danny Welbeck featured in the teams the Reds beat in those finals. To me, it highlights what a good team spirit and professional attitude Liverpool's youth side had back then, but without doing what it needed to do: produce first-team players. The overhaul in 2009 has certainly rectified this, and rather than win FA Youth Cups, the Reds are now producing first-team players.)

At 23, Sturridge has shown at Liverpool that he's ready to be a star. After a promising break-through at City (but where he was never first choice), he perhaps chose the wrong option in going to Chelsea, where politics appears to play a part in who plays. He had shown on loan at Bolton (eight goals in twelve games) that he was capable of transferring his talents to the highest level, and he excelled under Andre Villas-Boas in the first half of last season when back at the Bridge, but he was never the big-name striker that the owner seemed to demand in the team.

Chelsea's loss is Liverpool's gain. Sturridge has skill, pace, power, reasonable height and a sweet left-foot, plus a coolness in front of goal. It seems that all he needed was someone to put their faith in him, and at Liverpool he has that. At City the club were starting to spend big money on major names, and at Chelsea there was Drogba, then Torres.

Going forward it's all coming together for Liverpool. Yes, the big wins have been against the sides in the bottom half of the table, but the Reds troubled Manchester United, Arsenal and City in spells of varying length.

Given the age of Suárez, Sturridge, Coutinho and Sterling – and the evergreen nature of Steven Gerrard and Glen Johnson (the best progressive full-back in the league) – I can only see Liverpool's attacking getting better with time, experience and practice (although it's never 100% guaranteed).

And if the attacking can be improved due to individuals, pairings, trios and quartets being more devastating, then the balance of the team can be stronger, as not as many men will need to go forward for each goal scored, which in turn protects the back four. Get that right, and top four could be possible next season.

LIVERPOOL FC'S ROAD TO THE FUTURE

By Paul Grech

July, 2012

One of the first was Dominic Matteo; a classy if injury-prone defender who had bags of talent but not really the application to make the most of his abilities. Before him there had been Steve McManaman, whilst Robbie Fowler and Michael Owen came afterwards; each one immensely talented and worthy of being labelled as world class. In turn they were followed by Jamie Carragher and Steven Gerrard; two players who would shape Liverpool's fortunes for over a decade.

And then ... nothing.

For ten years there has been a big question mark surrounding Liverpool, one regarding the reasons behind the lack of homegrown talent coming through. What happened? Where did all the talent go?

The successes of the nineties had raised hopes and expectations for the new academy facilities opened in 2001, especially when Gérard Houllier – famed for laying down the plans for France's highly successful Clairefontaine academy – was appointed as manager.

Yet rather than providing the basis for Liverpool's return to the top of English football, the Academy became a battleground of ideologies and personalities. It is one of the saddest episodes of Liverpool's recent history, yet one that is so symptomatic of the club's inability to get its act together. It is, in many ways, an unbelievable story. One in which Academy directors were appointed without any form of consultation with the club's manager. One in which the reserves set-up at Melwood was practically excluded from those players coming through the Academy. It seemed that an us-against-them mentality between the Academy and the first team was not only tolerated but even actually encouraged.

Given all this, it is hardly surprising that only two players – Stephen Warnock and Danny Guthrie – have managed to make it and obtain a degree of success at Premier League level. Amazingly, the bulk of two FA Youth Cup winning sides (2005-06 and 2006-07) vanished without leaving a trace, with only Jay Spearing making anything like a substantial number of appearances for Liverpool.

It is difficult to determine why this situation was allowed to develop, for there is no reason other than lack of leadership and vision. It is impossible to explain otherwise why the club would continue its significant annual investment in the Academy whilst at the same time allowing it to become a black hole for talent.

Eventually it came down to a battle of wills between Rafa Benítez and those running the club; a battle that the Spaniard won not because others had been convinced by his arguments but because politically he was too important for the owners in their desperate battle to keep hold of the club. Getting control of the Academy was one of his key requests when it came to signing a new contract and, given that it was seen as a way of quelling the club's rebelling fans, eventually it was what he got.

That was the chain of events that led to the defining shift in strategy at the Academy. Out went a host of coaches who were deemed as not being good enough and in came three men hand-picked to start the revolution.

Scouser Frank McParland had worked with Benítez as a scout before joining Sammy Lee as General Manager when he was named manager of Bolton Wanderers. That didn't last long (Lee was sacked within six months of him getting the job), so he was available when Benítez came calling with the offer of a position as Academy Director, which was the fancy name for a rather administrative role that involved overseeing all that happened at the Academy.

For the technical side, Benítez turned to the most famous academy in the world: Barcelona. Specifically, he turned to José 'Pep' Segura who had worked with both Barcelona's youth and their B side before going into management, winning the Greek league title with Olympiakos. His role was to be that of shaping the Academy's technical strategy: outlining the way teams played, what type of players Liverpool should be looking for, and educating the coaches.

The third member was also hand-picked from Barcelona's academy. Rodolfo

Borrell had been so highly thought of that he been re-offered his job after a short stint as assistant manager at Greek side Iraklis went wrong. Despite this offer, Borrell knew that at Barcelona he was unlikely to progress beyond managing at Under 17 level (former players tend to land higher jobs there) and that he would have to move for his talents to be appreciated. When Liverpool offered him the chance to manage the Under 18s, he saw it as the opportunity that he was looking for. His role, however, involved more than simply coaching: having grown through the Barca system he could guide other coaches on the principles they had to follow.

Those three were the ones charged with reshaping the Academy, and they made the first step in that direction by setting a playing philosophy. They did this by canvassing the opinion of as many people as possible to come up with a system that closely mimics that of Barcelona whilst, at the same time, taking into consideration the nature of English football.

Thus the 4-2-3-1 that was eventually adopted by the Under 18s was something of a compromise between the 4-3-3 with which Segura was more familiar and English football's historic reliance on 4-4-2. The physical side of the game, which at Barca is of no importance, was also considered, with the decision being made to focus at least partially on this because otherwise they would be producing players who wouldn't cope with the demands placed on them by English football.

Both of these were inspired decisions which were aided by the 'pass and move' philosophy already at the club. Suddenly there was a system in place that updated the mentality that had been the club's ethos for decades with a tactical approach that was more in line with modern thinking.

Of course 'the plan', as Liverpool's strategy came to be called within the walls of the Academy, involved more than that. There were new approaches to training and greater attention to how instructions were communicated to the players, whilst setting the profiles as to what was needed from players for each position. From a philosophical point of view, however, those were the most significant modifications.

No matter how well thought out, it is in the implementation that the success of any new system will be determined. And it is here that the appointment of Borrell proved to be particularly important. At the most basic level he is, quite simply, a terrific coach. There isn't a player who has come into contact with him who hasn't improved. He pushes hard, criticises (even in public) when he feels the need, but knows both how to teach and how to motivate. It is a combination of attributes that inevitably leads to improvement.

Perhaps the finest example of Borrell's abilities is Stephen Sama. When he joined from Borussia Dortmund, it was clear that Sama had a lot of physical strength but there wasn't similar certainty about his technical ability. Sometimes, it looked like he had been placed in defence purely because of his size. Slowly, however, he started to improve. He began adding tactical intelligence to his game, with his positioning consistently improving. It was clear that he had been subjected to some serious coaching. Whether he'll ever be good enough to play for the first team remains to be seen, but he's got much closer to achieving that by playing under Borrell – and surely there isn't a better compliment that can be given to a coach in charge of a development squad?

It also helped that Borrell set high standards both for himself and for his players. Irrespective of the result, rarely does he fail to point out little things that could be done better. What might seem like nit-picking to most is in truth a very valuable trait as it teaches his charges that at the highest level they cannot afford to relax and have to keep working harder no matter what.

For all the criticism over the end result, Liverpool's Academy teams had been doing well before Borrell's arrival as the two FA Youth Cup triumphs testify. The Spaniard continued this good work, finishing second and reaching the quarter final of the FA Youth Cup playing a brand of attractive football reminiscent of that for which his previous club is famous. The new style of coaching seems to be working.

Coaching, however, wasn't the only aspect that changed; there was also a shift in beliefs. Under Steve Heighway, the mentality had always been that of focusing as much as possible on local players with only one or two brought from the outside. That started to change when Malcolm Elias was brought in from Southampton, where he had been a key member of one of the most fruitful academies in English football, one that had produced the likes of Theo Walcott, Gareth Bale and Alex Oxlade-Chamberlain. Just as it had been at Southampton, Elias' remit at Liverpool was that of finding and recruiting players, something that he was almost instantaneously successful with when acquiring the services of fourteen year old defender Andre Wisdom from Bradford.

When authority over the Academy was handed to Benítez, Elias opted to move on, joining Fulham a few weeks after compensation had been agreed. Eventually he would be back at Liverpool but only to point out Alex Kačaniklić and Lauri Dalla Valle (both of whom he had spotted for Liverpool) as two young players that his new club should include in the deal that took Paul Konchesky to Liverpool. Sixteen months down the line, Kačaniklić would be impressing for Fulham's first team.

Given Elias' track record, it was perhaps the most negative fallout from the internal restructuring, especially as Liverpool were about to get more aggressive in his area of specialisation.

The first indication of Liverpool's new strategy came in February 2010, when they agreed to pay £600,000 for Queens Park Rangers' fifteen year old winger Raheem Sterling. It was a bold and ambitious move, one that not only landed Liverpool one of the most talented young players in the country but which also showed that the club was willing to elevate its youth operations to a whole new level.

There was still a huge belief in local players – Benítez, Segura, Borrell and McParland all spoke at different times about the importance of retaining a Scouse heartbeat – but there was also an acceptance that Liverpool had to aggressively go after the most talented young players in the country to either fill any gaps that there were or to improve on what was available.

It was this decision that resulted in the purchase of Jordon Ibe, Suso, Shinji Ojo, Lloyd Jones, Dan Smith and Joao Texeira who, between them, cost a little over three million pounds. If just one of them were to be even a reasonable success, Liverpool would recoup their outlay for all of them by selling him to a smaller Premier League team. It isn't fool-proof but, as a strategy, it is a pretty low-risk one. It is also one that is already bearing fruits. Sterling has progressed well, making fleeting appearances for the first team and hinting that there is more to come.

In truth, that isn't the only change in the recruitment strategy that has been witnessed over the past months, for Liverpool are also trying to be more creative in the places where they look for new talent. This idea is one that Rafa Benítez had actively pursued in the form of a deal with the Hungarian side MTK Hungaria, guaranteeing that their best talent would come to Liverpool. Whilst that deal initially raised eyebrows because of Hungary's current standing in the international game, given the relative success of that deal – Peter Gulacsi and Kristian Adorjan are two highly promising players who are still on Liverpool's books whilst Kristian Nemeth and Zsolt Poloksei were possibly even more highly rated but were unfortunate in that injury curtailed their chances – it is something of a disappointment that with Benítez's departure this agreement seemed to die out.

Fortunately, new avenues seem to have been identified. The arrival of American midfielder Marc Pelosi might have been down to his performances at the Under-17 World Cup but Villyan Bijev's signing at around the same time hints at a widespread scan of the American youth movement; a view confirmed by the trial given to another young American in the form of Andrew Oliver. Although developed before Fenway Sports Group took over the club, it is easy to see why such a policy might resonate with them.

Soon after his appointment as the Boston Red Sox's General Manager, Theo Epstein declared that his aim was to build a "$100M player development machine" where the goal was to "develop a constant flow of impact talent". This wasn't some jumped-up comment from a manager eager to show just how much he wanted to win; instead, it formed part of an over-arching plan that had carefully considered the potential benefits of acting in this manner.

In a 2003 interview with the Boston Dirt Dogs, Epstein would go on to list these benefits. Included among his reasons were the access to talented young players who were more likely to stay healthy and improve than older ones, access to inexpensive talent which would free up financial resources to strengthen in other areas and, poignantly, also the "added pride in the Red Sox uniform".

Lift those points out of a baseball context and they could easily slot into any vision aimed at improving Liverpool FC. How much money has been spent on squad players like Salif Diao, Paul Konchesky and Philipp Degen – players with clear limitations but who were signed in the hope that they would give the squad added depth – which could have been diverted to get one player of established class had there been faith in the players coming out of the Academy to fill those squad-padding roles?

That question isn't an original one, nor an overly imaginative one. Yet the faith quite simply hasn't been there, just as it wasn't there for the Red Sox before FSG changed the set-up.

What the Red Sox did do was to develop a plan for the identification and development of players throughout the whole organisation. There was to be a holistic approach to playing, a certain style that was to be reflected regardless of whether a player was in the major league roster or whether he was affiliated to one of their minor league teams. They cemented what now is known as the Red Sox Way.

One way of achieving this was by putting a lot of focus in the baseball academy that they operate in the Dominican Republic, where the aim is to be able to discover the next star to come out of this country rich in baseball talent whilst at the same time using it as a base from which to scout the Latin American baseball market.

A parallel of sorts already exists at Liverpool, where Damien Comolli set up a link with Uruguayan side Nacional when Sebastián Coates was signed. With Uruguay's rich history of producing good technical players, that deal theoretically gave Liverpool an advantage should there be another talent like Luis Suárez or Edinson Cavani.

Whether that link will last given the Frenchman's departure is doubtful, but it wouldn't be surprising if Liverpool were to pursue a similar strategy – and do so more aggressively – in the future.

There is, of course, another very important reason why Liverpool should look overseas: learning. Whilst in their ability to successfully transition youth talent Barcelona remain the most famous example to be followed, they aren't the only one. The NextGen series showed just how impressive Sporting Lisbon's system is, whilst it also confirmed that the Ajax tradition is still strong. There are others – Atlético Bilbao, Atalanta, even Crewe – whose continuous success dictates that their methods have to be looked at in order to see what aspects Liverpool can integrate into their approach.

Again something has been happening in this area with Steve Cooper, Liverpool's highly thought-of Academy manager, spending some time at Ajax looking at how they operate even if, perhaps worryingly, that trip was also set up by Comolli. Given the potential benefits, the hope is that such visits do not cease now that Comolli has left.

One of the things that Cooper will have noticed is the heavy involvement there of former Ajax players. Current Ajax manager Frank De Boer started his coaching career at the Ajax academy, whose current structure includes Bryan Roy, Wim Jonk and Dennis Bergkamp. The presence of such iconic players not only provides the young players in their charge with a living example of where hard work can lead them but also they know that whatever advice they receive will be borne of their experience.

With the exception of Under-18 manager Mike Marsh, at Liverpool's Academy there are no immediately recognisable names. Perhaps former players, even those of the recent past, aren't too comfortable with the system adopted. Or else their ambition is to coach higher up than at academy level. Whatever the reason, Liverpool do need such people around.

Then again, the opposite should be avoided as well: Barcelona have lost some top youth coaches (including Borrell) because of an unwritten rule to let only former players coach the older age groups.

Yet, having former players around would be proof to the players that it is possible to progress because, ultimately, that is what all this work should lead to. And it is where Liverpool have faltered.

The difficulty, it seems, is one of bridging the gap that exists. Whilst players might appear good enough at reserves level, making the step to a team that is challenging in the top half of the table is perhaps one too far. Liverpool need to find a way of getting players an intermediate step; one that allows them to gain the experience that they cannot gain in the reserves.

This could be achieved through better use of the loan system – Liverpool have traditionally failed to provide players loaned out with clubs who can provide them with the platform they need – or, perhaps, through something more adventurous. There is no sure-fire system, just as there is no guarantee that can be given about a player developing in a way that fulfils what potential he shows as a youth.

And that is the cardinal rule of youth football. At 15 or 16 – even older – a player has a lot of growing up to do. Physically he might not develop as hoped. He might suffer injuries at a crucial stage or find himself lacking motivation when not given opportunities to progress. Or, quite simply, he might not be good enough no matter how well he does against players his own age.

With Liverpool screening a large portion of all the U18s and reserve games live on LFC TV, there is the danger that this rule gets forgotten. People will see a player doing well and quickly demand that he be given opportunities. Such elevated expectations are hardly beneficial for players who are still so young and lacking the maturity to handle such pressure.

Here it is the coaches' role to shield them; to remind both the players and those watching that there still is much to be done. It is a role that both Borrell and Marsh do well – neither one is quick to praise players, at least in public – and it is a talent that others will have to develop as well.

Indeed, developing coaches will be as crucial for the Academy's future as doing the same with players. The higher the quality of the coaches, the better the players will do. The more they know how to teach Liverpool's way of playing, the more comfortable and proficient they will be in doing so. And getting there will take time – which is an important note to keep in mind. For all the progress that has been made over these past three seasons, the inescapable fact is that Liverpool are trying to short-circuit the system in order to make up for all the wasted years. But it will still take a lot of effort and – just to stress how crucial it is – time to get to a stage where the development between second and first team will be seamless and continuous.

That will require patience, but the wait will be aided by the knowledge that the structure that is already in place ensures that it won't take a decade for Liverpool to produce another player good enough to play regularly for the first team.

JOHN BARNES: BLACK MAGIC

By Paul Tomkins

June, 2012

An outstretched left boot, planted on halfway-line chalk: a perfectly executed block-tackle. A spin into space, and half of the Anfield pitch opens up; new-boy John Barnes is away, running at the defence of table-toppers QPR. The ease with which, having approached the edge of the box, he jinks to his left, past a lunging tackle, transforms a great skill into something effortless. But it is the way he drags the ball to his right, and somehow readjusts his balance, that defines one of the greatest goals the famous stadium has ever seen; it defies belief, not least because he somehow manages to accelerate in the process. England international Terry Fenwick is bypassed – a *Tussauds* waxwork in blue and white hoops. England international full-back Paul Parker slides in, but is not quick enough. England international goalkeeper David Seaman – beaten by a Barnes curler into the top corner earlier in the half – is left helpless again, as the Reds' no.10, with right instep, nonchalantly slips the ball beneath the man in green.

John Barnes had impressed in the early part of his debut season, but this is the moment the Jamaican-born winger arrives. The Kop, who'd been deprived of the chance to see the new man due to a collapsed sewer that saw the stadium closed until mid-September, were finally getting to see his genius first-hand. His home debut had been against Oxford United, and he scored a fine free-kick. The Reds then beat Charlton, Derby and Portsmouth at home – Kenny Dalglish's side scoring eleven goals in a trio of victories – although Barnes was not amongst the scorers. But then came that QPR game, and an idol was born. In his 1999 autobiography he noted that it was the most memorable moment of his Liverpool career.

For the next four years the new no.10 absolutely terrorised English defences, scoring 75 times in all competitions in the process. His versatility was showcased in the way he went on to excel at centre-forward in 1989/90 (having ended his time at Watford in the role), and when, after an achilles tendon injury in 1991 sapped his acceleration, he later rebuilt his career as a deep-lying central midfielder, recycling possession and, at the age of 32, earning an England recall in that particular role.

It's fair to say that John Barnes was viewed with suspicion when, in June 1987, Dalglish signed the Watford winger for £900,000; a fairly hefty fee that was 60% of the then British record (at a stage when Liverpool had never broken the £1m barrier; that happened a month later, with the procurement of Peter Beardsley). There were no black players at Liverpool or Everton at the time, in an era where racism from the terraces was still rife. To make matters worse, Barnes' heart had been set on a move to Italy – at the time the leading league in world football. While Watford contacted Spurs, Liverpool and Manchester United, the player's agent, Atholl Still – a former opera singer – was hawking his client to leading Serie A clubs. It was widely known that a video had been produced to try and seduce AC Milan and Juventus, but only Sampdoria and Verona were interested. A quote appeared in the *Liverpool Echo* saying that Barnes wanted to move abroad or stay in London; the latter being patently untrue. There were also doubts about a player moving from a long-ball, low-expectations side with no great top-flight history, and whether or not he could adapt to the pressure and style of play at Liverpool. Those fears, expressed far and wide, were shown to be truly and utterly misplaced.

Barnes was nothing short of sensational. Despite his solid frame (before it became more – how shall I put it? – *meaty*), he glided across the pitch, moving with grace and poise. And for a silky-skilled winger, he had end product. He got into positions with pace, power and skill, and then found the killer pass or the inch-perfect cross (how many times did John Aldridge have to just nod in from the six-yard box, so delightful was the curve and weight on the centre?). In an era before assists were recorded, by viewing all the league goals from the late '80s and early '90s (courtesy of grainy videos located in the attic) it's clear that he never once failed to get into double figures in those first four campaigns.

Despite a full decade at Anfield, did Barnes ever perform better than in his first year? – with those constant mazy dribbles, astute passes and 15 league goals. Or did the shock and awe of that first season create a fantasy, where anything less than beating several men and providing a cool finish, produced disappointment? Had he painted himself into a corner of perfection? Maybe it's an illusion, but by his second season he already seemed a fraction heavier, and only registered eight times in the top division. But this bulk and strength, allied to pace and quick feet, made him a hugely effective centre-forward, and he featured there on occasions when he won his second Football Writers' Player Of The Year award, after finishing the league's top scorer, with 22 goals, plus six more in the cups. Another fine goalscoring season followed, and in those first four years he was averaging over 15 a season. That dropped to less than four a season for the next six years, to highlight how his game had altered. Still, in ten straight seasons – with Watford and Liverpool, between 1981 and 1991 – he never registered fewer than 13 goals in a season, and for the Reds he managed 108 goals in 407 appearances. To put Barnes' scoring record into perspective, Ryan Giggs – another prodigious winger whose game was reinvented in a similar way, but who has spent his entire career at a dominant club – had scored 163 goals in 909 club games, as of the summer of 2012; by contrast, Barnes, in his 19-year career, scored 35 more in 128 fewer matches.

One hallmark of greatness is just how good the player was at his peak; just how brightly he burned. Another is the duration of his excellence; precisely how long the flame lasted, even if it wasn't quite as luminescent. Barnes had ten years in Liverpool's first team, but it was those first four years that mark him out as a legend. The question for such players becomes whether or not their legacy is ruined by their merely human years. Is that perfection blemished, or can you place those vintage years into a glass display cabinet, and label them untouchable? Had Barnes stayed as a winger, struggling, short of the old pace, he may well have eroded some of those memories. The fact that he managed several more years in a completely different role – performances that, on their own, would not see him in a best-ever Liverpool XI – probably helps, because he wasn't damaging the memory of Barnes the Winger.

Perhaps the hardest question to answer is just how Barnes would be remembered had he arrived in 1994 as a portly possession master. Would people see a Xavi-esque ball retainer, whose appreciation of time, space and the weight of a pass, kept Liverpool ticking over with metronomic rhythm, or would he have been viewed as a lazy, tackle-dodging midfielder who failed to burst with dynamism into the box? Perhaps it didn't help that he was partnered with Jamie Redknapp, who was brave in always wanting the ball, but like Barnes, not much good at fighting to win it. By the time Roy Evans plumped for midfield steel, it was Barnes, now almost 34, who made way for Paul Ince. If those first four seasons saw a 'ten out of ten' player, he added six more as a seven or eight. Despite 224 games for the Reds after his achilles dulled his verve, his legendary status was confirmed by the first 178.

To be recognised as greats, players are often expected to be part of a successful side, and there's no doubt that Barnes, at his best, fits the bill – because he elevated an excellent Liverpool side to a sensational one. His less remarkable incarnation was in keeping with the club as a whole; when his achilles snapped in 1991, Liverpool's demise was hastened. Due to the post-Heysel ban, Barnes also missed out on appearing in the European Cup, which, through no fault of his own, left one major question unanswered; most greats lit up that particular stage. Having said that, he was the undoubted creative light in what Tom Finney described in 1988 as the best English side he'd ever seen, and it almost didn't need that highest-level participation; at the time, only AC Milan – whose first of three European Cups in six seasons was still a year away – looked capable of matching the Reds.

As an individual – albeit one finely attuned to the team's needs – Barnes had it all. He displayed skill without excess; flair without showboating. There were nutmegs and drag-backs aplenty, but perhaps as a result of Graham Taylor's hard-line Watford drilling – and the military discipline of his colonel father – the aim was always to be as direct as possible: get into the heart of the opposition box, or get to the byline to deliver a cross. If space was tight, and there were three men around him, then the tricks might come out – but only to work himself free. Nothing was overdone or overblown. No blind alleys were wound down. Nothing was done to humiliate an opponent. He'd shift the ball one way, then the other, and the balance was perfect. The acceleration would do the rest.

Barnes was also excellent in the air. Every headed goal seemed to be met with the commentator noting "a rare headed goal by John Barnes", yet he got several each season. His upper body strength was immense, aided by the thighs of a bodybuilder. Matthew Le Tissier – himself no lightweight – once remarked that, in going shoulder to shoulder, he just bounced off Barnes. In his 1996 autobiography, Ian Rush describes Barnes thus:

"A beautifully balanced runner, who could glide past defenders seemingly effortlessly. He also had great vision and the ability to split defences with one telling pass [...] But his greatest asset of all – and one that a lot of spectators have never fully appreciated – has been his sheer physical strength. When he had the ball he could hold off two, or even three, defenders with his power. At his devastating best, Barnes was a player of true world class."

In 2006, John Barnes was voted 5th in the official Liverpool website's '100 Players Who Shook the Kop'. Had serious injury not robbed him of one of his greatest assets, he would surely have ranked even higher.

CULTURAL EXCHANGE: AMERICAN IDEAS & 'OUR FOOTBALL'

By Simon Clancy
November, 2010

Players vs. Managers

Excuse the cliché but Chapter One of Michael Lewis's book *Moneyball* is called 'The Curse of Talent'. Be it Major League Baseball, the NBA or the NFL, the curse of talent is what haunts owners, general managers, coaches and fans. How else can you explain the popularity of the NFL Draft as a spectacle? The most watched non-sporting sporting event in history. And how else can you explain the day in, day out, week in, week out, 365 day pursuit of talent in American sport? Scouts follow every move of high school kids; men like Tom Lemming are so important that they can make or break the future of a prep athlete, and websites such as Rivals.com and Scout.com provide a living, breathing heartbeat to every high school kid from Helena, Montana to St Petersburg, Florida. And where National Signing Day – and the announcement of where one 16-year-old boy is going to play college football, baseball or basketball for three, maybe four seasons – is broadcast live on ESPN.

Why? Because the player matters so much.

Look at Lewis's other best-selling book about former 'Ole Miss' left tackle Michael Oher, *"The Blind Side"*, or Willie Morris's remarkable account of the recruiting process of Marcus Dupree, *"The Courting of Marcus Dupree"*, and you'll find a significant part of your answer as to why managers take more responsibility in English football;

the players are the focus in American sport, so much more than they are in European football, because those players are household names from the age of 12 or 13. Excuse me if I continue to use (American) football as the example but it's where I'm most comfortable. Now if a tape of Reggie Bush (pre USC) and Noel Devine (pre West Virginia) is getting a million hits on YouTube then you understand why the players are always going to be King.

Only in America can you debate to death the ramifications behind whether Cam Newton really did cheat in an exam (or three) at Florida, or whether his father really did ask Mississippi State for $180,000, for his son to sign with the Bulldogs upon leaving the JUCO ranks. Yes, you can debate those issues here and they'll get talked about a little bit on the football phone-in and the media discussion shows, but within a few days people move on. The analysis involved in English football is much more subjective than that of the American version. It allows for agendas to be formed and carried out. It allows for the indefensible to be defended. It allows for blame to be incorrectly attributed and it masks a multitude of failings.

As much as doing the right thing is important, to be perceived to be doing the right thing can carry you a long way and buy you time. It's why the Premier League is full of players with 'unfortunate' transgressions in their past, yet who are able to carry on their business, without the sort of ramifications that the same incidents present in the US. And it's only when you drive through Texas and listen to the callers berating Mack Brown and his players, stand in Death Valley on a Saturday night watching LSU, listening to the Tiger faithful bemoaning Les Miles and his players, or drive through Alabama the week of the Iron Bowl against Auburn that you realise why the player carries more responsibility for his performance in the US than he ever would do in the UK.

It's cultural for sure. But it's also historical.

History

If you look back over the history of football in this country, you'll rarely hear stories of players losing their jobs because of bad performances. Yes, they lose their place in the first team and will end up in the reserves, but the opportunity to play again with the first team is usually available very quickly. It's something of a rarity when players physically lose their jobs and end up on the unemployment line. What happens, of course, is that they get sold. And when they do, the selling club still makes money; albeit often not a profit, but money nonetheless. For argument's sake: a player is sold to Crystal Palace from Liverpool, a lower division club perhaps more suited to his abilities, and he may well flourish. But there's a great deal tied into the original deal that brought him to Liverpool in the first place.

It's still relatively rare that Player A is signed for £10 million, plays poorly for six months, then is sold on quickly. Sometimes the player is loaned out; Alberto Aquilani being the perfect example. Bought for a figure in the region of £20 million from Roma in the summer of 2009 (after the departure of the tremendous Xabi Alonso to Real Madrid) he arrived with an injury that wasn't responding well to treatment, and it's understandable that when he finally did play, he struggled at times with the pace of the English game, having come from the much more sedentary Italian league.

However, a decision was made – a wrong one in the eyes of many fans – to loan Aquilani back to Italy and Juventus where he's subsequently had a terrific first quarter of the season. But, rightly or wrongly, the blame for Aquilani's poor performances at Liverpool didn't rest on the shoulders of Alberto Aquilani; it rests on the shoulders of the man who bought him: Rafa Benítez.

I touched upon it earlier, but player indiscretions are treated in a different light in European football. There is still something of a Playboy culture that surrounds professional footballers and whilst elements of drinking and other high jinks have to some extent been eradicated, there are still weekly occurrences of players ending up on the front page of the national papers, falling out of a nightclub in the arms of a woman who clearly isn't their wife. The same wife they were recently photographed with in a glossy magazine. Somehow though, the blame is levelled at the club they represent and the game of football generally; it is expected that they'll behave like that. 'It's in a footballer's nature', is the stereotypical response. That, then, gets passed off as fact.

Despite being born a Liverpool fan 36 years ago, I've also spent nearly a quarter of a century immersed in the NFL and college football and to me there are subtle differences, but differences nonetheless; an NFL roster is made up of 53 players. Of course, the top echelons are generally untouchable. You only have to look at the indiscretions of Michael Vick (jail sentence for involvement in a dog fighting ring), Ray Lewis, Terrell Owens, etc. to know that. Regardless of what happened with Vick in Atlanta, Arthur Blank was left with a very difficult decision to make about a player he'd drafted first overall out of Virginia Tech, and who he nurtured like a son. When he was released from his jail sentence, the Philadelphia Eagles immediately picked him up and he's now arguably the 2010 NFL MVP to the midpoint of the season.

Ray Lewis is a first ballot Hall of Fame linebacker, his arrest and subsequent trial for murder still didn't cause the Baltimore Ravens to sever ties. And if you look at Terrell Owens, the vast majority of his 'situations' have come within the confines of the sporting arena. And yet, year on year, he winds up with another suitor: the 49ers, the Cowboys, the Eagles, the Bills or the Bengals. Owens is considered a 'cancer' in the locker room and yet he still gets a job.

But, what about those not in the top echelon of players? It's much, much easier for teams to take a cap hit and cut a player. An average starting defensive lineman or a back-up point guard or a second baseman gets caught doing something wrong by the police, and often it's easier to cut them and get someone else in, because there's a big pool of players waiting in the wings. And many from that pool of players will have gone to the Final Four or played in the BCS Title Game; they're still household names and have been since they were 14/15 years old. Therefore, the onus of responsibility lies much more on their shoulders.

Unless you follow an English football team religiously, your average fan isn't going to know the starting eleven of the reserve team. But your average college football fan knows that at Alabama, Will Vlachos is the center, Greg McElroy is the Quarter Back (QB) – he hands off to Heisman winner Mark Ingram who throws to Julio Jones. Your average Duke Blue Devil basketball fan will know the one to five starting line-up, and the bench. The player as an individual means more in the US, and that comes from the pressure cauldron of college sports. Hell, after Dan Okrent created Rotisserie Baseball back in 1980, he made players personal. He made them the focus of the attention of the sports-watching nation. More than 19 million people in the US alone play fantasy sports. So when a pitcher doesn't live up to the hype, he's cut. When the 3rd round pick QB can't break the roster, he's cut.

But when the right winger struggles for five seasons to make the team consistently, then it's as much the fault of the manager, as it is that of the player. More so, if for example you're like Ryan Babel or Royston Drenthe, who proved to be two of Europe's brightest young talents at Ajax (and in the Dutch U21 side up to 2007) before flattering to deceive at Liverpool and Real Madrid respectively.

The Way the Games are Played
European football, baseball, basketball and gridiron are, to a greater or lesser degree, team games. But within that team ethic, there are great distances between what that actually means: the pitcher has a specific role on the diamond, as does the point guard on the hardwood or the wide receiver on the gridiron. If the wide receiver is dropping catches and not doing his specific job, then it's the wide receiver's fault, because he has a more defined role than a left midfielder.

By the very nature of the way gridiron is played compared to the way that soccer is played, positionally you're more vulnerable to criticism with an oval-shaped pigskin than a soccer ball.

Take Brandon Marshall of the Miami Dolphins on Thursday night against the Chicago Bears; he dropped two critical passes on the same drive and then gave up a 15-yard unsportsmanlike conduct penalty for under-arming the ball in the direction of his friend and former QB Jay Cutler. Friday's papers and message boards were ringing with discontent, directed squarely at Marshall. It's hard to find the same levels of vitriol labelled at a Premier League player who didn't do his job correctly.

Of course, soccer is much more fluid in terms of where the ball goes, but the fact remains that in the US, the way that the games are played opens up the players to far more criticism than their European counterparts. The concept of open play is what soccer is all about, whereas American sports – football and baseball anyway – are more focused on execution.

The focus is on developing certain specialised skill sets that are used tactically as part of a whole. In that sort of environment, with a multitude of coaches and on-field captains, there is an onus on the player to get his job right. That's not such an issue in soccer. And, it's certainly a strong part of the explanation as to why players don't get as much of the blame.

General Managers

Most US sports teams have general managers (GM). That's a totally foreign concept, certainly in English football. It's why Damien Comolli was viewed through such disconcerted eyes when he was first appointed into a GM-type position at Tottenham.

If you look back over the history of English football and it's successful managers, the names that will always stand out are those such as Herbert Chapman, Bill Nicholson, our own Bill Shankly, Bob Paisley, Matt Busby, Brian Clough, Don Revie, Alex Ferguson, Arsène Wenger and Jose Mourinho.

Successful teams always carry the imprint of the manager and all those aforementioned names did that in their times at the clubs they represented. Managers who fail are often men who simply don't have the personality to make the club theirs. Take Wenger as a perfect example. Bookish and rather nervous looking when he arrived from Japanese football, he was seen as something of a strange appointment by Arsenal and was laughed at by fans and sections of the media. No-one's laughing now. Whilst Arsenal may be trophy-less for several seasons, you simply cannot argue with the vision he had when he joined and the remarkable legacy that he will leave the club with if and when he chooses to depart.

Alex Ferguson has done the same thing at Manchester United. There's a famous quote attached to his appointment back in November 1986, coming as it did during a period of dominance for Liverpool. Ferguson stated that he wanted to "knock Liverpool off their fucking perch". It may not have been the quote that you'd repeat to your mother, but it set a benchmark and, despite some early, rocky patches, that's exactly what Ferguson has done at United, laying down his marker and changing United's fortunes forever.

Of course, all of those names worked with coaches and assistants who helped them change the course of their respective clubs; Fergie and Archie Knox, Peter Taylor and Brian Clough, Shankly's Boot Room or Jimmy Murphy and Matt Busby.

Where the waters get muddied is with what Americans would call front office members; Mourinho's relationship with Peter Kenyon was cited as one of the reasons why the mercurial Portuguese left Chelsea for Inter Milan.

The successful managers have always been responsible for their purchases and to a greater or lesser extent have lived and died by them. No-one would ever have told Matt Busby that he should buy Harry Gregg or Tommy Taylor, just as no-one would ever tell Arsène Wenger to buy Theo Walcott or Alex Song. They do it themselves, because that's their job.

The concept of a GM managing the playing staff and a coach concentrating solely on the on-field stuff is so alien to a UK audience. And yet in the US, it's the most natural thing in the world; GMs are known across the league, be it the NFL, MLB or NBA. New England Sports Ventures' Theo Epstein is far more well-known than manager Terry Francona. In fact, I would hazard that Dustin Pedroia is better known than Francona. That's no disrespect to Francona, but it's the underlying point of this whole piece.

Chelsea was Mourinho's team. Yes they had Terry and Lampard and Drogba but they were Mourinho's team. Manchester United are Ferguson's team. No-one player is bigger than Sir Alex and that has been proved time and again through history, especially when he's sold off players like David Beckham and Jaap Stam. Nottingham Forest was Clough's team and Clough's alone. His much publicised 44 day stint at Leeds United highlighted perfectly what can happen, when the power of the player restricts any managerial imprint being nailed down.

Of course that's not to say that US sports haven't had their fair share of statesmen-like coaches; Lombardi, Stram, Landry, Shula, etc. But those types of coaches, these days, are becoming the exception rather than the norm. Part of that is a generational thing but it's also because of a change in the dynamic of the front office, where yesterday's cheque signers have become today's personnel decision-makers. Even in today's NFL there are very few joint GM/coaches. Perhaps only Andy Reid in Philadelphia and Bill Belichick in New England still exist (Bill, who is a throwback to the older generation of NFL head coaches, but who is also very similar to the statesman-like English football coach.). Belichick's hooded top could be Brian Clough in his green jumper, Mourinho in his Prada suit or Alex Ferguson's chewing gum. His imprint and legacy is long lasting but he's a rarity. You only have to look at the longest serving head coach currently in the NFL to realise that; Tennessee's Jeff Fisher is a great man and a terrific coach, in his own right, but you'd never mistake him for a *statesmanlike* coach.

When the Red Sox traded for Jarrod Saltalamacchia, I'm 99.9% sure that it was Theo Epstein making the trade, not Terry Francona. On NFL Draft Day, it's Rick Spielman not Brad Childress at Minnesota making the final call; it's Jeff Ireland, not Tony Sparano in Miami; Ozzie Newsome not John Harbaugh in Baltimore; Scott Pioli not Todd Haley in Kansas City. That simply wouldn't happen in English football.

Over here, the manager is the ultimate arbiter of the kind of player a team strives for. Yes, coaches in the US generally decide whether teams will run a 3-4 or a 4-3 defence, whether their identity on offense will be that of a conservative-run first attack or an all-out pass attack. But the round pegs, for these holes, are ultimately selected by the GM. The area scouts report back to the general manager, not the head coach. Therefore the onus of failure and responsibility is shared amongst the coach and the GM.

If Team A loses three seasons in a row then the GM who signs the free agents and makes the draft picks will take as much, if not more, of the rap as the coach, who couldn't get them to win. But if the GM was signing mediocre players, then there's an element of sympathy with the coach, who did his best with a bad lot. In the Premier League, the onus of buying and selling players has traditionally fallen on the manager's shoulders and his alone.

He picks the tactics, he decides whether to play a 4-4-2 formation, or 4-5-1, 4-2-3-1, 4-3-3, and so on, and he moulds the players into his vision. He does that because they're *his* players. So with the freedom of selection, come the pitfalls of poor judgement.

(The appointment of Comolli raises some interesting questions, as it removes some of the 'blame' from the manager when it comes to transfers. If successful, it will provide a long-term overview from a 'GM'/Director of Football whose job is not dependent on winning matches, but on securing talent. The 'problem' is that the DoF and the manager have to share a vision, because the manager – unless he is a real magpie, who can flit between various methods – needs players to fit his tactical system and football ideology. Some players are versatile enough to fit any system, but others only excel in certain set-ups.)

Despite all his marvellous success at Manchester United, Sir Alex Ferguson's job came under severe threat a few years ago due to several poor purchases: Eric Djemba-Djemba, Kleberson, Liam Miller, Juan Sebastian Veron, Massimo Taibi, *et al.* This led to three years without the title. He managed to pull it round as some of his younger players – Cristiano Ronaldo, Darren Fletcher, etc., started to progress into international-calibre performers, but even an untouchable such as Ferguson felt the pressure for his poor purchases. It wasn't perceived as the fault of the players, it was perceived as the fault of the manager for buying mediocrity in the first place.

No manager is sacred in the English game because almost all have the weight of responsibility that comes with picking your squads.

After all, as Lewis himself once wrote:

"If Billy Beane is such a goddam genius, how come he's paying Jermaine Dye $11 million a year?"

But, Beane probably wouldn't get fired for that. Jermain Dye probably would, when it was financially viable to do so. Roy Hodgson definitely would. And that's the difference.

A DOCTOR AT HILLSBOROUGH

By Neil Dunkin

April, 2010

This piece was originally written for the Sunday Express in 2009 – and, as they only published half of the article, Neil offered the full text to TTT. We were only too glad to accept.

A perfect day for an FA Cup semi-final. As Dr Glyn Phillips drove with his brother Ian and two mates from Merseyside to Sheffield, they all agreed the weather could not have been better. April showers had been replaced by radiant sunshine and the Pennines looked stunning beneath the immaculate blue skies.

A beautiful day for the semi between Liverpool and Nottingham Forest.

Although he lived in Glasgow and worked as a GP in Lanarkshire, Dr Phillips, 34, had been born and bred in Huyton, Merseyside. A devoted Liverpool supporter, he had achieved the Holy Grail of every fan by obtaining a season ticket for Anfield, and he travelled down religiously to see the Reds. Now he was on his way to the Cup tie at Hillsborough where the four pals had tickets in the end allocated to Liverpool fans.

Once they arrived in Sheffield, they parked their car and strolled to the stadium, arriving half an hour before kick-off.

At the ground, they joined the throng of supporters and walked through a central tunnel into the Leppings Lane terrace, behind the goal:

"As soon as we got in, we knew it was an abnormally packed crowd," says Dr Phillips, now 55. "We were carried along on our feet by the crowd. We got split up from our mates and Ian and I found ourselves near the front, on the pitch side of a steel crowd barrier."

Dr Phillips had been in lots of packed football terraces but he soon realised the pressure of bodies in this pen was of a different magnitude.

"I've been on the Kop many, many times, and I've never been in a crush like that before. It was on a completely different scale to my previous experiences. I'd been going on the Kop since the age of 12, for big, big games, derby games, Leeds and Man United games, European games. We always used to go right in the middle behind the goal and I'd enjoy the movement, the surges, the swaying of the crowd. It was part of the fun. But this was abnormal, quite sinister.

"We had to get away from there. I knew this was not a good place to be and we decided to move higher up the terrace. People couldn't stand aside so we went down on hands and knees and crawled through legs. Higher up it was still so tight that standing up was difficult but we did it and even managed to meet up with our two friends. Then we were looking at each other with faces of incredulity. What's going on?

"There wasn't much you could do, though, because you were stuck, penned in by the side against railings. Imagine having your elbows down by your side and your hands up in front of your chest. You just couldn't move your arms because you were so crammed together. Even then, as kick-off approached, we assumed the crush would ease and everything would be all right. I remember vaguely the match kicked off and Peter Beardsley hit the bar but you couldn't watch the game because you were so conscious by then that it was a dangerous situation.

"You were constantly making sure your footing was right because if you went over, loads of other people were going to go over. There was a lot of shifting of position. You were getting moved to and fro, only small distances but it was impossible to resist. Then I became aware of people climbing the fence, trying to get out, and police paying increasing attention. To the side of us, on the right, down towards the pitch, alongside the fence running perpendicularly up the terrace, people were becoming very agitated. That was an area with loads of space to move around, in contrast to where we were.

"Lads were yelling: 'Get back, get back. There's fans crushed at the front', and they were becoming very upset because people didn't realise what was going on. And you see very limp bodies getting hauled out and you think: 'Oh shit, something really bad is happening.' Then someone ran on the pitch, yelling at Liverpool's goalkeeper Bruce Grobbelaar to stop the game.

"Minutes later, we'd climbed over the railing into the next pen which was relatively empty. I was looking down at the pitch and could see the state of some people and I thought: 'God, they're dead. I'm going to have to go and try to help.'

"So I made my way down to the front where there was a gate in the fence, on top of a low wall. I shouted to a policeman: 'I'm a doctor. Let me on the pitch.' I put my hand out to him and he pulled me up the wall, but we didn't realise there was a cross bar in the gateway. As I leapt up, I cracked my head on this bar."It nearly knocked me out. I was seeing stars. A hell of a blow, causing a scalp laceration. Blood was streaming down my face. I shook the blow off and walked on the pitch, which was full of people milling around. Chaos, chaos.

"I'm thinking what to do and literally the first body I came to was this young lad, a teenager. He wasn't breathing, no pulse, ashen, grey, clinically a cardiac arrest, and I knelt beside him and started doing CPR [cardio-pulmonary resuscitation]. There was a guy next to me — he said he was a male nurse — so while I did mouth-to-mouth, he did chest compressions.

"As we worked away, I was aware of a lot of people suffering in the pens. I thought if this lad is this bad and he's on the pitch, then the ones still in the pens have no chance. I thought I've got to give him a decent chance, so I stayed with him. I asked some policemen for oxygen and an oxygen cylinder arrived. This is a big bone of contention in the statement I made afterwards and the subsequent inquiry into the disaster. To my best knowledge, the oxygen cylinder was empty. The gauge was reading empty. But this was part of the inquiry when at least one QC wanted to discredit my evidence. It was eventually deemed that on the balance of probabilities I was wrong because I admitted I was angry and I'd had a heavy blow to the head.

"Anyway we carried on working on the boy as he didn't have a pulse. We must've been there five, 10 minutes and I was on the point of giving up when I felt a femoral pulse. He had developed a healthy, bounding pulse. Against the odds, his heart had spontaneously started again. He was completely unconscious but he started making some efforts at breathing.

"So we got a stretcher and carried him into an ambulance behind the goal. There were two others on the floor inside but they were dead. We put the lad on his side in the recovery position and I decided there wasn't a lot more I could do. I don't know if that was the correct decision, if I should've stayed with him, but his heart was going, he was breathing.

"I remember saying to the ambulanceman: 'Keep an eye on him. If there are any problems, give me a shout.' The daftest thing to say, with all this chaos going on, but you didn't think that at the time.

"As we had carried the lad to the ambulance, I'd been aware of eight to 10 bodies in the goal area. Inside you're struck with this desire to be professional and do what you can but at the same time incredulous this has happened in the space of half an hour, at a semi-final, on a sunny day. There are all these young lads lying dead.

"I went back looking for others to help. I tried CPR on a few more people but they were gone. It's horrible trying to resuscitate people who are effectively dead, the taste of vomit and all that kind of thing, but I have to say there was no hint of alcohol on any of the young people I attempted CPR on.

"And getting into the game we did not observe any misbehaviour. A bit of boisterousness you get with any football crowd but no bad behaviour, nobody inebriated or out of control, in contrast to the allegations made later in some newspapers. By now I was basically on the pitch scouting for somebody to help. It must have been after 3.30 and by then people were walking and talking or sitting and talking or they were dead. Nothing much in between.

"The last person I tried to resuscitate was in his 20s. I think his brother was trying to revive him and I remember this girl wearing a Celtic top saying: 'Leave him, he's gone, he's gone.' I had a go but he was dead. Now I was down the far end of the pitch, where this mass of Forest fans were just standing, watching in stunned silence. I saw two photographers by the goal and what was growing in my mind, among all this clinical stuff and the incredulity, was that I was very conscious of what the media did to Liverpool after Heysel, where the majority of 10,000 fans did nothing wrong and as a result of the incompetence of stadium officials, UEFA and Belgian police, 26 nutters were able to cause mayhem. Juventus had their share of morons, too, but that was conveniently forgotten.

"I thought they will try to blame this on the fans. I can't let that happen. So I went up to the photographers and said something along the lines of: 'I hope you're going to stuff this ground when you write it up.' I made a few remarks about the lack of facilities and they asked what I did. I said I was a GP and I've just been trying to resuscitate dead lads. As soon as they heard I was a GP, not just an overgrown scally fan, they thought here's someone worth quoting, so the notepads came out and photographs were taken.

"Then I thought I've got to speak to someone from Liverpool Football Club, to make sure they don't let the fans get the blame. I boldly went to the players' tunnel. There were police all around. I said I was a GP and had to speak to someone from LFC. They didn't even attempt to stop me. I think they were all stunned. Anyone who sounded as though he had any degree of intellect they let through.

"I made my way up the players' tunnel and by chance Kenny Dalglish was there, looking ashen-faced because, as I learned later, his son had been in the crowd. I introduced myself and told him very, very quickly what I'd just witnessed and I said you mustn't let them pin this on the fans. This was not fan trouble. The crowd conditions here were a disgrace. He said something like we didn't want to play here but had little say in it.

"Unbeknown to me, Alan Green, the BBC football commentator, was standing there listening and he asked if I minded repeating it on radio. Next thing he was introducing me live, I was saying what I'd witnessed and it came out, almost in one breath."

Dr Phillips told the radio audience: "There's no doubt this crowd was too big for this ground. Liverpool just filled the end they were given. The police allowed the fans to fill the middle terracing section to the point where they were crammed in like sardines. And yet the two outside portions of the terracing were left virtually empty, and I stood and watched police allowing this to happen.

"It got to a point where they lost control completely. Lads were getting crushed against the fence right down near the pitch and there were so many people in that part of the ground that nobody could even move to get out. I climbed sideways into an emptier section and then made my way on to the pitch to try and help.

"Now unfortunately there are guys who have died down there on that pitch. I've seen about eight to ten, I don't know how many there are.

"There was one chap I went to, he was clinically dead. He had no heartbeat. Myself and another guy – I think a nurse – we resuscitated him for about 10 minutes. We were just about to give up when we got his heart beating but I don't know what the state of his cerebral functions is going to be like.

"We asked for a defibrillator. I've been informed there isn't a defibrillator in the whole ground, which I find appalling for a major event like this. We were given an oxygen tank to help with our resuscitation and it was empty. I think this is an absolute disgrace."

With that, Dr Phillips ended his comments and walked back on the pitch, returning to the Leppings Lane end.

"I made my way through the gate I'd used to get on the pitch," he says.

"I went up the terrace and rejoined my brother and two friends at the top where they'd stayed while I was on the pitch. They were stunned, disbelieving what had happened. I'd done what I could. I'd tried to help revive people. I'd also made sure people who needed to know what really happened had somebody with some credibility telling them. Bizarrely, I'd got a chance to speak out on the radio, which had one personal advantage.

"My wife was at home in Glasgow, very upset and anxiously watching events on telly, knowing we were in that terrace. Thankfully one or two friends heard me on the radio and phoned her within minutes to say I was okay."

The four mates left Leppings Lane and returned to their car for the journey home to Merseyside.

"I was in the back, reflecting on events and listening to the radio," says Dr Phillips.

"They replayed my little outburst two or three times, leaving me with a total sense of disbelief. What my friends couldn't quite get was how dispassionate and comprehensible I was, which surprised me because when I was speaking I thought

I was shaking with anger. More importantly, we were all horrified and upset by the steadily increasing death toll.

"We made our way back to Rainhill where my folks lived and I made an emotional call to my wife. By this time I was feeling quite numbed by everything and very conscious of the media interest. Papers wanted to get hold of me. They'd heard about this GP from East Kilbride, so the press officer for Lanarkshire Health Board had to come in off holiday and field calls.

"Next day, Sunday, I drove to Glasgow and realised how preoccupied I was because I made it in three hours, about an hour quicker than normal. I just clogged it. I was back before I realised it. I got into work on Monday morning and knew I couldn't do the job. It felt as though I shouldn't be there. I needed to be in Liverpool. So I told my partners in the surgery: 'I'm going to have to go off for the rest of this week.'

"That evening I returned to Liverpool and we went to Anfield where we tied some flowers with our scarves to a barrier. That was emotional, but I had such mixed feelings. It had been pointless and preventable. Innocent lives had been lost and in the midst of all this, you've got despicable elements in the media attacking vulnerable people, bereaved parents, brothers and sisters having to read or hear rubbish about their lost loved ones.

"I was increasingly angry with the media and notably the most astute observation of that whole week came when Neil Kinnock, the Labour leader, was being interviewed on the pitch at Anfield. He was surrounded by scallies and whatever and this teenage voice piped up about the police: 'The bizzies fucked up.'

"I thought that sums it up. Why isn't he being interviewed? Absolutely dead right, and subsequently it was established he got it right. The stewarding and policing were incompetent.

"While staying on Merseyside with my family, I gave interviews to ITN, Granada, an American TV company at Anfield. Then I just had this sense I wasn't going to resolve this. By now there was a video running in my head about the events of the day, what I did, what I should've done. I thought I've got to go to Sheffield to find that boy on the pitch, find out what happened to him.

"The following Friday I drove over on my own and went to the ground. People were there to offer support and I was met by a woman social worker, Dee, who was great. She allowed me to walk all the way around the pitch and I told her my story, what had happened, what I'd witnessed. She was very, very supportive. That was therapeutic."

After qualifying as a doctor at Leeds University, Dr Phillips became a medical officer in Royal Navy nuclear submarines and he says:

"In military psychiatry, there's a well-known phenomenon, a need to resolve traumatic events. It's called revisiting the battlefield. Being back there on a calm, sunny day when the chaos has gone, that helps put the matter into perspective. Going back certainly helped me. When you've been part of a traumatic event with loss of life which is very upsetting, returning to the scene and seeing it's no longer going on definitely helps people get through these things.

"From the ground, I went to the two main Sheffield hospitals to find the boy. I thought he'd be in intensive care if he'd survived. I was discreetly allowed to look at some people who were being cared for and I didn't recognise him. I now know why, because he was totally swollen up. But he was there in intensive care.

"I came to the conclusion he'd died and I felt pretty low about that. I beat myself up, thinking I should've stayed with him. Having got him going again, I should've made sure he was okay."

After the tragedy, West Midlands Police launched the biggest inquiry in British legal history to ascertain what happened at Hillsborough, and in March 1990, Dr Phillips was asked to watch video footage. He went to Knowsley Hall, Lord Derby's home just outside Liverpool, where investigators had temporary offices for the examination of tapes which they hoped would establish where people had been on the fateful day.

"I was watching this video with a police officer," says Dr Phillips, "and by chance I fleetingly saw myself on the pitch, on my knees over this body. I said that's the first lad I tried to help. The constable said: 'We've got his name and I don't think he died. I'll look through the records and get in touch with you.'

"A week afterwards, the police officer phoned: 'We know who it is, an 18-year-old lad, Gary Currie. He survived and his family is very keen to meet you.'

"So we arranged to go down to Huyton and see Gary. Coincidentally he lived about half a mile from the primary school I'd attended as a young boy.

"Meeting him was a moving experience. Sadly he hadn't survived unscathed. His heart had stopped and he suffered some anoxic brain damage, so he's not as he was. He's disabled, on permanent medication, and can't work. But he can walk and talk and has still got his sense of humour. And he is still a massive Reds fan.

"His family were just delighted he lived. Two years after the disaster we were invited to his 21st and have kept in touch occasionally ever since. In fact, every Christmas he and his mother Alice send me a Liverpool FC calendar and a kind gift for my son."

Dr Phillips was also called to give evidence to Lord Justice Taylor's inquiry into the disaster, but oddly he wasn't invited to the subsequent inquest. He says: "At the Taylor inquiry, a panel of barristers represented various bodies ... South Yorkshire Police, Sheffield Wednesday, South Yorkshire Ambulance, St John's Ambulance, the stadium engineers. There was a row of them. On his high desk was Lord Taylor and below him the Treasury Solicitors, QCs representing the Government.

"I naively thought I was providing a public service but only after my questioning started did I realise this was a game, not a very funny game. At least one QC wanted to discredit me, basically a dirty tricks technique. I had been widely quoted as being critical because there wasn't a defibrillator and the oxygen cylinder was empty, so they wanted to make me look like an idiot.

"I was handed this photocopy of a series of heart readings, ECGs. They were very poor quality and it was time for trick questions. A QC asked: 'What do you think this first tracing is?' I looked at it and it was just a squiggly line.

"The subject under discussion was a condition called ventricular fibrillation where the heart has effectively stopped beating but is electrically quivering. I said it could be VF and he jumped right down my neck, smugly saying: 'Actually, Dr Phillips, this is a recording where the leads of the machine have been loose.'

"I thought what a smart arse. I instantly went from naivety to the full realisation this was to make me look stupid. I could feel my hackles rise. If it hadn't been in that setting, I'd have given him a piece of my mind. We're trying to find out what happened to young people who died unnecessarily and you're trying to make me look like an idiot, having volunteered to give evidence! I thought, all right, that's what we're playing, are we?

"Then he brought my attention to another tracing and asked: 'How would you treat that?' As disdainfully as I could, I said: 'Well I wouldn't treat it because it's a piece of paper. What I want to know is some detail about the patient it represents. Is he conscious? Is he breathing? Has he got a palpable major pulse?'

"And the QC just looked at Lord Justice Taylor and I looked at the two Treasury Solicitors. They both had broad smiles on their faces because I was playing the game how lawyers play it. And this first QC said: 'Oh, we've already had expert witnesses about defibrillation. I think I'll leave it at that.'

"That was distasteful. I really felt quite low at that point. I'm offering some helpful observations and you want me to look like an idiot and you weren't even there. I felt disgusted. Anyway my evidence was over pretty quickly and I just left feeling totally deflated. We'd had it from the media and now we were getting it from the legal profession. In all fairness, though, I believe that Lord Taylor was more than a match for such tactics and that in general he did a great job in deciding what was the root cause of the disaster."

Now, every year on the anniversary of Hillsborough, Dr Phillips thinks back to what happened and still feels a sense of utter disbelief. "For decades, fans had been treated appallingly by football clubs, treated with contempt," he says. "At away games that contempt was shared by local police forces. If you went on the terraces, you were basically unworthy. We put up with it because we loved the game. We didn't realise the danger we were in.

"When you were in a crush, there was always an assumption it would ease, the wave of pressure would go. The difference at Hillsborough was it didn't ease. It just got worse. This had happened before when Tottenham played there. People had to be put on the pitch because the crush was dreadful.

"What made it deadly this time is they didn't police or steward the influx of fans and this crazy notion they would find their own level was literally a fatal mistake.

"I still feel a terrible sense of waste. These young lives were lost pointlessly through going to watch a football game and the families feel their case hasn't been properly listened to, especially at the inquest.

"There's another abiding memory, my disgust at the legal profession. An hour later they'll all be in the bar, having a drink and having a laugh about that witness who's got one over on the opposition. It's a game. But this was literally talking about life and death. My brother and I had been on the pitch side of the barrier which subsequently broke. It could well be that our instinctive decision to crawl up the terrace saved our lives because we got away from where half an hour later 80 or more died.

"Ian is 13 years younger than me and I'd introduced him to being a Kopite from an early age. I had nightmares for months about what so nearly might have happened to him.

"We were the lucky ones though."

Neil Dunkin is the author of 'Anfield Of Dreams: A Kopite's Odyssey From The Second Division To Sublime Istanbul'.

BRENDAN RODGERS – FROM THE TAWE TO THE MERSEY

By Swansea City supporter Matthew Harrison
August, 2012

18th May 2012: Relief. Swansea City manager Brendan Rodgers rebuked an approach from Liverpool FC. Relief. Unlike his predecessor, Roberto "they kicked me out as a player, they'll have to kick me out as a manager" Martinez, Rodgers had always stated that he was highly ambitious and I felt that an approach by Liverpool would probably turn his head. Amazingly, he chose to stick with the Swans and we looked forward to the good times and the stylish football continuing. Just over a week later, much of the local press had confirmed that Swansea had all but secured the permanent services of their highly talented loanee Gylfi Sigurdsson, subject to the usual medical, agreeing personal terms etc. on the Monday following. All was rosy in SA1.

30th May 2012: Rodgers is gone and a revolution at Liverpool Football Club is on the horizon. Swansea fans mourn the loss of the Ulsterman and the Sigurdsson deal falls through. Twelve days: a lot can happen in the perpetually changing world of football.

Over the past few seasons, as the unfashionable Swansea City morphed into 'Swanselona', the Jack Army have got used to losing their best players to vultures high above them in the league, but the most unsettling aspect of the Swans' success has been the repeated poaching of their managers: Martinez to Wigan; Sousa to Leicester (thank God!) and now Rodgers to Liverpool. Swansea fans are used to it. Once again, there was little panic from Swansea fans as they know that in Huw Jenkins, we have the most reliable of chairmen. Jenkins has clearly enjoyed the brand of football that has become Swansea's calling card, and has always appointed managers that he felt could carry on and further the Swansea ethos. In stepped Michael Laudrup of 1990s Barcelona 'Dream Team' fame to replace Brendan Rodgers.

Rodgers v Martinez: Did Liverpool choose correctly?
Rodgers introduced the Swansea philosophy to a global audience after his amazing feat of getting the Swans to the promised land of the Premier League; however, the club's footballing philosophy was forged years before by an ex-club captain and legend: a rookie manager named Roberto Martinez.

Martinez took over the reins at Swansea in the closing months of the 2006/07 season after Kenny Jackett, the manager who released a distraught Martinez from Swansea as a player, was sacked with the side languishing mid-table in League One. Martinez immediately made Jackett's players, many of them former team-mates of his, into a tidy, passing team thanks largely to a more ball-based training regime. Amazingly, Swansea's new style seemed to be paying dividends quickly, as the club came agonisingly close to claiming a highly unlikely League One play-off berth. In his first full season in charge, after a number of shrewd, bargain purchases including Jason Scotland, Ferrie Bodde and Angel Rangel, Swansea romped to the 2007/08 League One title in style, with pundits repeatedly praising the newly-established 'Swansea way'. Swansea were simply stunning at times that season. After further impressive performances in the Championship, Martinez departed for Wigan, taking much of Swansea's backroom resources with him, something many fans have not and never will forgive him for.

Whatever grudges some areas of the Jack Army still hold, Martinez gave birth to the Swansea philosophy you see gracing today's football's modern amphitheatres such as Old Trafford, The Etihad, The Emirates and Anfield, and we should at least thank him for that.

I noticed when Martinez became the frontrunner for Liverpool's vacant managerial chair, some areas of the Liverpool support claimed they would prefer the Spaniard to Rodgers, as Rodgers had only achieved success with a system and squad he had inherited from the man dubbed 'El Gaffer' by the Jack Army. Rubbish. Although Martinez introduced the more 'continental' approach to our football, I believe that Swansea would never have achieved promotion to the Premier League under Martinez. We owe Martinez gratitude, but Brendan was the true architect behind the building of Swansea's promotion to the Premier League and he evolved the playing style of the years previous.

We had many good times under Martinez. His style of football was centred around a much faster-paced passing game than the 'tiki taka' of Rodgers; I probably preferred watching the style of football under Martinez to the slower-paced ball hogging football of Rodgers' Premier League Swansea. Ultimately though, Martinez displayed tactical naivety at times, especially defensively. Martinez also had a habit of leaving substitutions too late when things were not going the team's way. Many winning positions were squandered under Martinez and a series of 'should have been wins' were downgraded to draws. Thank you Roberto, but Rodgers, following a Paulo Sousa interlude, made Swansea a far more efficient unit and still maintained the pass, pass, pass philosophy that had become Swansea's trademark under Martinez.

Anyway, enough of Swansea City, now Liverpool have gone for Rodgers over Martinez, what can Liverpool expect from Rodgers? Well let's start with the things Liverpool fans should look forward to....

Rodgers' strengths

"If God had meant football to be played in the air he would have put grass in the sky."
– Brian Clough

Who doesn't like seeing a team play football the way it is supposed to be played? Well, judging from the reaction during the recent European Championship, not everyone, but I am sure well-educated football fans like Liverpool's will appreciate the eye-pleasing style that is soon to grace (or at least be attempted to grace) Anfield's hallowed turf. Watching Swansea over the past two years has been a joy. The only team I can honestly say I've enjoyed watching more in past couple of years is the mighty Barcelona (oh, and 'boring' Spain of course). Ball retention was the key to Rodgers'

Swansea philosophy, with a reliance on waiting for opportunities to arise rather than forcing the issue. Swansea's possession statistics are incredible for a team built for a pittance by Premier League standards. The team's average possession was the same as champions-elect Manchester City on 57% and Swansea were also second only to City in making the most passes in open play (OPP) with an impressive total of 20,791; Swansea's OPP completion was the highest in the league at 86% (once again the same as Manchester City's OPP completion figure).

Similar to the alumni of Barca's La Masia, Swansea are not blessed with height, an include two of the shortest players in the league last season, Joe Allen (5"6) and Leon Britton (5"5). Fortunately for Swansea, size isn't everything, and the Allen/Britton carousel proved to be the heartbeat of Swansea's 'tiki taka' style. Britton had the highest pass completion rate in Europe (93.5%), even managing a 100% pass completion in a game against Bolton in a 3-1 win in October 2011. Allen followed his partner in crime's example and had a pass completion rate of (91.2%), perhaps more impressive considering the broader and more adventurous range of passing that the little Welshman demonstrated.

Allen is a perfect example of another one of Rodgers' trump cards: developing and improving footballers. Allen had always been a good player since his introduction as a 17-year old under Martinez, but he could sometimes be overwhelmed in games and go missing. Sousa's ultra-defensive tactics and a series of niggling injuries hindered Allen's progress, but Rodgers' moulded Allen into a defensive midfield general and arguably one of the most promising midfielders in the league. Allen could play a pinpoint pass, but he was no longer daunted by opponents and he became a highly determined tackler with the third highest amount of tackles in the league last season (110). Even the fairly average Mark Gower, once a winger, was converted by Rodgers into a formidable centre midfielder and was one of Swansea's best players in the first half of their promotion-winning season. Two and half months into the Premier League season, Gower was statistically the most creative player in Europe! Good players become great players under Rodgers.

Another integral ingredient of Swansea's success under Rodgers would prove to be the fortress created back in South West Wales. One thing Rodgers was keen to do when he arrived in SA1, was to make the Liberty Stadium a stronghold from which to base the Swans' success. Rodgers' determination to make Swansea's home form formidable proved crucial to his success and even helped raise the volume and improve the Liberty Stadium atmosphere; the Jack Army had never truly found their voice at the Liberty until the Rodgers era, with the backbone of its success underpinned by impressive home form. In Swansea's 2010/11 Championship season, they only lost three games at the Liberty out of 23, and after an early February home defeat to their fierce rivals

Cardiff, Swansea went undefeated for the final seven home games (winning six) to help secure their highly impressive 3rd place finish. Swansea's maiden Premier League voyage would run in a similar vein at home; Swansea only lost four times at home, with their first home loss not coming until mid-November when the then Premier League champions, Manchester United, visited the Liberty Stadium and narrowly defeated the Swans 1-0.

Coupled with the fine form at the Liberty Stadium, Rodgers formed a fantastic relationship with the Swansea City support – the Jack Army. From day one, Rodgers could not laud the Jack Army enough and he dedicated many of the team's most famous results to the fans and the city of Swansea itself. The fans were very much central to Rodgers, with nearly every one of his press conferences featuring a tribute to the Jack Army. Even after he had departed the club, Rodgers praised the Swansea fans in an open letter published in the local press; Rodgers signed off from the Swansea faithful with "Brendan – Forever a Jack".

Rodgers' Weaknesses

Rodgers was brilliant at Swansea and despite some of the bitterness that resides from certain areas of the Jack Army, he deserves to go down as one of Swansea's great managers – who knows, if he had stayed he could have gone down as the greatest. But the man is mortal, as his spell at Reading showed and at times during his tenure in South Wales.

I noted one of the best aspects of Rodgers is the style of football he deployed at Swansea, but Swansea's elegance also proved to be his downfall at times. Ultimately, Rodgers will very rarely stride away from the 4-2-3-1 set-up even when things are not going to plan. There was one question that was repeatedly raised throughout last season by press and fans: what is Swansea's Plan B? Simple answer: there wasn't one. The lack of Plan B was almost a source of pride for Swansea City fans, who enjoyed the fact that Swansea were so ruthless in sticking to their principles, in a similar fashion to the stubbornness of Spain and Barcelona. Unfortunately, Swansea do not have the same talent at their disposal as Barcelona or Spain. In the harsh lands of Premier League football, Swansea's inflexibility led to dropped points, especially against sides such as Stoke, Everton and Norwich who had come up with plans to counter 'Swanselona'. At Liverpool, Rodgers has a ready-made Plan B in Andy Carroll – whether he uses him is another story. Rodgers will certainly need to learn how to become more streetwise to managers countering his tactics, especially now he's at a club of Liverpool's stature with teams gunning for their scalps. Also, will Liverpool's fans be as patient as Swansea's in regard to the team potentially passing backwards and sideways for long periods?

Some might even tell you that Swansea, like their doppelgängers Spain, play boring football ("Boring, boring Swansea" went the chants at Loftus Road). Some areas of football cited Swansea as a team that could only pass backwards and sideways; the Swans had the lowest percentage of forward passes in the league with only 40.49% of their passes going forward. Against Newcastle the Swans made an incredible, unheard of *900 passes* ... but still lost 2-0.

There are some other stats that maybe vindicate the idea of "boring, boring Swansea" with perhaps Swansea's goalscoring being the most blatant example. Swansea striker Danny Graham was the only player to reach double figures and only Nathan Dyer, Scott Sinclair and loanee Sigurdsson, who joined in January, scored more than five. Until the arrival of Gylfi Sigurdsson in January, the Swans only scored 20 goals in 20 games compared to the 24 they scored in 18 after his arrival; half of Swansea's goals in the second half of the season came through Sigurdsson's seven goals and five assists, showing how dependent Swansea became on the Icelandic midfielder. Gylfi would prove to be Swansea's only escape from 'tiki taka' with his ability to play a killer pass and shoot (and score) from distance.

Swansea scored 44 goals all season, fewer than relegated Blackburn and Bolton and only better than four other teams in the league (Stoke 36; Aston Villa 37; Wolves 40; QPR 43). Discovering goalscoring strikers has always been a problem for Rodgers at Swansea. On arriving at the club he deployed Stephen Dobbie, more of a number 10, in the lone striker role; when Dobbie didn't work out there was a succession of failed attempts at finding a first choice striker: Shefki Kuqi, Craig Beattie, Frank Nouble, Jermaine Easter, Luke Moore, Tamas Priskin – all failed the audition. Swansea's goalscoring prayers were answered by a young Italian striker called Fabio Borini just in time to lead Swansea to a play-off place. Borini left for Italy and once again Rodgers struggled to find a goalscorer, as Swansea took five games to score their first Premier League goal. Although Swansea record signing Danny Graham would find the net regularly (eventually), Swansea's other strikers, Leroy Lita and Moore offered little competition to Graham with both backup strikers only scoring two Premier League goals all season.

Winning away from home also proved a tough thing for Rodgers to master during his time at Swansea. The determination to create 'Fortress Liberty' and his obsession with 'tiki taka' could have been the two main factors for Swansea's poor away form last season; in fact Swansea's away form under Rodgers was dire for most of his tenure. Swansea lost 11 of their away games in 2011/12 and they would not record a win on the road until January 2nd at Villa Park. Swansea would win four away games all season, largely thanks to man of the match performances by Gylfi Sigurdsson at West Brom, Fulham and Wigan. Rodgers could have really done with bringing Sigurdsson to Merseyside when looking at his importance to Swansea last season.

A lot of Swansea talk there, but from the evidence above, I feel that even despite some glaring weaknesses his arsenal, Rodgers will prove successful on Merseyside – if given time.

Rodgers' signings: The Swans that flew away

"Joe is a player whose profile will fit perfectly with the ideas of this group. His ability to control and dominate the ball is an important ingredient in our attempt to gain success on the field." – Brendan Rodgers

Rodgers has stepped away from the Moneyball-orientated transfer policy of Damien Comolli (now relieved of his duties at Liverpool) and stuck to what, and who, he knows by signing two players that have served him well in his past two years at Swansea.

The signing of Joe Allen could prove to be inspirational. The Allen and Britton combo was essential to Swansea's success last season and Allen will be a tough act to follow for his replacement at Swansea. Despite claiming in a previous piece that I felt Liverpool could live without Allen, after watching the 2nd leg of their Europa League qualifier against Gomel, I could make out a very clear Allen-shaped hole in their midfield. He will slot in perfectly next to Lucas. Ostensibly, Lucas and Allen will act as midfield destroyers, freeing Gerrard up to return to his attacking role of old, although both players are far more than that. In the Gerrard/Lucas/Allen triumvirate, Liverpool have the makings of one of the most all-rounded midfields in the Premier League.

The lack of fanfare that has surrounded Fabio Borini's capture has surprised me. Bluntly, Borini is lethal in front of goal, probably more so than Kop-favourite Suárez. Last year in Serie A for Roma, Borini scored a goal every 187 minutes – the best rate in the league. Borini was a crucial factor in leading Swansea to play-off glory during his three-month loan spell in South Wales. Six goals, two on his debut, in nine appearances helped secure 3rd place in the league. Aside from his goalscoring exploits, Borini is an absolute dynamo who never stands still. At Swansea, Rodgers also relied on Borini to press opposition defences and to get the ball back high up the field. Liverpool fans need not worry about that 'adapting to British football' tag that so often is placed on foreign exports, after Borini cut his teeth in the unforgiving second tier, having previously spent time in Chelsea's youth set-up. Early signs are that Rodgers will deploy Borini out on the left of an attacking trio with him constantly switching roles from the left to centre with the equally mobile Suárez. From the brief glimpse I had of their partnership in Liverpool's game versus Gomel, I feel the Suárez and Borini partnership could be lethal. Expect goals from Fabio.

How and why Rodgers will succeed at Liverpool

Kopites will love Brendan. The idolisation of Shankly and King Kenny just shows how much the Liverpool fanbase adores someone that engages with them. Obviously,

Rodgers has a long, long way to go until he has anything like the rapport with the fans that the two previously mentioned Kop legends had, but his letter to fans thanking them for travelling and supporting the club out in Gomel for their recent Europa League qualifier is a good place to start. Rodgers was adored by the Jack Army and winning over the Kopites could prove crucial after the dethroning of the King – just look what happened to Hodgson who never really got the fans onside.

Similar to his arrival at Swansea, Rodgers will look to make Anfield the intimidating arena it once was. Rodgers, like he did at Swansea, will look to rally the fans, but also get them to be patient like the Swansea fanbase who never displayed frustration with their ball-hogging ways. It took Swansea fans time to get to their high level of patience and Liverpool fans will have to be the same if they want the Rodgers way to work. Remedying Liverpool's stuttering home form could prove the difference between European qualification (Champions League? perhaps too soon for now) and a mid-table finish. Liverpool only managed six wins at their once imperious ground last season and drew nine times, mainly to supposedly 'smaller' teams; one of these 'smaller' clubs drawing at Anfield was Rodgers' Swansea, who were even applauded off the pitch by the Liverpool faithful for their ballsy display of football that earned them a 0-0 draw.

John Henry and FSG obviously have a lot more money than Huw Jenkins at Swansea and the quality available to Liverpool is far beyond Swansea. Rodgers, with the right purchases, could adapt his ball-passing philosophy and make it more expansive and move away from the safer game that he deployed at Swansea. Also with players such as Suárez, Gerrard and Downing, he has attacking players ready-made to sharpen the point of the Rodgers philosophy.

Rodgers loves to use a 'sweeper keeper' and at Swansea he had excellent distribution from the back with Dorus De Vries and then Dutch upgrade Michel Vorm; Rodgers has a ready-made 'sweeper keeper' in the excellent Pepe Reina. In Johnson and Enrique he also has upgrades on the attacking full-backs he had as part of his system at Swansea. I believe the personnel at Liverpool are ready-made for Rodgers' philosophy and system.

Under Dalglish, many Liverpool fans criticised the team's tendency to grant opposition teams space to play in – this will not happen under Rodgers. Rodgers, very much a disciple of Barcelona's philosophy, will look to implement Pep Guardiola's 'four second rule', involving forward players trying to press high to retrieve the ball back four seconds after losing it – an exercise he would introduce into his training sessions. Rodgers would regularly state his frustration at the media's failure to acknowledge how well Swansea pressed the ball when they were out of possession. When Stuart James of *The Guardian* visited a Swansea training session, Rodgers told him beforehand:

"You'll see in some of our exercises this morning, a lot of our work is around the transition and getting the ball back very quickly. Because I believe if you give a bad player time, he can play. If you give a good player time, he can kill you. So our emphasis is based around our positioning both with and without the ball. And for us, when we press well, we pass well."

With talent such as Shelvey, Henderson, Sterling and young full-backs such as Flanagan, Wilson and Kelly, Rodgers has a whole plethora of talent to nurture and develop and I am sure he'll thrive on it. The largely unknown Adam Morgan has even demonstrated in pre-season the injection of confidence Rodgers can give a young player.

I do not think that Rodgers' plan will come to fruition quickly and I think it'll take a season, at least, for Liverpool fans to see the best of Rodgers' team. He stepped into Swansea with the players already used to a similar system to his; although I think he has the players to pull it off, they may take time to adjust. Liverpool have a tough opening to the season and I hope for Rodgers' sake that if things don't go to plan early on, the press, the board or the fans don't get on his or the team's back. Patience is the key to success under Rodgers, off and on the field.

A TACTICAL GLOSSARY – SOME TERMS FOR THE MODERN AGE

By Mihail Vladimirov

September, 2012

In the past ten years or so, there has been a constant major tactical evolution happening in front of our eyes. There were always innovators in the past too, but right now more or less everyone is an innovator. In the past, someone had to be an ideologist to dare threaten the status quo and try to invent something new. But in the modern era, given the tactical and statistical tools available, everything is much easier – you don't need to be an ideologist to use them, you only need to be initially curious and then hard-working and patient enough to dig out the required information, analyse it from a context point of view and then think about how you could use it for your and your team's benefit.

In the modern era the knowledge is openly available for everyone who seeks it. And as the saying goes – more people means more ideas. More ideas means more approaches and counter-approaches. That constant battle for superiority is the driving power behind every single evolution.

In the past, a certain idea could be dominant for years. Right now it's a matter of months before it's found out and adapted to. This means new ideas must be thought up in the meantime or you will be left behind. In terms of style of play, everything is rather static and rigid – you either want the ball and aim for possession dominance, or you don't want it and are defensive-minded and counter-attacking. You either press fiercely in order to limit your opposition's time on the ball or you just sit back and absorb the pressure, suffocating them for space. You either mark zonally or man-to-man. Of course, in modern football the ends of the spectrum are much more blurred – some teams use possession as a primary source of defending, others are attacking-oriented via their constant smash and grab counters. But there is more-or-less nothing that wasn't used in the past, nothing new that could be invented in terms of general style of play.

But this is not the case in terms of players' specific roles on the pitch. Once it was rather unthinkable to have, for example, attacking full-backs, different types of playmakers, inverted wingers or "false" types of players. Now it's a matter of need if you want to be tactically flexible and able to compete at the top end in the modern era. If you are one-dimensional (no matter the exact dimension), you are going to struggle.

But what are the modern type of players known as? What are they doing on the pitch? How they can be combined to achieve maximum tactical balance within some of the modern formations? To answer these question we should be able to catalogue them and assign them different terms as per their role on the pitch in order to divide them and be able to explain the differences between them. Otherwise we risk being outdated in our thinking and expression. The evolution began long ago and is in full swing; we should evolve accordingly to keep pace and not be left behind, in order to have the required basic knowledge and glossary to see and understand what is going on down on the pitch.

Keepers

Shot-stopper: pretty much the archetypal keeper whose main job is to prevent the opposition scoring goals. He rarely ventures away from his comfort zone in the penalty area. His on the ball contribution is precisely zero – whenever he gets to the ball his main instinct is to just "clear the lines".

Sweeper-keeper: a more mobile (not in terms of pace but in terms of movement in and around the penalty area) version of the shot-stopper. This keeper is keen to go outside of his area if necessary and sweep-up any long balls that get behind the defensive line. He just looks to clear the ball, without any particular focus on ball-retention.

Recycling keeper: the most modern type of keeper. Perfectly capable of doing his goalkeeping duties but also cultured enough to be counted as the eleventh outfield player. His on-the-ball contribution is greater than his predecessors' as his main aim is to recycle the ball and initiate the initial build-up phase of his team, focused on bringing the ball out of defence with a chain of short and possession-oriented passes. He is often used as the "out" ball if the defenders are put under pressure. Then, only if he is closed down and he cannot see a short pass, would he aim to hit the ball long, directly feeding his attacking team-mates.

Centre-backs

Stopper: the classic physical central defender. Known for his last-ditch tackles and physical encounters. His main aim is to engage the opponents in order to prevent them reaching and/or controlling the ball or continue having the ball if they are already in possession. Offers next to nothing in terms of technical (passing, technique, dribbling skills) and mental abilities (composure, vision) on the ball. Generally seeks to hoof the ball out of danger. Due to his technical deficiencies it's counter-productive to field two proper stoppers in a team that is aiming to get a possession dominance and build up patiently.

Possession-friendly defender: has all the typical defensive skills for a central defender but in the meantime is much more cultured with the ball at his feet. His contribution on the ball is to just keep the ball ticking over via short passes to the nearest more creative team-mates. If the team has a ball-playing centre-back he will look to pass to him. If not he will wait for one of the midfielders to drop deeper and collect the ball. Only rarely, if there is a clear chance, will the possession-friendly defender aim for a longer cross-field pass in order to feed his attacking team-mates down the channels or over the top. This defender is generally seen as not having enough vision and technical proficiency to be able to bring the ball out of defence by himself.

Ball-playing defender: the most cultured type of centre-back. In short, the defence's chief playmaker and the player who is tasked to bring the ball out of defence either via carrying the ball higher up the pitch by himself, or by using his vision and passing skills to move it creatively to his midfield or attacking partners. Sometimes if the opposition is obviously sitting deep and not attacking in numbers, when his team is in possession the ball-playing defender could step out of the defence and join the midfield line as either an auxiliary deep-lying ball-player or additional player on-rushing from deep who joins the team's attack.

Full-backs

Defensive full-back: in short this is essentially a centre-back playing down the flanks. The solid defensive oak that Houllier so much rated in his time when he used Carragher as a right-back. This player will not venture forward, will not dribble down the line and will rarely provide a cross (and if he does, it'll be from deep areas and would be seen more as an angled hoof-ball than a proper cross). He stays deep and narrower to offer additional defensive stability for his team and cover for his central partners. Such a player could be useful if the team has a very attacking full-back on the opposite flank in order to provide a sort of balance, by remaining in his defensive position and forming a back three with the centre-backs, allowing not only the other full-back but the midfielders to push forward too.

Supporting full-back: generally a defensive-oriented full-back, but with little bit more attacking and ball-playing input. The supporting full-back will rarely if ever push forward beyond his wide partner but will aim to be closer to him in order to provide him with an "out" ball if the winger's path down the flank is blocked and there is no way he would dribble through it. In the meantime he will be an additional passing angle for the midfielders down the flank. This full-back will additionally join the recycling process of his team aiming to bring the ball out of defence and pass it to his midfield team-mates.

Overlapping full-back: overlapping runs and constant dribbles down the flanks are this full-back's main priorities. His aim is to be always in touch with his wide partner, aiming to constantly provide a 2 vs 1 overloading down the flank in the opposition half. The overlapping full-back's position is very dependent on the behaviour of the player ahead of him. If the winger is inverted, the full-back will seek to stay on the outside and act both as a passing "out" ball for his winger but also as a wide outlet for his team, stretching the play. If the winger is more of a natural wide player (i.e. a player who prefers to stay wider), the overlapping full-back will be forced to tone down his runs beyond the winger and generally remain closer to him, playing in a line, either to rotate who will push further forward down the line or to create a constant 2 vs 1 overload down the flank. If this full-back is inverted (i.e. playing on his "wrong" foot), then the player ahead of him should play on his natural side (left-footed down the left flank and right-footed down the right flank) in order to provide tactical diversity in their movements on and off the ball.

Wing-back: the most attack-oriented full-back. Also known as a quasi-winger. His attacking instincts and constant overlapping runs are so obvious that he needs to play either as the single wide player (in all 3-5-2 variants) or partnered with a wide player who will play higher and narrower up the pitch, constantly aiming to move diagonally and vacate the whole flank for his full-back partner. The alternative is to partner the wing-back with a wide midfielder who will stay wide but will remain in much deeper positions, allowing the wing-back to push beyond him. If the wing-back is inverted, then the player ahead of him (if there is a player ahead of him) should play on his natural side (left-footed down the left flank and right-footed down the right flank) in order provide tactical diversity in their movements on and off the ball.

Midfielders

Retriever (thanks to Dan Kennett for this particular term!): the archetypal ball-winning midfielder whose aim is simply to retrieve the ball from the opposition. He will do that by either going for the press and engaging his opponents or by holding his position, counting on proper positioning and timing as he seeks to cleanly nick the ball via interception or well-timed tackle. His on-the-ball contribution is to pass the ball short to his nearest midfield partner as soon as he regains it. However, an additional distinction could be made here by grouping both types of destroyers as either ball-winning midfielders (i.e. the one that relishes the press and physical encounters) or anchorman (i.e. the one that is pretty much static and counts on defensive intelligence to regain the ball). However, in modern football, especially in the dynamic environment of English football, rarely if ever do we would see a pure anchorman who is going to remain static just in front of the back four, only waiting for his opponents to come closer for him to nick the ball off them. He would be simply bypassed too often. Hence these roles should be merged in order to have the "full package" defensive capabilities. That's why Lucas is one of the best midfield retrievers – not only is he able to go for the press but also to hold his position and count on his defensive intelligence. It's his overall intelligence and decision-making process that enable him to choose the right decision more often than not.

Passer (also known as a *recycler*): this player is focused on retaining possession via constant "passive", short-oriented passes around the pitch. He could go for the more direct, crossfield passes, but only if the risk of the ball being intercepted is minimal. He lacks the vision and flair to be a constant creative threat on the ball in terms of always looking to send penetrative through balls, but he doesn't need to possess such skills. This player is not here to take risks and speculate with his passes, he is here to calm things down and just help his team dominate possession. His role is to be the link between his midfield partners in order to "glue" the midfield structure. As such he is often placed either between his midfield partners (if the team is playing with a three-man midfield) or between the defenders and the midfielders (if the team is playing with a two-man midfield). He is the man setting and controlling the team's passing rhythm. His defensive contribution isn't based on his individual defensive skills, more on joining the team's overall defensive strategy – be it pressing as a unit or standing off as a unit.

Recycling retriever: in short this is a cross between the two previous types. A defensively capable passer who could execute both roles perfectly. Such a player is essential for the modern-looking 4-1-2-3 system, as this player could sit at the base of the midfield triangle offering both defensive security and passing control, allowing the players in front of him to just focus on the creative and attacking side of the things. Also, this player is very useful in a two-man midfield as he is able to cover two roles, letting his midfield partner concentrate mainly on how to help his team from an attacking point of view. In essence, a two-man midfield would be able to perform the roles of a three-man midfield

Creator: the most creative midfielder in the archetypal retriever/passer/creator 1-2 midfield trio. As such he is tasked with providing that extra bit of magic on the ball, via dribbles or defence-splitting passes. He has the movement freedom to step out of the midfield line and link with the forwards, but generally will try to keep the midfield shape in order to provide the required platform for the rest of the team, to secure possession dominance. Ideally this player will be the most advanced of the trio (with the retriever being the deepest and the passer in between), with the aim of constantly looking for diagonal angles. This player will rarely, if ever, come deep to pick up the ball or he would risk ruining the whole midfield shape and not provide the required attacking angles through the middle. He will aim to receive the ball around the centre-circle but in the opposition's half, in order to be able to transform the recycling process in the transitional phase into more attacking-oriented possession, initiating the attacking phase. His defensive contribution is mainly to press from upfront, joining the forwards in the initial pressing wave, but he will rarely drop deeper to aid his team defensively in terms of positioning.

Deep-lying playmaker: a creative-oriented player but playing in the zone between his defence and midfield. Hence he is either the deepest midfielder in the 1-2 triangle or the more creative midfielder of the double pivot. His primary aim is to collect the ball directly from the defenders and either distribute it to the full-backs and his midfield colleagues with short passes or spray it with more penetrative and direct passes down the channels or over the top. This player is both a passer and a creator in that he has the tactical freedom to mix his passes and decide how to set the tempo and where to channel his team's attacks. His defensive contribution is minimal so he needs the players around him to cover for him when the team is without the ball – it's desirable in the 1-2 triangle one of the "2" to be a very competent presser and tackler; while if playing in a double pivot, the deep-lying playmaker's partner must be a proper defensive-minded holder. Otherwise, as much as he might be the team's primary source for creativity on the ball, this player would be a major liability for his team without the ball.

Number 10: the classic advanced playmaker who stays between the lines and roams all over the last third in order to receive the ball and create openings for his attacking team-mates. This player's vital attributes are all creatively oriented: vision, flair, passing, dribbling and brilliant technique on the ball. He will rarely if ever drop deep, either to collect the ball or aid his team defensively. As much as such as player might be a creative genius, he could be a real disaster from a defensive point of view – he wouldn't press or drop deep to help out his team-mates. Hence in the modern era there are very few proper number 10s. To have such a player you either need to be really sure you will have the majority of the ball during every match, or partner him with two defensive terriers in behind. Mesut Ozil is the only real notable example of such a player at the moment. As he is playing for Real Madrid, very few teams would be able (or dare!) to dominate possession against them. In the bigger matches Ozil is either played on the flank or benched – showing how much faith Jose Mourinho has in his defensive contribution and how prepared is he to risk his team to play with one man down from a defensive point of view.

False 10 (known also as a *second forward*): the modern number 10 – perhaps lacking in the creative department in comparison to the classic playmaker but with increased attacking and goal-scoring verve. This player's primary aim is to provide vertical runs in the last third, to aid his forward partner, level with him and be in position to create passing moves with him; or simply take advantage of the space opened up, and run beyond the centre-forward to become the team's primary attacking target. Often this player is a converted midfielder who showed exceptional attacking skills and instincts (see Steven Gerrard in 2008/09). Although he does not necessarily always play in the forward line, this player will rarely drop into the midfield, hence he is not seen as a third midfielder. Defensively he will act as a proper second forward – pressing from higher up the pitch but not dropping deeper to aid the midfield. As a secondary defensive function, this player could be seen as the natural marker for the opposition's deep-lying playmaker.

Box-to-box midfielder: this type was a dying breed in the last decade when played in a two-man midfield. With the rise of the three-man midfields, such a player was seen as a liability – he was the perfect all-rounder but not trusted enough to do any particular job particularly well. Hence why the modern tactician prefers to divide this role in two and form a three-man midfield instead. But recently, given that 90% of teams already use three-man midfields, there is perhaps a need for such players to re-emerge. The modern three-man midfield is usually comprised of retriever-passer-creator type of players. But if the opposition has a similar trio, both midfields can easily cancel each other out, and with the teams lacking a proper link between the midfield and the forward lines in terms of midfield runners, gaps start to open between the lines so that the teams start looking broken and the passes are often intercepted. That's why in the last couple of years, managers started thinking how to find something extra and find a way to provide the missing link. The box-to-box midfielder re-emerged, mainly in teams using a double pivot. Khedira (for both Real Madrid and Germany), Diaby (for Arsenal,) Schweinsteiger (Bayern), Lars Bender (Leverkusen), Gokhan Inler (previously for Udinese, now Napoli) and Nocerino (Milan) are some of the prime examples of players providing such a role for their respective teams. This player is seen as both defensively solid and capable enough going forward to contribute in both phases in equal measure. His main attribute is his physical power and energy, enabling him to execute his role tirelessly up and down the pitch.

Wide players

Winger: the classic wide player, aiming to hug the touchline and stretch the play by constantly running down the flank and providing quality crosses into the box. Starting in relatively deeper positions in order to have space in front of him in which to accelerate, dribble past his opponent and provide the cross, this player is seen more as a part of the midfield line rather the forward line. As a result he is a good fit for the typical 4-4-2, 4-4-1-1 and 4-2-3-1, but not for the typical 4-3-3 and its variations (4-1-2-3 and 4-2-1-3). Defensively this player will aim to drop deep and help out his full-back by generally tracking the opposition's full-back.

Wide forward: the winger alternative, capable of featuring in the 4-3-3 variants. This player will still focus on playing on the outside, stretching the play and dribbling with the ball, but will do all of this from higher up the pitch (hence seen more as a forward rather a midfielder), with the aim of reaching the byline and providing a neat cut-back or a one-two combination with his nearest team-mates (generally an overlapping full-back/wing-back, an on-rushing midfielder or a forward coming wider). When without the ball, this player's primary objective will be to press from higher up the pitch (joining with the rest of the forward line) and cut off the possible angles for the opposition's defenders to bring the ball out of defence.

Inverted winger/wide forward: generally doing the same things but by playing on his "wrong" foot, he will often cut infield. The winger will still aim to dribble and cross but will provide more of an in-swinging angle, while the inverted wide-forward will be even more suited to dribbling and then turning inside and feeding his nearest team mate or even shooting.

Wide creator: a ball-player placed on the flank. His general role is to move infield (preferably by playing inverted as he will find it easier to cut inside and either pass or dribble on his stronger foot) and aid the team's ball retention process by overloading the opposition between the lines. By making lateral infield runs this player will often end up in central playmaking positions, acting as sort of a quasi-Number 10, hence he will be in the perfect zone to see the majority of the pitch and thread through balls to his attacking team-mates. As with the natural number 10, this player's defensive contribution is minimal; even more so given his roaming presence. Hence it'll put increased pressure on the full-back and the nearest central midfielder on his flank.

Inside-forward (known also as a *wide poacher*): this player will act as the team's de facto finisher, but by starting off the flank and making diagonal attacking runs to occupy central goal-scoring positions. This player's on-the-ball contribution is seen mainly as joining in short-oriented give-and-go passing moves aimed at providing the required platform to push higher up the pitch and allow him the time and space to make his trademark off-the-ball runs. The other primary input of this player is to allow the overlapping full-back (preferably the wing-back) the space down the flank to push forward and stretch the play. This will create overload down this channel and force the opposition to second-guess who and where to try and cover, resulting in either a lapse in concentration or leaving a pocket of space somewhere in the last third that the inside-forward will relish exploiting. As with the wide forward, this player will contribute in defence by putting early pressure on the opposition's defenders and deep-lying midfielders in order to ruin their initial passing rhythm. This player is a nailed-on fit for the 4-3-3 variants but could be used in the 4-2-3-1 formation too if the centre-forward is more of a creator, and if on the opposite flank there is either a proper winger or a wide-creator to offer a sort of pure on-the-ball contribution.

Centre-forwards

False 9 (also known as a *roaming forward*): the modern-day lone forward – quick, technical, with excellent vision and on-the-ball skills. His roaming habit will force him either to drop deep and join the midfielders in the passing combinations, or to drift wider and create an overload on each flank before cutting inside with or without the ball. This player's primary aim is to create for others – either feed them with quality attacking passes or move in a way that vacates space for them to move into. Due to his technical on-the-ball proficiency and constant movement, often he will end up in good goal-scoring positions himself, making him more of all-round attacking threat. From a tactical point of view this player needs at least two direct attacking players (either two inside-forwards on the flanks in 4-3-3 or an inside-forward and a false 10 in a 4-2-3-1) around him in order to have someone to create space for and to feed with good passes in the last third.

Deep-lying forward: similar to the false 9, this player is seen more as a supporting rather a consuming forward. The difference is that this player generally lacks the technical expertise, dribbling skills and/or the mobility of the false 9 so is much more reliant on his pure physical presence. Hence this player's aim is to drop deep and play with his back to goal, aiming to help the midfielders transition the ball higher up the pitch with a chain of short-passes or just hold it up and allow the rest of the attacking players to occupy positions around and beyond him. (As Liverpool did in 2011/12 with Andy Carroll, who played deeper than Suárez.) Only then will this player seek to push forward and present

88

himself as an additional option in and around the penalty box, receiving cut-backs from the wide players or quality angled crosses from the full-backs/wing-backs. Another attacking contribution is that given his dominant physical presence, the opposition will always try to make sure he is properly covered, often with one player marking him and another covering in behind, hence leaving a shortage somewhere else on the pitch. His primary defensive contribution is to strike fear into the opposition's back line and force them to always double-up on him (hence leaving less attacking numbers to join or contribute to their attacks).

Poacher: the archetypal Number 9. This player is seen as the team's main resource for goals, the best finisher in the team. The whole tactical behaviour would be channelled to feed him with the required service in order to provide him with plenty of goal-scoring chances. This player prefers to receive the ball at his feet rather than trying to connect with crosses from out wide, always looking to work the channels and latch on to through balls from all possible angles. He lacks the ball-playing attributes to contribute to the build-up play but compensates with predatory instincts off the ball and a deadly finishing touch on the ball. When the team is defending he will remain higher up the pitch, lurking around the opposition's third waiting for the ball to reach him. In a way this type of player is seen as outdated and not needed in the modern era, but combined with capable on-the-ball midfielders, he is still able to deliver by scoring goals – and this is something that will be always needed in order to win matches. The current best example is Falcao – a fairly limited on the ball number 9 but a deadly finisher. In the past three years (since he came to play on the continent), he has scored 114 goals in 140 matches.

Target-man: similar technical abilities and tactical focus as the poacher – to be the team's main finisher – but his style is based mainly on brute power and physical presence rather than intelligent runs off the ball down the channels. This player relishes physical encounters in the air, aiming to head as many crosses as possible into the back of the net rather than sniffing on through balls on the ground. His play with feet is limited to passing the ball short distances to the nearest teammate before turning and battling his way towards a goal-scoring position where he would receive the ball in the air. The target-man will rarely drop deeper in order to join up the build-up play or shield the ball to provide time for the midfielder runners. Similar to the poacher, this player will stay high up the pitch when his team is defending, always in position to receive a long, direct pass from his own half.

Summary
Obviously there are plenty of different roles within the current tactical reality. This provides the managers with the tools to mix their styles and increase the team's tactical flexibility and potency. This in turn increases the threat they will offer to their

opposition on a match by match basis.

In the past, the players' roles were more generic and rigid, without so many nuances. This made the teams easy to be found out and nullified. Such tactical set-ups are now rarely seen in the modern era, even in some of the lower football echelons. Tactical flexibility, versatility and fluidity has been the order of the day since the turn of the millennium.

Granted, some of the roles listed here could be divided into sub-groups or merged to provide more of a complete player – for example there are target-men that are perfectly capable of playing on the deck and joining the build-up play as a deep-lying forward (Andy Carroll quickly springs to mind). But it's more a case of a certain player having the skills to do that than that the role itself invites or requires such dual responsibilities.

Bearing the current tactical terminology in mind for now, it'll be really interesting to see how they will evolve or completely change in the next few years or decade. Will new roles be introduced with new duties and aims? Definitely, as every new era brings its own evolution and changes.

What could they be? That's why the uncertainty is so interesting and tickles our curiosity. For now we can but appreciate the current palette of roles and enjoy watching their performances on the pitch.

WINNING BY NUMBERS

Lee Mooney
October, 2012

'A journey of a thousand miles starts with a single step' – Lao Tzu, Chinese philosopher

My career to date has largely been spent helping organisations to find and exploit the value that's hidden in their data. Generally, to frame initial conversations about projects, I've found the following structure to be helpful:

• What is the business question we're ultimately trying to answer?

• Can we prove/justify why having the answer to that question really matters to the organisation?

• Conceptually, to answer that question, what data would we need?

• How much would it cost to make the required data available in a usable format?

• Do we have the right people, skills and tools to understand the data and create value with it?

The outcome of this exercise is a matrix of 'questions', with each question located in terms of cost and value. The next step is to prioritise the various activities and build a more refined view of scope, timeline and cost. So, at least in theory, your initial areas of focus are those that matter the most, and are also those that can be transformed into value the quickest or at the lowest cost (depending on your circumstances). I've come to apply the same thought processes to football. What are the business questions that really matter to Liverpool Football Club and can we prove why they matter? What data would we need to answer those questions and how much would it cost to make that data available in a usable format? Finally, and perhaps most crucially, does the club have the right people, skills and tools to understand that data and create value from it?

You can't assess the significance of a particular question without first understanding the business

There's a fundamental difference between 'clubs' and 'businesses'. A football club, ultimately, exists to serve its supporters. I guess the easiest way to articulate what supporters want from their football club is to feel 'part of it' and to be 'made happy'. About as subjective and volatile a set of expectations as can be faced, I'd imagine!

A football business though, is different. A football business exists to deliver value to its shareholders through a return on their investments and the payment of dividends. Delivering those outcomes requires the careful management of revenues, costs and assets to generate profit. It was suggested to me that the 'entertainment business' might be a more appropriate paradigm to use here: think in terms of theatres, award-winning actors and the merciless shifting of high-margin merchandise.

Could it be argued that winning football matches is really just a driver of value in a football business – one of several that enable shareholder value?

Continuing my sacrilegious journey, let's think a little more about the Liverpool FC 'business' in terms of its revenues, costs and the management of its assets.

Putting football club revenues into context

In terms of income, Liverpool FC is already amongst the top ten revenue earners in European football. Interestingly, this position is achieved whilst being a relative under-performer in footballing terms (when compared with the other members of that list). I guess the sustained successes of the past have given rise to generations of fans that will take time to 'fade away'. Similarly, it will be many years before the recent successes of Chelsea or Manchester City will accumulate into a significant global following.

Thinking open-mindedly and perhaps with a hint of cynicism, could this be why FSG bought Liverpool FC in the first place? Does Liverpool, because of the 'stickiness' of its revenues, represent an 'easy' opportunity to grow shareholder value? Consider this possibility: increased shareholder value = avoidance of supporter protests +

reduced costs + better use of assets.

One thing that all fans, and 'fanalysts' (possibly a new term which I might have just invented) in particular need to understand, is that football clubs aren't large businesses at all. A typical 'Tesco Extra' store – that's one single store, just to be clear – can generate in excess of £200m per year in revenue (enough to place it 5th amongst Europe's elite clubs, according to Deloitte; Tesco numbers derived from average retail revenue per square metre of retail space for the last financial year).

Club	2010/11 Revenue (€m)	2010/11 Revenue (£m)
Real Madrid	€479.50m	£383.12m
FC Barcelona	€450.70m	£360.11m
Manchester United	€367.00m	£293.23m
Bayern Munich	€321.40m	£256.80m
a typical Tesco Extra store	€257.88m	£206.05m
Arsenal	€251.10m	£200.63m
Chelsea	€249.80m	£199.59m
AC Milan	€235.10m	£187.84m
Internazionale	€211.40m	£168.91m
Liverpool	€203.30m	£162.44m
Schalke 04	€202.40m	£161.72m

Now, I'm not saying that FSG should knock down Anfield and build a supermarket, or that they should turn Melwood into a housing development, but you do have to wonder why the 'smartest guys in the room' decided to buy a football club at all? Is this a short-term investment, a quick 'flip' to make a 'fast buck', or is something else motivating FSG? Perhaps, just possibly, they have a desire to achieve in ways other than returns and profitability?

Players are a significant and complex piece of the puzzle

One way to begin understanding a business is to review the balance of its assets and liabilities and put those in the context of the competitive marketplace. Improving the health of a business is basically about getting more value from its inventories, machines, buildings and employees.

I think a football business is a little different though, and it's different because of one unique element: the players. The players are really employees, but they're also machines and inventory (depending on how you look at it). Managing players effectively, at least in my opinion, is really about finding the right blend of principles from across the social sciences. Thinking of players as employees is possibly the easiest perspective for most people to relate to. Employees, generally speaking, require a range of environmental factors to be in place which enable them to perform at their best, in the role they were hired to fulfil. For the business, the goal is to continually have the right people in the right roles (either by recruiting internally or externally) and to ensure the headcount numbers and salary costs are carefully managed.

Thinking of players as 'products', or different types of 'assets', is a little more abstract. Individual players have the capacity to generate revenues through marketing, advertising and merchandising. Some players have immense merchandising value – perhaps far more than their ability to generate value through their playing abilities (see the increase in merchandising revenues for the LA Galaxy following David Beckham's arrival). I'm not sure if they're 'products' exactly, or if this is simply an aspect of their employee role that is frequently overlooked. One thing's for sure: a player's commercial revenue contribution, above and beyond his contribution on the field, is a variable that needs to be considered in the recruitment decision.

I find the 'asset' perspective possibly the most interesting of the three. From this view-point, players are like inventory, or cogs in a machine (good teams are often described as 'machines'). Players basically need to be acquired, maintained, replaced and disposed of with ruthless efficiency. As inventory, players effectively exist within a football business to be re-sold. As cogs in a machine they're really no different to parts on your car – they have a service interval, a maintenance schedule and patterns of usage which can either prolong or shorten their life. They need to be replaced in good time as their degradation can cause damage to other parts of the machine.

Which business questions should matter the most to football clubs?

The owners and managers of Liverpool FC will make hundreds of decisions every day – so, which decisions are the most important ones to get right? Surely it's the questions underpinning these decisions that need to be the most well-informed – and therefore the focus of the 'fanalyst' community (if we want our efforts to have a positive impact)?

My personal opinion is that player trades and wage decisions matter more than all the other decisions combined. Throughout the club's history, we've grown when we've traded well and we regressed when we've traded poorly.

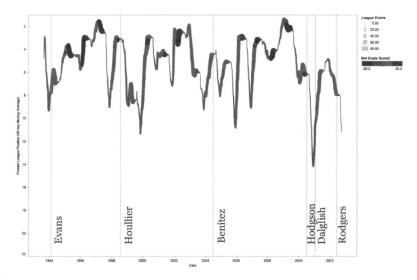

Obviously other factors play a part. But, I personally don't think incredible coaching, tactical acumen or motivational ability will ever compensate for the loss of £40m in value resulting from poor purchases or sales. Such write-offs, particularly when your rivals don't have to make them (or are successfully pumping in even more money), are just too big a hit to absorb. Sadly, Liverpool fans know this better than most.

Rafael Benítez was (and is) a top European coach with a proven track-record of winning at the highest level. His systems and techniques were well-established at Liverpool FC over a period of six years. In his final year, despite all the meticulous attention to detail and the proven elite coaching and tactical acumen – capabilities that delivered Liverpool FC to the pinnacle of European football – it was restrictions on player trading, at crucial moments, that broke his regime (and broke it fast). This decline was accelerated by the Roy Hodgson regime and was compounded further during the Comolli/Dalglish era (where good players were bought but for fees clearly calibrated against those being paid by clubs like Chelsea and Manchester City, rather than Arsenal, Everton and Newcastle).

Opposite to the above example: Alan Pardew's time at Newcastle. A succession of excellent transfer deals in a short space of time effectively propelled Newcastle – a club only recently promoted and having just sacked a manager – into the upper echelons of the Premier League.

Player wages generally account for 50% to 70% of turnover – if you add in the value of players sold and bought then you're talking about a massive overall 'impact' given the size of the business. The conclusion then: the following 'big questions' can effectively set the operating level of the club for a number of years:

- Who are the right players to buy/sell?
- When is the right time to buy/sell these players?
- What is the right price to buy/sell these players for?

The last of these three questions is really what separates the winners and losers for me. It's not enough to just buy good players, you need to be paying fees and wages in-line with or lower than your rivals (obviously excluding those clubs that have a sugar daddy). Arsenal, Newcastle and Everton currently set the standard in my opinion. Newcastle's last two years, in particular, highlights this key point really well in my opinion. The price you pay is so important – the right price means you can 'live to fight another day' when you make a mistake and need to sell that player on. With these critical questions identified, and the reasons for highlighting them explained, I've quickly come to challenge the value of my own 'fanalyst' contributions to date. Too much time has been spent thinking about performance analysis and tactical content. Looking at the bigger picture logically, I've come to conclude that this content really doesn't matter that much. Here's some more detail to help explain why.

Performance analysis doesn't matter much in the big scheme of things

The 'on-ball event' data is pretty much used by everybody in sports journalism and analysis. Surely it's an accurate record of the events that matter in a football match? Surely understanding this data is the key to unlocking new levels of understanding and insight? Or maybe, just maybe, it's not the 'goldmine' of insight that many think it is.

On-ball event stats capture 193 measurable events during a game for each player involved. My extensive analysis of this data, requiring many thousands of individual calculations, is presented in the visualisation below:

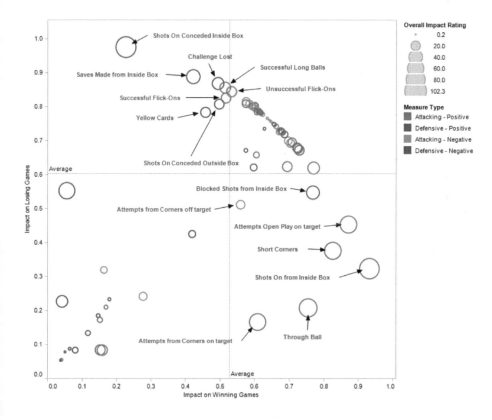

[PT: Using Lee's interactive graphic, I have created my own illustration (see overleaf) to show how direct game tactics – successful long balls, successful flicks-ons and successful crosses in the air – are grouped in a very mid-range band in terms of their impact on winning games, and also their lack of impact in avoiding losing games. By contrast, approaches that you'd associate with cultured football – short corners, successful dribbles, successful final third passes and successful through balls – are in the areas of the graphic you want to see them: lower down, and further to the right.]

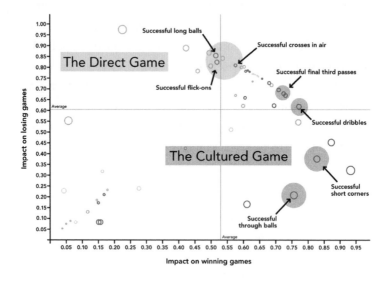

Teams that win tend to dominate their opponents in terms of:

- Shots on-target inside the box
- Use of the through ball
- Attempts on-target from open play
- Short corners played
- Attempts from corners on target

Teams that lose tend to lead their opponents in terms of:

- Shots on-target conceded inside the box
- Challenges lost
- Use of the long-ball and flick-ons
- Yellow cards
- Shots on-target conceded outside the box

So, games are largely won or lost as a result of key moments in and around the penalty box. There's little evidence to suggest that passing better in any area of the field directly results in wins unless that pass is a through-ball. What really matters is what you do with the ball in the vital areas (or when trying to penetrate those vital areas). Could it be that the current Liverpool philosophy places too much emphasis on the general dominance of possession? How strong is the relationship between possession and winning? Perhaps one for Brendan Rodgers to think about.

The availability of data, and the ability to analyse it in this way, might be modern – but is this new knowledge? Could it be that this generation has forgotten the early lessons of those managers that pre-dated the 'data era' and perhaps what we're seeing now is the rediscovery and re-learning of old lessons via new means? Could the drive for footballing 'modernity' actually be damaging, rather than improving decision-making?

Let's put this 'on ball' data into context. A football match is 22 players contributing (excluding stoppages) 90 minutes of output each – so 118,800 collective man-seconds are spent in every encounter. Last year there was an average of 1,260 'touches' on the ball in a game (maximum of 1,586 and as low as 914). Considering a range of values from two seconds per touch to ten seconds per touch, 'on ball' activity only accounts for as much as 13.35% of the overall contribution and as little as 1.54%.

Seconds	Touches			% of Match		
	Min. 914	Avg. 1260	Max. 1586	Min.	Avg.	Max.
2	1,828	2,521	3,172	1.54%	2.12%	2.67%
4	3,656	5,042	6,344	3.08%	4.24%	5.34%
6	5,484	7,563	9,516	4.62%	6.37%	8.01%
8	7,312	10,083	12,688	6.15%	8.49%	10.68%
10	9,140	12,604	15,860	7.69%	10.61%	13.35%

If the 'fanalysts' are to have an impact then we need to focus on identifying the 'right' data for the 'big questions'. Thrashing the data available is leading some of us to lose a bit of perspective – we're also potentially ignoring a huge proportion of what's actually happening in a game. From now on I'll be focusing much more on how players acquire and deny space, how they move, and the intelligence of that movement in relation to the other players on the field.

If a football match is so much more than the 'on ball' events, with the margins between winning and losing in those terms being very small indeed, what are the big differentiators? Does one 'style' of play really dominate the other? Clearly aimless long-balls and flick-ons aren't a durable platform for success, but other than that? Surely if you can get the ball into the box quickly to someone who's ruthless at putting it in the net, whilst giving away nothing at the back, then surely you'll do okay – could Sam Allardyce actually be smarter than many give him credit for?

I've heard accounts from ex-Liverpool players who played for both Bob Paisley and Bill Shankly. They described managers who brought 'footballers' to their teams – players who were smart enough to modify their style of play when faced with a situation. These weren't players that slavishly followed a script – they read the play and made the right choices as a unit. They were expected to solve problems themselves. What data would enable objective analysis of these characteristics and does it exist? I'm not sure it does.

The exploration of 'off ball' event data is possible today via camera systems like Amisco. Such systems increase the amount of information collected per game from approximately 2,000 events to around 4,500,000 pieces of information. However, analytical costs increase with increases in data volumes and data complexity. This is especially relevant given the size of football businesses as analytical tools, and large-scale data handling capabilities can be expensive. The potential of exploration to deliver new insight needs to be balanced against the costs of those potential discoveries.

I suspect football clubs will rely upon packaged software offerings to manage the presentation of information from these large sets of data. If this is true, then this means that any rival who's bought the same product will know everything you know – so what's the point other than to keep pace? How should Liverpool FC use data to achieve competitive advantage whilst operating within the boundaries of financial viability? My recommendation– at least as far as the 'big questions' are concerned – would be to look away from packaged software and towards some smart innovations using data that is overlooked because it isn't 'reassuringly expensive', a kind of 'Moneyball' for data so to speak. For example, the piece I did earlier this year ("Solving Liverpool's Goalscoring Woes") was developed entirely using free data from Wikipedia and other free web sources.

Achieving competitive advantage whilst operating within the boundaries of financial viability

"It's the economy, stupid". If you've got something worth buying, a bigger club will eventually come along and buy it from you. Sustained success then, sadly, is all about the economics – so it's in the economics that clubs should seek to gain or cement an advantage.

If 'fanalysts' are to have the impact on the club then we need to turn our collective energies to the three 'big questions':
- Who are the right players to buy/sell?
- When is the right time to buy/sell these players?

• What is the right price to buy/sell these players for?

Manchester City FC has led the way in terms of engaging with its 'fanalyst' community to harvest usable insights in a low-cost way. However, by focusing on the 'on ball event' data, I don't think they're harnessing that energy in the most valuable way. Perhaps Liverpool FC can do things differently and take the lead?

In any case, a key priority for FSG should be, in my opinion, the building of an enduring capability that is the best in the business at answering these 'big questions'. This capability should be on the permanent payroll and have enduring principles which are embedded deep into the 'constitution' of the club. Such a vital capability has to be built within the organisation and endure, despite changes in management. Managers should be appointed with their first duty being to honour and preserve that constitution. For example, if Liverpool's constitution had strict standards for passing and control ability – would they have hired Ryan Babel? Would tests of attitude and character have let El Hadji Diouf through the Shankly Gates? If Bob Paisley's view that 'legs should go on someone else's pitch' was still enforced, would the Reds have hired Poulsen, Konchesky or Cole (or still have Gerrard or Carragher playing regularly)?

Modern managers operate in the face of intense short-term scrutiny. Success, sadly, is also measured on the same timeline. I believe that genuine understanding and insight is being drowned out by the noise of 24/7 talk radio, media hype and cheap ex-player punditry. It's easy to see why many managers might just 'play it safe' and aim to acquire household names or adopt a 'reassuringly expensive' approach to transfers – the 'short-game', for many, is the only game worth playing.

Personally, I'm often encouraged when Liverpool are linked with players that the vast majority of fans haven't heard of. I'd also actively welcome a 'panning for gold' strategy that quickly filtered through potential 'rough diamonds' that we'd bought cheaply. Data can help to identify these opportunities and to ensure that the fees being paid are properly calibrated. Sometimes it will mean walking away, and taking some heat from the fans, but that's what real leadership is all about – it's not a short-term popularity contest.

According to Albert Einstein, *"Not everything that can be counted counts, and not everything that counts can be counted"*.

When you think about these 'big questions', what really matters and can these elements actually be counted?

The autobiography of Brian Clough identifies a number of desirable player characteristics. These characteristics are introduced by first emphasising that player recruitment is "vital" to success and that managers should invest carefully and with skill. All these years later, the available data is now able to support that message:

- Ball control is three quarters of the challenge – must be automatic
- Teams must have real talent in goal, at centre-back and striker
- Confidence with the ball
- Bravery, courage and no fear
- Discipline, respect for referees
- Familiarity and comfort in their role
- Smart enough to handle your tactics
- Everyone gives everything to the team

An objective assessment of some of these qualities is totally possible. I expect it would be difficult to assess these qualities from afar though, using secondary data. But, an assessment centre environment that creates primary data could work. Many organisations use this method today in recruitment, so why should football clubs be any different? However, some of these items are also abstract and as such would be almost impossible to quantify. That said, perhaps they're not impossible to engender through the right processes and systems? When you look at Cuban boxing, the Chinese approach to Olympic sports and Barcelona's 'La Masia' academy – you see three 'systems' that are all highly capable of transforming people and delivering a required level of capability.

The same 'data guided' approach could be turned to Liverpool's youth development. Imagine, as a youngster, if Liverpool FC had operated an 'open-door' talent policy. You could put yourself forward at any time for assessment with a view to getting into the club and 'unlocking' further opportunities and support. If you passed, you'd be one step closer to the team. If you failed, you'd get objective feedback so that you knew exactly what needed improving and how you could do it – with the door always remaining open. What kind of players would this approach introduce? Now, imagine extending a proven model of this type on a global scale – avoiding all of the restrictions on catchment areas and the 'ivory tower' Elite Performance Plans (which will limit access to those children whose families can afford to support the logistics associated with that). This is just one idea from one 'fanalyst'. Can you imagine the creative and practical potential of the wider community if it was engaged effectively?

To conclude, I would encourage Liverpool FC to really engage with the 'fanalyst' community and set it challenges in five key areas:

- Player life-cycle tools (buy – use – sell);
- Youth development initiatives;
- New wage and incentive models;
- Financial ratio analysis of competitors;
- Innovations that open up new revenue streams or increases in existing revenues.

'FANALYSTS', POSSESSION AND PANNING FOR GOLD

By Tony McKenna

November, 2012

Note: this was originally posted as a comment by Tony in reply to Lee Mooney's 'Winning by Numbers' article. We then made it into an article in its own right.

Volume, Intensity and Intelligence

This resonates with me because, for a long time, I have acknowledged the limitations of the most quoted and sourced stats. This acknowledgement stems from none other than Bill James himself; the following quote is one of my favourites since it is a definitive warning from probably the most revolutionary of statisticians there is:

"It is one thing to build an analytical paradigm that leaves out leadership, hustle, focus, intensity, courage and self-confidence; it is a very different thing to say that hustle, focus, intensity, courage and self-confidence do not play a role in real world baseball teams." – Bill James, quoted from *Mind Game* – p177.

Here we are talking about variables pertaining to the human condition. Bill James' list is certainly not exhaustive in that sense; and you have added other considerations such as game intelligence. In this sense, I am also very interested in a player's movement in time and space – his positional play – off the ball. The problem with these entities is that they are infinite and abstract, and being abstract they cannot be easily measured or quantified, and therefore represented as statistics.

Even crucial 'on the ball' skills defy easy explanations. I recall many years ago, the late George Best, speaking on the Parkinson show; he referred to the time a reporter was asking him to verbalise his thoughts when engaged with the ball and beating opponents. Best was dismissive – laughingly so – saying it was impossible to verbalise instinctual aptitude in such conscious manner. Instead, the Belfast wonder referred to what Shankly termed as the "football brain". Unfortunately, this too, is an ineffable entity.

Nonetheless, it does not negate the need for future research into means that may help to attain such calibrations. This must also try to incorporate the 'off the ball' qualities since, as Lee points out, these are the more numerous events.

I do think that a strategy exists already that circumvents the unquantifiable and the unknown, albeit one not at the disposal of every football club. Economically, a multi-billionaire owner can purchase a surplus of players until the wheat emerges from the chaff; the latter can just languish on the bench and/or be sold at a loss – because the

101

cost is less punitive when, for example, you are bolstered by the petro-dollars in your artillery bank account. Any deduced inference, here, to existing real life football clubs is totally intentional on my part!

The Question of One Style over Another

Tiki taka has been eulogised and blogged to death, and rightly so. But Rafa Benítez, in a blog post called "Quo Vadis, EPL?" (July, 2012), advises caution about influences other than the particular style itself: Barcelona is a team that has practised this for an inordinate amount of time, and it is also about the players as individuals. These are Rafa's assessments, not mine; I just happen to see the validity in what he says. It also means something to me that Rafa neglected to import a style from his native country to the Premier League when managing Liverpool. Instead, his eclectic style was much his own – to the point that he was hard to second-guess.

Undoubtedly, in this way, he attained a high standard by making infinite use of a finite squad; one that had limitations in terms of intrinsic value and quality. Did Liverpool really have the right to go 'head to head' with the likes of Chelsea in those glorious – now seemingly distant – Champions League nights? Abramovich's riches should have been an unassailable advantage.

Support for Lee's hypothesis – about one style not necessarily eclipsing another – comes from a very credible and very timely source; *The Guardian* of Saturday 10th November 2012. A quote from none other than Iniesta:

"But the football that Spain and Barcelona play is not the only kind of football there is. Counter-attacking football, for example, has just as much merit. The way that Barcelona and Spain play is not the only way. Different styles make this such a wonderful sport. But what we do is not easy, either."

We should also appreciate the ridiculous amount of time and energy devoted to the underpinnings of La Masia, not to mention resources; which may explain why Barcelona has substantial debt – despite a flourishing academy. Truth is that La Masia trials thousands of youngsters from very young ages. A gigantic net is cast and unwanted produce is dismissed at later intervals. Most clubs will operate similar principles, but it is the scale to which Barcelona takes it where the difference lies; its early recruitment policy far surpasses the lengths to which all PL clubs go. So, as Rafa promotes, their success is clearly more than just the style of football they play; and it is still the case that Barcelona has won 3/4 of its European Cups in just the last six years. Was this also the outlier occurrence of a golden generation? Despite their exhaustive recruitment policy, they may never replicate the likes of Xavi, Messi or Iniesta– a cautious consideration emanating from within the Nou Camp itself:

"Barca has been lucky", the club's then chief executive Joan Oliver admitted to us

in 2009. Yeah, good fortune exists always in the world, in every kind of industry. It's not possible always to guarantee that we will have a Messi or an Iniesta or a Xavi from the academy." – Soccernomics, 2012 edition.

Whilst looking to Barcelona, one must first consider that Liverpool do not have Barcelona's squad. Perspective and context may help to curb the hedonism that threatens the mother of all hangovers should failure ensue. If someone, within Barcelona itself, happened to respect the potential of serendipity – as well as the elements of more purposeful design – it may be prudent for us outsiders to embrace the same uncertainty when trying to emulate the blueprint.

It upsets some people when I suggest that we should not be singly seduced by the tiki taka fame. But fashionable allure is underlined by one important observation. Jonathan Wilson's *Inverting the Pyramid* is a seminal work exploring the history of football tactics. Naturally one would expect to find tiki taka listed in the index; but it is not. Crucially, the book was first published in 2008, the year that Guardiola became manager of Barcelona; only hereafter did tiki taka's fame begin to mushroom. No doubt Wilson will cover the subject in a later updated version of his book, but as it stands, there were a plethora of other successful styles covered; tiki taka does not have an historic monopoly on success.

The Transfer Market

"Personally, I am often encouraged when we're linked with players that the vast majority of fans haven't heard of. I'd also actively welcome a 'panning of gold' strategy that quickly filtered through potential 'rough diamonds' that we'd bought cheaply." – Lee Mooney

I wholeheartedly agree with these above sentiments, and Lee puts them so eloquently. First, the notion incorporates a risk management strategy from the outset; second, the losses are more comfortably absorbed; third, the failures or flops are mostly forgotten – unlike the damage caused by huge investments blowing up in your face and generally calling the club's business acumen into question. The plaudits David Moyes receives for his 'achievements' in the transfer market seem hard to deflect. But, turning it on its head, here is a question: does Moyes actually enjoy an advantage?

The less you have to spend the more you will look in arenas where the bigger clubs have a lesser presence. In this sense, at least, you are 'away from the crowd'; there are fewer competitors in that market place where price inefficiencies are still likely to figure; in short, bargain buys without waiting in a queue. Indeed, Everton utilise the *Football Manager* database to gain an advantage. The big spenders do not always get to the best players first; this is important. This is, for example, how Wigan got Antonio Valencia before United did, and before he became a household name. And if a purchase does not work out then Moyes certainly eludes the criticism of too many flops; for example, no one berates him over James Beattie, Diniyar Bilyaletdinov, Andy Johnson or Yakubu.

Stats that Matter and the Fanalyst

Bill James was such a Fanalyst; it is remarkable not only what his work achieved but the manner in which it was achieved. A lone wolf knew more than the collective authorities on baseball; his strength lay in not being contaminated, or influenced, by the prevailing belief systems of 'insiders', irrevocably stuck on the wrong data and on data that is over-revered.

But finding the right data, especially data that may be new, is a bit like trying to catch the first autumnal leaf to parachute from any particular tree. Where do you look first? Where do you go? It is a hydra task; and, as such, one that requires the attention of a many-headed beast.

This is why I absolutely like the idea of access to low cost and extensive research bases provided by fans themselves; an inexpensive harnessing of endeavours and intellects of many different minds, something that *Soccernomics* espouses as a virtuous strategy, calling it the 'wisdom of the crowds'.

Here, Simon Kuper and Stefan Szymanski even talk about this in the context of fans actually picking the team. Well, Henry and Werner may not want to go that far, but certainly, in other regards, this is something that can be utilised – was it not TTT's Dan Kennett who spotted the value of Steven Fletcher who, almost single-handedly, has kept Sunderland – and Martin O'Neill – afloat this season?

Lee's reference to the qualities that Shankly/Clough valued is crucial in my opinion; and they are no less important today. Their success, based on a possession/passing game, proves that you do not necessarily have to look to carbon copies of the latest blueprint espoused by the Most Successful Team. I see a danger in the latter.

Barcelona are unique, and so are the processes that created them; the design has longevity in terms of application and rehearsal. Messi, for example, has been at Barca since he was 13 years of age, Iniesta since he was 12 – these boys have practised football with many of their current playing colleagues, from the inception of adolescence.

We talk about the successful individual attaining his 10,000 hours of practise; we must, in similar fashion, consider the merits of a group rehearsing, as a collective unit, for inordinate amounts of time. The same principle applies when the best orchestras consist of the same musicians for long periods; because team pursuits are disadvantaged when the carousel change of personnel impacts upon the development of twin necessities: mutual understanding and bonding.

Possession:

"How strong is the relationship between possession and winning? Perhaps one for Brendan Rodgers to think about."

My final feedback had to be on this. First, I note the distinction; Lee is not saying that possession is unimportant, and neither am I; we know *it is*. But the question is in the strength of the correlation between possession and winning; and the attendant need to study accompanying variables. In support of one of Lee's other themes, whereby a focus on specific data may detract from other more significant data, Dan Kennett tweeted to highlight a superb article by Mark Taylor, 'The Power of Goals', from which I quote:

"... raw possession isn't as important as what you actually do with it and Swansea aren't Barcelona ..."

Indeed. Whilst the fanbase finds solace in great football and the possession stats, there are other issues that need our focus. They should recall too that last season we were not that bad on possession either; currently, EPLindex has Rodgers' average shading Dalglish's (57.57% compared to 55.48%); hardly a cause for celebration though, admittedly, Rodgers' is a much smaller sample size and he may go on to increase that; then again, it could go the other way. Additionally, this season an allegedly 'poor' United now have an average possession of 58.65%; as such, exceeding that of Rodgers. Yet, I do not hear United fans eulogising about their possession prowess; I think their league position is more the issue and the fact that they score goals.

Winning 79% of the Time

Brendan Rodgers states, and often, that the team 'better on the ball' will win 79% of the time. I was intrigued to know the source of this study; was it Rodgers himself who conducted the research or was it an independent study? I hoped that I could locate it on the Internet. This was not too fanciful, I thought, since most other aspects of his game plan are readily accessible; unfortunately, I could not find anything.

My intrigue was born out of confusion, and I was confused about this for a long time. I asked Mihail Vladimirov, via TTT's tactics thread, whether he could direct me to the evidence base corroborating the 79% edge hypothesis. Mihail was unsure but we agreed that the theory sounded logical enough. 'Mdonald1987' also replied to my query confirming that it was Rodgers' own research project.

Yes, Rodgers' research does sound logical indeed, but allow me to explain the context of my caution. Consider the following: the players 'better on the ball' will belong to those clubs that collectively have the biggest economic resources. Since the best players normally have the most talent, we can safely correlate this with superior general ability on the ball – including the specifics of passing skills, ball retention and most importantly, goal scoring prowess.

We also know that such assets would normally cost you more in terms of transfer fees and wages. Surely, and rationally, it follows that the most economically blessed clubs will inevitably glean the vast majority of those players.

So, what comes first the chicken or the egg? Any study evaluating the most successful clubs may engage a forgone conclusion: these are the homes of the best players, therefore, amongst other things, better passing ratios and possession stats should ensue. If you research which English Universities boast the best brains and superior intelligence, it should not be a surprise if Oxford and Cambridge came out on top.

Possession: Nine Tenths of the Law?

The oft-quoted comparison, borrowed from the legal profession, is a square peg in a round hole when transposed to a game of football. Possession, of a physical asset, may render a legal advantage if ownership is in dispute; you may get to keep the prized possession. Yet, in a football game, possession is not the 'be all to end all', nor is it necessarily the hallmark of ultimate victory, as Celtic, with their victory over Barcelona, just reminded us. Instead, we look to earn points and you do not earn them just by bossing possession; even if you do enjoy the lion's share, it is goals that are key; you still have to score more than your opponent.

Better conversion ratios than your opponent – of all the chances coming your way – mean you will win 100% of the time. But, as we know, goal-scoring players are not replete in Liverpool's current team in the same way that they are in that of United and Chelsea – from different positions on the pitch. Look at Gary Cahill's goal ratio at Bolton and continuing with his move to a bigger club; this is exemplary from a defender. And once again yesterday, United showed how to turn around a losing game – just score one more than the opposition.

Even Everton have now come back from behind in half a dozen games. Liverpool need to stockpile chance *converters*, as well as chance creators throughout the team, so that a variety of options can be called upon. Fanalysts may have been able to help Rodgers in that pursuit.

As the January window approaches we see this as the opportunity for solution. But we must bear in mind that prior sought targets, Gylfi Sigurðsson and Clint Dempsey, are not quite cutting it at Spurs.

January could still be a curse in disguise.

BOSTON RED SOX VS. LIVERPOOL FC

By Simon Steers

August, 2012

One of the unique selling points for Fenway Sports Group when they talk about a desire to 'win trophies' and get Liverpool back to where they belong is that they have done it before with the Boston Red Sox.

There have been a lot of similarities drawn between the situation at the Red Sox when FSG took over, and the one at Liverpool.

The methodology and blueprint that FSG have used at the Red Sox can give us some insight into how the Liverpool journey may unfold. Whilst baseball is a very different sport to football, there are some business and sporting principles that can be integrated across sports.

I thought it would be interesting to look at the Red Sox journey under FSG and try and draw some parallels with how that might influence the direction of Liverpool. To help me understand and assess that journey, I have asked two Red Sox fans to give a view as to how successful FSG have been at the Red Sox – one of those is a Fulham fan as well, to give an 'impartial' view of the FSG model when applied to football.

Background

Having recently celebrated 100 years at their famous home 'Fenway Park', the Boston Red Sox are one of the oldest baseball franchises in the US. The Red Sox have a rich heritage, but before the arrival of FSG had a reputation as 'always the bridesmaid but never the bride', fuelled by the failure to win a World Series since 1918.

NESV (New England Sports Ventures), fronted up by John Henry, arrived at the Red Sox in 2002, acquiring the franchise for around $600m in a deal that also included NESN (the real money maker in the FSG portfolio, generating around a billion dollars in profit each year), Fenway Park itself and some other minor stuff. There was some initial controversy over the sale concerning a long standing relationship the previous owners – the Yawkey family – had with a Boston cancer charity 'The Jimmy Fund'.

These issues were resolved quickly as Henry and co set up the Red Sox foundation (see later in article) which has kept the relationship between the Red Sox and the Jimmy Fund strong – with over $10m in donations and fundraising over the past four years alone.

The reaction to the new owners was initially one of caution and distrust, recalls Russ Goldman, a lifelong Sox fan:

"I think many Red Sox fans were very sceptical of John Henry and his partners.

This group was not from Boston, and I think that bothered many fans. I feel Bostonians wanted owners that knew the history and the passion of the club."

NESV were very clear from the outset that they wanted the Red Sox to win the World Series and to be competitive right at the top of the sport. But they were also pragmatic enough to recognise that the spending power of the Yankees meant that they would have to follow a different journey – one where money was invested wisely, and where a focus on youth and development would have to be the foundation of the blueprint.

Methodology

The Red Sox, when NESV acquired them, were a franchise with a great heritage and fanatical support. They were playing in a ball park that was steeped in history, but wasn't fit for purpose in a modern game. They were also a distance behind the Yankees in terms of revenue and ability to compete financially.

With Henry and Werner at the helm, the blueprint developed into three key areas which can probably be categorised as:

– Sporting

The Red Sox approach to the game is again nicely summed up by Russ:

"The blueprint I believe is a version of Moneyball that is based on statistical analysis to get the team built in a certain manner, and actually play a certain way."

One of the qualities that NESV brought into the Red Sox was a strategic view and approach – everything was about planning for long term success. There was also a pragmatism that recognised innovation was going to be critical to beating the Yankees – so once a certain Billy Beane starting making waves over at the Oakland A's, he naturally attracted the attention of Henry. The Moneyball theory has a number of facets, but at its heart is excellent scouting and sourcing value, with a strong emphasis on statistical and data analysis to match player qualities with the requirements of the team. But Moneyball can only get you so far. Matt Lyke, another lifelong Red Sox fan, observes:

"Overall they have done a good job of buying established well-known players as well as developing unknown talents in the farm system. The teams that won the World Series in '04 and '07 were a mix of big money free agents/trades and home-grown talents."

The 'farm' or 'academy' system is something that is absolutely critical to the success of the blueprint at the Red Sox. The development of youth has played a huge role in the two World Series wins under FSG's ownership. The model that FSG have used at the Red Sox is a hybrid of developing youth with investment in established players. Russ points out:

"The Red Sox do spend a tremendous amount of money, and are just behind the Yankees in payroll."

So, there is a real financial commitment from the owners – where the profits that the franchise makes are reinvested back into the team. One of the things that the owners have also demonstrated at the Red Sox is that they are not afraid to make risky or unpopular decisions. In the first year they were at the Red Sox they installed Theo Epstein as General Manager – at 28 years old. The sacking of Terry Francona in 2011 is clear evidence that they will take unpopular decisions if they feel it is in the long-term interests of the team. Another important area of the approach FSG took at the Red Sox is also summarised by Russ:

"The owners certainly know how to delegate and surround themselves with the best people in sports."

This is a critical point – listening to experts is the only way that you will make the right decisions to see success on the field.

– Commercial

One of the things that NESV recognised at an early stage is the potential of the Red Sox to increase its revenue streams. This is the key strength of Henry and Werner – and both bring a great deal of business and media acumen to the table. Increasing revenue is the key to competing.

The commercial side of sport doesn't always sit easy for supporters – as Russ notes:

"I don't like everything they do as they market everything under the sun with the Red Sox logo on it. But, they do put it back into the team, so I try to look over all the ads at Fenway Park along with the other ideas they have come up with to build up the Red Sox brand."

But the key point is that increasing commercial income can increase the team's ability to compete. FSG have done an excellent job of leveraging the Red Sox 'brand' (like I say – the commercial side doesn't always 'sit easy') – and they now sit second behind the Yankees in terms of the revenue they generate ($272m). One of the methods that FSG have used successfully at the Red Sox is to work with subsidiary sponsors. The Red Sox have a staggering 95 commercial partners – all of whom contribute to the bottom line. Whilst baseball is a huge sport in the US, it doesn't have the global footprint of football, so leveraging revenue from sponsorships has been a big part of the Red Sox approach. Another area where FSG have added value to the Red Sox brand is through digital and media. Werner has a strong background in this area, and FSG's ownership of NESN has enabled them to use this channel 'to take the Red Sox product to market'.

– **The ball park**

One of NESV's biggest challenges on acquiring the Red Sox was Fenway Park. Many observers felt that a new ball park was the only long-term solution – but FSG took a different view.

Russ sums up the Red Sox stadium issue as:

"Before NESV became owners, the Red Sox were in discussions regarding building a new ballpark. If I can remember correctly, it was after a few seasons of ownership when they made it known that the Red Sox would be staying at Fenway Park. I was actually against this, and wanted them to build a new ballpark. I haven't changed my stance on this at all. However, to their credit they have done a wonderful job with the re-development of Fenway. The Park is now 100 years old, and FSG have done what they can to modernize it."

But instead of building a new ball park, $285m has been spent on re-developing Fenway Park, the spiritual home of the Red Sox. This has included installing extra seats, and a complete renovation of a ball park that was in decay. In 2011, team president Larry Lucchino announced that after ten years of investment, the renovations were complete. The approach that the owners look to have taken was to assess all options before making a decision. The renovation of Fenway was a decision that will have been weighed up against the economic challenges of building a new stadium. Whilst prices have gone up at Fenway, the game day experience has been improved by the renovations to the ball park.

The comparisons with Liverpool FC

One of the most important comparisons to make is between the cultures of Liverpool and the Red Sox. Russ gives a fantastic insight into this:

"The culture is a crazy passionate fan-base that is very similar to Liverpool. Many fans analyse and dissect almost every move the team makes. The fans are extremely knowledgeable about the team and the game. It is a place that a player should want to come to because the fans care. They will let you know when you have done well, and when you have not. The players have to take the good and the bad if they want to play in Boston. Many players that leave Boston often miss it a great deal, and the fans have so much to do with it I feel."

Both Boston and Liverpool are port cities, and sport is a key part of the identity of both cultures. As Russ points out, there are real similarities between the supporters, which should act as a good foundation for FSG at Liverpool, having been through similar scepticism in the early days at the Red Sox. In terms of the methodology that FSG used at the Red Sox – the 'blueprint' – there are obvious similarities that jump out. Indeed Henry himself noted:

"A number of parallels emerged with the situation that existed in Boston when we arrived."

The obvious similarities are the stadium and commercial opportunities at Liverpool. Whilst the Red Sox are a cherished institution in the US, they do not have the global appeal or opportunity that Liverpool presents. The commercial potential at Liverpool is enormous – but it also has constraints with TV rights being a barrier to fully realising the club's potential. The Liverpool 'blueprint' has undoubtedly been influenced by the approach that FSG took at the Red Sox. The appointment of Comolli in a 'GM' type role had a similar feel to the appointment of Epstein at the Red Sox.

But, as Henry points out: *"Choosing players in any sport is an imperfect science. We certainly have been guilty of overspending on some players and that can be tied to an analytical approach that hasn't worked well enough."*

The Moneyball theory is a more difficult concept to apply in football.

My view is that when FSG came into Liverpool, the belief was that the model that they have used so successfully in Boston could be applied directly to football. But football is a very different game, with different dynamics, and it has become clear that whilst there are sporting parallels between Liverpool and the Red Sox, the 'blueprint' needs tweaking if it is going to work in football.

Some of the principles remain the same – such as a focus on the academy, development of youth and investing big money in the right players. The structure at the club has also moved away from the baseball 'GM' model as things stand – although there may still be a longer term role for a 'Sporting Director' that will bring Liverpool's ideology closer to that of the Red Sox.

Whilst it is disappointing that Pep Segura is leaving the club, there is a commitment from the owners that the club will progress towards a continental structure. I think they are giving Rodgers some time before making the long-term structural decisions that will provide continuity.

As Russ pointed out, FSG have historically surrounded themselves with experts to help inform decision-making; and it is reported that FSG were advised by both David Dein and Johan Cryuff when reviewing the Liverpool structure, who were at the heart of restructuring Arsenal and Barcelona respectively; clubs that have robust, sustainable models that can influence long-term success.

The biggest elephant in the room for Liverpool at the moment is the stadium. And it is clear that FSG are keen on taking an almost identical route to the Red Sox, with a redevelopment of Anfield the favoured option. But as with the Red Sox, they will not be rushed into a decision that will require huge investment. There are also political complexities to be overcome, and a process that requires support from Anfield residents.

By looking at the approach FSG took with the renovation of Fenway Park, you can perhaps begin to see how they may approach the issue of redevelopment at Anfield. I think they will add additional capacity and upgrade the facilities over a period of time – so it could be that the 'stadium solution' is a gradual process – the same as the renovation of Fenway Park.

On the commercial side we are seeing a number of new partnerships – Warrior, Chevrolet and other smaller deals. The Fox documentary *Being:Liverpool* is a mechanism for taking the Liverpool 'brand' to market. The appointment of Billy Hogan will give Liverpool the expertise and insight as to how the Red Sox have grown revenues, and with Ian Ayre's understanding of the Asian market and Jen Chang's understanding of digital and media, this is a team well equipped to leverage our global footprint.

On the pitch, FSG have recognised that the 'blueprint' has to be tweaked – but off it the journey Liverpool are following looks to be very similar to that of the Red Sox.

The Red Sox and Liverpool foundations

Another important initiative that FSG take seriously in Boston is the Red Sox Foundation; the RSF is a charity and community programme that was set up in 2002 once FSG acquired the Red Sox. Henry's wife, Linda Pizzuti, is a Director of the RSF.

On arrival in Liverpool, FSG also created the Liverpool Foundation, which has a very similar structure to the Red Sox counterpart. Linda Pizzuti is a Trustee and has been heavily involved in its development. Recently Liverpool appointed a Foundation Director to take this work forward, and on Liverpool's recent trip to Boston there were some joint initiatives where Liverpool had the opportunity to get involved in local communities.

The Red Sox and Liverpool Foundations are an important part of retaining the identity of both institutions. And it is encouraging to see that the Red Sox Foundation has made a real difference in Boston since its inauguration.

What the future may hold

Nobody can see what the future holds for FSG's ownership of Liverpool, but if you look closely at how they have managed the Red Sox, the signs are promising.

FSG may well be at both the Red Sox and Liverpool for a financial return, but they are not afraid of the long-term. They have been in Boston for ten years already, during which time their $600m investment has increased to a $912m valuation (*Forbes*). This has been based on a model of self-sufficiency, solid business acumen, but also – and most importantly – sporting success.

In recent interviews Werner has confirmed that FSG are at Liverpool for the "long haul" with Henry stating that they're "just getting started".

Although the Red Sox are currently going through a turbulent period, the majority of FSG's ownership has been a success, cemented by two World Series titles. The current issues at the Red Sox are a direct result of the owners taking action after a season where the team failed to perform. As Russ says:

"Lately, it has been about how they have spent their money that has been an issue."

Owning two sports institutions the size of Liverpool and the Red Sox is a challenge – and the owners are reliant on the teams that run both organisations to perform. The owners do take a hands-on approach when needed – and employees are left in no doubt that they expect high standards. They will back you with whatever resources they can leverage from the business – but they expect results.

There has been some noise in the Boston media lately about FSG's interests in Liverpool. The key point with FSG's interests in the Red Sox and Liverpool is that there are more opportunities than risks. FSG do take an active interest in both – but they also rely on the people they employ to manage day to day operations.

The commercial opportunities provide access to two passionate sets of fans – taking the Red Sox product worldwide through the Liverpool fan base, and taking Liverpool into the US market. This can translate itself into revenue that can be re-invested onto the pitch. I don't think it is a case of the owners having more of an interest in Liverpool or Boston – they want the very best for both.

Whilst there are 'sporting' issues in Boston at the moment, the foundations are in place for success. Liverpool are trying to build those same foundations – so that will translate itself into time and resources being diverted towards that goal. That is against the backdrop of trying to understand a different sport and culture.

Liverpool's recent trip to Boston was an opportunity for both the Red Sox and Liverpool FC to start building a relationship that can provide long-term benefit to both organisations.

Essentially, what FSG do well is to build a sports franchise (forgive the phrase!) business from the bottom up, increasing revenue and driving growth to invest back into the product 'on the pitch'. They aim for the top on the business side – and expect that to translate into winning on the sporting side.

FSG do not on the face of it look to be in the business of sport just for a big return – as two World Series titles with the Red Sox demonstrate. They are competitive, and they want to win. As Russ sums up:

"In the end they are great owners because it is about winning, and they have done that. I have always said that Liverpool will win the Premier League soon, and the Champions League because FSG will not stand for anything less."

There will always be short-term decisions that do not sit well with supporters, such as managers or players leaving the club. But the judgement on FSG will come not now, but in 5-10 years when they have realised the vision they have for Liverpool.

If they can translate the success they have had in Boston into football, then Liverpool are in good hands. It may be a big 'if' – and the decisions they make will always rightly be scrutinised – but they have shown at the Red Sox the ambition, investment, and methodology is there. The trick is getting it to work for Liverpool.

The logical conclusion to this piece is to put the question to Liverpool's new commercial director, Billy Hogan, on how FSG's experience at the Red Sox might influence Liverpool's journey. Billy said:

"We are focused on significant commercial growth over the next several seasons. We know that driving increased revenues will allow ownership to invest in the football side. Ownership has shown a willingness to invest in players – in both Boston and Liverpool – and our job is to generate income to help that process. While there are a number of similarities between the Red Sox and Liverpool, one significant difference at Liverpool is that we control our rights globally – the Red Sox don't control their club rights/marks outside of New England, those rights are held by Major League Baseball. The Liverpool fanbase is global in nature and our commercial business will be as well. We are intent on establishing partnerships on a worldwide basis, for example our two newest club partnerships with Chevy & Garuda show the global appeal of an association with LFC. Another example of our growth globally is our recently-opened online store for China, serving our fans in China, Macau and Taiwan."

Big thanks to Russ Goldman and Matthew Lyke for the contributions to this article. Russ is a lifelong Red Sox fan who lives in the Boston area and has supported them for over 40 years. Russ is also a Fulham fan. Mike is a lifelong Red Sox and Liverpool fan. Also thanks to Jen Chang and Billy Hogan for providing a LFC perspective.

INTO THE RED: THE FINANCIAL FAIR PLAY RULES AND LIVERPOOL FC

By Daniel Geey

June, 2013

The aim of this article is to set out briefly the rationale for the new UEFA rules, then go into some detail about what they say, and finally offer some insight into their significance for Liverpool Football Club. The article will try and demonstrate that, in the short term at least, due to the unfortunate timing of the proposed takeover and the lack of any significant funds in the last few transfer windows, Liverpool Football Club has not been able to take advantage of the UEFA rules used to calculate whether a club has broken even.

Background

UEFA and its president, Michel Platini, have long been concerned that clubs who continually make losses and, as a result, accumulate debt, are not playing by the rules of fair competition. The Premier League, and in particular its chief executive, Richard Scudamore, has been wary of lessening the global attractiveness of the Premier League by curbing the ability of owners to subsidise their clubs or, in some cases, milk their clubs dry. Tellingly, however, UEFA has implemented, as part of its already functioning club licensing system, the Financial Fair Play Rules (FFPR) to ensure a club, more or less, has to balance its books.

UEFA's overall aim for the FFPR is for its affiliated football clubs to balance their books, not spend more than they earn, and to promote investment in their stadia and training facility infrastructure and youth development. This idea of self-sustainability relates to UEFA's underlying belief that transfer fee and wage inflation continues unabated because each set of new club owners injects more money into the European football club market. This 'keeping up with the Joneses' effect spirals further because a new owner then has to outbid other high-spending clubs.

Whilst the beneficiaries are no doubt the players who are earning ever more lucrative salaries, the clubs (through their representative ECA body) have been seeking ways with UEFA to actually limit their own spending. This may seem rather ironic in the case of Chelsea, given their £120m loss in 2004, but it actually makes perfect sense; Mr Abramovich, after spending over £800m+, sees the fallacy of football clubs constantly outdoing one another. The very clubs that are being restricted by these rules are the ones that have actively participated in, and consented to, the proposals. Clubs are asking UEFA to save them from themselves. UEFA, along with the various interest groups, put forward proposals in order to create a deflationary effect across UEFA-affiliated national football associations.

The Basics

In summary, the following points need to be understood (there are quite a few!):

• As part of its already functioning club licensing system, the FFPR are to ensure a club, more or less, has to balance its books;

• At its heart is the break-even criterion. Each club that believes it can qualify for next season's European competitions must, prior to the beginning of that season, apply for a UEFA Club Licence. From the 2013-14 season, the licence stipulations will include adherence to the break-even element of the FFPR. Until at least the 2013-14 season, there are no sanctions for breaching the FFPR break-even requirements;

• The FFPR promote investment in a club's stadium, training facility infrastructure and youth development schemes by excluding such costs from the break-even calculation. Any club has the incentive to spend in these areas, should they wish to participate in European competition, because the FFPR does not count such investment as expenditure for the purposes of its break-even calculation. Therefore, any new funding for a proposed Stanley Park stadium or upgrading Anfield will not impact on Liverpool's ability to pass the FFPR because such finance would be excluded;

• UEFA FFPR relate only to Champions League and Europa League participation, and not to domestic league participation. It should, however, be borne in mind that the Football League (FL) has just implemented its own version of FFPR for the Championship, while the Premier League (PL) at the time of writing has just voted in various cost saving measures;

• A wide variety of clubs (through the European Club Association) were consulted by UEFA over many months. The regulations have been drafted and implemented with the consent of the clubs;

• The break-even aspect of FFPR will start to bite from the 2013-14 season. The rules needed to be borne in mind, however, from the 2011-12 season onwards because the 2011-12 and 2012-13 season accounts are used to determine a club's licence application in the 2013-14 season;

• Acceptable deviation is the term used to describe break-even. Acceptable deviation allows clubs to pass the FFPR break-even test without actually breaking even. The acceptable deviation provisions allow a club with some losses over a certain number of seasons to 'break even' and therefore pass the FFPR.

UEFA has also been at great pains to stress that they are not anti-debt. With Manchester United's huge reported debt and Liverpool's own debt inching towards it, Platini placated various debt-ridden clubs with the distinction that so long as the debt is being serviced (i.e. profit is covering interest payments), UEFA does not have a problem. Issues become more delicate when interest payments to service the debt do not cover the profit made.

Acceptable Deviation = Break Even (ish)

Usually, break-even means expenditure must equal revenue. Not in this case; at least not at the outset of these rules. This is because included in the break-even calculation are the acceptable deviation provisions (code for a little bit of a loss is acceptable in the first few years). Clubs will not have to break even until 2018-19 season at the earliest.

The revenue that is taken into account for break-even purposes includes gate receipts, broadcasting rights, commercial sponsorship details and profit on player transfers. Expenditure includes player transfers, wages and associated costs and other operating expenses. There are also anti-evasion mechanisms like arms'-length trading and related-party transaction requirements.

The acceptable deviation provisions allow a club with some losses over a certain number of seasons to 'break even' and therefore pass the FFPR. Without trying to get too technical, below is a table that I have amended slightly from an excellent Swiss Ramble blog on the FFPR.

Acceptable Deviation Levels

Reporting Period	Number of Years	Years Included			Acceptable Deviation (€m)	
		T-2	T-1	T	Equity Investment	Non-Equity Investment
2013-14	2	N/A	2011-12	2013-14	45	5
2014-15	3	2011-12	2012-13	2014-15	45	5
2015-16	3	2012-13	2013-14	2015-16	30	5
2016-17	3	2013-14	2014-15	2016-17	30	5
2017-18	3	2014-15	2015-16	2017-18	30	5
2018-19	3	2015-16	2016-17	2018-19	<30	5

The table shows that the acceptable deviations (i.e. losses) vary quite considerably. In taking the first row as an example, the rules come into force in the 2013-14 season. The reason why this is important is because, in the first year, two years' worth of accounts are used to assess whether a particular club can successfully apply for its UEFA Club Licence. The first point to stress is that if an owner does not put any money into a club by way of cash for shares, each club's acceptable deviation (loss) (by reference to the last column in the table) is a mere €5m over three years (i.e. €1.3m per season). For the 2013-14 season when the rules come into force, an owner can inject up to €45m over two seasons to cover the losses of the club. After the 2013-14 season, an owner can on average exchange only €15m worth of cash for shares each year to spend on transfers and wages. That figure is reduced to €10m per season (€30m over three seasons) for the 2015-16 season. Should Liverpool FC wish to pass the FFPR break-even requirement, and it makes for example a €35m combined loss for the first monitoring period ('13-14), the owners will have to inject €35m worth of equity into the club. If they do not, Liverpool FC will breach the rules.

Explanation of some Important FFPR Concepts

Transfer fee amortisation
Very simply put:
'When a player is purchased, his cost is capitalised on [a club's] balance sheet and is

written-down (amortised) over the length of his contract.' – Swiss Ramble

For example, a player signs in January 2010 for a transfer fee of £10 million on a five-year deal. Thus the transfer fee in the club's accounts will show the amortised amount of £2 million each year for five years. The basic point for FFPR break-even compliance is that even a transfer that occurred in the 2010-11 season can have an impact on a club trying to break even in the first monitoring period in 2013-14, because clubs amortise the player's value over the length of their contract.

The Annex XI Provision

In the final annex of the FFPR is a provision that permits clubs to remove some of their wage expenditure from the break-even calculation. It is not necessary to go into the details of the provision, but needless to say it allows clubs to remove the wage costs of players who have contracts that have been in place prior to June 1st, 2010. For clarity's sake, any contract renegotiations after June 1st 2010 for an existing contracted player would be classed as a new contract. This was the date the rules were first published and it was seen as unfair to punish clubs who would not have been aware of the rules prior to them being made public.

Therefore, even if a club fails to meet the standard deviation target (i.e. losses of up to €45m) in the first two monitoring periods when applying for a UEFA license, the club can remove all wage costs from their 2011- 12 accounts for players whose contracts were already in place prior to 1 June 2010. If that cost reduction takes them inside the €45m loss figure and the club's cost trend is improving, they will not be sanctioned.

Sanctions

The Club Financial Control Panel will conduct club audits to ensure that the system is applied correctly.

The relevant UEFA regulations do provide for a whole host of possible sanctions including a reprimand, a fine, disqualification from competitions in progress and/or exclusion from future competitions or withdrawal of a licence.

Although the above are all possible sanctions, it appears likely from the outset (from the 2013-14 season) that a soft-touch approach may well be applied, simply because these rules were in part drafted by the clubs not wanting harsh sanctions for breach of the rules. This is unless presumably there is a blatant flouting of the rules (i.e. someone posting a loss similar to Chelsea's £140m in the 2004/05 season).

Why a soft-touch approach? Because there is nothing set in stone in the rules which says a club falling outside of the break-even parameters will automatically have its licence refused. Indeed there is even a provision where clubs can be in breach of the break-even calculation and still not be sanctioned at all! (Annex XI(2) as explained above).

It should be borne in mind that Real Mallorca and more recently Malaga have been sanctioned with expulsion because they failed to meet the UEFA Club Licensing entry criteria. This decision can however be appealed to the Court of Arbitration for Sport.

Such an instance does illustrate the powers UEFA has to refuse a club licence application. When the FFPR get added to the licence criteria in time for the 2013-14 season, the rules will be stricter than those applied to Real Mallorca. A future high-profile UEFA refusal of a club licence application should not however be ruled out.

How will Financial Fair Play and the Break-Even regulations be implemented?

FFPR is already in action and has allowed UEFA to sanction a number of clubs for overdue debts. As mentioned briefly above, the initial step is for all clubs wanting to play in UEFA competition to submit the required licensing documentation to their national FA. The FA then makes the licensing decision which is then communicated to UEFA. UEFA, through its newly constituted Club Financial Control Body (CFCB) has the power to conduct club audits and ask further questions to ensure that the national FA approval/rejection system is applied correctly. If the Panel believes that the FFPR have not been correctly applied, it has the disciplinary power to sanction clubs in breach. Bear in mind that FFPR apply not only to ensure that clubs break-even, but cover a wide range of licensing conditions to ensure clubs pay their debts in a timely manner.

UEFA's CFCB has the power to sanction clubs for breaches of the FFPR. Such sanctions include a reprimand, a fine, withholding of prize monies, points deductions, refusal to register players for UEFA competition, reducing a club's permitted squad size, disqualification from competitions in progress and/or exclusion from future competitions.

How the rules constructed and what was their ultimate aim? What is the current political situation?

Clubs have had a large say in the drafting of the rules and as a result some provisions do give clubs leeway to comply with the FFPR (see Annex XI as described above). The rules are a product of collaboration and negotiation between UEFA and the many interested parties in European football. The FFPR have been implemented in such a way to ensure gradual adherence (with certain acceptable losses) in order to give clubs time to comply.

My understanding of the consultation process with UEFA and the ECA in particular is that a number of concessions were made (i.e. the Annex XI provisions, the staggered acceptable losses approach and the removal of all infrastructure and youth development costs from the break-even calculation) in order to get clubs across the finishing line.

My belief is that the rules are not in place to catch clubs out. Rather they are there to guide clubs into a more responsible era of spending where everyone plays by the same rules of the game. UEFA describes it as adding "rationality" into the football finance landscape.

I think fans need to understand the overall objective for the rules is to bring clubs into line. This may not happen overnight and people may not be happy that break-even is not actually break-even. However, the benefit of this incremental approach is that the top clubs will have to ensure that after a bedding-in period, they will have to break even.

Everyone that I have spoken to at UEFA is consistent in insisting the CFCB will sanction clubs who breach the FFPR. UEFA's general secretary, Gianni Infantino, has stated:

"We would bar clubs in breach of the rules from playing in the Champions League or the Europa League. Otherwise, we lose all credibility."

Sanctions as explained above, will take many forms. It should be stressed that it is far from certain that a club that breaches the FFPR will be automatically excluded. High profile club sanctions should not be ruled out but exclusion will certainly be saved for only the most blatant offenders. Note: The text I have crossed out already appears verbatim on the previous page.

Could non-compliant clubs just start a European super league?

Clubs may make rational decisions not to comply but that would certainly be a high risk strategy. They could theoretically breakaway from UEFA (and FIFA) and form their own competition and thus not be bound by the rules anymore. It could become rather complicated because players for those clubs may not be eligible to play for their national team as a result. My own belief is a somewhat more straightforward theory. There are some very large clubs in the main European leagues like Real Madrid, Arsenal, Manchester United and Bayern who all posted profits in their last accounting period. Barcelona made a small loss and can thus be added to the list. It means some of the giants of European football are almost certain to pass the break-even criteria.

There are then clubs like Zenit, PSG, Monaco and Manchester City that have recently spent considerable sums in order to break into the established order. These aspiring clubs are the teams most at risk of non-break-even compliance. They are most at risk because they want to compete with their larger revenue-generating European rivals.

The top clubs that are making profit have a competitive advantage to maintain the break-even model because they have the ability to generate the highest revenues. They are incentivised to remain in the competition because the very rules that bind them provide them with the greatest advantage over their lesser competitors. They thus have a greater chance of sporting success in European competition.

The more recent free-spenders like Manchester City and PSG have historically not had such high levels of sporting success. In order to attract more fans, sponsors, players and TV exposure, they require high-profile matches against the highest-profile teams. Should such aspiring clubs fall foul of the regulations and be excluded (the harshest possible sanction) because of their quest to compete at the very highest levels, if the top clubs are relatively content with the status quo, it would be difficult for such clubs to breakaway. This is because the product would be less attractive without the top headline clubs to compete against.

One caveat to my theory concerns the three largest Italian clubs by revenue (Milan, Juventus and Inter). They all made losses of around £50m in their last set of accounts. Milan for example, by selling Ibrahimovic and Silva to PSG for a combined €65m, have saved over €150m on future wages and transfer amortisation according to their owner Mr Berlusconi. Should the Italian clubs and other clubs in UEFA competition breach the break-even rules it is less likely they will be expelled unless, as stated previously, their losses are abnormally large. As such there is less risk of expulsion which would calm any threats of a break-away. Recently the head of the ECA (the representative European club association) Karl-Heinz Rummenigge said:

"It seems that quite a few clubs have not understood the message. Time has come to take the new rules seriously. ECA will continue to support Financial Fair Play."

It appears the majority of clubs are in favour of the rules. Some clubs may however not be so polite if, and when, they incur the wrath of UEFA for FFPR infringements.

What does this all mean for Liverpool?

Longer Term Significance
I may be proved wrong, but this is where I believe the rules are in Liverpool's favour. Unlike smaller Premier League clubs who will probably have only a finite level of commercial income (mid-range stadium capacity, merchandising sold only in the local area, limited commercialisation of overseas markets), Liverpool are one of only a small number of global football institutions that have the ability to expand their international commercial activities.

Additionally, and most importantly, the club has the potential for a much larger stadium to bring vastly increased revenues. Liverpool's annual match-day income is dwarfed by Arsenal's and Manchester United's. Being debt-free (a big 'if') and having

£60m worth of additional revenue each season creates a much larger revenue stream with which to break even.

Therefore, in the long term, Liverpool's hopefully increasing international commercial performance (perhaps into China) along with the potential revenue windfall of a new or expanded stadium should allow the Reds to keep within the rules by having larger revenues to balance against larger transfer spending.

Liverpool's global following should give the club a disproportionate revenue advantage when compared with probably all but two or three other Premier League clubs. The fact that Liverpool were 9th (measured by revenue) in the Deloitte Football Money League 2012 for Europe shows the potential for further revenue growth.

Is Liverpool FC likely to comply with its break-even obligations?

It is a very tricky answer to give without having in-depth access to the club's accounts. Swiss Ramble has explained that had it not been for the current owners having to write off £59m in stadium development expenses, Liverpool would have made a £10m profit in its last published set of accounts. However, excluding the Torres sale, it would have realised a £20m loss. Remember, the break-even calculation in the first monitoring period is based on two, and then in subsequent monitoring periods (usually) three sets of accounts. So long as the Reds make a loss of no more than €45m in the first monitoring period (as you can see from the table at the beginning of this article) and the owners are willing to cover that loss, Liverpool will not breach the break-even criteria. The only individuals that know for certain whether the Reds will break-even under the UEFA regulations are likely to be the board and the club's accountants. This is because certain cost deductibles (Annex XI, youth and training development costs for example) will be difficult to extrapolate from the club's accounts.

That said, here are a few reasons why LFC may be in a healthier position to comply with the regulations than other clubs across Europe.

Champions League Shortfall

Over the last three seasons, and I believe set out in the two previous sets of the most recent accounts, Liverpool FC has lost out on significant Champions League revenues. In the 2011-12 season Chelsea made €60m, Manchester United €35m, Arsenal €28m and Manchester City €27m. The Europa League is very much small change. Even without the golden prize of Champions League revenues, Liverpool has not been making astronomical losses (taking away exceptional items). Indeed, Liverpool continues to feature in the Deloitte Football Club Money list. Most recently in 9th position earning €203m for revenues generated in the troubled '10-11 season. Should LFC achieve Champions League status once more, this should provide the club with greater revenues to offset against costs.

Premier League TV Deals

The latest £3bn domestic PL TV deal that was announced (which was a 64% increase on the previous deal) will significantly increase the revenues of all PL clubs participating in the league come the '13-14 season. Those that finish higher in the PL (hopefully including Liverpool) will benefit from higher-placed payments as well as a greater likelihood of more frequent TV appearances, thus benefiting from larger facility fees. Under the current distribution system and factoring in an increased foreign TV rights deal, Swiss Ramble believes there may be an additional £30m per season on offer for the PL's top clubs. Manchester City received £60m from the Premier League for winning the title. That could rise to over £90m from the 2013-14 season. This additional revenue, so long as it does not spark another round of transfer and wage inflation – although that is likely, based on past evidence – will assist PL clubs, including Liverpool, in complying with the FFPR.

Stadium Redevelopment

As explained above, the cost of refurbishing Anfield, which appears the preferred option, is excluded from the break-even cost calculation. This is to Liverpool's benefit. UEFA is keen to incentivise long-term revenue-generating projects like stadium construction and/or improvements. The net result of an improved capacity and a higher proportion of corporate seats will certainly dwarf current home match day revenues. By way of brief comparison, Manchester United makes £3.7m per home game, Arsenal £3.3m, Chelsea £2.5m, Spurs £1.6 and LFC £1.5m. The potential revenue growth is obvious.

Stadium Naming Rights

Linked to stadium revenue growth is the underlying issue of how to raise money to fund the stadium. Until recently it was unclear whether Fenway would consider a naming rights deal for Anfield. In answering questions posed by *Tomkins Times* members, John Henry did not rule out such a move. While I am a firm believer in Anfield remaining as Anfield, I challenge any Liverpool fan to argue against the value of giving a naming rights deal serious consideration if it halves the construction costs for the stadium and consequently allows LFC to continue to compete in the transfer market during the high financing construction phase of the project.

Commercial sponsorship arrangements

With reference specifically to shirt sponsorship, LFC have the 5th-largest deal behind Manchester United, Barcelona, Bayern Munich and Real Madrid. Manchester United recently announced a jaw-dropping £45m new shirt deal with Chevrolet starting in time for the '14-15 season. Their innovative approach to sponsorship has also led to a massive new training kit deal. Where once Liverpool was on par with United, our neighbours have soared ahead. It does however open up the possibility in the future that a sponsor may wish to pay similar amounts for a club with such global appeal (if not the recent success that United has enjoyed). Similarly, Liverpool's kit deal with Warrior has boosted the club's coffers significantly. The deal is over double the amount of the previous Adidas deal. Importantly, Liverpool FC is also able to have control over non-branded merchandising. The club naturally believes this will significantly boost club revenues.

Lastly, and a somewhat more tenuous point, the FFPR may just provide opportunities for clubs like Liverpool who are more likely to comply with the break-even criteria to take advantage of any difficulties large spending Premier League clubs may face should they breach the break-even criteria by a large margin. If so, the next best placed club in the PL would take their place. That may be Liverpool Football Club.

Daniel works as a solicitor for Field Fisher Waterhouse LLP and advises entities wishing to invest in the football industry, specifically in relation to Premier League, Football League, FA, UEFA and FIFA football regulations. He has a website (www. Danielgeey.com) and you can follow him on Twitter at (@footballlaw). He is also a subscriber to The Tomkins Times.

I HATE RODGERS (CLEARLY)

By Paul Tomkins

May, 2013

Of late a few people have accused me of being anti-Rodgers; even going so far as to say that I *hate* him. Even remarking on Twitter a few weeks ago about Jupp Heynckes being a free agent this summer despite possibly leading Bayern to a remarkable treble was translated as "advocating that he replaces Rodgers".

No, it was pointing out that a brilliant manager, who, if he decides against retiring, will be free after a quite remarkable season.

The Heynckes debate got me thinking. In truth, how can I tell the difference between Rodgers and Heynckes? They are different managers at different stages of their careers in different countries who have faced different situations, and most of their weekly work is done behind closed doors. Even if they had identical talents and approaches, they are using different sets of players to achieve their ends (and in Bayern's case, a far better set).

Like all other managers they have their own philosophies, and tactics, but it's what each does with them that counts. Managers are judged on results because everything else seems rather abstract. "He's a good man-manager". Well, does it show in the results? "He's a good tactician." Well, does it show in the results? "He's had 35 years of experience." Well, does it show in the results?

You have to put those results into context, but that's the hard bit; that when it starts getting subjective.

People seem to mistake my ambivalence for Rodgers as negativity. I still haven't formed a solid opinion on the current Liverpool manager. Some things he does I am genuinely impressed with. Others leave me nonplussed. Of course, I don't think we should have to *understand* a manager's ideas. I don't understand medical science, after all; I just expect my doctor to know his stuff, and to get results. And even then, he can't know it all. *Science* doesn't know it all.

So far, Rodgers' overall results are worse than last season's. He's won 23 from 52 games (44%), when last season Liverpool won 24 from 51 (47%). Liverpool's cup games, bar this season's ties against Udinese and Anzhi, were clearly more difficult on the whole last year: City (twice), United, Chelsea (twice) and Everton. Equally, Liverpool have marginally improved in the league, and are scoring more goals overall. If you label this a transitional season, then it it's hard to call it a failure. But then it depends what the targets are during a transition.

Hand on heart, if you told me that Rodgers would definitely be Liverpool boss next season, I'd be fine with that. And if you told me that he was to be replaced by someone of Heynckes' calibre (if not necessarily Heynckes, who is 67 and speaks no English), I'd be fine with that. I am neither convinced that Rodgers is the right man nor that he's the wrong man.

It probably took me six months to fully click with Rafa Benítez (at which point I became convinced he had something special) and about three games with Roy Hodgson (at which point I would rather poke my own eyes out than watch his football again). With Rodgers I vacillate, and in many ways that's my problem, not his.

I get plenty of tweets telling me Rodgers is "shit", or worse. But I don't understand the antipathy. People have decided that because he brought a certain level of success to Swansea that means that mid-table is his level. To me, his achievements in Wales prove he did a fine job, and indicate that he's a *good* manager.

I don't think Rodgers is mediocre, or worse, as so many like to tell me. But he is still, in many ways, unproven.

As things stand, proof of Rodgers' qualities only stretches so far. He has no trophies, and he's never tasted the top six of the Premier League. My problem is that, almost a season into his Liverpool tenure, I'm no clearer as to his true level. I'm pretty sure that he's better than his critics suggest, but equally, I don't know how brilliant he is.

Liverpool have been breathtaking at times this season, but also have a dreadful record in the 'bigger' games. The XI is far better now than a year ago, especially with injuries meaning that Spearing and Adam were the two most frequent central midfield starters in 2011/12, and Suárez scored one goal in five months from the day of the Evra incident, only returning to form once his ban was out of the way. With worse players, and greater distractions, the team of Dalglish and Clarke got better results.

Since January, Coutinho and Sturridge have added new dimensions, and a true cutting edge – both have a good amount of goals and assists – although Liverpool have also started drawing blanks (and drawing games) in recent weeks.

While I'm all for focusing on getting back into the top four at the expense of cups (in that my belief is that the Champions League is a virtuous cycle, attracting and paying for better players so that you can compete in all competitions), so far Liverpool have swapped cup success for one place in the league table.

Liverpool are now much better at home – a major problem last season – but only marginally better off in the league table (one place). And yet you could quite legitimately argue that Rodgers is starting a project; in which case you say that instant success is not to be expected.

Success

Most successful managers at the top end of the 'modern era' Premier League have certain traits, certain achievements under their belts.

Two things that stick out are, a) previous notable success, and b) doing something *remarkable* in terms of impact in their first year. Most can boast one or the other, and some can boast both. There's also a third factor, which I will come to later.

First, prior success.

Before arriving in England:

Ferguson had Aberdeen, where he broke up the Rangers/Celtic duopoly with two league titles and four domestic cups, and won a European trophy.

Wenger had Monaco, where he won the league, the cup and took the French team to the latter stages of the Champions League.

Ancelotti had two Champions Leagues, a Serie A title and an Italian cup.

Benítez broke up the Barcelona/Real Madrid duopoly with two league titles in three seasons, and won the Uefa Cup.

Roberto Mancini had three Italian league titles with Inter and had won the Italian cup with three different clubs.

Jose Mourinho had two league titles, the Portuguese Cup, the Uefa Cup and the Champions League.

And while he's not quite up to the same standard, Gérard Houllier won the title with PSG.

The same applies to Claudio Ranieri, who is below the standard of the other managers in terms of trophies (he's never won a league title), but he had won cups with Fiorentina and Valencia.

I believe that these are all of the managers to finish in the top two (having managed the *whole* campaign) since Wenger's first full season in 1997/98. That's fifteen years of top two spots limited to eight managers. Whilst Liverpool are not expecting to be competing for the top two at this juncture, it does show the quality other clubs have chosen.

All of these successes were achieved with different circumstances and different resources. Therefore they are not easily compared with one another. Perhaps weaker managers could have matched some of their achievements, given the budgets some had to work with. Still, they in the record books all the same.

Some subsequent "failures" arrived with good CVs, too. Andre Villas-Boas at Chelsea, and at the same club, Phil Scolari. Previous success is clearly no guarantee, although neither of those were given full seasons. But does it help with *future* success? With all of the best jobs going to men with impressive records, it's hard to know how the likes of Rodgers would do across a larger sample size. It's a bit chicken and egg: do they not get the jobs because they are not good enough, or do we never get to know if they are good enough because they never get the jobs?

What's also true is that some of those managers achieved their first home-country success "out of nowhere". Benítez, Mourinho and Villas-Boas were given jobs at Valencia and Porto based on potential. Their previous records, and their ages, when racking up those home-league successes were not so different to Rodgers' in the summer of 2012. They were appointed because someone saw something in them. All three won the title in their first season, although in the case of Porto, they often won the league anyway.

Di Matteo, who can be added to the list by virtue of his Champions League success, had no great credentials (he was similar to Rodgers in getting a smaller club promoted) but *did* do something incredible in his first season, even if he took over when some of the hard work had already been done (it was March, after all).

Mourinho also did something incredible in his first season at Chelsea: winning the title with a record 95 points (plus the League Cup). His first season was his best season. Ancelotti did something incredible: winning the double, with his team scoring a phenomenal 103 Premier League goals. His first season was also his best season. Benítez did something incredible: winning the Champions League against all odds with a side containing players like Djimi Traore and Milan Baros (and he also took a young team to a second final). It wasn't Rafa's best season in terms of overall quality, but it remained his best *achievement*. In Wenger's first full season (1997/98), he led them to the double, playing some of the best football England had ever seen. Admittedly Alex Ferguson didn't do something incredible in his first full season (1987/88), although he did take United to their best finish for almost a decade (2nd, with their last appearance in the top two in 1979/80) before falling away for a couple of years. And it may be a stretch to include Mancini's FA Cup in his first *full* season (2010/11), but it was their first trophy since the 1970s, and that can be a mental hurdle to overcome. Clearly the investment in players was behind much of their improvement, as it had been with Chelsea, but Mancini instantly put a trophy on the table in addition to Champions League qualification.

So seven of the nine managers made *significant* first season impacts in England, either in the league, the Champions League (or both), and with one landing the club's first trophy in almost 40 years. Of the two exceptions, Gérard Houllier, did partially improve Liverpool in his first season in sole charge, but not to any remarkable level, and Ranieri, who didn't make much of an impact at Chelsea until his final season, when Roman Abramovich arrived and began heavily investing. Houllier second full season, 2000/01, was his most memorable, with a fairly remarkable treble.

(Note: Ferguson, Wenger, Houllier, Mancini, Ranieri and Di Matteo all took charge midway through a season. Only Di Matteo made a *significant* impact in this initial part-season, and perhaps starting your first full season after a few months on the staff getting to the know the club and the players is helpful. Of course, Rodgers' replacement at Swansea – Michael Laudrup – also did something remarkable, based on their resources and history, in landing the club its first-ever trophy. For context, he was building on the good work of Rodgers, who got them promoted, but then Rodgers was also building on the good work of others.)

Cachet

The third factor is 'player cachet'. This is perhaps the least important, but having played at a massive club, and having represented a major international nation on many occasions, can surely help a young manager acclimatise to the pressures and expectations of clubs where success is expected (with the expected success often out of keeping with reality). Of the nine managers discussed, only three had that level of cachet: Ancelotti, Mancini and Di Matteo (all Italian internationals, incidentally, but none world-class, averaging about 30 appearances apiece).

In recent times we've become accustomed to "non-players" like Mourinho, Villas-Boas and Benítez landing top jobs. Like Rodgers, these are men who spent their 20s studying the sport in great detail, at a stage when a lot of players were just thinking of their own game. With Wenger and Ferguson also far from great players, but having played in their country's top division, clearly we now accept that having been a big name player is not essential in the modern age. Indeed, the old way of becoming a player-manager has all but vanished from the landscape.

However, a lot of big-name ex-players are amongst the most successful young coaches this season: Antonio Conte has just led Juve to another title, having played 419 league games for the Old Lady. (In his first year in charge he won the Serie A title, having been appointed on the back of Siena finishing runners-up in Serie B). In each of his three seasons as Ajax boss to date (his first managerial job), Frank de Boer has won the league title. No-one needs reminding of Pep Guardiola's credentials, and of course, at the other end of the spectrum, Jupp Heynckes, now 67, played many times for West Germany. On top of these, Ancelotti is cleaning up in France, albeit with riches. In Italy, Vincenzo Montella is making waves with Fiorentina.

Of course, most of these are big clubs, used to success, or laden with new money. Perhaps Jürgen Klopp is the standout, as someone who wasn't an international footballer. He did play hundreds of league games, but at lower levels. He is the obvious model for Rodgers, with Dortmund an obvious model for Liverpool.

Even Klopp did something remarkable in his first year at Dortmund: adding an extra 50% to their points tally in lifting them from 13th to 6th. So that seems clear.

But then they only moved up to 5th the next season, and perhaps what we're seeing with Rodgers is that stage of Klopp's team development. However, as with all of these examples, the situations are different, so nothing can ever be certain.

A worry with Rodgers would be that the first season is a good chance to excite and inspire your players, and your fan-base. I don't think Rodgers has succeeded in that sense, although unlike Hodgson, for example, he hasn't terrified those who watch the Reds.

Clearly being an ex-player isn't essential (Mourinho, Villas-Boas, Benítez). Clearly you don't *have to* make a significant impact in your first season, although of the nine singled out as top-two finishers and/or Champions League winners, only two (Houllier and Ranieri) failed to pull up any trees in his inaugural full campaign, and both of those managers are 'good' rather than 'great'. You don't have to have had previous top-level success, as Di Matteo showed, but some might argue that he is a mere flash in the pan.

But out of the three categories (which you might find random, but I think have some validity), seven of the nine have ticks in two of the three columns, and Mancini and Ancelotti tick all three.

Rodgers, alas, has none. He has no notable prior success at the sharp end of a top league as a manager; he has not made a significant impact in his first season (fractionally better in the league, worse in the cups); and he was never a player.

This is not to say that he has no skill, no talent, no potential. What he achieved at Swansea was very commendable, although if we laud managers who gain promotion as greats, we need to talk about Steve Bruce, Neil Warnock, Phil Brown, John Gorman, George Burley and assorted other mediocre managers.

Of the managers to finish in the top four this millennium, but not get any higher than third, there has been David Moyes, Bobby Robson, David O'Leary and a cluster of Chelsea managers. A fairly mixed bunch, although none of those, bar the Chelsea ones, have occurred since 2005. Clearly it's getting tighter at the top, with Spurs now a better side (based on selling well and reinvesting smartly), and Manchester City's wealth making them shoo-ins for the top four. Perhaps it is this group of managers against whom Rodgers should be judged. However, without oligarchs and sheiks as owners, Liverpool need to rely on their manager's wits.

Some of the Reds' attacking play this season has been excellent, with the goals scored and the number of clean sheets kept both impressive. The problem has been that a lot of the goals have proved fairly meaningless (some big wins that served only to boost goal difference), and when the Reds haven't kept a clean sheet they've tended to concede two or more.

Of course, there almost certainly wasn't scope to storm the top four anyway this season; it was an outside chance at best. And not being an ex-great hasn't hampered other managers.

I guess my uncertainty – and uncertain is what I am about Rodgers, rather than decided either way – stems from the fact that the cachet he lacked from not being an ex-player and not being a title-winning coach in a major league has not been redressed by anything *remarkable* this season.

No remarkable improvement in the points tally.

No remarkable cup exploits.

No remarkable victories against the odds or biggest sides, with a home win against Spurs the most celebrated result. (One win in fourteen games against the other seven teams in the top eight.)

Some *excellent* performances, particularly in a spell of home games against poorer sides, but nothing out of the ordinary when the heat was on. Nothing to scream that

Rodgers is the future, just as there's nothing to scream Rodgers is the past.

Rodgers has had to deal with far fewer injuries (for which he and his medical team deserve credit); he's spent c£40m net, but lost Maxi, Bellamy and Kuyt for pittance; and he did not (until bitegate when the season was all but done) have a massive Suárez sideshow; nor did he have two runs to cup finals to detract from league form. However, unlike Dalglish, who had 14 years, plus 18 league games at the end of 2010/11, he has had to get used to Liverpool FC. I also don't think *Being: Liverpool* helped his bedding-in period or his credibility.

So comparing with last season is fraught with pitfalls due to radically different scenarios, albeit many of which arguably favour Rodgers.

We all think that building a great side takes time, and it does. And perhaps what Rodgers is doing is building a great side (although until the future, who knows?). But there's also that crucial initial impact, when fresh ideas fire the players with enthusiasm. That hasn't quite happened, at least in terms of results.

On the plus side, Rodgers seems to have a certain level of respect from his players. He's a good man-manager, so they like him (although England internationals like Roy Hodgson more than they liked Fabio Capello, but they've dropped from winning 67% of games to 53%). Rodgers has bright ideas, such as enlisting the help of Dr Steve Peters. But do the players believe he can lead them to glory? Hopefully they do, but they are having to take a leap of faith, just like a lot of the fans.

Future

I don't believe in chopping and changing managers. Equally, I don't think you stick with a manager for the sake of it. If there's someone better out there, you have to consider it. It doesn't mean you have to make that move. It's the same with players: if someone better is available, wants to come and you can afford him, you make the move. Changing manager is obviously more disruptive than replacing a full-back, but if you have a consistent vision at the club, and don't chop and change between *incompatible* football philosophies, then it needn't be disastrous. And it's not like Rodgers is the only manager in Europe whose team can pass a football. He's fairly unique in terms of British coaches, but the continent is full of managers for whom this style is second nature.

Can Liverpool attract the best players? Obviously the very top tier are hard to procure, but it's still a special club in the eyes of the world. Both Suárez and Coutinho agreed to join, as did Nuri Sahin, although he left distinctly unimpressed with Rodgers (although he didn't appear too eager to do all he could to impress).

You could argue, however, that a big-name manager would help matters. It's not necessarily Rodgers' fault that he's not yet a star manager, but are players eager to come and play *for him*? Or is the club's fame on its own still enough of a draw? I don't think Liverpool should stick with Rodgers simply because no-one better would say yes. (There are good arguments that can be made for keeping Rodgers, but I'm not sure this is one of them.)

The way I look at it, if you're a top manager, would you be put off joining Real Madrid, Barcelona, Juventus, AC Milan, Ajax or Bayern Munich if they were 7th in the table? Do you still think it would be great to manage Brazil, even though these days they're ranked 19th in the world right now?

Liverpool still has the magic of a great name and still has those five European Cups, dozens of other trophies, 18 league titles and the most famous stand in the world. Clubs that have been in European finals over many different decades have an aura about them. Liverpool remains such a club. It's had a difficult few years, and miracles should not be expected. But mediocrity (if that's what this season has been) should not be easily accepted, either.

Part of me feels that if Rodgers goes out and replaces Carragher, who is retiring, Downing and Enrique with three better players for the XI, this team could really click into gear. And another part of me remains unsure about his killer instinct. Is he a winner? I think he has a pleasing *edge* to him, in that he can seem a bit steely. But I need more proof.

Whatever happens, next season needs to be better. If you want to write this off as a transitional season, then who am I to argue? But next season needs a proper challenge for the top four, even if the Reds fall narrowly short. The good news is that summer always brings fresh optimism, and unless FSG bring back Roy Hodgson, I'm already looking forward to next season, whoever is in charge.

ENTITLEMENT, EXPECTATION AND THE MODERN FAN

By James Keen
October, 2012

The Internet age has caused a seismic shift in the role of the football fan in the context of running a football club; or rather in the perception of that role by the fans themselves. As society has loosened up and the demographic of football supporters generally has changed, we now demand to be proactive consumers of a product, consulted and kept informed of all that goes on behind the Shankly Gates. As capitalism in the modern world has developed since the '60s it has recast all of us citizens as consumers and customers. In modern business parlance, Liverpool Football Club now has customers rather than fans.

This shift in emphasis changes the dynamic between the club and the supporters – often in a largely positive way. Clubs today cannot afford to take the fans for granted, legally or financially, in the way they perhaps have before. Fan welfare and creating a positive and safe experience are the tenets of the modern match-going concerns. But of course the match-going fans account for only a small percentage of worldwide support. We live now in a post-Taylor report era, the era of Sky and the Premier League. The old First Division was a very different beast from the modern Premier League; it had no idea what it would become and seems a lot less self-conscious than the vast entertainment industry we have now. Setting itself up as a rival to pop music and movies, the English top division has learned to sell its product all over the globe. But in the modern world we demand interactivity, we deplore passivity; this is the age of social media and consultation. Our fathers and grandfathers stood on terraces and watched versions of themselves play the game. Now we sit in vast coliseums and temples, and worship heroes and titans as they compete in the arena. But all of this interactivity and expense implies a sense of entitlement amongst supporters and creates demands for a certain level of treatment and service.

With the Internet at the centre of many of our lives now, suddenly everyone is empowered to have a voice. It is almost a non-negotiable aspect of the modern world that we are constantly asked what we think. Regardless of experience or knowledge, as consumers of media we now create content. We are all just a few mouse clicks away from having a Twitter account, and from there we can all bombard the world with our thoughts and dreams, hates and prejudices, or simply sit and read other peoples' thoughts. To an extent there is no limit to what we can say in the virtual arena. The law is struggling to keep up with the new and fast-moving ways in which we can stretch the boundaries of acceptable comment, whilst at the same time balancing our outrage at being offended, which has taken on a far more sinister undertone in recent times.

The news has changed in that time as well; vox-pops are not new but the media now demands input and viewer-created content (after all, they have 24 hours of TV to fill each and every day). News programmes have tweets in their coverage, YouTube has become a way for ordinary members of the public to track and film events and share them with the world. This includes the news media that would in the past have created that content for themselves; entire programmes are set aside for YouTube clips and they play a very large role in the online life of a newspaper.

In short, "our" views are important and seemingly valued by the society we live in. It seems that there is no barrier to my views on any given subject being presented as being of equal importance as that given by an expert in the area being discussed. Radio phone-ins perhaps give the best example of the conflict between knowledge and emotion – and the extent to which emotion appears to be winning that fight. Twitter is like a hysteria button to these discussions; the minute a discussion enters Twitter, the sane voices are quickly drowned out by the screams of outrage, the pompous taking offence and the childish sniggers of the Trolls as they run away after napalming the conversation with their lack of irony and wickedly blunt 'wit'.

Since the arrival of the Premier League, the game has undoubtedly been gentrified, and just like the run-down areas of towns and cities all over the land that were gradually overrun with the moneyed classes, there are positives and negatives associated with that change. The positives are massive injections of cash, capital and business acumen into the sector. The downside is the people who did live there have been unceremoniously dumped out of the places in which they have for years been happily living. Where once the Fast Show's middle-class football fan "prawn sandwich man" was funny because it was a new thing, now he is common, desired even. Witness the new Wembley and the lack of interest any of the corporate ticket holders have to get back to the game after half-time; it is no longer odd or unthinkable for middle-class people to be football fans.

With the change in make-up of the supporters themselves and the influx of Roy Keane's "prawn sandwich brigade" (perhaps the reason the Wembley buffet is so desirable), a strange new and uneasy relationship has been established. Liverpool Football Club and its followers perhaps represent this shift in our game more starkly than any of the other clubs. Liverpool has always prided itself on being different and the fans are regularly described by us and by many outsiders as "the best in the world", but with the power of the Internet, the supporters are managing to infiltrate the club to a previously unheard-of level. No longer kept at arm's length and literally caged, the modern fan has demands of the entire organisation and wants to know the details of the ins and outs of running a modern football club. As customers and emotional stakeholders, we want more involvement. But the change in Liverpool sits perhaps most uneasily of all, since historically the city of Liverpool prides itself on its working-class values. It has always been one of the bedrocks of trade unionism and was at the forefront of anti-Thatcher feeling in the '80s. As such, the gentrification of anything associated with the city is a philosophically difficult thing to accept.

One of the biggest changes in recent times is the rise of the fan sites, not least in as much as they symbolise the extent to which the Internet has irrevocably changed the way in which we are football fans, in which we discharge our role as fans. All clubs have them now, and within the walls of these sites, the team and the club are analysed minutely, and dissected. They are analysed to an extent that football clubs and teams have never been subjected to in the past. TTT is an excellent example – we have articles and discussions beyond the usual line-up and tactics. Our group knowledge extends to finance, legal and communications issues.

Shankly did not have to perform well on TV – though as it happens he did, and the extent of the success of his televisual presentation is part of his legend. But it is a pre-requisite that a modern football manager has to be able to deal with the press and cope with press conferences and TV appearances. Brendan Rodgers has had it more severely than most, having to deal with *Being:Liverpool* within hours of being made manager. Media training is a given now for coaches and players, to a large extent it is employed simply to mitigate problems arising from the forensic analysis of the club and of the club employees as individuals.

But most importantly, the fan sites are a massive influence on fan opinion. An article in the right place and with the links retweeted by the right people can disseminate the arguments from these sites in minutes, and before the mainstream media outlets have even boiled the kettle in the office in the morning, the clubs fans can have discussed, dissected and come to a conclusion on the latest news to hit the club. In the past there were blokes in pubs talking about the team and in a sense that discussion was pissing in the wind – at no stage would the chairman walk into the pub, sit down at the bar and listen to the conversations and ask for their advice. But now (taking TTT as an example) that pub is worldwide and all the blokes from the different pubs are talking to each other and we know people from the club are listening to what we have to say. Which is both an inspiring and a terrifying prospect.

This has positive outcomes. If you know where to look, it is possible to have a level of detailed discussion about our club that you just wouldn't get through a newspaper or mainstream media outlet. It also provides somewhere to go to discuss Liverpool; personally I do not have enough well-informed non-tribal football friends to have a decent discussion with. Now I am spoilt as to where I can get the latest news and views and contribute to the debate about the issues surrounding my club.

But I worry that the 24-hour news cycle and the obsession with vox-pops and viewer-created content is making us believe we have a bigger influence than we do – or should have. The supporters of the club historically filled the stadium twice a week and paid to see the local team. The gate receipts and tickets were affordable to the largely working-class fan base, who would follow the team, living vicariously through the side's and players' achievements, and for 90 minutes every few days would be able to switch off from whatever may have been happening in their lives and come together to support the team and the players. That idea has become obsolete. For better or worse, the major income now comes from TV and sponsorship. Gate receipts are a factor, but more than just filling a big stadium, the clubs now must allow and make provision for the corporate entertainment industry. The stadiums are becoming revenue generators not just by filling the stadium with fans but by allowing sponsors and the high-level and high-earning leisure industry into the game. To an extent the traditional supporters' model has been lost.

The Liverpool supporter base is now vast and international. It is perhaps more important to the future of the club that we all buy shirts and Sky subscriptions than it is that we turn up every week to fill the stadium. There are too many of us now to be ignored; the wider fan base must be appeased along with the locals and season ticket holders. We are all being squeezed for more money and alongside our emotional involvement we are expected to make a financial contribution.

But with an increase in investment financially from the fans comes a greater sense of what they want from the club, and this is where the world has changed: fans historically didn't make demands of the clubs. A similar situation is being created with the introduction of tuition fees in higher education. As the students are now paying relatively massive amounts of money for their education, the universities are no longer able to get away with the relaxed and laid back manner in which that education was provided in the past. Suddenly the students want their money's worth and, rather than all the demands being made by the institutions on the students, there is now a two-way demand process.

The same thing is beginning to happen in football. The fans now have expectations about how they will be treated. They have expectations about the quality of the pie at half-time, the toilet facilities or the provision for their families. The cost of football now rivals and in most cases eclipses taking the children for any other day out, therefore the amenities are expected to be up to standard with other leisure activities. The spectre of the middle-class football fan is massive in this new world – people with the means and the experience to challenge a lot of these ideas and change the status quo that existed up until the Premier League started – has meant that the conditions and opportunities available to the average fan have increased hugely, but the tradition of top flight football being a largely working-class concern has gone. Just because football was historically a certain way does not mean it has any compulsion to sustain its history. The Pravda-esque way in which all football history and statistics seem to exist in a purely Premier League context is proof of this. You must convert to the new faith or be ignored.

But from the clubs' perspective, they need these more affluent supporters to increase revenue to compete in the financial realities of the Premier league. They are getting their heads around treating their customers properly and we are thankfully miles away from the herding and physical abuse of the caged terraces as they were. But as fans of the team, should we have a say or even an opinion on the way the club is being run?

If we are to have a genuine discussion of the chances that the team may have, we need to discuss the reality of all aspects of the club. With the expansion of the supporter base and the proliferation of fan sites, we have access to a collective knowledge that extends all the way round the world and encapsulates all the experience and knowledge that that level of reach implies. Therefore, we now understand how player contracts are amortised, we understand how wage bills work and how important they are in terms of cash flow. This is light years away from the black and white days when flat-capped, Woodbine-smoking blokes would urge their players to get stuck in. Indeed it is possible – and even more likely when you consider the size of the global fan base – that the average modern football fan does not go and watch the team play anymore. The games can be followed on the Internet. The discussion happens on the Internet and the people who have never been to Anfield or ever set foot in the city of Liverpool can be better informed than some of their local counterparts.

This last couple of weeks has thrown up again the uneasy relationship we now have with the club and with new technology. The club has made big efforts to embrace new media and the press conferences where the fan sites have been invited to talk first with Brendan Rodgers, and then Lucas Leiva, have been well received and actually more successful in many ways than the traditional press conferences. Certainly I feel Rodgers was asked more detailed tactical questions than he would ordinarily be, and there was very little evidence of trying to tie either person into a preconceived media narrative or to catch them out.

What has become painfully apparent is that the traditional print media, with their army of football writers, are likely to have no more knowledge or expertise than a well-informed and tech-savvy fan. This has created some fantastic discussion sites and information-gathering services. People who have contacts within the construction industry have been able to glean little details about the stadium refurbishment or rebuild process that even the traditional sources are not privy to. In terms of dissemination of information this is clearly the future. Revelations of injuries or incidents is spread around Twitter faster than any newspaper can ever hope to get the news online. But of course the club does need to keep us at arm's length to an extent. Any business needs to do its negotiating behind closed doors. However, our obsessive following of the club means we *demand* to know what's going on. The problem is exacerbated by the aforementioned sense of entitlement. If the club says nothing about an issue we assume that there is something to hide or that something untoward is going on. The perpetual online conversation can go from supportive to paranoid in seconds. Because the club has started to talk to us more, we expect it to talk to us all the time, and to tell us everything.

The fans' self-perception has changed most dramatically following the ousting of Hicks and Gillett. The establishment of the Spirit of Shankly group and the Share Liverpool idea, and the concerted effort by fan groups to get rid of the former owners made the fans into activists against people working for the club for (I think) the first time in our history. There were marches in support of the manager and videos decrying the owners. The club and fans were in a state of civil war (with each other and amongst themselves) for months, we were abusive to each other and deeply sceptical of each other's motives and opinions. The constant unease within the supporters became heightened by the very real possibility that the club we all love and fixate over might actually cease to exist. This unthinkable idea drove the supporters forward to attempt to positively influence the future of the club.

Despite the good work and passionate exchange of ideas, how much influence they actually had on the selling of the club is debatable. The club was sold by the bank when it became concerned the club would not be able to service the loans it had provided to buy the club in the first place. This process was followed in great detail by the fan groups and sites, which is only to be expected – this is our hobby, and thinking about and debating ideas surrounding the team and the club takes up a great portion of our waking time. But I find it hard to accept that RBS based any loan policy decisions on what Liverpool fans were saying or demanding. It seems likely that if Hicks and Gillett had found a way to pay then they would still be in control of the club.

But the thought lingered that in some way "we" had got rid of them. The club at the time was being run by charlatans and liars, certainly no-one that we could identify with or trust, so we had to take on the responsibility for ourselves. This does seem in my view to have altered how we view our role and influence over the club. *We* got rid of the cancer spreading through the club, and as a result here was a bright new dawn. The problem is the world is not that straightforward. There were many more factors involved than simply the wicked witch is dead, now we have lovely fairy godmother looking after us.

The club was in dire straits and the new owners (FSG) were not prepared to put themselves in a position to instantly pump into the club the amount of money that would be required. We have looked with some degree of jealousy at Chelsea and Manchester City and wanted a similar injection of capital, we have waited so long for the 19th title, and the fan base's patience has been stretched. The issue with the club has always been the speed with which things happen, because we can see the problem and think we know what the solution is, and because – with a greater sense of involvement, a greater sense of influence and with a greater sense of entitlement – the belief arises that things should be happening faster. This combination of increased knowledge, a pile up of impatience accumulated over 20 years of relative under-achievement, multiplied by the Twitter factor, and we assume a much greater idea of what should and shouldn't be done than perhaps we can, given the actually small amount of factual information we have about how the club is run. The club is obviously reluctant to discuss the minutiae of its business dealings with the fans but this has been perceived as shiftiness, or dishonesty. There is a sense that we are not yet over the Hicks and Gillett debacle, which is understandable, but the feeling has remained that we can influence the club to do whatever we want.

Now the club is reaching out to the Internet and the fans sites like TTT and TAW, that sense is even bigger. The regular sites that interact with the club at these press conferences now have a direct line to the club's press office. So suddenly the blokes in the pub have a direct line to the club they support and they can get ideas across; indeed they are being canvassed for opinions and ideas about who the club should employ. We are being asked for ideas about other people to talk with to decide keys areas of how the club will be run, and of course we are delighted to respond. But not just because it is a novelty; we expect it, because our opinions are important in the modern world, and we now know this. We know what we think *matters*, but in the day-to-day running of the club that influence and opinion only goes so far.

The owners must be allowed the time and space to employ people – and they will make mistakes. We are several years away from challenging for the title so my view is that as a group we should stay calm and wait and see. Trying to second-guess every decision that is made by the club in whatever department a decision is taken is exhausting us all. My observation is that we are forensically examining the club in order to find the smoking gun that proves FSG are going to screw us over and ruin the club.

Now, that may or may not be the case but at this stage, nothing of an incriminating nature has been uncovered. But we will have to wait and see. It's frustrating, but the only way to discover their true intentions is to wait until they are revealed. Besides which, we can't *make* them sell the club. Hicks and his cronies were made to sell by RBS. FSG own the club outright – we can moan all we like, it won't make any difference if they do not want to sell. All we can do is support the club and continue to produce the frankly staggering level of writing, podcasts, online TV and other media that are created by fans and groups about our club. If the club is listening (and we know it is), then surely the better way to approach it is to present our views calmly, cogently and logically on one of these outlets, because sending Linda Pizzuti abusive tweets if we disagree with something her husband has done only makes it less likely we will be asked our opinions, not more.

I want to be clear that for the most part all of this is largely positive and accelerates the death of the traditional print media, which in turn will democratise the dissemination of information, but I wonder whether, despite the increased interaction between the club and supporters, the stain of the Hicks and Gillett era has us watching and waiting for the next time when we will need to rise up and campaign against the club in some way. When coupled with the heightened sense of hysteria that Twitter fosters, it means that to an extent any little thing (even rumours and unsubstantiated stories) has us ready to believe the worst.

But despite the sophistication of the means by which we now follow the club, there are some behaviours that are seemingly ingrained in the football fan's psyche; we all follow the same team but there are millions of interpretations of how things should proceed and how the clubs and fans should behave. There are traditionalists who want the traditional local teams back, and conversely there are modernists who want to see us capitalised and monetised to a far greater degree, as well as all opinion points in between on all subjects. And they will never agree.

But the tribalism of our support has separated the fans. Where you log on can be as important now as who you support. The Internet is great at providing access to information to everyone, but the downside is anyone can use it and anyone can claim to be a good source for that information. It can be hard to see fact from fiction and objective analysis from self-serving posturing. The emotional nature of football support, aided by the accelerant that Twitter can be, means that rational discussion is very difficult. We all value the sense and calm that TTT provides. But out on the rest of the Internet it can be a bear pit.

I have spent my career thus far working in libraries, and over the last ten years the amount of trained reference librarians has reduced drastically, and our reliance on the Internet has ballooned, which in many ways is as it should be. The Internet can be the greatest reference tool any human has ever had access to. But when I first started, the librarians were an educated and experienced filter through which members of the public had their information rated and appraised. Without that filter it is harder to be sure that you are getting, or indeed in my case giving out, good information. That is a problem in all forms of life. The phrase "I read it on the Internet" has huge caveats attached to it, and a large number of questions immediately follow: "What site was it on?", "Who wrote it?", "What is the context?" Bad information and uninformed comment can now be trending on Twitter before anyone can refute it.

Rather than the worldwide pub meaning the supporters are joined and united, it has meant that personal agendas and ill-informed nonsense have become genuinely debated and have influenced opinions. At our worst we represent an ignorant rabble rather than a coherent and united fan base. We are too willing to believe the worst and assume the worst about the club and the owners, even about each other. A healthy dose of cynicism is always a good way to approach any subject, but when the accumulated weight of bullshit starts to obscure our view of anything even resembling an attributable fact, it becomes hugely damaging to us as fans. It damages us and our view of each other, and it damages our reputation externally.

Ultimately this is our hobby and it is supposed to be fun. It is important to remember that we all want the same thing; much as we may disagree about how that end can be achieved. But as we have no real control of the situation, we can debate and discuss the team between ourselves but we will never be privy to the full extent of the club's business, on or off the pitch. There needs to be a widespread acceptance of that truth; we can speculate but that's all it is.

It's fun to speculate and talk about players we like and don't, or the tactics we prefer or the way the club is dealing with certain things – let's be honest, there are an infinite number of things to concern ourselves with! But we have to remember who we are and what we represent. We are Liverpool supporters – not only do we represent the club in many ways, more importantly we represent each other. If one of us behaves like an idiot, it will be assumed by many that we are *all* idiots. We also need to accept the limits of our knowledge and influence, and falling out with ourselves is the most counter-productive thing we could possibly do. We can dissect the club and its dealings to the nth degree, but we have to be able to walk away at the end of the conversation because ultimately it is only ourselves we are harming.

SHOW ME SOMETHING I CAN'T SEE

By Bob Pearce

February, 2013

When I was a teenager in the 1970s, football was rarely shown 'live' on TV. If you couldn't go to the game, the next best thing was to listen on the radio as the commentator described what the listener could not see. 'This player passes to that player. One player tackles another player. Someone shoots and someone else saves'. You could tell when the action was moving towards one of the goals by the change of gears in the commentator's voice. Moving from interested, through excited before reaching ecstatic anticipation (and usually rapidly deflating unfulfilment). It was the listener's job to provide the pictures in his or her own imagination.

I'd argue that with football coverage on TV today, what we have is the same radio-style coverage, but with the pictures. The commentator continues to describe the same things. 'This player passes to that player. One player tackles another player. Someone shoots and someone else saves'. Except now they are describing what the viewers can plainly see for themselves. It is still a commentator who reads the names that are printed on players' shirts, and occasionally yells their name to indicate they are directing the ball towards the goal.

What are the criteria for a TV football 'expert'? Are you a current or ex-player or manager? Yes. Do you have a recognisable 'football face'? Yes. Can you behave yourself? Yes. Can you speak with an air of confident certainty in answer to any question we put to you? Yes. Are you fluent in football clichés? Yes.

One indicator of just how bland and stale TV pundit opinions are is the genuine surprise that is felt when something of actual interest and value is said. It is like looking at an endless wall full of charming but crude children's paintings and suddenly finding a Van Gogh.

*'I thought he was half-decent today...' *

We are often told that these highly paid modern-day footballers should remember that they are role models to fans in general, and young fans in particular. I would argue that the lazy clichéd comments of TV 'experts' serve as a role model just as much as the players' behaviour on the pitch. These 'expert' clichés are adopted and used as a means to convey knowledge of the game without having to consider their accuracy. TV coverage is the young fan's introduction to the game. What are TV's 'experts' educating them to believe is most valued in the game?

Goals.

Individuals.

Effort.

*"Lots of energy, lots of work rate, lots of passion. That's what fans want to see. Blood, sweat and tears for the shirt." *

Currently, football coverage on TV is almost indistinguishable from game to game, from week to week. The same tired focus, with the same weary comments, like a diet of microwaved ready meals. If you listen closely you may even hear the microwave 'ping' as the theme tune ends. Football coverage on TV could be so much more.

John Walters (producer of the unique BBC Radio DJ John Peel) would often have to pound the table and remind BBC executives that "We aren't here to give people what they want. We're here to give people what they didn't know they wanted!" Walters was only reminding them of what Lord Reith had set out, as the aims of a public service broadcaster. Reith believed the BBC should always be demonstrating high quality, originality, innovation, while being both challenging and engaging. Part of the BBC's role, said Reith, was to introduce viewers to subjects they might not know about.

"A massive win." *

We should not lose sight of the different roles here. Fans are the paying punters so they are entitled to make judgements about what they get for their money. Pundits are not punters. They are paid to provide high quality originality and innovation, while being both challenging and engaging. As such they should have their performances judged too. I don't need pundits to make my judgements for me. What I want is for them to present relevant information and helpful perspectives and allow me reach my own conclusions.

For me the two simple guiding principles would be 'Show me something I can't see' and 'Remember, you are a role model'. Help me to look at the same thing and see something 'new'. Offer me someone I can to aspire to become.

What I am proposing here is not a detailed 'pitch', but simply a handful of alternatives to illustrate just how stale the current approach is and the sorts of alternatives that can be conjured up with a little time and a bit of imagination.

"Makes this a must-win game." *

As an absolute minimum I'd introduce a cliché alarm. Any commentator or pundit who uses a footballing cliché will be shown a yellow card, a red card, sent from the studio, and then given a 'stating the bloody obvious' ban, and even fined. I don't want to hear their lazy words. Make an effort to have an original thought or you are off. Shouldn't FIFA be declaring clichés from the mouths of TV role models to be a 'cancer' that is destroying football?

'Show me something I can't see'. Surely we can see all the 'who is passing to who' on-the-ball action. Why not leave us to do the ball watching and describe some of the off-the-ball action? The commentator could stop reading the names on players' shirts as they receive the ball and begin describing something that we can't see for ourselves. There is so much they could bring to the viewer's attention about off-the-ball movement, the inter-play and cohesion between players, the stretching and compressing of space, probing and repelling, the changes of tempo, the split second doubts and hesitations, and occasionally where that ball thing fits into all of this constantly changing concoction. 'Remember, you are a role model'.

"Just three changes from the team that won last week." *

'Show me something I can't see'.

When team line-ups are shown at the start of the game, don't just scatter the names across the pitch as though they'll stay put for 90 minutes. Add a little animation to the formations. Show how the structure will change in and out of possession. Show the team breathing in and out. Not just with arrows. Let us see the roaming players dropping back and wide, the wide players cutting inside, while the backs push forward and wide. Bring it to life. Then, having shown that for both teams, let's have them overlaid and see the two living and breathing formations interacting. You could even go as far as highlighting a couple of interesting zones and battles we can focus attention on.

Too often, 'experts' refuse to acknowledge their lack of knowledge about the thinking behind a substitution or tactical change; instead they resort to questioning the competence or sanity of the manager with a dismissive comment. Is it acceptable to mock what you don't understand rather than acknowledge you have reached the border crossing between your knowledge and ignorance? Let's have someone who does know, so that we can come back to formations within the game to show what has been happening, when tactical changes are made (either by substitutions or the manager gesturing from the side lines), to show what changes this might make, and what to look out for. 'Remember, you are a role model'.

"Everton include three Manchester United old boys." *

The *FourFourTwo* StatsZone chalkboards would be a great way to instantly demonstrate a tactical point, from where particular passes are received, the dominant passing combinations, the impact of a tactical change with 'before' and 'after' images. These could be used to rapidly convey tactical information mid-game so that viewers can be more aware of the development of the game. Use the periods when a player is injured and getting treatment for an expert to step up and succinctly explain a change in tactics that recently occurred, and illustrate it with a chalk board.

"A team that look like they know exactly what they're doing." *

When a manager is making gestures to players, rather than the commentator guessing like someone projecting human thoughts onto their pet cat, find someone who has a tactical understanding about what it is he could be communicating.

"Possession exactly split down the middle. 50:50." *

Currently, any statistics used are simply data 'droppings' that are given no context or analysis. They fall well short of being information that we can do something with, as they lack anything of nutritional value which can be digested and developed over time into knowledge.'Show me something I can't see'. The use of statistics should go way beyond possession percentages, number of shots, fouls, yellow cards, red cards, and corners, that are delivered with no context or meaning. At best they allow the 'wise fool' pundit his once-in-every-game opportunity to make his signature comment that the only statistic that really matters is the score. It is never explained why these are seen as the key performance indicators. That suggests to me that they are simply the numbers that are easiest to measure and so collect (the statistical equivalent of being paid to read the names from players shirts), but we have never stopped to ask if these really have any relevance.

"And their lead is doubled." *

'Let's make statistics 'sexy'?

Let's give the statistics the context and meaning needed to help us make use of them. Let's have a statistician providing not just lists of numbers in isolation, but a wide range of visual illustrations of relevant statistics at various stages of the game. They could start with basic pizza charts of possession that are maybe broken down further into zones where possession has taken place, which player has possession, which player to player combinations are the most frequent, or any other views that may play a big part on whether possession is being used effectively. Let's have the possession versus space battle demonstrated and explained for all to see.

When there's something wrong in the commentary, who you gonna call? Myth-busters!

I want statisticians who challenge the media created myths and show they are based entirely on guesswork. Maybe they can present their evidence to the supposed 'expert' and ask them to offer some kind of explanation of why the facts don't match their repeated claims? After a few weeks of having their lazy comments held up for close examination, these 'experts' may think twice before they open their mouths. 'Remember, you are a role model'.

'There was no doubt in Mark Clattenberg's mind.' *

'Show me something I can't see'. Do we need pundits giving vague and ill-informed comments about how they 'feel' about a refereeing decision? Their default starting point is to presume the ref and linesman were likely to have got it 'wrong', while the 'expert' requires the benefit of hindsight and multiple camera angles to eventually and grudgingly admit that the ref got it 'right' with one look and in real time. I'd argue that his constant drip, drip, drip questioning of the referee's decisions throughout every game, season after season, is serving to erode and undermine the authority of referees at all levels in the game. Why not have qualified referees to comment? They know the letter of the law. They know the spirit the law. They know the realities of the human judgements referees make. They will have the experience to know what it is like to make yellow and red card decisions, make an offside judgement, whether a tackle was a foul, when to play an advantage, the type of message that is being given when the referee speaks to a player, and the type of response the fourth official will give to the manager chewing their ear on the side lines. 'Remember, you are a role model'.

"An unsung hero. He doesn't get mentioned enough." *

'Show me something I can't see'. Isn't one of the deadly sins of football 'Thou shalt not be caught ball watching?' Isn't that precisely what the TV cameras are guilty of? Camera angles tend to remain with the ball at the centre of the frame. This is interspersed with close-up shots focused on specific players but still with the ball as the central focus. This suggests the ball is the most important thing in the game. It ignores the importance of space and team cohesion almost entirely. It does not allow us to view the movement and timing of the 21 players who don't have the ball. It does not show the vulnerable space that is becoming exposed for the counter-attacking team to exploit when they seize possession. The camera is focused on the 'now' of the game when it could just as easily focus on possibilities of what could happen 'next'. Let us see the passing options, the 'windows' of vulnerable space being prised open and slammed shut. There could be overviews of the zone showing how space has been created with players making runs and 'magnetic' fields around them showing how they are attracting players, a trail left behind the ball's progress that changes colour to show the change in pace of the ball. 'Remember, you are a role model'

"It just didn't go in for him." *

'Show me something I can't see'. Why not have a sports psychologist who can comment throughout the game on what an individual player's body language may indicate about their mind-set? Let us know what to look out for to know it has changed. Let us know how this may be impacting on others in their team. Let us know how this may be impacting on the opposition both individually and as a team. Describe a player's response to a moment of poor judgement or plain bad luck. Describe a player's apparent mind-set and confidence when executing a free-kick, clear cut chance or particularly from both perspectives at penalty shoot-outs. With so much else to talk about, do we really have time for the sidekicks to the commentator anymore? Someone whose job description seems to be 1) all-seeing judge with total confidence in your opinions, 2) mind-reader who has no doubt that the thoughts you project on to people are reality, and 3) a 'bit of a character' who can frequently tell me things that I can see for myself are just plain not true. Aren't these similar requirements for the job of the 'expert' that sits on the park bench, drinking cider, and muttering about the pigeons?

"167 Manchester United goals. Eight of them have come against Everton." *

And we won't have time for the trivia that commentators compile and then scatter through their commentary like confetti, delivered in a tone that suggests that apparent coincidences and data from a random selection of historical circumstances have some kind of significance and meaning (this player, as part of a number of different teams, has scored against this club when it has been represented by a number of different groups of players). They may as well have astrologers giving observations based on players' zodiac signs. And what do we get from an interview with a player or even the manager after the game? Do we really expect them to reveal their thinking? Isn't it more realistic to expect them to be like a poker player who wants to keep his cards close to his club crest? At best they'll repeat a series of guarded footballing clichés. At worst they have to endure an inquisition on some current media invented speculation. Is there really any point in talking to him at all? What is that giving the viewer? Why not give the time to one of our panel to 'Show me something I can't see'.

"That's when you want your keeper making these big saves. In these big moments." *

Do we really need a 'Man of the Match' award? Really? Even putting aside the award criteria which dominates the judgements currently (scoring goals or 'hard graft'), the very idea of the award encourages a focus on individuals over teams. If we feel the need to be giving out awards in every single game, even 'Partnership of the Match' would at least be a step in the right direction.

'That is one he'll certainly remember.' *

And if 'Man of the Match' is to go then 'Goal of the Month' should go with it. It encourages and perpetuates a view that goals are the key part of any game, and again they are attached to the individual that was the last person to touch the ball before it entered the goal. Month after month, season after season, it continues to dismiss the team work, the space creation, the timing, the passing, the delivery that led to the final touch being in a position to be delivered. If we really cannot live without the need to select the 'best' of something and put an award in its hand, at least move to something like 'Move of the Month', even if it doesn't result in a goal! It would show the finest interplay of team work, co-ordination, manipulation of space, precise timing, and changes of pace.

Who will this role model 'showing me something I can't see' be?

Will it be a current or ex player or manager with a recognisable 'football face'? Or will it be someone from the infinitely deeper meme pool of non-current and non-ex-players and managers with a 'nobody face'? I really don't care where they come from. I'd be happy to have musicians, chefs, engineers, architects, scientists, you name it. If they can add a fresh way to describe and think about maybe how players work together, or perhaps the interplay of parts, or even the construction of the formation. All I ask is 'Show me something I can't see' and 'Remember, you are a role model'.

"Letting him know he is in a game." *

What is the role of the host in this new format? I'd suggest it is to have the ability to question the experts further to drill down into the detail and implications of their comments, and to be able to summarise and re-present them in every day terms. Would we need all these new experts for every game? Not necessarily. There could be a squad of panel regulars that could be rotated. There would be different perspectives for each game, which allows the exciting potential of different combinations of perspectives rubbing up against each other to produce new and fresh insights.

"A couple of big performances." *

Some may argue that football fans could find these types of changes 'boring'. I'd suggest they are 'bored' right now. It could be argued that all this extra information would be giving away too much. Revealing too many secrets. 'Letting daylight in on the magic'. What is it that we think will be revealed? The game is taking place in public, sometimes watched by millions around the world. Do we really think that highly paid opposition managers are watching TV coverage praying that someone is going to reveal the secrets to them of how to do their job? What about that nagging doubt that all this detailed scrutiny of the each game will take the magic out of it? Just stop to think about what that statement means. Isn't it like saying don't tell me there is no Santa Claus?

The 'magic' will be taken from the game if we 'understand' how it works.

Really?

Are we any less amazed and awed with a scientific explanation of how the universe works compared to a version that says 'Well Brian, it was God what done it'? Just ask yourself which of those two points of view is the more likely to lead to discovery and result in progress?

"What a vital touch." *

As a wise person must have said at least once, 'The act of observing a thing changes that thing'. I'd suggest that not only could TV coverage be an important factor in the future evolution of the game, I'd go as far as saying that the current 'pop-pop-ding' ready meal coverage is actively inhibiting the growth and development of the game. To finish I'll blatantly copy and paste what I said earlier. What I am proposing here is not a detailed 'pitch', but simply a handful of alternatives to illustrate just how stale the current approach is, and the sorts of alternatives that can be conjured up with a little time and a bit of imagination.

* *All quotes from Match of the Day 2, 10/2/13.*

FAIR PLAY FOR FENWAY

By Dan Kennett

June, 2011

(With expert review and contributions from site members Graeme Riley, Zach Slaton, Taf McDonald, Daniel Geey and Paul Tomkins.)

"UEFA Financial Fair Play": A phrase that has been used in recent times by even the most lay of football fans. But what is it? And does it matter for Liverpool FC? This article attempts to keep things extremely simple but at the same time demystify UFFP and explain how it impacts Liverpool Football Club.

Our principal owner, John W Henry, has given two interviews to *The Guardian* in which he has talked definitively about FSG's approach to ownership and UFFP. First of all in November 2010:

Henry said UEFA's impending financial fair play rules, which will be introduced in 2012-13 and eventually require clubs to break even on football operations, had been a key factor in persuading NESV (now FSG) to buy the club. He said they would leave Liverpool much better-placed to compete with such clubs as Manchester City and Chelsea: "They are operating under the current rules. The rules are going to change."

Then in an extended interview in February 2011:

"The big question is just how effective the financial fair-play rules are going to be. Perhaps some clubs support the concept in order to limit the spending of other clubs, while implementing activities specifically designed to evade the rules they publicly support. We can only hope that UEFA has the ability and determination to enforce what they have proposed.

"We've always spent money we've generated rather than deficit-spending and that will be the case in Liverpool ... it's up to us to generate enough revenue to be successful over the long term. We have not and will not deviate from that. We intend to get younger, deeper and play positive football ... our goal in Liverpool is to create the kind of stability that the Red Sox enjoy. We are committed to building for the long term."

So there we have it, straight from the horse's mouth. Not only do FSG embrace UFFP but they're already planning to exploit it. However John Henry is right to raise the one big unknown about UFFP: how strictly will the rules be enforced? In a nutshell, if a club wants to compete in UEFA competitions it needs to be granted a UEFA licence.

The UEFA licensing system is already in operation. In recent times the highest profile club to have been denied a licence is Real Mallorca, who were unable to take their place in the Europa League. (UEFA say a total of 27 clubs have been refused a licence over the years.) For 2011-12, three clubs have been refused a licence – including FC Timisoara – for next season's Champions League. UFFP is simply a complicated extension to the UEFA licensing system. So, in theory, a team in breach could be denied entry to the Champions League group stage and the £25m minimum that comes with it. There are a lot of cynics and sceptics who think that UFFP will come to nothing and when push comes to shove UEFA will not stand up to the big boys. There's also been a lot of far-fetched discussion about loopholes in the regulations and scenarios that will never be allowed, like the £100m half-time pie for Sheikh Mansour or the £250m Chelsea sponsorship deal with Sibneft.

However, a lot of the concern is valid – but is not in scope for this article because it's too early to tell how possible any workarounds for clubs are. Instead my starting assumption is: can any owner or chief executive of a major club accept the risk of UEFA strictly implementing the UFFP regulations? For example, will any club be brazen enough to spend with impunity and carry on regardless? Or will in fact all clubs come in line to some degree?

Why is UEFA doing this?
Despite the game being more popular than ever and with more money than ever, UEFA says that:

- 37% of clubs are in negative equity (their debts are more than their assets).
- The total income of all European clubs is 11.7bn EUR but the total costs are 12.9bn EUR.
- No less than 7.4bn EUR of total costs are players' wages.
- The average club in Europe spends 64% of its income on player wages.
- 73 clubs spend more than 100% of their revenue on player wages (note in '09/10 this included Manchester City).

UEFA wants to start forcing clubs to live within their means, almost to save the clubs from themselves. It's also no coincidence that the momentum behind UFFP grew during the global credit crunch that had been caused by too many people spending too much money today in the over-optimistic hope that they would be able to pay it off later.

How Do The Rules Work?
All terms used in this section are defined in great detail in the UFFP regulations:

Break Even Result = Relevant Income - Relevant Expenses

Deviation = Sum of Break Even Results for each year in Accounting Period

What is "Relevant Income"?

Revenue + Profit From Player Trading (Revenue is income from media, matchday and commercial).

(Profit from player trading is not as most football fans see profit on trading – more on this later. There are a host of caveats and clarifications in the detail.)

What is "Relevant Expenses"?

All Staff Wages + Cost of Transfers + "Other Costs" (e.g. finance costs)

("Other Costs" excludes the costs of youth/academy programmes, community programmes and stadium development. Technical note from TTT's head statistical historian, Graeme Riley: this also includes interest on the development, which can be capitalised and amortised, rather than immediately expensed).

This is because UEFA wants clubs to plan for the future by investing in these things rather than spending all their money on players' wages.

The "Cost of Transfers" will be discussed later on, alongside amortisation. Understanding this as well as the profit from player trading is absolutely essential if you want to realise how FSG are likely to exploit UFFP.

What Are The Rules?

UFFP has "Accounting Periods" that are aligned to the UEFA licensing cycle and came into effect on 1st June 2011. The first "accounting period" is two years, 1st June 2011 to 31st May 2013. The niceties regarding exchange rates have been ignored for this article.

For each year in UFFP, a club's "Break Even Result" is allowed to be up to a 5m EUR loss. This is known as "acceptable deviation". Clubs are allowed to make bigger losses for "Accounting Periods" but only if their owners invest more of their own cash into the club to cover the loss.

For the first two-year accounting period, clubs are allowed a maximum "acceptable deviation" of 45m EUR but owners will be tasked with finding up to an extra 35m EUR in cash to cover losses. The grey areas will start with aggregate losses of more than 45m EUR, and the question of at what point UEFA will draw the line. The general feeling is that clubs who are significantly reducing their losses year on year will still be given a 'pass' (Annex XI of the regulations).

The first serious impact on licensing decisions will be in place for the 2014/15 season (i.e. the first time a club may be denied entry to the Champions League is 2014/15). Things get gradually stricter from that point on. The 2nd accounting period extends the 1st by a year licence (i.e. to May 31st 2014) and from this point, three years' worth of accounts are required to be submitted in order to gain a licence. However, acceptable deviation is *still* an aggregate 45m EUR. Then there's a rolling three-year accounting period where acceptable deviation reduces to 30m EUR and finally to less than 30m EUR in 2018/19.

What About Liverpool?

The two articles below have recently looked at Liverpool's last financial results in fantastic detail and are an absolute must read for those interested in off-the-pitch matters:

http://swissramble.Blogspot.com/2011/05/liverpools-future-strategy.html
http://andersred.Blogspot.com/2011/05/liverpools-200910-results-underline.html

The AndersRed article contains a detailed analysis of what our "Break Even Result" for 2009/10 might look like. The Swiss Ramble one takes a more forward-thinking look and outlines a 15-point strategic business plan. While taking a lead from both and summarising some key points, I believe I have one major advantage over Swiss Ramble and AndersRed in that I'm a Liverpool fan and consume Liverpool news and information in great detail every single day.

Based on their public statements about no deficit spending, it's a reasonable assumption that FSG will be attempting to ensure Liverpool have a UFFP break-even result within the 5m EUR acceptable deviation. Therefore the rest of this article will look at two angles:

1. How to increase relevant income, particularly the importance of the Champions League and player trading.

2. How to reduce relevant expenses, particularly the "bad contracts" that John Henry has frequently talked about. As we can only estimate wages for most players, I will be performing a player/wage value analysis to show where FSG could look to make savings.

Liverpool's "Relevant Income" for UFFP

One way for FSG to ensure compliance with UFFP is to increase revenues. This is what they've done at the Boston Red Sox and fits with John Henry's approach as quoted at the top of this article. Let's look at the club's recent financial results. Liverpool first started reporting revenue in the categories of Media, Matchday and Commercial in 2001/02. The results for all nine seasons are:

	Total	Media		Matchday		Commercial		ROTW Commercial		CL (Est.)	PL Finish	Europe
2001-02	98.6	42.6	43%	30.6	31%	25.4	26%				2	CL QF
2002-03	102.5	44.2	43%	28.6	28%	29.7	29%				5	CL Group
2003-04	91.5	33.4	37%	26.4	29%	31.7	35%				4	UC R32
2004-05	122.4	51.0	42%	33.1	27%	38.3	31%			33.3	5	CL W
2005-06	121.7	49.7	41%	32.7	27%	39.3	32%			19.0	3	CL R16
2006-07	133.9	52.2	39%	38.4	29%	43.3	32%	2.3	5%	21.9	3	CL RU
2007-08	161.7	68.3	42%	39.2	24%	54.2	34%	1.7	3%	21.1	4	CL SF
2008-09	184.8	74.6	40%	42.5	23%	67.7	37%	5.3	8%	19.9	2	CL QF
2009-10	184.5	79.5	43%	42.9	23%	62.1	34%	4.3	7%	27.2	7	CL Group

Note 1: The Champions League revenue is estimated because UEFA annual reports were in Swiss Francs and now Euros. A relevant conversion to GBP has been calculated based on the exchange rate on 31st May of the relevant year. Also, this is only Champions League TV money, not Champions League gate receipts or Champions League-related payments from Liverpool FC sponsors. From the accounts there is no way to establish the whole value of the Champions League to Liverpool.

Note 2: In 2009/10 the revenue from the run to the Europa League semi-finals was a tiny 3.1m EUR compared to the 29.3m EUR from the group stage exit in the Champions League.

Note 3: The ROTW Commercial column is the proportion of commercial revenues coming from outside the UK. This would appear to be an immediate area where FSG can look to improve.

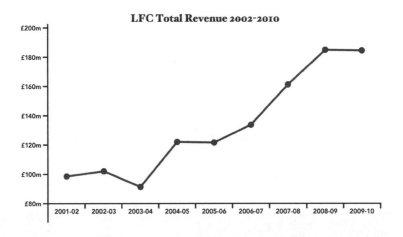

The overall growth in Revenue during the Noughties is quite remarkable. In fact from 2003/04 the total revenue *more than doubled* in just five years (£91.5 to £184.8m). (NB: Included in this are rises seen throughout football relating to TV deals.)

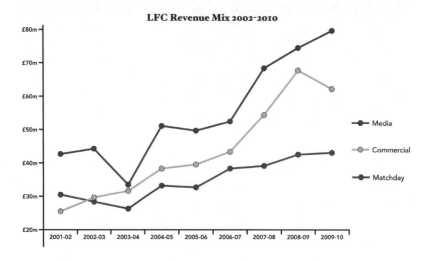

LFC Revenue Mix 2002-2010

Note 4: The nine-year trend shows a steady decline in the proportion of revenues that come from Matchday (31% to 23%). This explains why the new/upgraded stadium remains at the very top of FSG's to-do list. Another reason why is because Swiss Ramble calculates that Man United and Arsenal earn £2m more than Liverpool from every home game.

In that same period, Media has remained in the low 40s but Commercial shot up from 26% to 37% in '08/09. Expect this to further increase in the 2010/11 results due to the Standard Chartered shirt deal (a £12m p.a. increase on Carlsberg) and from 2012/13 due to the Warrior kit deal (£13m p.a. increase on Adidas). The accounts put the 2009/10 decline in commercials down to "reduced merchandising" (e.g. many fans buying less in the final year of Gillett & Hicks); however the experts suspect clauses in sponsors contracts related to loss of Champions League football.

Over the nine years, Commercial increased by 167%, Media by 86% and Matchday by 40%. Throughout 2002-10, Media was the biggest proportion of Liverpool FC revenue. The tables below are a detailed look at the Media breakdown from 2004/05 onwards.

	Media	CL (cGBP)	CL Share	Other	Overseas TV	Equal Share	Facility Fees	Merit Payment	Domestic TV	Other (WCC, ESC, FAC, LC)
2004-05	51.0	21.3	42%	29.7	4.0	9.1	6.8	7.8	23.7	2.0
2005-06	49.7	12.0	24%	37.7	4.0	8.9	6.7	8.7	24.3	9.4
2006-07	52.2	21.9	42%	30.3	4.1	8.9	6.7	8.8	24.4	1.8
2007-08	68.3	21.1	31%	47.2	9.1	13.2	12.0	12.2	37.4	0.7
2008-09	74.6	19.9	27%	54.7	9.6	13.9	12.3	14.5	40.7	4.4
2009-10	79.5	27.2	34%	52.3	10.1	14.6	12.1	11.2	37.9	4.3

Note 5: Yellow/bold-boxed cells indicate estimates as I've been unable to obtain a copy of the Premier League Annual Report for those years.

Note 6: Equal Share is the part of the TV deal distributed equally to all PL clubs. Facility fees directly results from the number of times you are shown live on TV and Merit Payment is the PL place money which is on a sliding scale from 1st to 20th.

Note 7: WCC = World Club Cup, ESC = European Super Cup, FAC = FA Cup, LC = League Cup.

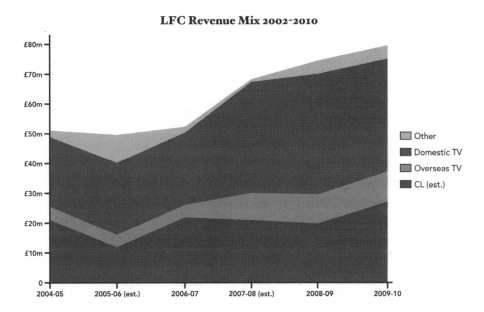

The thing that stands out is just how much of our Media revenue comes from the Champions League. It's a fair bet to say that the 2010/11 results where we are not in the Champions League will see Commercial overtake Media as the biggest source of revenue even though 2010/11 sees the start of a new PL TV deal period.

PL TV Deal History (£bn)

Start of Deal	Total Value	Domestic	%	Overseas	%
2004-05	1.454	1.13	78%	0.325	22%
2007-08	2.503	1.877	75%	0.625	25%
2010-11	3.513	1.953	56%	1.56	44%

What's most interesting here is that for the first time, the proportion coming from overseas is threatening to overtake the value of domestic rights. It's also worth noting two things at this point:

• The PL TV deals exclude mobile and online content, another clear immediate opportunity for FSG to focus on

• The EU is currently hearing a benchmark case from pub landlady Karen Murphy, which threatens the nature of all current TV deals. No-one yet knows the real impact if Mrs Murphy wins the case.

For the season just gone 2010/11, Liverpool's revenue's will almost certainly decline due to the absence of Champions League football. The amount of that decline will be decided by how much cannot be offset by an increase in Commercial, although bonus payments from sponsors and facility costs are also likely to decrease. For the upcoming 2011/12 season and the start of UFFP, revenues could return to 2008/09 and 2009/10 levels thanks to the new PL TV deal but due to lack of CL once more, it's unlikely that there will a return to 20% year-on-year increases as seen in recent times. For much more on how Liverpool could increase revenues, please see the Swiss Ramble article.

Liverpool's "Relevant Expenses" for UFFP

With revenues unlikely to increase for the first year of UFFP it becomes critical for the club to cut relevant expenses to reduce the risk of breaching "acceptable deviation". John Henry has talked on a number of occasions about "bad contracts" and the poor value/depth of the squad for the size of the wage bill the club has. Both Swiss Ramble and AndersRed show how Liverpool compares unfavourably with their top six competitors, not least the seemingly rampant wage inflation of recent years. The Reds' latest wages to turnover ratio is the highest it's ever been at 62%, edging toward the UEFA "red flag" level of 70%. Liverpool's aspiration should be to become a lot leaner, like Spurs, who have a similar cost of squad with arguably better depth but with only 60% of the wage bill.

An aside here is that the leanness of the Spurs wage bill is no surprise given the acumen of Daniel Levy and the amount of players traded during the Damien Comolli era, hopefully Liverpool will benefit in the same way over the coming years.

The notion of "bad contracts" got me thinking, is there any way we can try to demonstrate what this means? At Hewlett Packard, where I work as a data analyst, we define new measures all the time to identify and track what is important to us. My idea was to create two new measures and plot them to see if they could be used as a way of identifying "bad contracts". In both cases, "Long Term" means five years:

1. Long Term Contract Commitment (LTCC)

A simple measure based on information that is in the public domain.

LTCC = Number of Full Contract Years remaining x Estimated Basic Annual Salary

For some players this is readily available e.g. everyone knows that Joe Cole is on £90k a week. For some, particularly the recent contract renewals and new signings under FSG, it is not made public at all (something that I do welcome) and estimates have been made.

[2] Long Term Player Value (LTPV)

Elements of this measure are subjective. The primary elements are a player's *age* and *quality* (the subjective part).

• Age has been scored as follows: under 23 (5), 24-25 (4), 26-27 (3), 28-29 (2), Over 30 (1). Goalkeepers receive a bonus point due to their longevity.

• "First Team Quality Estimate" has been assessed as follows:

• World-Class (acknowledged world-class level performer) = 5

• Top International Class = 4 (not every international will be rated as this. It's more for the "best" players from the "top" countries)

• Established Premier League performer = 3

• Fringe international = 2

• Club (or Youth) level performer = 1

• An additional multiplier is then applied for "fitness risk".

• High Risk means likely to miss up to 50% of games through injury and multiplier is 0.7.

• Moderate Risk means likely to miss up to 30% of games and multiplier is 0.9.

• Low Risk multiplier is 1.

LTPV = ((Age rating + Goalkeeper Bonus) x First Team Quality Estimate) x Fitness Risk

If I was presenting this in my day job I'd say I had an 80% confidence level in its accuracy – sufficient that any inaccuracies are unlikely to have a significant impact on the results.

No.	Name	Homegrown	Pre-June 2010 Contract	Age	1st Team Quality Estimate	Fitness Risk High = Likely to miss up to 50% of games Mod = likely to miss up to 30% of games	Long Term Player Value to LFC (3-5 years) (Age * Quality) * Fitness Risk	Contract Ends	Full Contract Years Left	Conservative Salary Estmate £m (all youth = 0.5)	Long Term Contract Commitment (years*salary) < 2 = Green 3-4 = Amber 5-9 = Yellow > 10 = Red
Goalkeepers											
1	Brad Jones	Y	N	29	Club	Low	3	2013	2	1.5	3
25	Pepe Reina	N	Y	28	World	Low	15	2016	5	5	25
Defenders											
16	Sotirios Kyrgiakos	N	Y	31	Club	Low	1	2012	1	2	2
22	Danny Wilson	N	N	19	Club	Low	5	2013	2	0.5	1
23	Jamie Carragher	Y	N	33	International	Low	4	2013	2	4.5	9
37	Martin Skrtel	N	N	26	Established	Low	9	2014	3	3	9
5	Daniel Agger	N	Y	26	International	High	8.4	2014	3	3.5	10.5
	Emiliano Insua	Y	N	22	Fringe	Low	10	2011	0	1	0
6	Fabio Aurelio	N	N	31	Established	High	2.1	2012	1	1.5	1.5
2	Glen Johnson	Y	Y	26	Established	Moderate	8.1	2013	2	4	8
3	Paul Konchesky	Y	N	30	Club	Low	1	2014	3	3	9
34	Martin Kelly	Y	N	21	Fringe	Moderate	9	2014	3	1	3
Midfielders											
21	Lucas Leiva	N	N	24	International	Low	16	2015	4	2.5	10
26	Jay Spearing	Y	N	22	Club	Low	5	2015	4	1	4
8	Steven Gerrard	Y	Y	31	World	Moderate	4.5	2013	2	6	12
28	Christian Poulsen	N	N	31	Club	Low	1	2013	2	3	6
4	Raul Meireles	N	N	28	International	Low	8	2014	3	3	9
33	Jonjo Shelvey	Y	N	19	Club	Moderate	4.5	2014	3	0.5	1.5
4	Alberto Aquilani	N	Y	26	Established	High	6.3	2014	3	5	15
14	Milan Jovanovic	N	N	30	Fringe	Low	2	2013	2	4	8
17	Maxi Rodriguez	N	Y	30	Established	Low	3	2013	2	4	8
10	Joe Cole	Y	N	29	Fringe	Moderate	3.6	2014	3	4.5	13.5
	Jordan Henderson	Y	N	21	Fringe	Low	10	2016	5	2	10
Strikers											
24	David N'Gog	N	Y	22	Club	Low	5	2012	1	1	1
18	Dirk Kuyt	N	N	30	International	Low	4	2013	2	3.5	7
39	Nathan Eccleston	Y	N	20	Club		5	2013	2	0.5	1
12	Dani Pacheco	Y	N	20	Club	Low	5	2014	3	0.5	1.5
7	Luis Suarez	N	N	24	World	Low	20	2016	5	3.5	17.5
9	Andy Carroll	Y	N	22	Established	Moderate	13.5	2016	5	3.5	17.5

The colours (for those on electronic devices) are used as indicators specifically relating to each column of data. The purpose is to allow for a targeted deeper analysis of the 'red' cells and maybe the 'orange' ones too. For Age it's simple, the 'red' zone is over 30, for contract length it's any player with contract ending within one year, for LTCC it's any contract with a total monetary commitment over £10m.

Examples of deeper analysis could be:

1) For LTCC. It's important to understand what is driving the high monetary value. Is it annual salary, length of contract or both? Management focus should be on players with high LTCC because of the former.

2) For Age, not all 30 year olds are 'melting' at the same rate. Contrasts would be Joe Cole and Steven Gerrard with Ryan Giggs and Gary Speed. The indicator would flag up the need to go and investigate other data sources before making a decision.

Some 'reds' are also red herrings. For example, Pepe Reina, because his LTCC may be £25m but he also has the 3rd highest LTPV behind Suárez and Lucas. So in short, don't focus too much on the colours in this chart; instead focus on the results when

LTPV and LTCC are plotted against each other on the chart below.

With some invaluable consultancy from Zach Slaton, the data was transformed to make it 'normal'. In the final chart below, the square root of the LTPV is used.

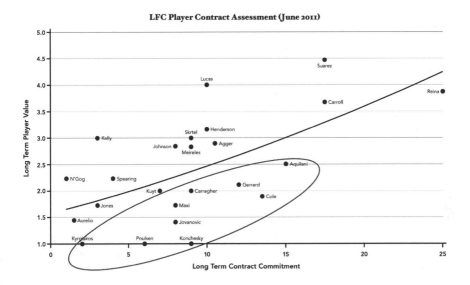

The key is the distance from the line. Those far above the line like Kelly, Lucas and Suárez need to be retained at all costs. Looking at the chart, it's interesting that most of players above the line have signed contracts under FSG: Kelly, Spearing and Lucas have extended, plus Henderson, Suárez and Carroll. Only one player who has signed under FSG is below the line, and that is Kuyt, and even then it's marginal. However the exceptions are Ngog, Johnson, Škrtel, Agger and Meireles. If we examine the reason for the distance from the line we can make intuitive decisions about what needs to be done next. The reason for Ngog and Johnson is shortness of contract remaining. Based on this fact, both need to be re-signed on a new deal ASAP or sold. Meireles, Agger and Škrtel fall into a different category. They all have three years remaining but they all have significant resale potential. I fully expect all three to be the subject of significant internal discussion about whether we cash in or retain.

"Bad Contracts?"

After defining the measures and collecting the data, my conclusion of what John Henry meant by "bad contracts" is the ellipse on the chart. And yes that includes Steven Gerrard.

Nine first team players, with a cumulative estimated weekly wage of over £700,000 *per week*.

Or £3m a month.

Or about £36m a year.

Just what kind of return are we getting from those nine players for c£36m p.a.? Especially when you consider that these players are supposed to be the senior players in the first team and taking responsibility in the drive to make the club successful.

Of the nine, seven of them are already 30 or over (Joe Cole is only six months away). Only Aquilani has age on his side at 26 (hence his slightly higher LTPV but not enough to justify his LTCC).

Contract length remaining is critical for three players: Konchesky, Cole and Aquilani all have three years left so they are likely to be the highest priorities for FSG to resolve.

Those with two years are Gerrard, Carragher, Rodriguez, Jovanovic and Poulsen. Carragher and Gerrard are assessed as having a "First Team Quality Estimate" of international or above but both are borderline. Those assessments, plus the number of first team games they can still play – and make a difference in – should mean they are excluded from this summer's transfer plans.

If I was looking at this as presented and with no idea of who those players were then I would conclude that none of them would be offered another contract when their current ones expired – and yes, that includes Steven Gerrard.

The chart below shows how much of our total wage bill (players, manager, directors, coaching staff, reserves and youth – including bonuses) is consumed by the estimated basic salary of the first team squad. Of those you can see how for 2011/12 and 2012/13 about half could be considered "bad contracts" (and they don't disappear completely until 2014/15 season).

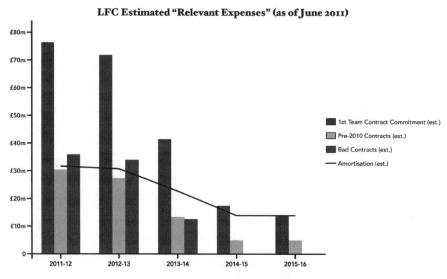

LFC Estimated "Relevant Expenses" (as of June 2011)

The other bar on the chart is the potential UFFP "joker in the pack". There is an annex in the regulations that states that pre-1st June 2010 contracts will be excluded from the break-even calculation (because UFFP was only finally approved in 2010). Of course, the number of pre-1st June 2010 contracts will diminish over time but in the first two years of UFFP, Liverpool could have almost an aggregate of c£56m potentially excluded. It's also worth noting that thanks to Pepe Reina's six-year contract signed in April 2010 the Reds have c£5m get out of jail card right up to 2015/16. The line on the chart brings me to the final part of this article: how the cost of transfers is handled.

A Different Way of Thinking About Player Transfers

Under UFFP, players are assets and player transfers are handled following standard accounting practices for fixed assets. The transfer fee for a player is written down (amortised) over the length of his contract. Let's take the example of our most expensive player, Andy Carroll.

As we all know, he signed for £35m on a 5.5 year contract which is an amortisation of £6.36m per annum.

£6.36m will already have been charged to the Profit & Loss Account in 2010/11 and £6.36m will be charged every season until he leaves the club or signs a new contract.

Liverpool also have some other very big contributors to amortisation in 2011/12: Suárez £4.2m, Johnson £4.5m, Aquilani £3.6m *[technical note from Graeme Riley – fee to be amortised is £18m. Add-ons will be separated out under "contigent liabilities"]* and Henderson £3.2m (£16m over five years).

However, consider this. By the end of the first accounting period, 1st June 2013, Carroll will be 24, Suárez 26 and Henderson 22. Yet their transfer values will have been amortised by £19m, £12.5m and £6.4m respectively. On the Liverpool books the player's values would be:

Carroll – £16m

Suárez – £10.3m

Henderson- £9.6m

Yet all would still have three years left on their contracts and in football terms, yet to hit their peak years; a fantastically strong position that could only be undermined by (1) catastrophic injury (2) the three turning out to be duds.

Right at the start, when I explained about "Relevant Income", I mentioned how under UFFP, profit from player trading counts as income alongside things like TV money.

The best example of this happened this season. Under UFFP, Ryan Babel would have made Liverpool a profit on player trading.

How I hear you say?

Well we think of profit as what we received minus what we paid but this isn't how player sales are calculated for profit (or in Babel's case it's the other way around – a loss). As Swiss Ramble explains, in 2007 we signed a 20-year-old Babel from Ajax for £11.5m on a five-year contract so the amortisation was £2.3m a season. After 3.5 inconsistent seasons his value on the books was just £3.4 million. His £5.8m transfer to Hoffenheim will actually bring a £2.4m profit to next year's accounts.

The same method will mean approximately £13m profit for Mascherano (value on the books down to £4.5m) and somewhere around £42m for Torres. This means that the 2010/11 accounts (the year before UFFP) are going to see a huge profit on player trading of c£58m, when in reality we know that the cost of Carroll and Suárez was almost exactly offset by Torres and Babel. Accounting, eh?

The same practice also gives us a clue as to what could happen with Alberto Aquilani. As we speak, his value on Liverpool's books is c£10.8m *(18-((18/5)*2))*. A transfer fee of 12m EUR this summer would ensure no loss counting towards year one of UFFP. Another option would be *another* year long loan followed by a cast-iron, unbreakable commitment to buy at, say, 8m EUR. Madness I hear you cry! But from a UFFP perspective, c£5m would be saved in wages during year one and a sale at his accounting value would ensure no loss in year two.

Conclusion

Based on Liverpool's last set of accounts (2009/10), our elements for a high level UFFP equation were:

Relevant Income = £184.8m (Revenue) + £22.8m (Profit from player trading)

Relevant Expenses = £114.3m (Wages) + £40.2m (Amortisation) +£27.7m (Other Costs)

£207.6m (Relevant Income) – £182.2m (Relevant Expenses) = £25.4m

Obviously this ignores things like interest paid under Gillett and Hicks, but fingers crossed that is a thing of the past going forward under FSG.

The interesting thing is that without the profit from player trading (mainly Alonso in this case) Liverpool are getting close to making a loss.

Then you need to factor in the loss of the Champions League: a minimum £25m in TV money plus gate receipts and extra payments from sponsors. No wonder it's estimated that our replacements in the top four, Spurs, made a total of £39m from their run to the quarter-finals last season.

When the 2010/11 accounts are published in May 2012, the loss of the Champions League will not be apparent in the bottom line because we will make almost £50m profit on player trading.

However, for year one of UFFP things looks more serious. If we take that Spurs figure as a benchmark then all of a sudden Liverpool are in the UFFP red zone:

2011-12	UFFP Year 1 High Level Estimate
£185m	2009-10 revenue
-£35m	Total estimate for the CL
£12m	Difference in StanChart deal vs Carlsberg
£162m	**RELEVANT INCOME**
£114m	Total Staff Wages (assume the same)
£32m	Amortisation (after Henderson)
£27m	Other Costs (fairly static over last five years)
£173m	**RELEVANT EXPENSES**
-£11m	**BREAK EVEN RESULT**

There's going to be deductions for the Academy and pre-2010 contracts (such as the earlier example of £5m per season for Reina) but it shows you how borderline the situation is. Every expensive transfer will increase amortisation. Every dead-wood player that isn't moved on maintains the wages. The only players who will yield an accounting profit in 2011/12 are those "above the line" plus the unpalatable prospect of selling academy players. Ngog's value on Liverpool's books is c£350k, Agger c£600k, Lucas c£900k, Kuyt c£1.1m and Škrtel c£1.6m.

If the status quo is maintained, FSG are facing the prospect of writing a hefty cheque to cover the loss above 5m EUR – something which they will be extremely reluctant to do given their policy on deficit spending. On the other hand, with a successful cull of the wage bill the scope for further signings increases again. Even getting rid of Cole, Jovanovic, Poulsen, Konchesky, Rodriguez and Kyriagkos on free transfers will free up about £20m in wages to be used for new player wages and the first year's amortisation on new transfers. Any transfer fee for any of those players would be a bonus. It's not all bad news though.

The problem most clubs face is lack of cash flow to make transfer signings happen in the first place. FSG appear to be the opposite – a cash-rich organisation who will not have any problems meeting onerous up-front payment terms when buying new players. When they took over Liverpool, FSG talked about needing three to five years to make Liverpool genuinely competitive again, both domestically and in Europe. After even this high level look at the figures it's easy to see why. For the next couple of years, FSG are going to be very, very busy.

A MODEL TO IDENTIFY PLAYERS

By Lee Mooney

March, 2013

I left the Swansea game at Anfield a couple of weeks ago feeling inspired. Not because we'd won the game, though that was brilliant, but because I feel I got a glimpse of the future under Brendan Rodgers. The balance of the side was great and the gaps seemed clearer than ever. As is often the case, rather than argue in a pub like a normal person, I turned to the data. In this article I've used analysis to identify key areas of the field that need to be invested in. I've also offered detailed rationale as to how much should be invested and suggested likely candidates for each of the key roles. The Liverpool side that faced Swansea last week looked like this:

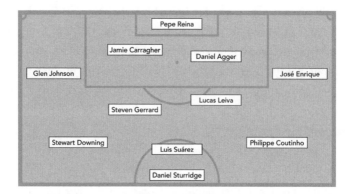

It is my opinion that the Liverpool squad is being re-configured to fit the following tactical frame:

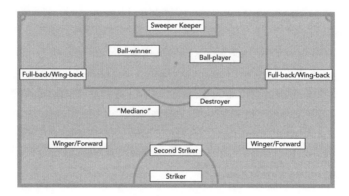

Despite playing a weakened opponent, the side against Swansea seemed balanced and equally 'able' across all areas of the field (perhaps with the exception of Downing who didn't appear to fit well with the movement of Suárez, Coutinho or Sturridge). The team on Sunday also seemed to be the closest yet to having the right quality of player in the right role. So, for Liverpool to move forward, which areas of the field should be invested in, how much should be invested and who should be bought?

How much money should Liverpool FC spend on players?

One of the things that I've found particularly frustrating recently has been the talk about transfers. Fan expectations around the fees that should be paid seem to have no relation to the club's financial position. What follows is a very simplistic attempt to understand how a squad budget might be broken down. Hopefully those who specialise in the club's finances will provide deeper insights than I will here. What I'm positing is really just a starter to encourage debate, discussion and further refinement.

I know it's delicate to use Manchester United as a benchmark for any analysis. But, given the sheer volume of winning they've done in the last 20 years, it seems reasonable to assume that they know a thing or two about assembling a squad.

For this exercise I've used the squad values for Liverpool and Manchester United, as estimated on transfermarkt.co.uk, along with the 2012 revenue figures published by Deloitte as part of the 2013 *Football Money League*.

I appreciate that these transfer valuations alone will be hugely open to debate, but if the base of data is consistent for both clubs then we should arrive 'close enough' to the desired end-point. The distinction between 'starting XI' and reserves has been made based on appearances this season. The diagram below shows my suggested starting XI for both clubs (again, I recognise the simplicity here and that tactical variation is required):

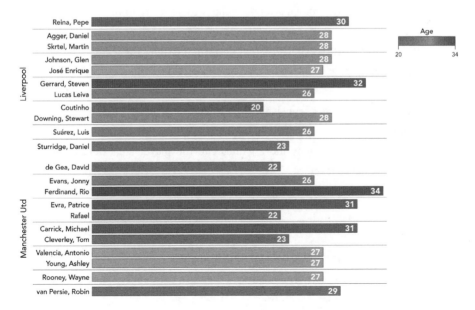

Taking these two starting XI lists, I've produced the graphic below which shows the ratio of average player value to club turnover, by club and the generic playing position:

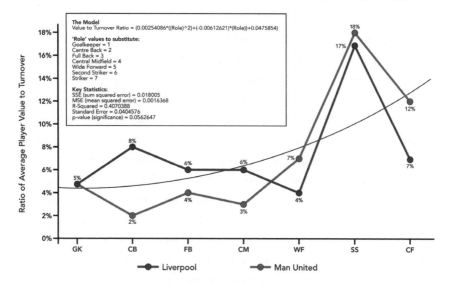

If I was the Liverpool FC Director of Football (no protests please), I would be obsessed with reconciling a number of potentially conflicting key concepts:

• Budget: how much should I be spending to staff a particular first XI or reserve role?

• Cost: how much has/will it cost to recruit and retain a player?

• Value: how much is a player worth in the transfer market today?

• Value Forecast: how much is a player likely to be worth in the transfer market in the future?

• Benchmark: what level of consistent performance does the team require?

• Capability: what level of consistent performance does the player offer to the team today?

• Potential: what level of consistent performance is a player likely to offer the team in the future?

• Shelf-life: for how many more games can the player consistently sustain the required performance level?

• Capacity: how many match-play minutes can a player sustain to maximise his total return?

• Utilisation: for how many match-play minutes is a player being used?

I would also operate under two bold guiding principles:

• The right player is *always* available at the right price and at the right time – the challenge is finding him.

- Always walk away from a deal that doesn't meet the club's expectations of quality and value.

Looking at the current squad through this lens, the 'shelf-life' concept would have me thinking very carefully about any player that is 28 years old (or older). Being older doesn't always mean a player lacks 'capability', but it may limit his 'capacity' to perform consistently at the required performance level. With the market value of an outfield player deteriorating so rapidly beyond the age of 29, reaching the age of 28 is a key opportunity to ask some difficult questions:

- Is the on-field value the player has left to offer less than his current market value?
- Is the player operating consistently at the required level and how likely is this to continue?
- In real terms, is the player worth more today than the club originally paid for him?
- Can I replace this player with somebody younger and/or cheaper and re-invest my budget in another area?

- Do we have first-team-ready replacements for this player in the current squad? With the exception of Pepe Reina (because goalkeepers have a longer shelf-life than out-fielders) I'd be asking these questions in relation to the following players:

- Steven Gerrard
- Daniel Agger
- Martin Škrtel
- Glen Johnson
- Stewart Downing

Looking at the differences between Manchester United and Liverpool on the chart, the following observations also jumped out at me:

- Squad values, when seen in the context of club turnover, are largely comparable.
- The depreciation of Ferdinand, and the absence of Vidic, deflates Manchester United's centre-back ratio.
- The gap between 'strikers', especially when you consider the cover Manchester United have, is 'striking'.
- The gap between 'wide forwards' is worth further investigation.

The money 'league table' produced by Deloitte also suggests that Liverpool, at least in revenue terms, should be strong enough to achieve 5th place in the Premier League. Given the near-fatal management of recent years it seems, at least to me, grossly unfair for anyone to expect Liverpool to reach that level this season. It also suggests that Liverpool fans have no 'right' to expect regular participation in the Champions League;

only that Liverpool should be generally competing for a qualification place.

So, how much should Liverpool FC spend on players? To estimate this theoretically we need to consider two more variables:

• The probability that the transfer will be a 'success'

• A limit for the value of the squad based on club turnover (budget)

To populate these variables, I need to refer to the 50/50 'rule of thumb' from '*Pay As You Play*' with reference to a teams' transfer success – the basic suggestion being that a good manager gets as many deals right as he does wrong. To me this means, at least in theory, that a manager's track-record should directly affect his budget.

I've based the budgets for the first XI and reserve XI on the squads of Manchester United and Liverpool (both show approximately 70% of turnover is allocated to the starting XI and 50% of turnover to the reserve XI – so overall it seems we're looking at a hard ceiling of 120% of turnover). Notice we're talking about value, not cost. So, in an ideal world, the value of the squad in real terms would be higher than the cost of building it. The Academy could really be seen as a 'value factory' where value is made rather than bought.

Turnover	£188,700,000
First XI Ratio:	70.00%
Reserves Ratio:	50.00%
Total Cost:	£226,440,000
Budget Cost:	£113,220,000
Cost/Turnover	120.00%
Success Rate:	50.00%

Group	Ratio	Position	Model	% Budget	Budget Limit	Imposed Limit
First XI	70%	Goalkeeper	4.40%	5.80%	£7,655,479	£3,827,739
		Defence (CB)	4.55%	5.99%	£7,915,947	£3,957,974
		Defence (CB)	4.55%	5.99%	£7,915,947	£3,957,974
		Defence (LB)	5.21%	6.86%	£9,060,976	£4,530,488
		Defence (RB)	5.21%	6.86%	£9,060,976	£4,530,488
		Midfield (CM)	6.37%	8.40%	£11,090,565	£5,545,283
		Midfield (CM)	6.37%	8.40%	£11,090,565	£5,545,283
		Midfield (LW)	8.05%	10.60%	£14,000,714	£7,002,357
		Midfield (RW)	8.05%	10.60%	£14,000,714	£7,002,357
		Striker (SS)	10.23%	13.48%	£17,803,423	£8,901,712
		Striker (CF)	10.23%	17.02%	£22,486,693	£11,243,346
Reserves	50%	Goalkeeper	4.40%	5.80%	£5,468,199	£2,734,099
		Defence (CB)	4.55%	5.99%	£5,654,248	£2,827,124
		Defence (CB)	4.55%	5.99%	£5,654,248	£2,827,124
		Defence (LB)	5.21%	6.86%	£6,472,126	£3,236,063
		Defence (RB)	5.21%	6.86%	£6,472,126	£3,236,063
		Midfield (CM)	6.37%	8.40%	£7,921,832	£3,960,916
		Midfield (CM)	6.37%	8.40%	£7,921,832	£3,960,916
		Midfield (LW)	8.05%	10.60%	£10,003,367	£5,001,684
		Midfield (RW)	8.05%	10.60%	£10,003,367	£5,001,684
		Striker (SS)	10.23%	13.48%	£12,716,731	£6,358,366
		Striker (CF)	10.23%	17.02%	£16,061,923	£8,030,962

What I found interesting from this simple modelling is the suggested budgets for each first XI role. It seems we're operating around the 'Imposed Limit' level for the more recent signings. Could this be the effect of recent purchases who weren't available prior to the January window? Obviously 'value for money' is a key element that needs to be kept at the top of the agenda – those charged with spending the club's money need to be doing so with ruthless efficiency, getting as much value as possible within these guiding limits.

Which areas of the field should Liverpool FC invest in?

The key gaps between the Liverpool and Manchester United squads seem to be in the 'striker' and 'wide forward' roles. The recent acquisition of Coutinho appears to be an attempt to reinforce in this area. With Henderson and Allen both operating effectively at first-team level, it would appear the most pressing priorities are to reinforce:

- First-team striking options.
- Right-sided wide-forward position (currently occupied by Stewart Downing).
- Left-back.

There are several options for meeting these short-term objectives. My personal preference would be to:

- Recruit a first-team-ready player who will be effective as a striker (and ideally as a second striker).
- Re-deploy Glen Johnson as a wide-forward and promote a youth player to the first-team at right-back.
- Sell Stewart Downing to release investment funds.
- Recruit a player who can provide cover for José Enrique and be ready to replace him within the next two years.

Which players should Liverpool buy?

Player recruitment has certainly become my specialist area. I see no other aspect of the football business where relatively small data and analysis investments have the potential to deliver such a big commercial impact (which, hopefully, translates into on-field growth and success on the pitch).

To make these recommendations I'll be using the same version of my recruitment model that I used recently to compare Liverpool and Manchester United. This time though, I'll provide more detail as to how the model works (and where it doesn't).

This first version of my model is limited. This is mostly due to the data that I've been able to collect within a time-frame that's relevant. For example, I could collect better data, but the process is so slow that getting to market with useful information is impossible. When time is critical, you either throw money at the problem (which I don't have) or you compromise quality. Keep in mind, 'good enough' might be all we need. So, players are rated based on the squad value of the club they play for today, not who they've played for before and not based on what any of those clubs have actually achieved in terms of league places. Similarly, domestic appearances are also not counted – so a squad player who never plays for Barcelona scores the same as a player who plays all the time. Addressing these two weaknesses is a priority for version 2.0.

The basic components of this version of the model are as follows:

• National Team Score: indicating the strength of the player's national team;

• Base Country Score: indicating the strength of the player's domestic nation (where his club plays);

• Club Score: indicating the value of a squad compared with that of the top club side (Barcelona);

• Weighted International Apps: measure of appearances based on the strength of the nation;

• Weighted International Apps Score: measure accounting for the player's age and playing position;

Four of these elements are then combined to create a Player Score using the following formula:

(Base Country Score x Club Score) + (National Team Score) + (Weighted International Apps Score)

The relative simplicity of these calculations, perhaps with the exception of the 'Weighted International Apps Score' which required a fair bit of engineering and testing, makes it possible to apply them consistently across a large dataset (in this case a reference catalogue of over 92,000 players).

Having a domestic and international perspective is also powerful. Using both perspectives helps to identify talents that have perhaps been overlooked. If a player is making regular full international appearances at 19 for a strong footballing nation, he's possibly worth looking at a little more deeply, even if he does play for a club you haven't heard of.

I was asked specifically about the scoring of Jamie Carragher compared with Nemanja Vidic. There are 1,208 central defenders in the model aged over 33. Carragher is ranked 15th (of those playing in England, only Rio Ferdinand ranks more highly – with the top of the list being occupied by Carles Puyol). Very few of the top clubs in world football have central defenders still playing who are over the age of 33. This doesn't mean that Carragher is 'better' than Vidic, but he is quite extraordinary to be doing what he's doing at 34 (hence the high score).

Before drilling into specifics about Liverpool FC, I thought it might be useful to show a 'dream team' that was picked solely by using this model and one filter – that the player must be under the age of 29. Here it is:

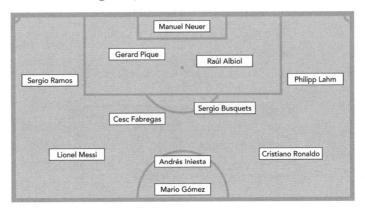

What do you think? Without any human intervention at all a simple set of data has been used to create a 'dream team' that would generally 'make sense' to most football fans with a basic knowledge of European football. Can we be more specific now and make suggestions about the current Liverpool squad – safe in the knowledge that the model isn't complete nonsense?

I concluded earlier in the piece that Liverpool should look to prioritise three specific on-field positions (from a recruitment perspective):

- First XI striker (budget up to £11.3m);
- First XI right-sided wide-forward (budget up to £7.0m);
- First XI left-back (budget up to £4.5m);

Identifying candidates for these roles requires some final filters to be applied (along with the financials):

- Define the target age-range;
- Define the minimum score a potential Liverpool player should have;

The ideal target age-range would appear to be 22 to 25 (my rationale for this won't win a Nobel Prize anytime soon). The work I did on strikers last year suggested a peak age-range of 26 to 29. The value of a younger purchase will have time to grow, so fees stand a chance of being recovered and re-invested. The lowest scoring Liverpool player in the model (remember the model data is over six months old now), is Jordan Henderson. Henderson scores 1.393, so to simplify we'll say that the recruitment process for the Liverpool FC first XI should not consider players with a score less than 1.300.

The first XI striker position (budget up to £11.3m)
So, having applied the filters and referenced www. Transfermarkt.co.uk to gauge

market values, the short-list of potential targets is quite interesting. The most surprising result was that Daniel Sturridge (valued at £13m), when at Chelsea, meets all of these conditions and has the highest value within reasonable reach for the 'Striker (Forward)' category (players like Lewandowski and Cavani obviously score very well, but they are way beyond the budget we've set here).

Full results below (only includes players valued at £1m or above to make the results readable):

Striker (Forward)	Score	Value
Gamiero, Kevin	1.377	£10,500,000
de Jong, Luuk	1.427	£9,700,000
van Wolfswinkel, Ricky	1.379	£9,200,000
Rémy, Loic	1.587	£8,800,000
Aubameyang, Pierre-Emerick	1.371	£8,800,000
Lens, Jeremain	1.548	£7,000,000
Matavz, Tim	1.438	£6,200,000
Hernández, Abel	1.454	£3,500,000
Obinna, Victor	1.744	£3,100,000
Mouche, Pablo	1.998	£2,200,000
Rojas, Joao	1.489	£1,600,000
Hoffer, Erwin	1.424	£1,300,000
Jackson, Simeon	1.374	£1,300,000

Striker (Target Man)	Score	Value
Caicedo, Felipe	1.991	£7,900,000
Perisic, Ivan	1.502	£6,600,000
Bendtner, Nicklas	1.716	£6,200,000
Long, Shane	1.539	£5,300,000
Necid, Tomas	1.957	£4,000,000
Petersen, Nils	1.734	£4,000,000
Maïga, Modibo	1.684	£4,000,000
Derdiyok, Eren	1.909	£3,500,000
Altidore, Jozy	1.845	£3,100,000
Beqiraj, Fatos	1.624	£3,100,000
Viatri, Lucas	1.945	£2,200,000
Moreno, Marcelo	1.497	£2,200,000
Blandi, Nicolás	1.606	£1,800,000

The first XI right-sided wide-forward position (budget up to £7.0m)

Objectivity can be a real pain! A couple of players score highly on this list but need to be excluded because of their estimated market value – players like Martin Harnik, José Callejón and Kevin Mirallas for example. When the rules are applied the list is as follows:

Right Wide Forward	Score	Value
Arnautovic, Marko	1.331	£7,000,000
Lee, Chung-Yong	1.597	£6,600,000
Vargas, Eduardo	1.371	£6,200,000
dos Santos, Giovani	1.860	£3,500,000
Pabón, Dorlan	1.693	£3,100,000
Weiss, Vladimir	1.509	£3,100,000
Beerens, Roy	1.351	£2,600,000
Elmohamady, Ahmed	1.572	£2,200,000
Barrera, Pablo	1.748	£2,000,000
Pérez, Hernán	1.389	£1,800,000
Villaluz, César	1.477	£1,400,000

The first XI left-back position (budget up to £4.5m)

Not many candidates are available that meet both the conditions of value and quality (it would appear). Do any of these players stand out for you?

Left Back	Score	Value
Bertrand, Ryan	1.303	£4,400,000
Pieters, Erik	1.852	£3,500,000
Elderson	1.493	£3,300,000
Torres Nilo, Jorge	1.800	£3,100,000
Monzón, Fabián	1.533	£2,600,000
José Ángel	1.304	£2,600,000
Contento, Diego	1.734	£1,800,000
Aldrete, Adrián	1.417	£1,800,000
Obradovic, Ivan	1.423	£1,300,000
Chávez, Darvin	1.350	£1,300,000
Iberbia, Raúl	1.331	£1,200,000

Conclusion

The recruitment model I'm developing is in the very early stages. There will be considerable variance in terms of the quality of recommendations. With time and investment though, this variance will be removed and the robustness of the model will grow. That said, even at this early stage, the analysis results when using this model produce some interesting insights. At worst it prompts thinking about players you'll most likely never have heard of (which in itself has to be a good thing). Some of its suggestions may be unobtainable due to price or because they are already at a rival club who won't do business with Liverpool – but they can easily be ignored.

During the review, Paul specifically asked me about Coutinho, and whether he would have shown up as a recommendation.

Coutinho is a left-sided attacking midfielder who's in the 16 to 21 age range. There are nine players within this segment that could potentially 'cut the mustard' for LFC. These are:

Mario Gotze (£37.0m)
Eden Hazard (£35.0m)
Lucas Moura (£31.0m)
Erik Lamela (£19.5m)
Coutinho (£8.8m)
Adem Ljajic (£5.7m)
Tommy Oar (£875k)
Yohandry Orozco (£450k)

Gai Assulin (£450k)

Once you apply the budgetary constraints, and perhaps consider that some of these players might already be getting Champions League football, you're left with five players to consider (three of whom would really be considered 'gambles'). So, using this model alone, if you'd have asked me a couple of months ago to find an attacking left-sided midfielder under the age of 21 within Liverpool's budget, I'd have recommended Coutinho or Adem Ljajic.

When Damien Comolli arrived I made a bold suggestion that he might not be as good as he was hyped up to be. The exact recruitment decisions that were made could have been prompted by simply analysing the prior year's fantasy football data alone (which emphasises assists, goals and a clean disciplinary record). The fees that were paid also seemed to be based on a crude average (an average that included the astronomical fees being paid by clubs like Manchester City and Chelsea – effectively doubling what we were spending compared with our comparable rivals).

The current regime does not appear to be operating in this way. With the exception of the deal to buy Joe Allen (whose £15m fee is way above the hard ceiling of £11m I'd permit and three times the budget limit of £5m), the transfers so far seem to be far more aware of the 'key concepts' outlined here than Comolli ever was – at Liverpool, at least. This has to be a good thing for the club moving forward.

EMBRACING UNCERTAINTY

By Tony Mckenna
March, 2013

The Southampton game, like the Anfield defeat to Villa, halted any burgeoning optimism amongst large sections of the fan-base. The doomsayers are often portrayed as negative dissenters; some optimists see them as traitorous and disloyal. All hell breaks loose. Yet, is the polarised battle necessary? Even the optimists may be misguided. There may be a third way to support our football team.

Throughout many of my own comments on TTT, I often refer to my approach of 'embracing uncertainty' in relation to Brendan Rodgers. I would like to expand on what I mean by this.

This approach is based on three crucial issues: first, we cannot predict the future; second, the information we receive, even hard statistics, can be misinterpreted by fallible human minds as a pointer to a brighter future; and third, we receive our knowledge base from others, we absorb it, and yet accepted facts can be disproved as time amasses new evidence. Is it wise to become inextricably attached to one viewpoint before the future unravels?

The Psychology of Winning & Losing

"I hate losing more than I love winning" – Billy Beane.

When sportspeople say something like this, they reveal as much about all of us as they do about themselves. Indeed, it is a psychological truism for all humankind. The despair of losing far exceeds the elation of a winning outcome. This should not be surprising; the impact of loss, in all its guises, pummels our emotions, defeats our morale and clouds us in abject misery. Loss is, in fact, a shape-shifter with a pernicious omnipresence in all our lives, and with varying degrees of potency: bereavement, a relationship break up, redundancy, losing a football match, or indeed, losing money. The last scenario typically applies to traders who pit their wits against the stock market; and any good trader must understand the psychology of trading as much as the markets themselves. Failure to grasp this could lead to an emotional ambush. The field of neuroscience flashes a warning:

"...the brilliant psychologists Daniel Kahneman and Amos Tversky have shown that the pain of a financial loss is more than twice as intense as the pleasure of an equivalent gain." – *The Intelligent Investor*

In other words, lose £1,000 and the emotional pain will be more than double the joy if you had won the same amount. Or, to apply a football analogy; imagine your mood when your team loses 3-0, as opposed to winning 3-0. Remember West Brom on the first day of the season? Now recall your mood when the Reds beat Wigan, Sunderland and QPR by the same score line; the contrast reveals your capacity to experience both ends of the emotional spectrum.

The problem is we often express a view when our emotions are clouded by the impact of those extremities; we are not in control and may err greatly in what we say. The sense of loss, being greater in impact, will motivate us much more in terms of extricating that mood. If you have the Internet accessible at your fingertips, then what better convenience of an outlet – to express your chagrin – could you have?

That said, being flushed with optimism can pose its own dangers; though not equal to being crushed by pessimism, our over-confidence can still render us irrational in mind, thought and emotion.

Trusting the Experts?

Many years ago, as a young man, I read a quote attributed to John F Kennedy following the Bay of Pigs fracas:

"How could I be so far off base as to trust the experts? All my life I have known not to trust the experts."

I did not really get it. Experts, in my mind's fledgling maturity, had superior knowledge in their recognised fields. It is they who we must look up to; and should even their advice be received with mistrust, then who the hell *can* you trust? The quote receded to the back of my cerebral attic – until quite recently. Memory smote: reading *'Thinking Fast and Slow'*, in which Daniel Kaheman had evoked Tetlock's citation of when so-called experts – no less susceptible to human fallibility than the rest of us – make erroneous applications to a viewpoint:

"Experts are led astray not by what they believe, but by how they think, says Tetlock."

"How they think?" That nailed it. Many people, including experts, become dogmatically fixated on one theory – their theory, and the only one they wish to hear. Their refusal to debate is a dislike of being disagreed with; they hate to be wrong. Theirs is a determined desire to win the argument rather than arrive at the truth; the essence of debate is lost. Personality-wise, they are bombastically opinionated, imbued with superiority complexes that say their predictions are right.

And, for Tetlock, it is in the very notion of prediction that the problem lies, because it assumes a future. The catch is that the future is wholly unpredictable, and even information accepted as fact can later be dismissed.

The Arc of the Pendulum Swing

If, like me, your Primary School teacher taught you that Pluto was a planet, it has since been necessary for you to revise your stance. But I actually believed this as fact for most of my life. As the Frankfurt Theorists warned, we take our ideological and cultural heritage as given. Our subscription to doctrinal beliefs is perilously prejudiced because most of us are mere vessels for the knowledge we receive; we can never test its validity ourselves since the scale is beyond us. Possibly, there are only a handful of people in the world who could corroborate the actual size of Pluto.

When we are given information, it should not necessarily follow that we become irrevocably affixed on the theory – or finding – imparted. Knowledge bases are not static entities, but rather a shifting sands phenomenon as the evolution of time facilitates additional findings. Even a genius can be bettered given enough time; Einstein built on Newton's work and the latter, in turn, has been surpassed by others who have added to his work.

Imagine a pendulum swinging between the polar opposites of sheer optimism and desperate pessimism. Somewhere, in between, the pendulum creates an arc where it may be preferable to posit oneself; not one extreme, nor the other, but somewhere in uncertain mode – until, of course, the time comes when the future delivers irrefutable outcomes – like finishing in the top four, or even winning the league. Until then, there is far too much that we cannot know.

Sfumato

One of the seven steps to genius that Michael Gelb explores in his beautifully written and illustrated book '*How To Think Like Leonardo Da Vinci*', *sfumato*, literally translated, means: "turned to mist" or "going up in smoke"; a metaphorical representation of uncertainty and ambiguity with the added expectation to embrace both. As Gelb explains:

"Leonardo's ceaseless questioning and insistence on using his senses to explore experience led him to many great insights and discoveries, but they also led him to confront the vastness of the unknown and ultimately the unknowable. Yet his phenomenal ability to hold the tension of opposites, to embrace uncertainty, ambiguity, and paradox, was a critical characteristic of his genius".

Well, I had to have that – abandon the fight with complexity and contradiction; embrace the fact that the search for knowledge and truth renders us forever playing see-saw with an elephant: the weight of what we know will be always be outweighed by what we don't know – ignorance renders us suspended at loftier heights than our knowledge base could ever attain.

All my life, ever since reading that book, I have retained that philosophy. I have endeavoured to utilise it in all aspects of my thinking, professionally and personally; and now include its reference in an article about football! Since the principle was harnessed by one of the greatest minds that ever lived – on which to predicate his thinking – it seemed a good idea to emulate the great man. Not that I expected to morph into a genius; but rather that I would, at least, appear less foolish.

And should a genius have cause to appreciate the 'vastness of the unknown and ultimately the unknowable', then as a lesser mortal still, I can only respect the existence of the same entities.

How Rodgers' tenure at Liverpool evolves, or how it ends even, remains one of those unknown entities. Even hard positive statistics can lead us astray; our brains are pattern-seeking organs, which is just as well so that we can go about our daily lives and find our way around. Ultimately, we need this skill to survive. But often the brain can deduce patterns and make erroneous correlations; possibly even engender misguided optimism as with the statistics I will quote at the end.

Since human judgement is so fallible, it follows naturally, for me, to think about the future, but not to try and predict it; I may have an opinion but I will not express it in commandment fashion.

The following section is a summary of my own latest thinking. It is not a prediction or forecast for the future, but rather a personal embracing of uncertainty relating to Brendan Rodgers. Neither should it be taken as criticism, but evaluation made in the knowledge that I may be totally wrong to think this way.

Uncertainty: A Personal Perspective

Imagine No Possession

I wonder if you can. Well, not *zilch* possession exactly, but the scenarios in which teams are victorious when having considerably less possession.

Take the Aston Villa game as a prime illustration. *EPL index* indicates that the Reds had an astonishing 72.1% possession; as good as that sounds, we know we lost the game. Such examples used to cause me irritable consternation; in what other game or contest can you achieve such an edge and yet still lose? But, of course, possession is not the pure essence of winning at football; *scoring goals* is what counts. Possession is the means to an end, but not the end itself.

Try turning it on its head: if Villa had just 21.9% of the possession, this still means that they had the ball for almost 20 minutes; of course that is in a collective sense, not an unbroken episode. Nonetheless, it is still a lengthy period to have had the ball. More importantly, it is how they made maximum use of that potential when in charge of the ball. It would be spurious to talk about the possession game if a team – as Villa did here – had not come to contest those stakes.

Instead, they were playing a different game, which maybe Rodgers needs to factor in during similar contests. Villa had set their stall out with a focus on counter-attack, physicality and pressing when Liverpool tried to play out from defence. Other than that they were content to defend and soak up the possession until it may have threatened: they made 53 clearances to Liverpool's 13. On the physicality front they won 62% of aerial duels, edged the ground duels 57%/43%, and committed twice as many fouls (10).

Attack-wise, Villa made the best use of limited opportunities: they had only five shots inside the box but scored two; Liverpool had 15 and scored one. Outside the box, Villa had six shots, scoring one; Liverpool had 12 and scored none. To ponder a thought: the notion of 'resting on the ball' seems paradoxical considering the amount of endeavour Rodgers' side implemented for such little return.

Pressing

"The players are becoming accustomed to how I want them to play, to pressing as a team." – Sunday Times, 3.3.2013

Brendan Rodgers was speaking after the comprehensive 4-0 victory over Wigan; it sounds like progress. Only recently, on this site we debated the absence of the pressing game. Rodgers' words may have answered those concerns; a wave of optimism may ensue and the problem may be considered fixed. However, uncertainty is where perspective lies.

Should it have taken this long to implement? Pressing is not the most difficult component of Rodgers' system to rehearse and learn. Notice I said *most difficult*; not that it is easy but, comparatively speaking, in relation to other aspects of the system – playing out from the back, for example – it is less of a task. A couple of months should suffice to adopt the technique of closing down the space in which your opponents are operating.

Neither are we talking about a new concept here; it has been achieved to great effect with players of lesser ability than those in the current Liverpool squad. Jonathan Wilson reminds us that the introduction of pressing – into the game – actually, has fairly uncertain origins. Allegedly it may have come from some Eastern European team, possibly Maslov's Dynamo Kyiv, later given prominence by Zubeldia and the notorious Estudiantes. Wilson, by contrast, is able to be more precise about who introduced the tactic into the English game; and it comes from a surprising source. No disrespect to Graham Taylor and his Watford, but it does seem incongruous that a team famous for long ball tactics nonetheless manifested innovation in a different aspect of the English game. One that prevails three decades later, encoded in the Brendan Rodgers philosophy.

But there are caveats. Pressing, we know, requires high levels of fitness; levels that can be unsustainable even for athletes, especially with the incidence of inclement weather. When unusually hot or cold environments apply, the task becomes more challenging on the human body, including those in peak physical condition. Even without those scenarios, the efficacy can be reduced the further into a game you progress; fatigue increases with the passing of time. Particularly if you are contesting a cup game that has gone into extra time, you must acknowledge the need to improvise and change tactics. Wilson, more significantly, highlights Taylor's concession when Watford's meteorite success was buttressed on the European stage:

"It's all very well until you come up against a team good enough technically to be able to keep possession even when under pressure."

Mutual Weaponry

That quote is pertinent whenever Liverpool do embark on European campaigns. But it also has a domestic relevance if we consider the Reds' current season in the Premier League. Liverpool do not possess a monopoly on pressing, and when other teams have employed it against Rodgers' side, they have floundered. The Reds' susceptibility to playing out from the back raises the question that the aforementioned quote begs: are Liverpool's players technically gifted enough to retain possession when the space around them is closed?

Rodgers' own statement of teams 'winning 79% of games if they are better on the ball' continues to haunt me; you can never find the evidence base of how he arrived at this statistic. For me, however, it is revealingly suggestive of more than just keeping possession; is it about having the 'better' players who have the confidence and ability to pull it off – particularly when playing at the back?

Early in the season, Manchester City forced an error from Škrtel who – strangely in the left back position at the half way line – was closed down. He was not comfortable, or else he would not have been panicked into a kamikaze pass back to goal that Tevez seized upon. Škrtel had not even looked up to check the terrain; if he had done so then he surely would have seen the danger. The problem for him, as for other Liverpool players, is they need to keep an eye on the ball at their feet. Barcelona players have been trained to look up and be aware of what is going on around them; such is their confidence on the ball they do not need to keep a focus on it; try and steal it and, matador-like, they can pull away at the crucial moment as the opponent kicks the air.

Similarly, but on the opposite side of the pitch, Aston Villa had pressed Joe Cole on the half way line. The latter had been in receipt of a rather bad forward pass despatched by Joe Allen. Cole has his back to the two Villa players bearing down upon him; Benteke is in front of him. The player supposedly 'better than Messi' (according to Steven Gerrard in 2010) is caught in a triangle – focused on taming the erratic ball – from which he cannot escape. He is dispossessed with consummate ease and Liverpool are caught – not for the only time this season – in a swift counter attack.

The ability to deal with pressing teams shows no signs of even gradual improvement; in fact, the Southampton defeat reveals the problem persisting into this season's last ten game finale. Mauricio Pochettino seemed gloatingly intent on confirming that this was a conscious tactic:

"We made Liverpool really uncomfortable by pressing them high up the pitch." – *Sunday Times* 17.3.2013.

Pochettino, we should recall, has been in charge of his team for far less a time than Rodgers. And neither has he had the same quality of players at his disposal.

Not Being Barcelona?

Here is the rub; I do not think Liverpool are playing like Barcelona. Or certainly, there is no sign of the patient build-ups denoted by intricate passing – with the skill and flair entailed to be able to achieve that standard on a consistent basis. At times the Reds seem far more direct than patient. This led me to a question premised on uncertainty: is Rodgers actually trying to imprint the Barca method? If so, are the players falling short of the required standard? Are the players performing in the only way that they can? Does this frustrate Rodgers?

My own admiration for the Barcelona philosophy is tinged with caution when wondering whether the system is imitable and transferable to other teams. We see Barcelona's success but we do not see the infinitesimal evolution of that success; a success that originated from the painstaking selection of boys whose playing style seemed predisposed to the system already in mind. And that those boys then rehearsed, endlessly, the recurring drills of rotundas, one touch, half-touch passing – from pre-pubescence until adulthood. By this time they had not only acquired the art, but had also gelled as a group whereby mutual bonding, empathy and understanding meant that they became a team in every sense of the word.

"Could the Barca model be exported by hiring exceptional coaches from within its system and handling them control of youth development at a club?"

This is not my own question but one that was asked in *Barca: The Making of the Greatest Team in the World* by Graham Hunter. The answer is more compelling because of the person who provides it; and, here, I must defer to a greater football mind. Rodolfo Borrell replies:

"No, that would be a serious mistake. Every country has its own football culture and you shouldn't try to alter their basic footballing essence. All you can do is work out how to complement what they do already with some new ideas."

Borrell goes on to say that he tries to incorporate some of the principles that made Barcelona what they are; and ensures that all the teams, at all age levels, learn the same basic playing philosophy. But, ultimately, it is not a lock, stock and barrel replication of the Barcelona model; I often wonder whether Brendan Rodgers is on the exact same page. I really do not know; uncertainty reigns.

Signs of Progress?

There have been many statistical signs of progress during Rodgers' tenure; I have read most of them but have neglected to quote any of them here. Not to be unfair to Rodgers but only because they are snapshots of what has occurred in the past. They cannot predict the future; so this remains uncertain. We have been here many times before; and, in fact, only quite recently.

Goal Differences:

From Jan 22nd 2011 to the end of 2011/12:

Liverpool +19 / Chelsea +17 / Man United +17 / Man City +9 / Everton +8 / Arsenal +6 / Spurs +3.

Points Per Game:

Chelsea 2.06 / Man United 2.06 / Liverpool 2.00 / Everton 1.75 / Man City 1.73 / Arsenal 1.56 / Spurs 1.56.

John Henry tweeted both of the above on July 6th 2011; and he does not tweet often. So clearly, he was enthused about the evidence emerging so soon after Kenny Dalglish's second tenure began. Henry prefaced the tweets with the word 'interesting'. I found them damned interesting too. In fact, those statistics were as powerful a sign of progress, if not better, than any I have seen used to confirm that of Rodgers. You could easily be seduced into thinking that a top four finish beckons, and even a serious challenge for the title. As a portent of the future, however, the statistics were useless … no one predicted what happened next.

"I always avoid prophesying beforehand, because it is a much better policy to prophesy after the event has already taken place." – Winston Churchill

BETTER WITH THE BALL? IT'S JUST A SHOT AWAY

By Andrew Beasley

March, 2013

Statistics are correct up to 29 March 2013, and were sourced from EPL Index.

I recently read a couple of very interesting statistics with regards to the bearing that having more shots on target (SoT) than your opponent has upon winning football matches. On 24th February, *The Guardian* advised us:

"Of the 181 games won in the Premier League before last weekend, the team who had the most possession only won 103 – 57% in total. The team who had more shots on target than their opponents won 128 matches – 71% of the total."

Then this article by Benjamin Pugsley on the blog *Bitter and Blue*, which used a larger sample of 987 matches, chipped in with:

"Winning the SoT battle in non-drawn games, results in a team winning that fixture 71.73% of the time and losing the fixture 19.35% of the time."

It seems pretty conclusive; have more shots on target than your opponent, and you'll win around 71% of the time (when excluding drawn matches). This isn't in itself that surprising, but it's valuable to be able to quantify it from a performance monitoring point of view all the same.

But a thought occurred to me; you could win the SoT battle by anything from one (in a close game performance-wise) to potentially any number (and for the record, Liverpool's best figure since August 2008 has been twelve – on two occasions). Surely accounting for this differential might provide an even better guide than simply who had more shots on target?

I therefore decided to look at 'TSoT%' (total shots on target percentage), which is the proportion of the shots on target that a team has in a match. As a simple example, if one side has six shots on target and the other four, then the former has a TSoT% of 60%, and the latter 40%. The following graph shows Liverpool's points-per-game and win percentages for ten percent slices of TSoT%, since the start of the 2008/09 season:

Liverpool FC Performance by TSoT% Since August 2008

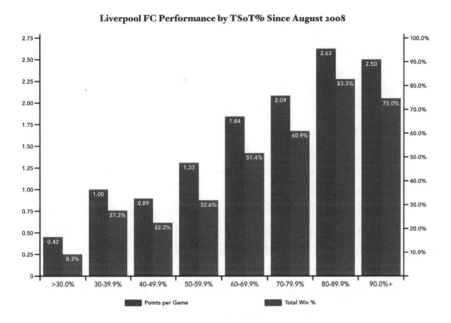

It may seem surprising that Liverpool have taken a lower proportion of the points and wins with 90% or more of the SoT than they have with 80-89.9%, but there is a much smaller sample (of eight games compared to thirty) for the highest section, so unlikely match results obviously have a bigger bearing on the average. The Reds have had four matches in this period where the opposition didn't have a single shot on target; they all came during 2008/09, and sadly two of them were (title costing?) 0-0 draws with Stoke City. In fact, adding 2011/12's 1-0 defeat at the Britannia Stadium to the aforementioned games makes a total of five points that the Potters have taken off Liverpool from three matches for a sum total of one shot on target, and that was a penalty. Typical!

The key thing to note with regards to the TSoT% data is that Liverpool have won just eight (19.5%) of the 41 matches where they had less than half of the shots on target. This has occurred twice in 2012/13; 3-2 wins against West Ham and Tottenham Hotspur. It's fair to say that the Reds were perhaps lucky to triumph in those matches on the balance of play, and the SoT figures back this notion up. As twenty-five of those forty-one matches were lost, Liverpool average just 0.78 points-per-game when they have less than 50% of the shots on target. At the opposite end of the scale, the Reds average 2.04 points across the 116 matches when they've had a TSoT% of more than 50%. Only 16.4% (nineteen) of those games were lost (including unlucky defeats against Manchester United this season, and Tottenham in 2008/09, for instance), illustrating again the value of out-shooting your opponents. The idea of being better in front of goal rang a bell with me in terms of a now famous quote Brendan Rodgers offered up at his fan site briefing in September 2012:

"I've always enjoyed and worked with the statistic that if you can dominate the game, with the ball, you have a 79% chance of winning a game of football. If you're better than the other team, with the ball, you've got an eight out of ten chance of winning the game."

Based on the question asked, it would appear that Rodgers was talking in terms of possession, yet *The Guardian*'s aforementioned research suggests his figure of 79% is a long way from the truth if so.

The interesting thing here is that of the 122 Liverpool league matches since August 2008 that haven't been drawn, and where one side has had more shots on target than the other, 78% have been won by the side who had the larger SoT figure.

Is this what should be meant by being better with the ball? It may likely be a coincidence, but Rodgers seems to have been close to the truth with his quote, though perhaps not in the way he actually intended.

Having seen the impact that TSoT% has on individual matches (for Liverpool at least), my next aim was to see how season long TSoT% performance corresponds to league performance. The graph below shows TSoT% against Premier League points for the period 2008/09 to 2011/12, and as you would expect, it displays a strong correlation:

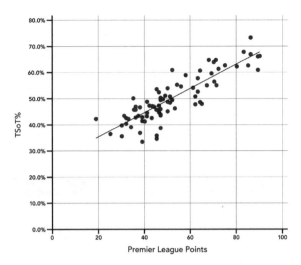

No prizes for guessing which dot represents Liverpool's 2011/12 campaign; one of the furthest from the line, where 52 points and 61% meet. In the past four years, the TSoT% of 61.1% posted by Liverpool last season is the highest by a team outside the top four, and better than three teams who have finished in a Champions League position. Had the Reds scored and conceded at a rate close to the line on the above graph, then they'd have bagged over seventy points, and a place at Europe's top club table. Instead, Kenny Dalglish's men scored with just 22.7% of their shots on target, which is the sixth-worst conversion proportion of the eighty teams in this study. Even matching the average conversion rate of 29.6% would've lead to fourteen more goals, which would have increased their goalscoring output by 30%. I have also plotted the average TSoT% for each league position over the last four seasons, to try to establish some benchmarks for future use:

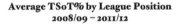

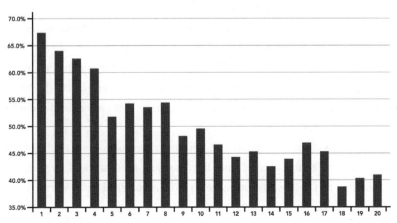

We can see that it broadly breaks down into four bands:

- 60%-plus should lead to a team being in the running for a top four finish;
- 50 – 55% puts a team in contention for a Europa League place;
- Comfortably above 40% should see a team stay up;
- Around 40% is relegation form.

Breaking it down into 5% chunks can also give an indication of the kind of points tally a team is likely to post depending on their TSoT% figure:

TSoT% Range	Number of Teams	Average Points
65.0+	7	81.9
60.0-64.9	8	73.4
55.0-59.9	7	64.6
50.0-54.9	11	51.4
45.0-49.9	22	47.3
40.0-44.9	16	37.7
< 40.0	9	37.0

But what does all this mean for Brendan Rodgers' Liverpool side? With a TSoT% of 58.8% so far this season (as of March 2013), they are not too far away from hitting the top four average of 60.7%, and they have also been floating around that figure at times during this campaign (with a high point of 61.8% after the 5-0 demolition of Swansea City), which is encouraging for the future.

Conceding just ten fewer shots on target this season would've put the Reds at 60.7%, and it's clear for all to see that whilst their attacking prowess has been admirable, Liverpool's defensive frailties have stopped them from kicking on into contention for Champions League football this season.

Obviously there is more to being a successful side than TSoT%, as spectacular under- or over-performance at either end of the pitch can make a massive difference; I've already demonstrated how the Liverpool side of 2011/12 under-achieved, but the opposite is true of the Manchester United side of 2012/13.

With a TSoT% of 58.5%, they should really be in the mix for fourth place at best, yet by converting 41.1% of their shots on target (which is 2.2% better than the best figure posted by *any* team in the last four complete seasons), this has enabled them to walk away comfortably with the league title.

It's also not as if other stats are not still important of course, as they indirectly contribute to TSoT%; the likes of final third passing accuracy and clear-cut chance creation are key up front, whilst defensive errors and blocked shots will play a part at the back of the field.

But if you want one simple indication of who deserved to win a match or which team should finish where in the league, this seems a very good place to start indeed.

THE SUÁREZ DECISION: LIVERPOOL FC GROUNDS FOR APPEAL

By Daniel Geey

January, 2012

Background and Introduction

The aim of this article is to put myself in the position of the Liverpool FC lawyers and to dissect a number of the Independent Regulatory Commission's Report (IRCR) conclusions, had the club decided to appeal to the FA Appeals Board. Although no appeal is to be pursued it may be helpful to disentangle a number of evidential issues that arose throughout the judgment and that have been commented on in the press in the last week or so.

This is not intended to be a comprehensive description of what the IRCR said. In fact, only the most significant evidential, credibility and consistency aspects of the decision are discussed. It means there will certainly be aspects of the decision that are not touched upon, in part because the judgment is 115 pages long and in part because it is important to get across the most salient and relevant points that Liverpool may have relied upon. The aim is not to go into every detailed issue but predominantly to pick out a number of key points or omissions in the IRCR and highlight their importance.

The structure of this piece is to (1) briefly set out the basic claims of Patrice Evra and Luis Suárez, (2) describe the legal tests that were used, (3) assess the key IRCR reasoning and conclusions, (4) assess a particularly key IRCR omission, (5) highlight corroborating evidential issues, (6) discuss the inconsistencies the IRCR find with Suárez's account, and (7) briefly discuss the procedural grounds of any appeal.

Points to note:

All that follows is based on the public IRCR document and not on the entire body of witness evidence before the Commission. All that is stated below is premised on the precise facts as set out and relied upon in the IRCR.

The assessment does quote the exact phrases used by the IRCR and as such may not be suitable for anyone who is easily offended by the use of abusive language.

In the absence of direct corroborating evidence to back up Evra's claim, unfortunately no one, including the Commission, could conclude that Suárez "definitely" said the things Evra claimed. As such, the Commission believed Suárez "probably" said them. This assessment is to do with the process of how the IRCR came to its conclusion.

The length of this article makes it appropriate to set out an executive summary.

Executive Summary

I believe LFC would have focused on:

• The fact that Evra only made reference to the precise number of times he claimed Suárez called him a negro four days after the event, and did not appear to tell anyone that the abuse happened more than once, points to a basic inconsistency in Evra's account. As such, Evra's story changes when interviewed by Canal+ and in the FA interviews. I think Liverpool would question why he did not make any reference to the multiple abuses he subsequently claimed up until that point. This points to numerous inconsistencies in Evra's account of what happened which goes directly towards his credibility as a witness as well as the underlying substantive nature of his claims;

• A complete lack of any direct evidence corroborating Evra's claims that he was abused more than the one time that Suárez admits to;

• The inconsistencies in Suárez's account of events not being as serious, substantive and detrimental to his credibility specifically in relation to differences in the accounts between Dirk Kuyt and Damien Comolli; and

• New evidence that could have been submitted to the Appeals Board to strengthen Suárez's credibility by clarifying inconsistencies relied upon by the Commission.

Standard and Burden of Proof

This is set out in detail in paragraph 31 where the Commission sets out "on the balance of probabilities, is the account of Mr Evra true and reliable?" and paragraph 74 onwards [1]. In effect, the Commission were asking "whose account was more probable" (paragraph 345).

[1] Burden of proof: *"It is not for Mr Suárez to satisfy the Commission that he did not breach the Rules. Rather, it is for the FA to satisfy us to the required standard that Mr Suárez did breach the Rules."* Standard of proof: *The applicable standard of proof shall be the flexible civil standard of the balance of probability. The more serious the allegation, taking into account the nature of the Misconduct alleged and the context of the case, the greater the burden of evidence required to prove the matter."*

The Basics and Contested Statements

Suárez admitted in his witness statement that in response to Evra saying in Spanish "Don't touch me South American", he (Suárez) replied with the phrase "Por que, negro?" (translated as "why, black?"). Suárez explained that the term negro was not intended to be offensive or racially offensive but in fact conciliatory. This is the only time Suárez states that he uses the word "negro". Evra claims that Suárez used the word seven times in total (six additional times to that which Suárez admits to saying). Paragraph 388 sets out what the IRCR believes probably occurred:

"(1) In response to Mr Evra's question "Concha de tu hermana, porque me diste in golpe" ("Fucking hell, why did you kick me"), Mr Suárez said "Porque tu eres negro" ("Because you are black").

(2) In response to Mr Evra's comment "Habla otra vez asi, te voy a dar una porrada" ("say it to me again, I'm going to punch you"), Mr Suárez said "No hablo con los negros" ("I don't speak to blacks").

(3) In response to Mr Evra's comment "Ahora te voy a dar realmente una porrada" ("okay, now I think I'm going to punch you"), Mr Suárez said "Dale, negro, negro, negro" ("okay, blackie, blackie, blackie).

(4) When the referee blew his whistle to stop the corner being taken, Mr Suárez used the word "negro" to Mr Evra.

(5) After the referee had spoken to the players for a second time, and Mr Evra had said that he did not want Mr Suárez to touch him, Mr Suárez said "Por que, negro?"

The disparity between both accounts is stark. Suárez only admits to saying point 5 [with negro meaning 'black', not as in 'a negro'] whilst Evra claims to have been racially abused six additional times. The rest of this assessment will establish how the IRCR concluded that based on the balance of probabilities test there was sufficient evidence to back Evra's account of the events in part because of the inconsistencies in Suárez's witness statement.

Evra's post-match account inconsistency

I believe Liverpool would point to one overarching inconsistency that the IRCR completely failed to consider. Each step in the process needs to be discussed as it relates to the number of times Evra says Suárez called him a negro. As will be discussed below, Evra does not mention the fact that he was called a negro multiple times. At least nine people appear to confirm in witness statements that this is the case before he says to Canal+ that he was called negro more than 10 times. I believe LFC would argue as a general point before looking into the specific factors below that it would appear strange for Evra (who had purportedly been racially abused seven times) not to tell anyone it happened more than once until a press microphone appeared. Even then, he did not mention the specific instances of the claimed abuse and was inconsistent in the number of times the abuse occurred. It means that the first time Evra claimed and set out that he was abused multiple times by Suárez was at the earliest on the 20th of

October in his first FA interview. Precisely four days after the match.

The circumstances begin when Evra states in paragraph 103 that "ref, he just called me a fucking black" (singular). The referee could not however corroborate that Evra said this. However, assuming he did, Evra only makes reference to Suárez "calling him a black" once. If this is a 'one-off' phrase because all the other accounts in relation to the abuse make reference to multiple abuse references, then Evra's contention that there were multiple references to the word "negro" ought to be called into question. The point however is that, this account appears completely consistent with what all other Manchester United and referee/fourth official witness statements appear to say in the IRCR.

Next Evra tells Ryan Giggs that he has been called black (with again no reference to the number of times this occurred). Giggs in paragraph 114 recounts that Evra said Suárez called him black (singular) and is silent about the number of times said. This suggests Evra did not tell him the number of times.

After coming into the dressing room at the end of the game Evra spoke to a number of United players. Antonio Valencia, Javier Hernandez, Nani and Anderson all provided witness statements and their evidence was accepted in full by Liverpool. All four players make similar claims that Suárez "would not talk to [Evra] because he was black". There is no mention in any of the witness statements (as set out in the IRCR) of the number of times or the other types of context where Suárez allegedly abused Evra. In paragraph 125 of the IRCR Evra goes on to say that he also told other players that Suárez had said "I won't talk to you because you are black" (single reference).

The IRCR raises no issues throughout their analysis about why Evra, after being called a negro numerous times, makes no reference of the fact to Giggs, his four team-mates and the wider team in the dressing room.

Evra then tells Alex Ferguson in the dressing room that "Suárez called me a nigger" (single reference). Ferguson in his witness statement told the referee that "Evra has been called a nigger by one of the Liverpool players". In paragraph 277 the IRCR noted that Ferguson:

"...did not recall having said specifically that it was five times and thinks it unlikely he would have done so. Mr Evra did not mention... any specific number that he told Sir Alex at the time."

Paragraph 130 clarifies that "Evra told the referee that Suárez called him a nigger" and paragraph 131 sets out in the referees witness statement that "Suárez had said to Evra "I don't talk to you because you niggers").

There remains no reference to Suárez calling Evra a negro more than once. The referee's report sets out in paragraph 153 that when Mr Mariner (the referee) and the fourth official were discussing the issue with Evra and Ferguson, Evra stated Suárez said "I don't talk to you because you niggers" (single reference). Next Evra is interviewed on Canal+, which reveals a fundamental inconsistency that adversely affects Evra's credibility generally. This is because he considers it appropriate to state something that according to the witness statement evidence, as set out in the IRCR, he has not stated to anyone else.

He claimed he was abused by Suárez more than once. I believe Liverpool would be puzzled as to why he uses this opportunity to accuse Suárez of multiple abuses when he has had ample opportunity to voice his concerns to a whole raft of people, with it fresher in his mind, but did not. I believe Liverpool would also challenge the "10+ times" inconsistency that was given three sentences worth of assessment (paragraph 281) by the IRCR. Specifically, the IRCR states that Comolli agreed with Evra's contention that Suárez racially abusing more than ten times was a French 'figure of speech' when actually Comolli did not believe that was the case (paragraph 160).

I consider Liverpool would argue strongly against the IRCR's belief that "there is nothing in the Canal+ interview which materially undermines Evra's evidence". Based on the above, I believe Liverpool would argue that Evra's account to Canal+ is inconsistent because it is inconsistent with what he has said (or rather not said) prior to giving the media interview. If he has been abused numerous times, he certainly needs to be more precise than 10+. Liverpool would also point out that the Commission came to the wrong conclusion that Comolli supported Evra's "common figure of speech" explanation. The only inconsistency in this chronology comes from Ray Haughan, the Liverpool administration manager who states that he heard Ferguson say "Suárez has called him… a nigger five times" (paragraph 135). However, the witness statements of Evra, Ferguson, the referee and fourth official do not appear to mention the number of times of any claim. Ferguson explicitly states in paragraph 277 of the IRCR that he does not believe he mentioned the five times point. As such, a panel would on the balance of probabilities probably infer that such a comment was less likely to have occurred because of witness statements of the accusers who do not appear to mention this fact (as set out in the IRCR). This point would then rule out the corroboration conclusion used the IRCR at the end of paragraph 382.

Summary

Evra claims to speak to the referee on the pitch, to Giggs on the pitch, to Valencia, Hernandez, Nani and Anderson in the changing room, to other United players and Ferguson in the changing room, to the referee and the fourth official in the referee's room and at no time does he mention the crucial fact that he was abused more than once. He is actually consistent throughout in his single claim that Suárez said he would not talk to him because he was black.

I believe Liverpool would argue that all of the above is not just one inconsistency. Each time Evra does not make a reference to the number of times the word 'negro' was used undermines his later evidence. This makes his subsequent FA witness statements at odds with his statements at the precise time of the events. This is in fact highlighted in the IRCR when it states in paragraph 288 that at least in relation to the referee's report:

"The referee's report was made on the day of the match. It should, therefore, be given some weight as a contemporaneous record of what people were told had happened soon after the incident, rather than what they recalled at some later date."

The Commission ignores its own directions to use the referee's report as the basis for the number of times Evra said Suárez abused him. I believe Liverpool would argue that this would cast serious doubts as to the substantive nature of Evra's claims and the consistency of Evra's post-match explanations, and as such should lead to the conclusion that material inconsistencies appear in his account which severely damages his credibility.

Corroboration

As a general point, I believe Liverpool would stress, as they have done in their public statements, that Evra's claims are not backed up with any direct corroborating evidence bar Suárez's admission of using the word *negro* once.

The IRCR stresses in paragraphs 214 onwards, for example, that "this is not simply one person's word against another" and that other evidence such as video footage, the evidence of others on the day and afterwards, documentation from the referee and the transcripts of interviews were all used. The Liverpool lawyer however stressed that the:

"...case turns very substantially on the evidence of the two main protagonists, that we should think very carefully before reaching a conclusion based solely on the word of the main protagonist for the FA, and that we should look at the other evidence, and see whether there is other evidence that corroborates Mr Evra's story."

I think that Liverpool would argue that the IRCR does not provide any direct corroborating evidence to back up Evra's claims. Indeed, the IRCR states that in the absence of being able to identify such corroborating evidence they "asked [themselves] which account was more probable". Based on the above arguments set out, I believe Liverpool's aim would have been for the Appeal Board to significantly downgrade Evra's credibility to demonstrate that his account was less probable.

Suárez Inconsistencies

If Liverpool had appealed the judgment, among other aspects of the IRCR, the club would have probably focused on at least three main grounds (there are of course others but these appear to be the most significant) that the IRCR used to discredit Suárez's statements. The Commission believed that Suárez's account of the incident was "flawed" and "profoundly undermined" the credibility of his evidence. Liverpool's aim would be to rebuild Suárez's credibility by attacking each one of the perceived Commission inconsistencies with the aim of showing that:

– *Less weight should be attached to the conclusions reached in the IRCR; and/or*

– *The conclusions reached by the Commission did not factor in, or at least discuss, other plausible alternatives.*

Suárez and Comolli/Kuyt inconsistent recollections: Kuyt and Comolli provided witness statements based on their interactions with Suárez. Comolli spoke with Suárez in the aftermath of the Evra complaint being made and was the second Liverpool representative after Kenny Dalglish to speak to the referee about what Suárez had said in Spanish to him. In paragraph 290, he said that Suárez had said "porque tu es negro" and not what Suárez had said in his witness statement i.e. "por que, negro". [2]

In Kuyt's witness statement, he explained how he spoke to Suárez in Dutch with the translation of their conversation recounting Suárez using the phrase "because you are black" (Paragraph 297). Both Kuyt and Comolli reference in their witness statements that something was 'lost in translation' in how the phrase was constructed. The question for the Commission to consider was whether this was a plausible explanation for two individuals who had spoken to Suárez about what was specifically said or whether this contradicted Suárez's account.

Countering any perceived inconsistency:

Comolli, whose mother tongue is French, spoke to Suárez in Spanish, which he then had to retell to the referee in English. He even admits in his witness statement that "he assumed [Suárez] would have used the words". Comolli may actually have been trying to make sense of Suárez's statement to the referee rather than quote exactly what was said. This therefore, if anything, should not demonstrate the inconsistency of Suárez's account but a problem with Comolli's interpretation of what was said.

It would be somewhat understandable if something got lost in the translation for Kuyt, having a conversation in Dutch with Suárez, about a specific and highly intricate Spanish phrase, and then trying to retell it in English through a witness statement; and that actually the IRCR ultimately backs Suárez account of the incident by setting out in paragraph 388 that "Mr Suárez said "Por que, negro?". They believed Suárez did use that phrase and not the one that Comolli and Kuyt originally believed was said.

I believe Liverpool would also highlight the fact that Suárez stayed consistent in what he claimed to have said to Evra, (por que, Negro?), yet because Kuyt and Comolli for differing reasons did not verify his precise Spanish phrase, this is held against

Suárez as demonstrating inconsistency. It would appear unfortunate that Spanish speaking players at Liverpool (Maxi, Lucas or Coates for example) were not asked to give witness statements to explain in Spanish what Suárez may have said to them. This could have given a more consistent and less likely to be 'lost in translation' approach. This is because the Spanish speaking players could have added additional precision to either back Suárez or give Kuyt and Comolli's account further strength [3].

[2] The difference being as explained in the IRCR that "If Mr Suárez had said "Porque tu es negro", then he would not be using "negro" as a noun to address Mr Evra, but as an adjective, meaning "Because you are black" paragraph 290.

[3] This is discussed in the last section about new evidence to provide to an Appeals Board.

Acting in a conciliatory manner (paragraphs 253 onwards):

For the one occasion that Suárez admitted to using the term "negro" he argued that it was said in a conciliatory context. The IRCR in paragraph 264 stated that "Suárez's attitude and actions were the very antithesis of conciliation and friendliness". The IRCR pointed to the video evidence demonstrating both players' hostility "before, at the moment of, and after" Suárez's admitted "negro" use. I believe Liverpool may have elaborated that:

Within the bounds of how arguments play out there can be, and are, conciliatory moments used by those arguing to defuse acrimonious exchanges. Liverpool may have claimed that the IRCR's perception that once an acrimonious exchange had begun, it remained acrimonious throughout is not so cut and dried. This would be of critical importance to Suárez and Liverpool because if this conciliatory approach was seen as more plausible, the context of Suárez using the word *negro* (based on the linguistic experts' opinion) could have been viewed as non-abusive. The IRCR not only dismissed Suárez's account of his conciliatory intention but used it to demonstrate that Suárez's evidence was inconsistent and "simply, not credible".

Pictures and body language (without actual audible words) would have been difficult to demonstrate continued, complete and total hostility throughout the exchange. Without audible conversation evidence in the TV evidence, alternative scenarios to simple continuous hostility should have been explored by the IRCR. Indeed no body language experts were brought in to examine how the two players acted throughout the exchange. Liverpool may have considered using such experts to cast doubt over the IRCR insistence that the actions of the two players were only that of continued acrimony.

Pinching (paragraphs 245 onwards):

Suárez stated in his witness statement that during the time of him pinching Evra, he was trying to defuse the situation.

Specifically:

"Evra did not back off and Dirk Kuyt was approaching us to stand between us. At this point I touched PE's left arm in a pinching type of movement. This all happened very quickly. I was trying to defuse the situation and was trying to intimate to Evra that he was not untouchable by reference to his question about the foul. Under no circumstances was this action intended to be offensive and most certainly not racially offensive. It was not in any way a reference to the colour of PE's skin."

Under cross examination Suárez accepted that pinching was probably not defusing the situation. The lawyer defending Suárez (Peter McCormick) put it down to "bad drafting" in the witness statement and furthermore admitted to the Commission in paragraph 250 that pinching was not the action of someone diffusing the situation. It appears Mr McCormick did not argue that it was not the actual pinch that Suárez's witness statement was making explicit reference to when saying he was trying to defuse the situation with Evra. The IRCR inferred that this was a material inconsistency (in saying one thing but doing another) on the part of Suárez.

I think Liverpool may have argued in any subsequent appeal that:

Although the pinch may or may not be seen to rile or aggravate further, Suárez's statement that he was trying to defuse the situation was more general in nature and was not in specific relation to the pinch; and/or

That the IRCR should not have inferred from his remark that this was anything close to a material inconsistency (albeit poor drafting on the part of the lawyer), when a number of apparent Evra inconsistencies are not addressed in any detail (e.g. Canal+ ten times issue above and Evra's use of the word "nigger" being changed to "black"). Inconsistency Summary: The reason these three issues are discussed in detail above is because the Commission uses these and other perceived inconsistencies to discredit Suárez's account of what happened [4].

Specifically, they make robust assessments that:

"We find it remarkable that [Suárez] sought to advance a case that was so clearly inconsistent with any sensible appreciation of what happened" and "Mr Suárez's evidence on these topics, which was shown to be flawed, profoundly undermined our confidence in the reliability of his evidence" (both in paragraph 357).

The way that the above inconsistencies can be countered by alternative arguments (with admittedly, varying degrees of strength) demonstrates that I believe Liverpool would have very strongly argued that such inconsistencies and conclusions were vastly overplayed by the IRCR in order to discredit Suárez and as a result favour Evra's account.[4]

There is one other relevant inconsistency issue relating to Suárez changing his account as to when he used the phrase *negro*, based on the video evidence he saw after he first made his FA interview statement. In the light of reports that Evra had up to three opportunities to see the video with the FA prior to making his statement, if true, should not therefore be used against Suárez as the basis for further IRCR conclusions of inconsistency.

Appeal Process

Whilst it has been reported that Suárez can only appeal against the level of the sanction and not the actual verdict [5], my initial reading of the FA Appeals Board Regulations is somewhat different [6]. Although the grounds for appeal may be deemed somewhat restrictive [7], regulation 3.3 states that among other things "The Appeal Board shall have power to: (1) allow or dismiss the appeal". This would suggest that the Appeal Board could find in favour of an Liverpool appeal, thus rejecting the IRCR findings. Additionally, the regulations allow in exceptional circumstances for new information to be submitted.

Such information could have included:

– New language expert reports questioning the accuracy of Evra's Spanish language claims [8] and body language experts to counter the continued hostility conclusion reached by the Commission;

– Evidence about Evra's past credibility as a witness (which was not used by LFC's lawyers as set out in paragraph 212);

– Witness statements of Maxi, Lucas or Coates as Spanish speaking players testifying about the exact phrase used by Suárez (if he spoke to them about it) to back up his version of what he admitted to saying and to reduce the Kuyt/Comolli IRCR inconsistency finding.

[4] There is one other relevant inconsistency issue relating to Suárez changing his account as to when he used the phrase negro, based on the video evidence he saw after he first made his FA interview statement. In the light of reports that Evra had up to three opportunities to see the video with the FA prior to making his statement, if true, should not therefore be used against Suárez as the basis for further IRCR conclusions of inconsistency.

[5] (see the document starting on page 425 "In the case of an appeal from a decision of a Regulatory Commission"

http://www.thefa.com/thefa/~/media/Files/PDF/TheFA/FA%20Handbook%202010-11/ FAHandbook-update-1011. Ashx/FAHandbook-update-1011.pdf

[6] See regulation1.1.4-1.5 "The grounds of appeal, available to Participants and The Association, shall be that the body whose decision is appealed against: (1) misinterpreted or failed to comply with the rules or regulations relevant to its decision; and/or (2) came to a decision to which no reasonable such body could have come. 1.5 In addition: (1) Participants only, may appeal on the grounds that the penalty, award, order or sanction imposed is excessive;"

[7] http://www.thisisanfield.cm/2012/01/professor-in-hispanic-studies-dissects-the-fas-Suárez-report/

Opinion, Speculation and Conclusion

LFC took under four days to consider a 115 page document and decide not to appeal. This suggests that not appealing was either a 'policy decision' taken from the top (in apparent conflict with the club's previous vehement statements to the contrary) or tactical. It is a long shot to suggest, however, that Liverpool may not quite have exhausted their appeal grounds. This all depends on whether an appeal to the Court of Arbitration for Sport (CAS) is still a possibility. The rationale being that Liverpool may take the ban (only four of the games being in the Premier League) but would argue to CAS (perhaps on the grounds of a lack of independence through the FA choosing the panel) that the evidence used in the IRCR needs to be considered afresh in order to partly or completely exonerate Suárez. It would appear however that this is unlikely to happen because:

There are explicit prohibitions against going to CAS in relation to regulatory commission procedures (3.2. of the FA Disciplinary Procedures Appeals);

The CAS code states that the club should have exhausted all internal remedies (i.e. to go to the FA Appeals Board first) which it appears they have not; and

This would embroil the club in an additional regulatory action (something they were presumably keen to avoid when they came to the initial decision not to appeal).

Regardless of whether this may happen or not, the above assessment illustrates potential examples of where Liverpool may have argued against aspects of the IRCR. Although this now appears impossible, the analysis may be useful in demonstrating why Evra's evidence was perhaps not as watertight as previously thought and that Suárez's lack of credibility as a witness may have been overplayed.

Thanks to Hal Cohen and my father David for checking the substantive points (though responsibility for all the assessments made above are mine).

THE BENÍTEZ MYTHS

By Paul Tomkins

October, 2009

First of all, let me say that anything in life has its good and its bad sides. Nothing, and no-one, is perfect. Football is not exempt. Every good player will have bad games, and every system a manager deploys will work sometimes and fail at others. Football relies on skill, and judgement, but also luck, run of the ball, force majeure, and the many facets of cause and effect.

A player making a great overlapping run is instantly a fool if the ball to him is cut out. A striker can miss with a technically brilliant effort but score with his arse. A goalkeeper can make 15 brilliant saves but be written off upon his first slip up.

For anyone who paints my viewpoint as one in which Benítez can do no wrong, let me make it clear that this is rubbish.

However, he deserves to be judged by the same standards as other managers and that clearly isn't the case with the British media, who seem to distrust his standoffishness (he's not their mate), his foreignness (he doesn't do things in the traditional way) and his intelligence (he uses technology, stats, etc).

Personally, I don't feel that the media is biased against Liverpool; big clubs are big news when they're doing well, and even bigger news when they're not.

But I do think that many of its more vociferous members are biased against Benítez. Andy Gray seems obsessed with questioning every Benítez method that he sees as failing, without praising the ones that work. Gray loves players like Gerrard and Carragher, but seems set against Benítez.

Henry Winter, who has written guest pieces for the official Liverpool site, recently said that "Unlike Sir Alex Ferguson, Arsène Wenger, Mark Hughes, Martin O'Neill, Harry Redknapp, Carlo Ancelotti and David Moyes, Benítez is an incredibly difficult person to warm to. Too detached, too cold."

I found that stunning, but it did explain why journalists are rarely in a hurry to give him the benefit of the doubt.

Brian Reade, noted Liverpool fan, columnist and author, believes that there was an agenda against Benítez from the start. His face didn't fit.

So I've compiled a list of what I see as the myths used to malign the manager, and given my explanations as to why they are untrue.

Myth: Benítez rotates too much.

Truth: In 2008/09, Benítez rotated quite a bit less, on average, than Alex Ferguson: 115

changes compared with 141. The same applies as a whole between 2006 and 2009: 364 by Benítez to 376 by Ferguson.

Myth: Ah, but Benítez rotates his key players too much; United keep a settled core.

Truth: Again, the facts don't bear this out. Benítez has a core of players – Reina, Carragher and Gerrard – who start pretty much every league match when fit, and several others, including Kuyt and Johnson (Arbeloa before him), who are not far behind. Torres is also entering this category.

Myth: Ah, but Benítez rotates too much given that his squad isn't as strong as United's.

Truth: This season Liverpool are being accused of having a weaker squad (although admittedly when several big names have been injured), but then so too are Manchester United, having lost Ronaldo and Tevez. However, Ferguson has made six and seven changes respectively in games United lost away and drew at home. By comparison, Liverpool's team sheet has been more consistent.

Myth: Rotation simply doesn't work.

Truth: Rotation *does* work. United have won the league by making the most changes. However, simply making changes means nothing in itself (drop your striker for the tea lady?), and there are thousands of factors that go into any single result. Sometimes fresh legs and a desire to impress means more can be gained from squad players than from tired stars, while sometimes a changed side will look disjointed and miss its main match-winners. In these cases, wisdom is easy after the event.

What is true, however, is that most players cannot play every minute of every game, and if they do, they cannot maintain their highest standards throughout. Any sports scientist working within the game will tell you as much.

The top-six team that rotated the least last season was Aston Villa; also known as the team which collapsed like Mary Decker in the run-in.

Myth: Liverpool are a two-man team, relying on Torres and Gerrard all the time.

Truth: No-one was saying that Xabi Alonso would not be missed when he left this summer, yet Liverpool were still a "two-man team" last season, when it suited pundits (even though those particular two men, Torres and Gerrard, only played 14 games together, and Liverpool had their best season in two decades).

Why is the league's best keeper, Pepe Reina (a Benítez signing) not considered worthy of addition to this "two-man" team? Why is the league's best defensive midfielder, Javier Mascherano (a Benítez signing), not considered worthy of addition? Why is Jamie Carragher, who so often has been heralded as someone Liverpool would be lost without, not considered worthy? (When just a couple of years ago, the two man team was him and Gerrard.)

Why is Dirk Kuyt (a Benítez signing), who scored 15 goals mostly from midfield last season, and who created countless others and worked like a dervish, excluded? Why is Yossi Benayoun (a Benítez signing), who was arguably the best player in England in the final months of last season, likewise overlooked? Why is Glen Johnson (a Benítez signing), who has already scored two and created several other goals, another exclusion? And for me, a fully fit Daniel Agger (a Benítez signing) is as good as anyone in the world in his position, and certainly worthy of addition to this "two-man" team. (Also, Škrtel is a top-class defender, when he hasn't got a broken jaw.)

All last season, the general consensus was that Liverpool had a title-winning spine, but not quite enough in wide areas. While Alonso has left, the other six spine members are still present, with Johnson added to the wings (albeit from full-back). Yes, Torres and Gerrard *are* the best two players, but take the best two players out of any top side and of course they will lose something. It shouldn't take an IQ of above 50 to realise this. (Unfortunately, some ex-footballers fall below that mark.)

Myth: Zonal marking doesn't work.

Truth: Liverpool have finished top of the set-piece defending league under Benítez (2005/06) using zonal marking, and did very well again a season later.

The truth is that Liverpool are on average now over two inches shorter than in the days of Sissoko, Crouch, Hyypia, Traore, et al, and therefore will always be more susceptible to a good delivery into the box. Insúa is a far better player than Traore, but the latter was about eight inches taller. Riise was 6ft and good in the air defensively, but his form fell away in his final season. Insúa is a better *footballer*, but the inclusion of such players will always come with a slight downside.

Experts who have used both methods (such as Gordon Strachan) can attest to the particular pros and cons of zonal and man-marking; neither is perfect, but you use what suits you. Such people agree that players "get a run" to attack the ball no matter which system is used. After all, has a man never lost his marker to win a free header?

It doesn't help that penalties are being included in figures damning Liverpool's set-piece defending this season. Who marks zonally from a spot kick? (Actually, everyone! – the keeper is the ultimate zone defender, who doesn't mark-up, but positions himself to deal with the ball.)

Myth: Benítez has spent £250m.

Truth: The current squad cost c£140m to assemble, with four rival squads currently costing in excess of £200m. Benítez has spent a lot *if you ignore how he's had to sell players to buy better ones*, making profits on many of his signings to reinvest. Sissoko led to Mascherano, Bellamy to Torres, and Crouch, indirectly (due to transfer fees owed), to Johnson. Surely the only gauge is what the current squad costs, as a manager will almost always put every penny available to him into the set up?

Ronnie Whelan said on Irish TV last month that the Liverpool eleven sent out to face Debrecen cost £250m. How many people will believe that? Quite a few, unfortunately.

It actually cost £78m. In what other profession would an "expert" get away with such utter mindless claptrap? Great player, but a total fool of a pundit. It's a bit like a film critic claiming that a low budget indie film cost more to make than Titanic; he'd lose his job and credibility in an instant.

What's clearly true is that Benítez has never been able to get anywhere near the British transfer record, whereas Alex Ferguson has smashed it several times.

What's also true is that the more Benítez has spent on a player, the better on average the signing has proven to be; however, the majority of his signings have been due to a compromise of one kind or another. Many of his main targets were deemed too expensive, even though players like Alves and Simao would not have cost even half the British transfer record (and both went on to be sold for far higher fees, suggesting they were the 'real deal'). There is no doubt that Chelsea and Manchester United could have afforded these two players, and that was a key difference; instead of Simao, Benítez only had enough money for Pennant.

Liverpool also lag seriously behind in terms of wage bill, and a club's wage bill heavily correlates to success; in other words, 90% of the time the biggest payers win the prizes.

Transfer fees can be arbitrary, but only the richest clubs can afford to keep a large group of top players on the payroll.

Myth: Benítez has a poor record in the transfer market.

Truth: Well, if you only list a manager's flops, then of course that's the case. By my reckoning, if 50% of a manager's signings succeed to any degree, he'll be onto something.

And, only around 10-20% need to be very special indeed.

What's strange is how Benítez's flops get scrutinised, and yet those of Wenger, Ferguson (and Mourinho) get totally overlooked. Some of that is due to the success those managers have had, although often that success was stymied following some really dodgy signings. In truth, Ferguson could only excel from his 7th season onwards,

Wenger has been unable to excel since the Premier League went über-rich, and Mourinho only succeeded with the help of an expenditure that puts Liverpool's in the shade.

Myth: Benítez's teams are too defensive.

Truth: They are attack-minded, and always have been, but not at the expense of *balance*. There's no point attacking too freely if your defence and midfield isn't yet capable of withstanding the counter-attacks. In his early big games, this was especially true.

A lack of sufficient goalscorers was also an initial problem, with Benítez struggling to find a centre-forward he could rely on prior to 2007 – he certainly didn't inherit one – but last season six players got into double figures, and that can easily be replicated this season.

The Reds finished last season as the league's top scorers – without Torres starting half of those games – and already have an even better goals-per-game average this time around, moving up from two per game to almost three.

Myth: Benítez prioritises Europe over the Premier League.

Truth: The Spaniard undoubtedly struggled in his first season in English football. Obviously, early on, he was more comfortable, in terms of the style of football, with the Champions League. And, winning that competition set in stone this particular myth; meaning, despite posting improved league showings, including the club's two highest points tallies for 20 years (plus its fewest *ever* defeats in a season!) and, a to-be-expected levelling off in Europe (still regular semi-finalists, and winning again would have been the ultimate miracle), the myth still persists.

There have been times when he's rested players in the league ahead of a big European game, but there have been European games, such as Marseilles at home, when he did the opposite (and he got slaughtered for that, too!). Once the Champions League becomes a knockout competition, there is no margin for error, but individual league games are rarely the be-all-and-end-all. Most managers will field a stronger team against Barcelona, Inter Milan or Real Madrid than against Hull, Stoke or Wigan, if there is not sufficient time to rest. That's how football works at the top level. Doing the opposite would be suicide.

This is especially true when teams are out of contention for the league title; both Arsenal and Liverpool fielded reserve sides – in the league – at the Emirates, days before the two met again in Europe.

Benítez was also widely castigated by Neil Warnock for fielding a weakened team against Fulham when the Reds were focusing on Europe in 2006/07, yet Warnock had fielded a largely reserve side at Old Trafford earlier in the season, effectively "throwing" the game, to use his own logic.

Myth: Benítez can't man-manage.

Truth: While he's not a cuddly, buddy manager, he has a way of working that separates the personal from the professional. That is his method.

While there may be some similarities with the goatie and the tubbiness, Benítez is no David Brent: "I've created an atmosphere where I'm a friend first, boss second. Probably, entertainer third."

Ultimately, Rafa tries to keep the same distance from all players. That way there are no accusations of favouritism.

However, there have been plenty of occasions when he's given very public support to young players or those under heavy flak from the press and fans, because they need extra protection.

I do get the impression that Benítez doesn't inflate the egos of the journalists who cover him, and has little time for pressing the flesh. His interpersonal skills, outside of those he trusts, may be lacking; especially as a man for whom English is not his native language, and who therefore has to be extra wary. He doesn't play the media in the perfect way Alex Ferguson does, which they lap up, even when he turns on them and calls them "fucking idiots".

Myth: Benítez manages by numbers/makes substitutions too late.

Truth: This is a dig at those who study the game, and use data to aid their decision making, such as Benítez (although Wenger, who does the same, is exonerated); indeed, it was a comment made by Andy Gray about Benítez only making substitutions around the 60-70 minute mark.

Against Chelsea – after 60 minutes – Gray noted that Rafa is right to have left things as they are; two minutes later, Chelsea scored. A couple of minutes after that, while getting ready to come on and receiving his instructions, Benayoun enters the fray. Gray says "it's almost as if Benítez is managing by numbers". How can a manager be right one minute, a robot following data the next, simply by reacting almost instantaneously to a goal?

Two things: first, a half-time team-talk is a chance to motivate and instruct anyone under-performing in the first half. Giving someone 10-15 minutes to put in every last ounce of commitment or risk being hauled off upon no improvement, is hardly revolutionary thinking. Second, Liverpool have a brilliant record of scoring late goals and winning games in the dying stages, which suggests that the players Benítez has on the pitch, whether brought on or kept on, are generally the right ones.

Oh, and a third thing. Benítez changes *tactics* during a game, switching players, and so on. So it's not like the only way to change a game at half-time is to bring on a sub. But when someone is truly hopeless, such as Salif Diao at Fulham in 2004, he will make an alteration at the break.

Myth: Benítez doesn't trust British players.
Truth: Benítez *can't afford* British players. This started when he wanted to sign Jonathan Woodgate in 2004, but was priced out of the market. The same applied with Gareth Barry four years later.

When he did buy Crouch, Pennant, Keane and Johnson, he was mocked for paying over the odds. Meanwhile, the best English players (albeit in very small clusters), were already at Chelsea, Arsenal and Manchester United – with Rooney and Ferdinand costing approximately £30m each – and therefore out of bounds (with Liverpool having their own untouchable pair in Carragher and Gerrard). Any England internationals at Everton will never head this way, either.

Clearly a manager knows a certain market best – for Benítez in 2004 that was Spain; which also happened to be the world's best league at the time. Benítez raided his homeland for its top talent, and internationals in the making: Alonso, Reina, Riera, Arbeloa and Torres – in the way Wenger did with France.

Unfortunately, the comparisons Benítez suffered with Houllier were not helpful; while his predecessor had success in other markets, unfortunately Houllier raided France for also-rans.

Myth: Benítez doesn't trust youngsters, especially local kids.
Truth: The Academy simply hasn't produced the players; maybe the rare gems never existed on Merseyside in order to develop, just as there haven't been many Geordie or Mancunian sensations of late.

These days, a top four squad is full of internationals, and the first-team full of world-class players. So it's inevitably harder for a young player to break through. Only now does Benítez have full control of the Academy; this, after it produced good teams with a great attitude, but no special players.

It could be a long time before any overhaul bears fruit; when Dalglish did so in 1986, it wasn't until between 1993 and 1998 that the big stars emerged (with the exception of Steve McManaman in 1989). When Ferguson overhauled the United youth system – also in 1986 – it was again around 1992/93 when the likes of Beckham, Scholes, Butt and Neville first started to emerge; only Giggs, a rare prodigy, broke through a little earlier.

Critics should ask themselves this: of any home-grown Liverpool players to emerge since 2004, *which of them have gone on to look good enough for the first team?* Nearly all have left, and aside from Stephen Warnock, which of them has looked even remotely worthy of a place in the match-day squad, let alone the XI? Danny Guthrie has Premier League experience, but that's about it, and he played in the Reds' strongest area of the pitch (central midfield). Instead, there are lots of good Championship players who will never get near the top four in the top league.

Therefore, would people rather have Neil Mellor, who will never be star, or a French 20-year-old who, though far from the finished article, has internationally recognised talent for his age group? Some of Benítez's alternatives may not prove much better in the long run, but at least they have the potential to be. At 26, Stephen Warnock was called up by England; at 20, Emiliano Insúa got his first full Argentina cap.

Myth: Benítez's goatee hasn't brought any luck.
Truth: Okay, I'll give you this one.

IT'S GETTING UGLY: HODGSON'S WAY

By Paul Tomkins
December, 2010

It's getting ugly. Well, technically it's been getting ugly for a while. But the Wolves debacle was the nadir of a trying season.

I hate it when people say that a performance "was the worst for 10, 20, even 40 years". You can't line them all up and compare at the same time. But really, that quite possibly *was* the worst home performance for 10, 20, maybe even 40 years. Even in the dark, dark days of Souness, I'm sure I recall the Reds at least trying to pass the ball, even if the players (Dicks, Stewart, Molby, Barnes *et al*) were generally too tubby to chase after it.

It has to rank up there, not least because, in all my time watching the Reds, I've never seen a game at Anfield where players were so scared to take possession in their own half of the pitch; it's been shook out of Brazilian, Spanish, Portuguese, Argentine and Dutch internationals, as well as two or three of the more technically gifted England stars.

Pass? No – get rid. But not just anywhere: into the floodlights, into the heavens, into their half.

Wallop!

From a total of just two long punts in last season's fixture, Pepe Reina sent an incredible 35 long-range missiles into the Wolves half the other night. So much for Spanish tiki-taka. The players were too scared to take a risk and play football, so the ball kept going back to him, and because coming short to receive the ball is now a definite no-no, it had to go long. It was pathetic.

At times, Glen Johnson was just kicking to touch like a rugby player; imagine Arsène Wenger managing a team doing that. Gerrard, back in his favourite central midfield position, was everywhere and nowhere at the same time. Hmmm...

Although Hodgson doesn't have many traditional wingers to choose from, he still opted to leave out Maxi – a cultured, possession-savvy Argentine with three vital goals of late – in favour of playing a defensive midfielder on the wing. Hardly inspiring stuff, given the opposition had the worst away record in all four divisions and were bottom of the table. Hodgson spoke of not disrespecting teams by thinking Liverpool should be beating them; setting his side out *to at least try* would be nice.

I noted several months ago that there was an obsession with calling a team with two holding midfielders 'negative' (naughty Rafa) and two strikers as 'positive' (brave Roy; see Andy Gray before Manchester City drubbed the Reds 3-0, saying that Liverpool fans will be pleased to see this approach, rather than the one taken at the venue by Benítez, who, though Gray neglected to mention it, had gained four points from the previous two visits to Eastlands. Er, yes, Andy, we were all absolutely chuffed to bits to be stuffed 3-0).

But under Benítez – whether Gerrard was in the hole or in midfield – against teams such as Wolves, Liverpool would have two incredibly attack-minded full-backs; not the horribly average Konchesky, and not the exciting quasi-winger Johnson hanging back for fear of a telling off from the sidelines.

If fit, there'd be Agger at centre-back, bringing the ball into midfield to change the dynamic. Kuyt, Gerrard and Torres would all feature – with the captain often in central midfield against the fodder – and basically, eight of the ten outfield players had licence to get forward, around the pivot of a holding midfield and one stopper at the back. The only teams to beat Liverpool at Anfield under Benítez in the Premier League were Chelsea, Arsenal, Aston Villa and Manchester United, plus Birmingham, in November 2004. Eight league defeats at Anfield *in six years*, and only one of them to a team who wasn't in the top six. Not quite half a season in under Hodgson, and Liverpool have already lost to Blackpool and Wolves at home. And even though a second-tier team did get the better of Benítez in a domestic cup, this season a *fourth*-tier team triumphed on the hallowed soil. Progress, eh?

But Hodgson couldn't even gamble with both Maxi and Kuyt on the wings; he had to play a holding midfielder on one side, and switch Kuyt to his unfavoured side. (I know Meireles isn't *'just'* a holding midfielder, but then neither is Lucas, and nor was Alonso, but they had the same label.) And it's not like Maxi and Kuyt can't defend, either.

Even with Meireles at right-midfield – a fine passer, but not someone who's going to play like a winger – there was still no scope for Johnson to get forward. Instead of three forward-thinking defenders (Johnson, Agger and Insúa), it was just Johnson, albeit now apparently scared of crossing the halfway line. Hodgson has at times opted for Carragher, Kyrgiakos and Konchesky, none of whom are comfortable moving into midfield areas.

The obsession with Gerrard in central midfield and two big strikers effectively becomes Liverpool managed by Andy Gray. No wonder he never criticises Hodgson. We've gone from a manager who averaged 72 points a season and racked up four Champions League quarter-finals or better, to one who's on course for ... 46 points.

Add to that a negative goal difference, a horrific away record and the worst turn-of-year position for Liverpool since the Reds were last relegated over 50 years ago, and you can conclude that in terms of unenviable achievements this season is set to break records.

Style

Liverpool have a group of players who are mostly used to playing between the lines; not in straight lines. While the Reds were no Barcelona in recent years, at least they'd take the game to teams at Anfield, and at least players weren't in regimented formations like a *Fußball* table. In the end, as well as just one forward-thinking defender (Johnson), there were only two forward-thinking midfielders, with Lucas and Meireles unlikely to pop up in the box. Two up front? Well, what good is that if the rest of the team is so negatively constructed?

If you leave out one of your in-form attacking players (Maxi) to play a holding midfielder on the wing, and it doesn't work, you deserve all the criticism you get. Remember, this was *Wolves* at home, not Inter Milan in the San Siro. If it had been a case of the tactics working but luck against Liverpool, I could have accepted that. I can handle defeat. But the tactics were shocking, and it contributed to an awful display.

At times, I find myself feeling sorry for Hodgson. Then, he opens his mouth. Or, I watch us play. From a distance, it may seem like he's been harshly treated. But the team's lack of ideas and his lack of understanding about the Liverpool way are 'crimes' against our club. It's also not the Liverpool way to publicly harangue managers, but if he doesn't respect our traditions, then the Kop will struggle to do likewise.

No-one expected Hiddink or Mourinho to pitch up at Anfield this summer. But Pellegrini – fresh from a club-record 96 points at Real Madrid, and, as also seen with his lovely Villarreal side, a purveyor of the kind of pass-and-move football Reds have grown up on – was passed up because the club (key executives and key players) wanted to go English. Quite why, aside from parochialism and xenophobia, is beyond me.

Ah, but Hodgson was a 'continental', too, after such a nomadic career. Except he exported a basic, solid English 1970s approach to Scandinavia at a time when English football was strong in Europe, and he took advantage of an out-of-date fascination with the sweeper system in that part of the world. But once back in England – especially at a big club in the new Millennium – he was in effect now importing ice to the Eskimos. And not even good ice at that; it was ice that was melting. Meanwhile, the big clubs had moved on.

Playing like an English team from the 1970s is what plenty of struggling and fair-to-middling teams tend to do in the Premier League; although to their great credit, the likes of Wolves, Bolton, Wigan, West Brom and Blackpool are all playing a far more progressive game than that; and indeed, in the 1970s and '80s, *Liverpool themselves* were playing a continental passing game, with brave centre-backs, not some basic homespun tripe. The Kop would have hated Hodgson's tactics then, so why accept them now, when the best teams all respect a possession-based game?

If Coyle, Holloway, Di Matteo and Martinez can get humble collections of footballers playing positive, expansive football, then there's no excuse for Hodgson failing with the current crop at Liverpool. No matter that he didn't sign them all (though he did sign five of the first team squad and release Aquilani); it took Owen Coyle next to no time to turn Megson's Hodgsonesque Bolton into something more Shanklyesque. By contrast, Hodgson has a squad full of stars that went to the World Cup, many of them integral to major nations, and has them chasing long balls and shadows.

Hodgson talks of a love of getting he ball quickly to the front men and midfielders then joining; in other words, pretty much the Wimbledon approach. What about passing the ball accurately into the front men having worked the ball upfield? Whatever he did at Fulham, including getting the ball up to Bobby Zamora and winning the LMA award, means nothing at Liverpool. The approach needs to be very different to a mid-table outfit. But Hodgson's whole career has been a 'one size fits all' approach. It fit Fulham brilliantly. Bravo. It fits us like Fatty Arbuckle squeezing into Cheryl Cole's bikini.

Even if he has target-men more suited to bringing the ball down (get rid of Torres, buy Carlton Cole), being so direct will never be accepted by the Kop. This is Liverpool; this is Anfield. We don't live in the past, and don't expect trophies every season, but certain qualities are part of the club's DNA.

Pass and move is one of those qualities. There are different ways to do it, but style has been so lacking. Right now, it's like going to a Michelin-starred restaurant, only to be served a Big Mac and charged £100 for the privilege. In Torres, Hodgson has a white truffle; the manager, it seems, would rather make use of a pickled gherkin and a ketchup sachet.

This is not to absolve Torres from blame for his sulking on the pitch, but *Jesus Christ*, if I'd been brought up in Spain and won every major international honour with my country, and was asked to risk blindness by staring into the floodlights to locate a snow-covered ball descending out of the haze – I'd be in a strop.

Again, I noted back in the summer that Benítez's high-pressing style got the best out of the Liverpool no.9. In his previous two injury-ravaged seasons he was still getting a goal almost every game, even if just coming back from a six-week layoff; now we're lucky if we get a goal a month.

If Benítez had to go, so be it. I've accepted that; that can't be changed, even though we have clearly traded down.

But the longer the media continue to blame solely him for Liverpool's woes (even though he left a team that finished with more points and more wins than the one he inherited in 2004, and had something like 15 World Cup participants), then the greater the outcry from knowledgeable fans who, whether they liked Rafa or not, know that Hodgson – with his kowtowing to 'Sir Alex', his disregard of the fans, his timid, gutless, artless football – is not the answer to our greatest question. No-one forces Hodgson to get so many men behind the ball, whether winning or losing. No-one forces Hodgson to have the defence sit so deep and hit the ball so long.

Mock us if you want – "they all laugh at us", as the song says – but we know our football, and we know our club. Patrick Barclay, Paul Hayward (who said Hodgson would replace Benítez's negative style with an exciting approach!) and their cohorts may know Roy Hodgson and Fulham Football Club better than us, but we know our standards. And if such people told us that 7th place with 63 points fell below the accepted standards – sack Rafa! (they did) – then this is so far below, it's almost off the scale. Frankly, it's an insult.

No wonder things began to get ugly on the Kop.

WE WERE THE VICTIMS; IT WASN'T OUR FAULT

By Chris Rowland

September, 2012

A 'From Where I Was Standing' account of being at Hillsborough on April 15th 1989

I could never forget the date anyway – April 15th is also my mum's birthday, you see. Every April 15th, I'm torn. I like to call my mum and wish her happy birthday without sounding how I'm actually feeling – overwhelmingly sad. It seems wrong to dampen her birthday every year by reminding her that's it's also 'Hillsborough day'. It's always a tough day. I don't know whether next year's will be any easier after the HIP report.

But at least my mum still has her son. She still says the phone call she got that day, after 6pm when we finally got far enough away from Sheffield to find a phone booth without a queue half way down the street (no mobiles then) was the best birthday present she ever had. Many other mums weren't so lucky.

Like Heysel, it was a beautiful sunny day. We drove up to Sheffield, met up with our mates from Liverpool, toured a few pubs, and headed for the ground. Usual pre-match routine. For those who later tried to blame 'drunken fans' for what happened ('the tanked-up mob', as Thatcher's pompous, prejudiced Press Secretary Bernard Ingham called us, despite not having been within 50 miles of the stadium – looking forward to the retraction Bernard, if you're man enough), do you really imagine there's ever been a set of fans, at any FA Cup semi-final like that one, or any match at all for that matter, who haven't been to the pub beforehand? If having a few pints before a match was the only precursor to Hillsborough, then every stadium in Britain would have been empty years ago.

When you even stop to think about it for a moment, it's too ridiculous to contemplate how that nonsensical version of events somehow endured for over 20 years. But that's the power of a coordinated smear campaign by the 'trusted', 'reliable' establishment, the police and the emergency services, the Government, the media. Who are people going to believe, them or a bunch of football fans? Fans who turned out to be bloody heroes as well as victims, who were reduced to ferrying out their own dead and dying on makeshift stretchers made of advertising hoardings as the authorities pretty much stood back and watched. To try and appreciate what that feels like, imagine other disaster scenarios – plane crash, train crash, multiple pile-up on the motorway, ship sinking, a major fire. Then imagine a world where the authorities, those whose job it is to respond to such emergencies – the clue's in the name 'emergency services' – not only didn't give a toss but actually blamed you for it. 'Ah serves them right for driving too fast. It's their own fault.'

I wonder whether that helps explain how let down we felt about Hillsborough?

It was about 2.30 as we approached the stadium, about a dozen of us. We walked down Leppings Lane – a name that still causes my stomach to knot to this day – and went to turn right into the enclosed area outside the turnstiles. We'd been there before, of course, so we knew what to expect. We'd been to games against Wednesday, to a Cup Semi-final with Arsenal, and to the same stage of the same tournament 12 months earlier, at this very ground against the same opponents – Forest – with the same ends allocated to the fans, the same ticket allocations – too many for them, too few for us.

That the area outside the Leppings Lane turnstiles was enclosed is crucial to this story, because what happened there led to what happened inside. It's a sort of triangular shape. One side is the sheer concrete wall of the stadium, with its small number of turnstiles for the Leppings Lane terraces and further to the left the turnstiles for seats above. The second side is a high fence separating the enclosed area from the river down below. The third is the road itself, a wall with an opening to allow fans in and out.

I said everything was the same as 12 months earlier, but there was one crucial difference. There was a different police officer in charge. Chief Superintendent David Duckenfield. The previous year, Duckenfield's predecessor had had a single line of fans lined up for each individual turnstile, separated by lines of police. It worked. In 1989 we turned from the street into the enclosed area and witnessed the world's biggest freeform jazz rugby scrum. It swayed this way and that as a single living entity, like coral responding to the tide. There was no attempt to form lines towards the turnstiles, it was everyone for themselves, an insane surging free-for-all. In the midst of the madding crowd were a few mounted police, yelling orders hysterically and not in a way that reassured anyone that this situation was under control. In no time we were consumed, all becoming separated and taken in whatever direction the surging mass took us. A police horse reared up, adding to the swaying heaving chaos. My face ended up squashed against the wall of the stadium, a turnstile no more than a few feet to my left, another a similar distance to my right. For all the chance I had of getting to them, they might as well have been on Saturn. I began to feel real primal fear as the extent of the potential danger I was in became apparent; I was in trouble, and it was deep, life-threatening trouble. Sweat trickled down my back, against the press of a thousand bodies with forward momentum. It was hard to see a way out. What felt like my body's entire supply of adrenaline went coursing through me. I began to try and push back, using the wall as leverage, arms and legs pushing back, back arched. I managed to break out, more than happy to trade my 'place' near the front for the chance to breathe again.

Many of our lot did the same, gave it up, and got out of it. These include some experienced boys from way back, Shankly boys. They were scared. One of the Liverpool lads suggested we try to get in to the Leppings Lane seats above instead. Our tickets were for the terraces, but these were dangerous circumstances. We headed for the stands turnstiles, and basically barged through them. 'You can't come in here; those are terrace tickets' shouted the operator. 'Well we're not stopping out there to be squashed to death, so bollocks' was basically our approach. That decision may have saved our lives. We'd have been in a very wrong place at a very wrong time otherwise. We'd probably have been in that tunnel, where so many lives were lost.

Meanwhile the chaos outside was getting worse, as more and more fans entered the enclosed area, many of those who travelled by coach having been delayed by long hold-ups on the M62. Remember, they couldn't see around the corner from the road into the enclosed area outside the turnstiles to what was ahead until it was too late – by then they'd added to the swell. The police opened the big gate – and later blamed it on drunken ticketless fans – to alleviate the mayhem outside. I actually think that's one thing they may have got right, given they'd created the mess in the first place. I believe there would certainly have been deaths outside if they hadn't. Tragically, by doing so they only transferred the problem inside and made an already-critical situation much worse. The chaos outside eased as thousands poured through the gate to escape the fear and the crush.

The first thing you see through that gate is a central tunnel leading to the terraces, and at the top a beguiling slice of green pitch. Not surprisingly, that's where most headed. What they found inside is now a matter of record. We stood gazing down from our lofty perch above the terraces in disbelief at the human gridlock in the two central pens below. We'd all been to Heysel. Surely it couldn't be happening again? We watched as bodies were carried onto the pitch, as fans desperate to escape the hell tried to clamber up to the safety of the seats above, those at the front reaching down to try and grasp the clutching hands below and hoist them to safety. We watched advertising hoardings being turned into makeshift stretchers.

The game began. We had one eye on the match and the other on the unfolding disaster below. Peter Beardsley hit the bar, it caused an 'oooh' and a surge. For many it was the final straw. Soon after the game was halted. Just as at Heysel, we were aware that something out of the ordinary was occurring, but had absolutely no conception of the scale or the consequences.

I mentioned the phone booth we called home from. It was on the outskirts of Chesterfield. There was a pub nearby. We wanted a pint and a time-out. There were about half a dozen locals in – and about the same number of Forest fans. As we entered, one said 'I've got a dead man's scarf here lads'. Before we could attack, the landlord stepped in, astoundingly quickly. 'Have a beer lads, I'll deal with this, not you.' He invited the Forest fans to leave without finishing their drinks and without a refund. They complied. Amazingly, an hour or so further south, in Ashby de la Zouch, we stopped again, and bumped into the same group of Forest fans. This time, one came over and apologised for their idiot mate, who had apparently been drinking all day (those drunken Liverpool fans eh?) and had been 'spoken to' by the rest of the group. We left it at at that. It's hard to describe what mood we were in – protected in some state of euphoric post-traumatic shock, yet aware that just beyond it lay unimaginable horrors.

In a police room somewhere inside Hillsborough, a cover story was already being concocted. It was the fans' fault, those Liverpool hooligans, those who caused Heysel less than four years ago. Football trouble was endemic in the English game at all levels, people would have no difficulty swallowing that version of events. The police version of events was the one adopted by the FA's Graham Kelly in the infamous TV interview, by Thatcher's government (hardly friends of the game of football and its followers, and hardly fans of the city of Liverpool either, the left wing politics of which presented an unaccustomed opposition to the general falling over backwards in fawning admiration for Maggie that seemed to have been adopted by so much of the rest of England). Bernard Ingham's crass comment added to the impression that was being artfully contrived. Then came Kelvin McKenzie and *that* headline, that article about us lot robbing and urinating on our own dead and attacking those 'brave cops'. Quite apart from the obscene nature of the unfounded allegations, anyone who had been there would have known it would have been physically inconceivable to do any of those things because those in the two central pens were hemmed in so tightly that even moving your hands to your own pockets was quite out of the question let alone bending down to steal. At the time of the allegations, people were frightened to breathe out in case there was not enough room to allow another in-breath. In those circumstances, it seems credible to believe that pillage is the last thing on your mind.

And a word about those two obscenely overfilled central pens when the two either side were barely more than half-filled; why wasn't there somebody – police or stewards – beyond that big gate, at the entrance to the tunnel, saying 'left or right boys but not straight on, it's full'? That's all it would have taken to prevent the tragedy. When the order was given to open that gate, there was no joined-up thinking to wonder what the consequences might be. Just a panic measure, the modus operandi of the police that day, and another shining example of the quality of Mr Duckenfield's work, to add to his utter failure in basic crowd control outside, his instructions to his officers to treat this as a pitch invasion, his refusal to allow the fleet of ambulances in at first, his part in concocting an alternative 'truth' under the chief constable Peter Wright, his involvement in changing officers' statements and the mysterious unavailability of the CCTV footage (oh it was broken was it? So which is it, incompetence or something much worse?), and his attempt to save face by pinning the blame on those who were already the victims of his incompetence. Just try to imagine how you'd feel if it was your husband or wife, father or mother, son or daughter, who'd been a victim of his bungling and then been expected to take the blame for it.

That's what I told countless people in subsequent years when people said 'when are you lot going to give it up? Just move on.'

'If it was your child and you knew the official story wasn't the true one, would you just give it up and move on? Or would it somehow be different then? We'll stop when the truth is finally told and those who lied and deceived get the punishment they deserve. That's when we'll call it a day.'

Well now, after 23 years of anger and frustration at the enduring lie festering within, we finally have the first part of that. We finally have the *truth*. We all knew it was, all along. The final instalment, the justice, will come when those who deserve to be punished for their parts in the Hillsborough cover-up get theirs. Of course there's no punishment, no sentence, that can ever come close to atoning for the suffering caused by what happened on the day, and what has happened subsequently. But it would at least allow us some closure, and enable us to 'move on.'

Some months later, when I was working in Birmingham, reception called me to say West Midlands police were in the lobby and would like to talk to me. About Hillsborough. The job of investigating what happened at Hillsborough was given to West Midlands Police. Some might question whether that might be the most neutral organisation to carry out the investigation, that they might seek to cover for their colleagues in the South Yorkshire force.

I went out. Two officers were there. We went into a private room. The conversation lasted barely ten minutes. It went something like this:

"Where did you travel from?"

"The Midlands."

"Who did you travel with?"

"My mates."

"How many?'

"Five of us."

"How did you travel?"

"Car."

"Who drove?"

"Me'."

"What time did you set off?"

"About 9.30."

"What time did you get to Sheffield?"

"About 11."

"That's quite early for a 3pm kick off isn't it? What did you do for all that time?"

"We had something to eat and went to few pubs."

"For three hours? So would you say you had a lot to drink then?"

"A few pints, nothing unusual."

"So you'd had quite a lot to drink before you got to the stadium, you and your friends?"

"Oh I get it, I see where this is heading. Do you want to ask any questions about what actually happened at the stadium, or is this just an attempt to get support for the theory that drunken fans were to blame?"

They said nothing.

"In that case I have nothing more to say."

They were just seeking corroboration of the lie which had now taken hold and which endured for 23 years. McKenzie, Thatcher and Ingham, all perpetrators of the evil myth, weren't there at Hillsborough. They took their 'information' second hand. All those who've taunted Liverpool fans ever since over Hillsborough, choosing to believe the 'official' version because it suited them to, weren't there either.

We were there, we saw what happened. So did the Chief of Police.

I was on holiday in Turkey last week when one of the lads I was with that day called to give me the news about the truth finally emerging. It felt good. At last a version of events that chimed with what I saw, what I knew. For a while I was elated. Then I started getting mad all over again. How dare they? How dare the police do that to protect their reputations? The realisation that even 96 deaths is of insufficient gravity for some people to suppress their wretched self-preservation instinct delivers a piercing jolt to your world view. And how dare McKenzie take the feelings of those who'd suffered so much so lightly? And why were so many, from leading figures in the government to the media, so quick to join in the chorus of condemnation?

My analysis of the day, what happened and why, and what went wrong, is reflected almost word for word by the HIP report. I find the desire and ability of the establishment to close ranks to protect itself deeply disturbing in a so-called modern democracy. I'm mystified how it can take 23 years for the truth about an event as momentous as Hillsborough to emerge. It feels odd that what I knew to be truth all that time is now also the official version. Whether it's also a universally accepted version time alone will tell.

I travelled to Anfield when it was opened to the public a week after the disaster, when the pitch was almost covered in bouquets. I went and stood on the Kop terracing where I'd stood so often, and the tears finally came, and kept coming, like there'd be no end. They come every April 15th. I looked at the scarves and tributes tied to the crush barriers and pillars – not just Liverpool but from virtually every club. Lots of Everton, which you might expect, and Celtic. But, lots of Man United too – I recall one saying 'United in Grief'.

We should try to remember that on Sunday when the teams match up again.

LIVERPOOL FC: AN ALTERNATIVE LESSON FROM HISTORY

By Andrew McKay

June, 2012

"A love of tradition has never weakened a nation, indeed it has strengthened nations in their hour of peril; but the new view must come, the world must roll forward." – Winston Churchill

The UK's wartime leader undoubtedly had many virtues, but an interest in football was never amongst them. Nonetheless, however unintentionally, his observation (quoted above) accurately summarises the current position of Liverpool FC, because if ever a football club has reason to be proud of its history and traditions, it's Liverpool. At the same time, if ever a football club was at risk of that same tradition becoming an unintended euphemism for inertia and underachievement, it's also Liverpool. Churchill is perceptive in his counselling that the past is there to be respected but should not be allowed to dictate the present.

The paradoxical trouble with Liverpool's tradition is that so much of it is very good indeed, which in turn can inspire so much respect that many are left unwilling to examine it too closely or think critically about what really built it in the first place – and so end up reluctant to countenance change. The irony is that Liverpool's proud heritage was not created by keeping things the same from generation to generation, however much some fans seem to think so, but the exact opposite. Most of the club's successes have in fact come when they've broken with tradition and done something differently, so what may misleadingly come to look traditional in hindsight was actually born out of constant change and innovation during its own era. Not only that, but the periods of drift over the years, of which the current example since the last league win is by no means the first, have arisen precisely because Liverpool were too much in thrall to what had gone before.

Take for example the domination of Europe in the 1970s and '80s, without doubt one of the proudest parts of the team's history for all supporters. As many histories of the club and former players have attested, the turning point came following their early elimination from the European Cup by Red Star Belgrade in 1973. Realising that their team had been outplayed, Bill Shankly and his coaching staff decided that if they wanted to capture the European Cup, changes would have to be made to the playing style.

As Brian Glanville put it in *Champions of Europe*:

"It was immensely to the credit of Shankly and his Boot Room brains' trust that they had the courage and initiative to admit to themselves that their traditional, often long-ball, English tactics were never going to gain them what they wanted in Europe, that changes must be made to a more continental style, with more emphasis on a patient build-up and on ball control."

The vision that this move took should not be underestimated, however inevitable the team's ruling of the continent may look in hindsight. Liverpool had already won six trophies under Shankly by this time, including three domestic titles and a UEFA Cup, as well as having reached another European final, the Cup Winners' Cup, seven years earlier. It would therefore have been easy and maybe even natural for the members of the Boot Room to have looked at the trophies already won and conclude that this defeat was simply a bad night that signified nothing. But they didn't. Shankly did publicly save some face by criticising Red Star's possession football as dull – "the Liverpool fans would never pay to watch that stuff"- but behind closed doors it was a different matter. To be at the bottom of the league and admit that things need to change is one thing, but to already be serial winners and yet still be prepared to do something new? As Glanville quite rightly says, that does take both courage and initiative.

Out went the traditional stopper centre-half (Larry Lloyd) and in came the more skilful and mobile Phil Thompson, later to be joined by Alan Hansen, so Liverpool could start building from the back as a basis for keeping possession of the ball and thus play the top European teams at their own game. Four European Cups in the ensuing decade or so, not to mention a whole host of domestic trophies, showed that the overhaul of the team's playing style was a break with tradition that worked out spectacularly well, but history may have been very different had the coaches not made the changes.

The converse – that not changing things can result in the club falling back into the pack rather than leading it – is also clearly demonstrated in the same era by the ultimately weakening legacy of the attitude to commercialism. Writing in 1990 in *Liverpool – The Glory Decade*, Ian St John commented that:

"There are no super-rich executive boxes ... it may well be that Liverpool undersells itself but this may not necessarily be a bad thing in these days of over-commercialisation."

This would doubtless have had many happily nodding in agreement at the time and given that English football was much less commercialised then than it is today, it didn't matter too much. But more than 20 years and a complete change to the game's financial landscape later, it simply reads as myopic and self-defeating.

Stephen F Kelly echoed this in his 1994 biography of Graeme Souness, bemoaning that Anfield was coming to represent "supermarket football" like the sort served up at Old Trafford – and making it clear that he doesn't care for it. It was easy to dismiss flash Manchester United with their soulless commercialism at a time when the league title count was still more than ten ahead in Liverpool's favour, but how hollow does such sneering sound now? Kelly was only half-right anyway, in that Liverpool's attempts to adjust to the new financial reality in the game – following the 1992 formation of the Premier League and first Sky TV deal – actually fell some way short of the speed with which United adjusted, as the growth of both their spending power and trophy count since then has all too bluntly demonstrated. When David Moores ruefully admitted, on the sale of the club to Hicks and Gillett in 2007, that "I don't think we have maximised our brand", it was with considerable understatement and may well be the defining comment on the club's history since the last league title.

Nothing epitomises Liverpool's damagingly slow adjustment to the new financial reality of football in the 21st century more than the lack of answers to the stadium question. It's widely held that Liverpool simply have to increase stadium capacity – and so the match day revenue – if they are to keep up with their rivals, either by redeveloping Anfield or moving to a new stadium entirely. It's been discussed plenty of times by various board-level figures over the years but broken promises have yet to turn into broken ground. Meanwhile, Arsenal have been playing at the 60,000 capacity Emirates since August 2006, while United reached their current 75,000 maximum at the end of that same season, yet all Liverpool have to offer in response is a lot of fiddling while they get burned financially. Perhaps the idea, backed by Liverpool City Council, of the

£125 million 60,000 capacity stadium shared with Everton should have been taken more seriously when it was proposed back in 1990. "But think of the tradition!" howl the diehard, "sharing with Everton is unthinkable!" As unthinkable as not winning the league title for nearly a quarter of a century?

Fans who prefer the traditional manner of doing things summarise it by referring to the "Liverpool Way", which is shorthand for "how things were done during the glory years after Bill Shankly arrived". A more objective observer, however, might note that The Way hasn't produced any league titles since 1990, and conclude that it was therefore something that worked at the time but doesn't anymore, although why anyone would think it should still work given the many changes in English football since 1992 is something of a mystery. What's more, like a Liverpool FC roll-call of sadly dwindling war veterans, only Ronnie Moran, Roy Evans and Peter Robinson of the men who built the Liverpool Way are even still living, and as none has worked at the club for at least a decade, it has to be conceded that The Way has long since passed into history.

As an illustration of how specific The Way was to its own era, take the widely held tenet that Liverpool give their managers more time than other clubs do. It may seem true but it's a myth. All four men who led the team during the glory years left of their own volition, but the six incumbents since the last championship in 1990 were all sacked or at least came close to it, jumping before they were pushed. The truth is therefore that Liverpool are actually like every other football club in sticking with managers when they win and sacking them when they lose, and the famed tolerance was nothing more than an illusion created by the exceptional circumstances of so much success. After all, why would Liverpool have sacked the manager during the dynasty era? The board certainly could have done, as secretary Peter Robinson hinted soon after Bob Paisley's appointment that he was at risk if he failed to keep the team at the top of the English game, although of course his subsequent success rendered that possibility academic. Even the two occasions where patience was apparently shown in the past 20 years, to Souness in the summer of 1993 and then Houllier a decade later, seem to have owed far more to sentimentality on the part of then-chairman David Moores than any official policy.

However, to concentrate too much on that period is to make the same mistake that the traditionalists themselves make, with their uncritical assumption that the answer to every question that might ever be asked about Liverpool FC is be found between 1959 and 1990. The reality, which anyone who looks solely at that era is liable to miss, is that the principle of change being good and conservatism bad has actually been embedded in Liverpool's history since its very earliest stages, and so is visible even in the case of Tom Watson, the club's first proper team manager.

In 1896, realising that Liverpool needed to appoint a man to deal full-time with the team if they were to stop the yo-yoing between the two divisions that had marked their first few seasons, Secretary John McKenna appointed Watson, already a winner of three league titles with Sunderland, to do just that. The ambition shown by the move was noteworthy in itself, as this club that had yet to win anything at league level targeted the most successful manager of the day and paid him what was thought to be the highest salary in the game at the time, but the benefits of doing so would soon become clear.

Watson's role wasn't quite what would be recognised as that of a manager today, with the most glaring difference being the board having more power over team selection than he did, but he did have sufficient influence over tactics and the leadership of the team to differentiate Liverpool from their rivals in an era when most clubs simply didn't have a manager in the modern sense. Everton in particular were dismissive of the need for such a role and, with one league title already to their name, might have been seen as the calm voice of reason and experience. Under their new manager, Liverpool would win two league titles before Everton managed to land their next one. Indeed, Watson's influence outlasted even his death in 1915 as a number of men he had signed – Donald McKinlay, Harry Chambers, Ephraim Longworth, Bill Lacey and Elisha Scott – would become key members of the team that won consecutive championships in the early 1920s.

However, the momentum generated by his regime was allowed to dissipate into inertia for the rest of the inter-war period, as Liverpool largely subsided into mid-table mediocrity. That the ageing title heroes were replaced with players of lesser talent was one reason, but there was also the significant failure to keep up with the changes in the game being instigated by Herbert Chapman, which included both tactical innovations and his reshaping of the manager's role. Tom Watson may have blazed a trail in his own era but Chapman took the manager's position further still and so rendered Liverpool's model out of date, illustrating that today's new ideas have to be constantly refreshed if they're not to become tomorrow's stale tradition.

Instead of stepping forward again themselves however, Liverpool responded by going backwards. The board gave George Patterson the job in 1928, despite his already existing one as club secretary, but importantly thus saved on a salary as one man was now doing two jobs. This uninspired appointment spoke volumes for both the directors' damaging penny-pinching, and – even more seriously – indicated how far the club's finger was from the pulse of the English game, as Chapman set about creating a faster, more skilful playing style at Huddersfield and Arsenal that would leave the strength and physicality of Liverpool in their title-winning years trailing in its wake, yet with Liverpool themselves in no position to respond.

Nonetheless, the harmful inertia that blighted the years leading up to the Second World War was replaced immediately afterwards by innovation once more, and Liverpool claimed the first post-war championship as a result. That the directors dispensed with their pre-war parsimony and backed the crucial signing of Albert Stubbins (24 goals in 36 league games) for a club record £12,500 was clearly one factor, but there was also the fresh thinking that saw manager George Kay take the squad to America for a shrewdly planned pre-season tour which allowed them to eat properly. Chairman Billy McConnell had been impressed by the dietary bounty the US had to offer compared to ration-book Britain while on a trip there for the Ministry of Food in 1945, and so returned home convinced that sending the team across the Atlantic was worthwhile. The players therefore began the season by putting on an average of half a stone and finished it as champions with both Kay and McConnell paying tribute to the nutritional advantage they had enjoyed. As George Orwell might have put it had *Animal Farm* been about another Red history rather than that of the Bolshevik Revolution, "new thinking good, traditional thinking bad".

However, the late 1940s' daylight was soon followed by darkness in the 1950s as the team of Stubbins, Jack Balmer, Bob Paisley and of course Billy Liddell aged and retired, while off the pitch the club was soon deprived of the drive of both McConnell and Kay, with the former's death in the summer of 1947 and the latter's retirement on health grounds four years later. It was time for conservatism to do its damage once more. Indeed, this constant oscillation between beneficial change and harmful conservatism was already so well established by this time that it would be at least half the truth to say that this, more than anything put in place by Bill Shankly or his successors, should be regarded as the real "Liverpool Way".

The ambition shown by McConnell in sanctioning the record signing of Albert Stubbins was cast aside by a board that would soon operate under a self-imposed unofficial rule that Liverpool wouldn't spend more than £12,000 on a player again. One needs only a passing acquaintance with the concept of inflation to spot the flaw in that policy. Trying to do things frugally also affected the manager's office as a young and inexperienced (therefore cheap) Don Welsh was appointed. He didn't turn out to be a particularly good choice anyway – it's hard to describe a man who oversaw Liverpool's relegation from the top division as anything else – but he was also hamstrung by an internal structure that had scarcely changed from the glory days of Tom Watson half a century before, in which the team manager was still subordinate to the board. (George Kay, with the benefit of both good players and a forward-thinking chairman, probably succeeded in spite of the system rather than because of it).

His successor, Phil Taylor, fared little better, and it was only with Bill Shankly in 1959 that Liverpool finally adjusted to the by now not-so-new world around them and appointed a manager who would actually pick the team himself.

Nonetheless, huge as Shankly's contribution to Liverpool's fortunes undoubtedly was, even he wouldn't have got very far without the backing of the board, and in particular Littlewoods' accountant Eric Sawyer. It was Sawyer who was installed by majority shareholder John Moores with a specific brief to open the chequebook and get the board to start spending money, which is something they hadn't done, figuratively at least, since buying Stubbins in 1946. Ian St John arrived in 1961 for a then record-busting fee of £37,500 (with Ron Yeats not far behind for a further £30,000); St John being the player that Shankly famously described to a hesitant board as the man Liverpool couldn't afford *not* to sign. Promotion back to the top flight duly followed at the end of that season. An out of date command structure and a hobbling fiscal prudence had resulted in relegation and eight lost years in the Second Division, while the casting away of such fetters reversed all of that and resulted in the birth of a dynasty, as change once again succeeded where traditional methods had failed.

That the dynasty era as a whole – the period most fans think of today when they refer to tradition – sustained itself on constant change is usually overlooked, as the fine detail is hard to see from the distance of a generation away, and especially so when sufficient time has passed for the whole era and its ethos to get collectively labelled as "tradition". There were always changes to what had gone before – how else can Paisley learning from Shankly's mistake and not letting older players go on too long, be understood, or Liverpool becoming in 1979 the first English team to have shirt sponsorship, or Dalglish – Howard Gayle's handful of appearances notwithstanding – signing Liverpool's first black player in John Barnes? What's more, the stories of Ronnie Moran handing out the previous year's title medals at pre-season training with as little ceremony as possible and a curt admonition that they represented *last year* and now meant nothing, so getting the players to constantly focus on the present and future rather than the past, symbolise how Liverpool's great dynasty was about constantly moving forward rather than looking back.

Finally, the principle continues to hold when applied to managerial appointments in the current, post-dynasty era, a generation removed from the most recent title. Of the five men to have held the manager's post since Dalglish resigned in 1991 who weren't Roy Hodgson, two were former players (Souness and Dalglish), one an internal promotion (Evans) and two were foreign coaches (Houllier and Benítez). The three with impeccable Liverpool – and by extension, *dynasty* era – credentials (Souness,

Dalglish and Evans) all won one domestic cup each but they also all returned home from Europe with nothing to declare at customs. In contrast, both foreign managers refurbished and extended the club's proud European reputation by one trophy apiece and both won more in total, with Houllier claiming four trophies and Benítez two, than the home-grown trio. They were also at the helm for the two nearest misses in the league since 1990, with second place achieved in 2002 and 2009. (Souness of course also finished second in 1991, but was only in charge for the last month of that season.)

The point couldn't be clearer. That Liverpool were close to getting it right when they broadened their horizons and appointed foreign coaches, but were less successful when their gaze strayed no further than former employees, suggests that a football club that first looks backwards in order to move forwards will achieve little more than merely tripping itself up. The most significant case is that of Dalglish, because if even the club's greatest player from the dynasty era and a formerly successful manager couldn't make it work in the 21st century, then surely no one else from that lineage can either, and it's therefore time for Liverpool to finally concede that asking the past to answer questions posed by the present has run its course.

FSG appear to have realised this with their appointment of the young and up to date Brendan Rodgers as the new manager ahead of any former players (of which there was a merciful dearth on the shortlist anyway), so signalling a break with tradition and thus a fresh start. Such a strategy has also worked plenty of times in the past, so why not again now?

L P Hartley may well have been right when he famously wrote that "the past is a foreign country; they do things differently there", as a number of people associated with Liverpool FC as well as a significant section of the fanbase seem to have spent the last two decades misunderstanding the club's past as if there was a language barrier in the way. The traditions produced by that past are indisputably proud ones, but as they were so closely associated with amazing success, the two concepts have mistakenly become intertwined and are seen by many as two sides of the same thing.

The truth from history is completely the opposite: success has come from changing traditional ways of doing things while sticking to them has resulted only in underachievement. This principle holds true, over and over again, wherever you look in Liverpool's past. So, giving Tom Watson a wider managerial brief than his contemporaries in the 1890s, or adjusting the playing style in the 1970s to better conquer Europe were undeniably changes that were to the club's benefit, while initially sticking to out of date tactics on the pitch between the wars and out of date financial attitudes off it after the founding of the Premier League were traditions that equally clearly were detrimental. Liverpool FC's true relationship with the past is therefore that they are successful when they learn from it and unsuccessful when they merely repeat it.

However, view Liverpool's heritage with too much reverence and this crucial lesson from history gets overlooked, a mistake that is especially likely if "history" is defined – and given the demographics and timescales involved it frequently is – as simply the dynasty era from the mid-1960s to the start of the 1990s. After all, how can anyone draw the correct conclusion if they're only looking at part of the evidence? It's a frustrating irony that Liverpool fans are deemed by the media to be more in touch with their history than supporters of other teams, yet the more conservative-minded of them do not seem to properly understand what that past is telling them.

Yet those who do understand the principle of change being good will see that FSG's appointment of Brendan Rodgers does represent the turning of a page and so something new. No one currently knows if it will work or not, but history is certainly nodding its approval.

THE GREATEST EVER LIVERPOOL PERFORMANCE?

By Paul Tomkins
April, 2013

Twenty five years, in the blink of an eye.

It was my 17th birthday, and I had carefully avoided the score to watch the highlights of Liverpool playing Nottingham Forest later that night. My mum joked that it wasn't worth watching, and like the idiot I was, I got angry at her for ruining the surprise.

Either she was right, and it was dull and Liverpool lost, or she was being ironic and the game was worth staying up for on a school night (these were not my rock'n'roll years). The latter proved to be the case. This was no damp squib. Indeed, in terms of squibs, this was bone-dry and connected to a ton of TNT.

No-one could recall such an impressive display of football; not even the greats of yesteryear, including Sir Tom Finney, who was 66 at the time:

"It was the finest exhibition I've seen the whole time I've played and watched the game. You couldn't see it bettered anywhere, not even in Brazil. The moves they put together were fantastic."

Maurice Roworth, the Forest chairman, added that:

"No one could have competed against [Liverpool]. They are the best team in

Europe, which is why they are not in Europe. They are too good."

Remember, this 5-0 routing came against the team who'd go on to finish 3rd in the league a month later, and who were also the vanquished FA Cup semi-final opponents of Dalglish's Liverpool, at a time when the FA Cup was still a national treasure. Forest were not so much taken down a peg or two as razed to the ground like their South American 'rainy' namesakes. All that was missing was Sting mounting a tree-top protest in Brian Clough's honour. (Meanwhile, Steve Sutton in the Forest goal should have been offered protection by Amnesty International.)

The football was slick, fast and brutally punishing. The visiting fans liked to sing "You'll never beat Des Walker". The pacy England centre-back, lining up in a back four that also included Stuart Peace, picked up an early injury and soldiered on until half-time, but he must have been wondering why he bothered, as the Reds swarmed past his colleagues.

It wasn't even Liverpool's strongest XI from 1987/88. Nigel Spackman was only playing because of an injury to Ronnie Whelan, and Gary Gillespie was in the side because Mark Lawrenson had just been forced to prematurely retire due to a serious Achilles problem. Both stand-ins were outstanding.

Everything clicked into place in that famous season, and this performance was the apotheosis of an epoch-defining team. John Barnes was mesmeric, Peter Beardsley a jinking magician. John Aldridge was more of a mere mortal in that sense, but his special power was that he knew exactly where to be. And Ray Houghton combined energy with intelligence.

Together they were unstoppable. At a time when English football was mired in a lot of long-ball nonsense, this provided pleasure for the purists, with the Reds showcasing possession with purpose. Perhaps it helped that Forest were also a passing side, as they weren't set up to stifle in the way that the Reds' bogey side, Wimbledon, tended to manage. However, Clough's men just couldn't get hold of the ball on the night for long enough periods to keep the home side at bay.

Watching the whole game again, two and a half decades later, the most obvious difference to the football of 2013 is the backpass rule. Having grown up with keepers being able to pick up passes from team-mates as part of the game, my first instinct – as pure reflex – was still "what the hell are you doing, Brucie!?". The outlawing of this tactic was clearly one factor in the speeding up of football in the intervening years, although this classic match still looks fairly frantic, with passages of chaotic play, and a fair bit of pace and athleticism.

Another difference is the tackling, and how forwards were far less protected back then. While I believe that Lionel Messi bears comparison with the great Diego

Maradona, the '80s were still a time of brutal punishment for flair players. John Barnes may not have regularly impressed on the world stage (in part due to England's lack of cohesion), but he tore international defenders apart in a red shirt. Had Liverpool been in Europe at the time I have little doubt that he'd have done the same.

Barnes had pace and skill in abundance, but what marked him out as the league's best player was the ability to ride a robust challenge. If he'd been a racehorse he'd never have fallen at Becher's Brook. And to mix in a few more animal metaphors, he was strong as an ox and as agile as a cat. No matter how he was clattered he always seemed to land on his feet, running off with the ball as the defender looked helplessly on. In fairness there were no nasty tackles in this match, although I counted at least ten occasions that could have led to a red card these days due to players leaving the ground with studs showing (all were playing the ball, but that's now irrelevant if deemed dangerous).

Barnes was just one of several stars on the night, and arguably not even the man of the match. Gary Gillespie was a revelation, at times pioneering the false 9 role from centre-back (including a sweetly struck goal), with his partner Alan Hansen also frequently joining the attack. At one point Hansen, a centre-back in his mid-30s, was in on goal *from open play*, but chose to square it, and overhit the pass; and therefore it wasn't one of 14 shots on target that I counted, to Forest's meagre two. (I also noted three passes by the silver-permed referee, Roger Milford, who seemed eager to show his skills and keep things moving whenever the ball went dead.)

I was fortunate enough to see Barnes, Beardsley, Houghton, Nicol and McMahon while they were still in their pomp, but my first game at Anfield was in 1990, two years after this classic, and those incredible heights were never quite hit again. Indeed, this incredible victory all but secured a 17th league title, and it's now been 23 years since the 18th.

Dividing the game into nine ten-minute periods, I went through and counted every successful pass, to try and get an idea of how it compared with modern football. While I may have missed the odd touch due to replays (although they were very sparse in those days, with the third goal *not even getting one*), I reckon that overall the Reds made 483 successful passes, compared with Forest's 291, to result in what I reckon to be 62% possession. To put that into context, Liverpool averaged 400 successful passes last season and 440 so far this season.

At no point in the game did Forest boss proceedings, or even get within ten passes of the Reds in any of those nine periods of play. Some of the one-twos between Barnes, Beardsley, Spackman, McMahon and the rest remain breathtaking. The way Beardsley shimmied in between defenders and the way Barnes glided past them helped make for one of the most inventive forward lines the British game has ever seen, and that pair, along with Aldridge, notched an incredible 64 goals that season.

To their credit, the much younger Forest side persevered, and four times in the final few minutes Steve Nicol produced a timely interception, with future Red Nigel Clough, then aged 22 (but looking about 11) showing form that he never managed to recapture after leaving his dad's club. With Forest piling forward for a late consolation, the Reds broke and added a fifth goal right at the death.

Twenty five years is a long time in football, and aspects of the performance (and hairstyles) have dated; just as looking at the 1954 Hungary team would have seemed quaint in the '80s. The English game is now full of many of the world's elite, whereas back then it was the best of British and a smattering of Scandinavians, with very few of those imports on a par with Liverpool's sub, Jan Molby. The only non-British/Irish starter out of the 22 on display was Bruce Grobbelaar.

But it was the same for everyone in the late '80s, and you can only judge a side within the context of the era. To put it into a modern setting, it was as if the Reds had Gerrard, Rooney, Wilshire and Bale, and the rest had Jenas, Zamora, Noble and Cattermole, to pick four random relative journeymen.

Liverpool were ahead of the times and ahead of the game, and that's what marked them out as special, even if Barcelona have taken the passing game to new heights. Although it remains debatable because the two could never meet, only AC Milan were on a par with the Reds back then.

And never did that Liverpool side put in a better display than the one that had the Kop chanting "Cloughie, Cloughie, what's the score?"

MAKING SENSE OF THE BLACK SWAN

By Tony McKenna
April, 2012

"The black swan theory – or theory of black swan events – is a metaphor that encapsulates the concept that an event is a surprise (to the observer) and has a major impact. After the fact, the event is rationalised by hindsight. Such events, considered extreme outliers, collectively play vastly larger roles than regular occurrences." –Nicholas Taleb

Andre Villas Boas was a great managerial appointment by Chelsea ... then he was not; 'Arry Redknapp is touted for the 'big job' based on Tottenham's success, but more recently they have earned just 12 points out of a possible 30; Arsenal's Robin van Persie scores "when he wants", then feast turns to famine – he has not scored for over a month; United are eight points clear in the league, the title race is over – but now it's back on … and, indeed, I could go on.

Kenny "must go"; Ferguson was on the cusp of going; Newcastle are now great; and so is Alan Pardew.

Football fans, journalists, pundits – and even the FA – are the most fickle of human beings; and the most reactive. The constraints of current events fix the mind-set in the present tense; knee-jerk assessments are made, yet the future is infinite and change is highly probable, as the above events will testify.

As Liverpool fans we are no less susceptible to the whim of strange occurrences – of both the success and failure kind. The 2011/12 season is already cast as one that is stranger than most. Random events have conspired to the point of disturbance for all of us.

Black swans, noted for their rarity, are bearable in small doses; but Christ, when you get a host of them in your back garden, in such a small space of time, it's overdose time. Until QPR, Liverpool had not surrendered a two goal lead to be beaten in 11.5 years (Opta Joe); Wigan had never won at Anfield, and then they did; West Brom hadn't won on our turf for 45 years … then came Roy Hodgson (who, since leaving, has had more success winning against Liverpool than he had winning *with* them.) Roy was kind enough to say, in his post-match interview, that Liverpool were the better team and had the best scoring chances. But then the Opta Stats gave him no choice; apparently 30 shots on target overall and the lion's share of possession was the Reds'.

West Brom's goal was the result of a Glen Johnson mistake; not singling him out for blame at all – Rio Ferdinand was arguably at fault for Everton's third and fourth goals (a header into the centre of his area was pounced upon in the first example, and poor marking denoted the second). It happens, certain mistakes are just bad luck. The problem for Liverpool is that we have incurred far too much bad luck.

How do we make sense of all this? The answer is we cannot. Rationale, logic, sense, dimension, rhyme and reason have all entered the place where Alice went; this season's script has been written in Jabberwocky format, making nonsense of our attempts to comprehend or appraise the situation. We are in the mode where tossing a coin gives us ten tails in a row when we called heads each time; unusual, but well within the realms of possibility. Maybe now is the time to appreciate this:

"Because our brains are bad at understanding randomness, probability is the branch of maths most riddled with paradoxes and surprises." Alex's Adventures in Numberland – Alex Bellos.

It snowed in June once – that is rare, yet it rarely snows on Christmas day. Regardless, for decades, an army of punters have consistently wagered bets on the latter outcome. Tell them that you placed a bet riding on a snowfall in June and they would laugh in your face. Yet, the potential reward – given the odds set for a summer month – would arguably outpace the return on any 25th December. What is more, you get 30 days in June as opposed to just one in December.

The cognitive bias of snow at Christmas is etched into our psyche; the gambler's fallacy is the bookie's best friend, and randomness compounds our rationale. Liverpool stocked up on 'chance creators' (Downing, Henderson and Adam), we expected the goals to ensue. They did not, not because the team is 'shit', but because randomness dealt us a bad hand.

Worse still, we are easily seduced by the current trend; a pattern we detect as a winning formula becomes the proverbial flavour of the month, and we would like to replicate the blueprint. It is a phenomenon that sees success only after the event, yet ignores the potential of randomness and serendipity – as well as genius – that may have occurred throughout.

It occurs in all sports:

"Baseball is a game of mimicry. Every year, someone wins the World Series and the twenty-nine other teams try to figure out the latest winning formula and copy it." Steven Goldman – *Mind Game*.

Who wants a manager whose stints at four different clubs saw him sacked twice, leave by mutual consent once and have an acrimonious departure at another club? Even better, he has limited experience in the Premier League. Better still, he becomes your manager because he frequents the same casino where your club's owner is also a member, and the Director of your club is also that casino's Managing Director!

Confused? You will be ... but that is how Alan Pardew became friends with Mike Ashley and Derek Llambias (Director at Newcastle) ... and the forewords to the above paragraph basically describe Pardew's CV.

Hardly a blueprint for success, and yet it's worked ... for the time being. I know Newcastle have their admirers but does this not appear to be a Black Swan of the fortuitous kind? Should appraisals be made three years from now to avoid the statistician's anathema of small sample sizes? Can Newcastle *really* continue to have unprecedented success with low budget forays into the transfer market? Sylvain Marveaux (yes he is still there) could easily become the norm in other seasons ... an array of poor signings is just as likely as the luck of signing two strikers who perform beyond all expectations. (Have Newcastle, like West Ham, got lucky with Demba Ba, whose knee is supposedly a ticking time bomb?)

Rare and random events have not only inspired our despair but also engendered our jealousy. Yet, at this moment in time, there is absolutely no evidence, or any reason, to predict that Newcastle's good fortune will see them pushing for a top four finish again any time soon. Everton did that once (emphasis on the 'once'). Nor is there any evidence to suggest that Liverpool's misfortune will continue to confound as it has during this season. Only the passing of time will reveal.

Whilst our emotions have been tossed and blown we would do well to appreciate that our biological and emotional tendency strings are pulled not by us but by those external random events and mishaps that occur in our lives:

"Paradoxically, 'you will be much more in control' explains neuroscientist Antonio Damasio, 'if you realise how much you are not in control." – The Intelligent Investor.

Which is why I praise Kenny's recent comments about Liverpool's poor luck, and Suárez's statement that people should only worry if we had not created so many chances, rather than lament our lack of conversion. Here, both manifest a higher understanding of what has gone wrong; endeavour, skill, talent and creativity have not been at fault, just some goddamn ridiculous probability twist giving rise to the incidence of too many unwelcome Black Swans ... and we will never make sense of them.

But people have tried. Some detractors dismiss Liverpool as a 'cup' team. This is utter madness; you cannot rationalise the irrational. Football games – like coins – have no inherent 'memory'. They do not conspire to upturn our fortunes in the knowledge that the Reds are now in a league game today. Those people also forget the number of *Premier League* teams vanquished in the cups: United, City, Chelsea, Everton, Stoke – translate all those games into Premier League points and deduce what we would have earned against top tier opposition.

You can have a strategy that is loaded up with the odds in your favour; chances created may be guaranteed but sequences of long bad runs are always an inevitable risk that will thwart the outcome of desire. Then is the time to hold your resolve and appreciate that, over the longer term, distorted spikes of bad luck will even out and revert to a more sensible mean, just like the MIT students who won millions counting cards beating the casinos at blackjack:

"Even when we were down $300,000 in 96-97, we had been successful so long, we never doubted". Mike Aponte – Massachusetts Institute of Technology.

... $300,000 down! And still held their resolve! But, of course, those people knew more about probability than most, that long streaks of bad luck are an inevitable consequence of any winning formula, even when meticulously and statistically appraised.

Lucas used to be 'shit'; now we miss him. Andy Carroll was a waste of money but he is now making people sit up and take note.

You either accept the longevity of a strategy resulting from meticulous design – the type that Liverpool's owners are trying to apply – and accept that Black Swans will eventually disappear, or else you buy into the 'Pardiola' hype that they bestow on the Newcastle boss.

Pardew has even become seduced and made dizzy by his 'success', by ignoring the randomness that entailed his own appointment – in a casino of all places. With feigned modesty, he claimed surprise that Newcastle were a 'year ahead' of schedule. So he had a Two-Year Plan to secure Champions League football?

Bullshit. As John Lennon sang:

"Life is what happens when you're busy making other plans".

GETTING LUCK ON OUR SIDE

By Aki Pekuri
March, 2012

Many Liverpool fans believe we have been unlucky this season. The woodwork has been tested as frequently as the net, and when shots have arrived, keepers from the opposing side have made world class save after world class save to keep us frustrated. (Just see the Match of the Day 'saves of the season' compilation.)

But what *is* luck?

Luck always comes into question when something unlikely happens and, depending on which side of the mean we are, defines its goodness or badness. This piece is about luck and how to stay out of its bad influence.

The mystery of luck is approached using Poisson distribution in analysis. Wikipedia defines Poisson distribution as:

"A discrete probability distribution that expresses the probability of a given number of events occurring in a fixed interval of time and/or space if these events occur with a known average rate and independently of the time since the last event".

Poisson is very good at predicting different outcomes in football when we know the above mentioned "known average rate". The first table (below) demonstrates its accuracy by using ten years' worth of Premier League data between 1995-96 and 2005-06. Known average rates here are the averages of goals scored per game for home teams (1.51) and away teams (1.10) during the period. To save space, only the distribution for home team goals is presented. Probabilities of different results can be calculated by simply multiplying all the different outcomes.

Premier League home goal and result distribution between 1995-96 and 2005-06

Home Goals	Poisson	Actual	Result	Poisson	Actual
0	22.0%	23.8%	1-0	11.1%	11.2%
1	33.3%	32.1%	2-0	8.4%	8.5%
2	25.2%	24.6%	2-1	9.2%	9.0%
3	12.7%	11.7%	3-0	4.2%	3.7%
4	4.8%	5.2%	3-1	4.7%	4.2%
5	1.5%	1.8%	3-2	2.6%	2.3%
6	0.4%	0.5%	0-0	7.3%	8.7%
6+	0.1%	0.0%	1-1	12.2%	11.7%

Poisson is not 100% accurate without some modifications which are mainly country- and league-specific. In some leagues there are, for example, more draws than the Poisson predicts, which could be taken into account to improve predictions. Here just the standard Poisson is used and as can be seen from the above table, results have about 2% confidence interval when the average rate is known. The problem here is that the known average rate is not available. Thus, a model was created to form average goal-scoring rate for each team.

At first, data for each Premier League team was compiled to show games played, goals scored (including all types of goals), clear-cut chances, clear-cut chances scored and total chances created. Data shows that after 26 rounds there have been 907 clear-cut chances (CCC) with a 39% conversion rate, so one CCC equals 0.39 goals scored. In addition to CCCs there are "ordinary chances" and ordinary goals, the remainder from total chances and goals scored after CCCs and goals scored from CCC have been deducted. Average conversion rate in the league for this kind of ordinary chance (OC) is 8%, ie 0.08 goals scored per created OC.

The next table shows total chances created, ordinary chance conversion rate, clear-cut chances, clear-cut chances scored and clear-cut chance conversion rate for each team. Goals "deserved" per game are calculated according to explained logic or models. Then deserved goals are compared to actual goals and the difference presented. Not surprisingly, Liverpool are at the very bottom and our Devilish rivals at the other end. First evidence of luck, maybe?

Who is scoring more than they deserve? Who is not?

	TCC	OC%	CCC	CCCS	CCC%	Goals Deserved per Game	Difference
Man United	333	12%	71	31	44%	1.89	0.54
Man City	382	10%	76	35	46%	2.10	0.48
Newcastle	237	11%	34	15	44%	1.15	0.31
Blackburn	211	11%	45	18	40%	1.20	0.23
Norwich	273	10%	34	13	38%	1.26	0.20
Chelsea	353	9%	47	20	43%	1.67	0.14
Sunderland	246	12%	35	8	23%	1.19	0.12
Bolton	241	10%	20	7	35%	1.00	0.12
Arsenal	359	9%	70	28	40%	1.96	0.08
Tottenham	364	9%	65	24	37%	1.91	0.05
Stoke	192	9%	32	11	34%	0.98	0.02
Wolves	231	6%	39	19	49%	1.19	-0.03
West Brom	292	8%	36	13	36%	1.35	-0.08
QPR	273	6%	31	13	42%	1.23	-0.19
Swansea	227	4%	48	20	42%	1.28	-0.20
Aston Villa	247	5%	48	20	42%	1.34	-0.23
Wigan	247	7%	29	7	24%	1.12	-0.24
Fulham	304	6%	44	16	36%	1.48	-0.25
Everton	247	5%	45	16	36%	1.36	-0.32
Liverpool	325	3%	58	17	29%	1.78	-0.78
AVERAGE	279	8%	45	18	39%	1.42	

Next the focus switches to Liverpool. Data was mined to discover how many ordinary and clear-cut chances had been created for and against Liverpool in each of their matches so far this season. Then the goals "deserved" were calculated and used as input (a known average rate) for the Poisson calculator to form after-match predictions for each match. Points deserved follow a simple logic of multiplying home win probability by three points and adding it up with draw probability. The compiled table (below) is full of interesting stuff, i.e. Stoke robbing the Reds twice and two thrown-away points against Blackburn. It shows that Fulham and Bolton equalled Liverpool in terms of goals deserved when Dalglish's men lost to them, while away at Aston Villa and Chelsea Liverpool hit lucky when winning. The most important thing, however, is that the Reds' performances have been worth 70 points if predicted to 38 games. That is Champions League form. Deserved goal difference (+0.74) looks promising too, because achieving a very respectable 55% winning percentage requires around +0.8 goal difference.

		Result		Deserved		Poisson Predictions			Deserved Points	Liverpool			Opponent		
		GF	GA	GF	GA	W	D	L		TCC	CCC	CCCS	TCC	CCC	CCCS
H	Sunderland	1	1	1.29	0.82	47%	30%	23%	1.71	12	1	0	10	0	0
A	Arsenal	2	0	1.68	0.96	54%	25%	22%	1.86	13	2	1	8	1	0
H	Bolton	3	1	2.23	0.88	67%	19%	14%	2.21	16	3	1	7	1	1
A	Stoke	0	1	2.40	0.16	87%	12%	2%	2.71	18	3	0	2	0	0
A	Tottenham	0	4	0.16	2.76	1%	9%	90%	0.12	2	0	0	15	5	2
H	Wolves	2	1	2.29	1.13	63%	19%	17%	2.09	13	4	1	10	1	1
A	Everton	2	0	2.12	0.58	73%	18%	9%	2.38	11	4	2	7	0	0
H	Man United	1	1	2.04	0.88	64%	21%	15%	2.13	10	4	0	7	1	1
H	Norwich	1	1	2.26	1.43	55%	21%	24%	1.86	20	2	0	10	2	1
A	West Brom	2	0	2.23	0.74	71%	18%	11%	2.31	16	3	2	9	0	0
H	Swansea	0	0	1.54	1.27	43%	26%	32%	1.55	15	1	0	8	2	0
A	Chelsea	2	1	1.19	1.54	29%	26%	45%	1.14	7	2	2	15	1	1
H	Man City	1	1	1.29	0.72	50%	30%	21%	1.78	12	1	0	5	1	0
A	Fulham	0	1	1.93	1.93	39%	22%	39%	1.39	16	2	0	16	2	1
H	QPR	1	0	3.25	0.49	89%	8%	3%	2.74	21	5	1	6	0	0
A	Aston Villa	2	0	1.51	1.76	33%	23%	43%	1.24	11	2	1	14	2	0
A	Wigan	0	0	1.60	1.23	46%	25%	29%	1.63	12	2	0	15	0	0
H	Blackburn	1	1	3.09	0.41	89%	9%	3%	2.75	19	5	1	5	0	0
H	Newcastle	3	1	1.35	0.55	56%	29%	15%	1.96	9	2	2	3	1	0
A	Man City	0	3	1.35	0.96	45%	28%	27%	1.64	9	2	0	8	1	1
H	Stoke	0	0	1.51	0.16	72%	25%	4%	2.40	11	2	0	2	0	0
A	Bolton	1	3	1.43	1.37	38%	26%	37%	1.39	10	2	1	13	1	1
A	Wolves	3	0	2.03	0.49	73%	19%	8%	2.38	21	1	1	6	0	0
H	Tottenham	0	0	1.54	0.80	54%	27%	20%	1.88	15	1	0	6	1	0
A	Man United	1	2	1.10	1.96	21%	22%	57%	0.85	6	2	1	9	4	2
		29	23	44	26	54%	21%	24%	70 = end of season points projection						
		1.16	0.92	1.78	1.04										

Next, we take a look at how unlucky Liverpool have been given that the record is not as good as statistically predicted. The red/right-hand line in the figure below indicates the probability for each goal haul with the Reds' 1.78 *deserved* goal rate. It should entitle Liverpool to 44 goals, which is in the middle of the distribution field. With those chances Liverpool have created and the model explained in this piece, the probability that they would have just 29 goals or less after 25 games is an absurd 0.92 %.

In other words, Liverpool shouldn't be expecting a similar period for the next century or so. The Reds' opponents, however, are only goals away from average.

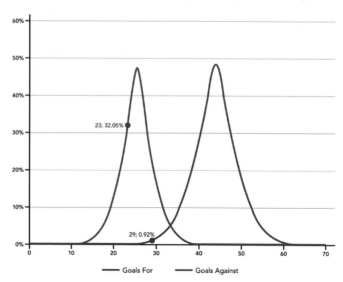

The next graph shows the gap between deserved and actual goals. As the trend seems to be continuous, it may indicate that Liverpool's chances are not as good quality as some others. But it is hard to believe that the Reds' chances would be much worse than the average clear-cut or ordinary chance in this league, which this research is all about.

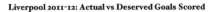

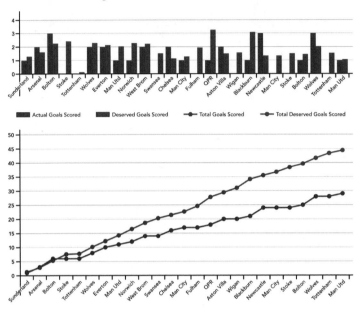

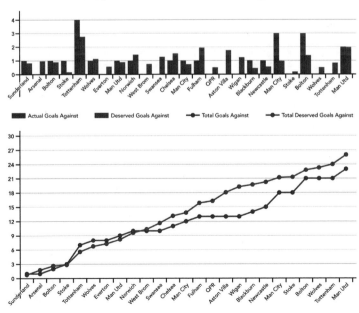

Then come similar figures for goals against, and how Liverpool's goal difference should be evolving (but is not):

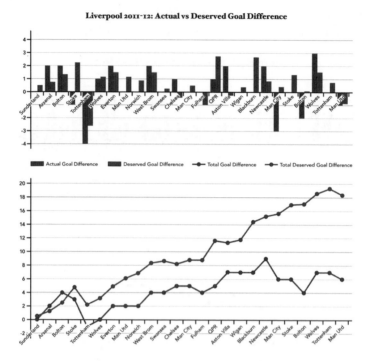

Liverpool 2011-12: Actual vs Deserved Goal Difference

As it seems, the Reds' *have* been unlucky in front of goal, but exactly how big an influence on the points haul has this bad luck had?

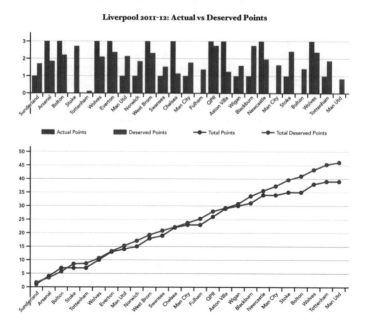

Liverpool 2011-12: Actual vs Deserved Points

In the last figure the blue/right-hand bar indicates deserved points while the red/left-hand bar tells the actual story so far. The difference is seven points (scale on left) which would put Liverpool nicely in line with rivals in London with a game in hand (against Everton).

"Destiny is a good thing to accept when it's going your way. When it isn't, don't call it destiny; call it injustice, treachery, or simple bad luck." – Joseph Heller

A EUROPEAN HANGOVER? LIVERPOOL'S RECORD AFTER EURO GAMES

By Graeme Riley

March, 2011

One of the following statements is true – can you guess which one?

a) Liverpool's record in matches after a European game is much worse than in fixtures when they have not just played in Europe.

b) Results of matches after European games were worst in the 1990s.

c) Liverpool perform better in homes games after European games than in away games.

d) Liverpool have only lost one game on neutral territory after playing a European fixture.

Read on to find the answer.

A frequent complaint amongst fans is that Liverpool don't play well after European fixtures, but does this belief actually hold water? In order to assess this, it was necessary to establish some ground rules. The most important of these is that only those games (regardless of the competition) that took place within five days of the European match were considered. So for example, a match after a European final would typically be in the following season, so it would be unreasonable to include this in the analysis, since a totally different team could be fielded.

Similarly, matches taking place six days later will put less pressure on squad resources, as they are effectively in the following week, and so I have discounted these as well. Contrast this with the match against Stoke in April 1966, which took place just two days after the away leg of the European Cup Winners' Cup semi-final against Celtic.

In order to make the analysis more meaningful, I've broken the data down into three distinct periods: pre-Heysel; 1991-2001 (ie pre Champions League involvement);

and post 2001, when most of the Champions League involvement has occurred. The results are somewhat unexpected.

Pre-Heysel (124 games)

Although Liverpool won marginally fewer games after a European match than when no match took place, the number of defeats was disproportionately lower. Somewhat surprisingly, the record in games was better in the immediate aftermath of an away international night than one at home. The win record was very similar (31 from 60 games for home compared to 33 for 62 away), but defeats were turned into draws (18 draws and 11 defeats after home European clashes, compared to 21 draws and only eight defeats after away games). Perhaps those trips to the far flung corners of Europe hardened the team and made them take fewer risks, settling for draws rather than chasing the victory and conceding defeat in the process.

Pre-Champions League (44 games)

It would be fair to say that in domestic terms at least, Liverpool were probably at their weakest during this decade. With what seemed like clockwork regularity the Reds were eliminated by perceived weaker opposition (Brondby, Celta Vigo, Strasbourg) and struggled to adapt to UEFA's new nationality (and assimilation) rules.

In those games where there was no preceding European match, Liverpool won 46.3% and split the draws and defeats almost equally (27.4% to 26.3%).

It is therefore surprising to see such a high percentage of successes *following* Europe – 61.4% wins, with a relatively equal distribution of draws and losses. Precisely at the time when Liverpool were struggling in Europe and the League, form picked up in the aftermath of a European match.

Even more surprisingly, the form after away matches outperformed the form in home games. Liverpool's record after home games in Europe was only 10 wins from 21 ties, whereas the form improved after Europe away days – 16 wins from 22 games, with only two defeats.

Champions League era (115 games prior to Braga)

The more recent period is probably the one that remains most vivid in our minds. The numbers are skewed by the volume of matches and quality of opposition in Europe, and the knock-on effect of this in subsequent matches. When there had been no European match in the previous five days, Liverpool won 62.3% of games and lost just 18.0%, but when there had been a European game this changed to 50.4% and 28.7% respectively.

The split of victories was roughly the same, regardless of whether the game following Europe had been home or away, at around 50%. Strangely, defeats were more frequent when a match followed Europe at home rather than away – 33.3% to 24.1%, with a corresponding increase in draws.

Conclusions:

So taking each of the questions at the start in turn:

a) *Liverpool's record in matches after a European game is much worse than when they have not played in Europe* – No, overall it is remarkably similar, with 53.0% of games won following Europe and 53.7% where no European match has taken place.

b) *Results of matches after European games were worst in the 1990s* – No, the complete opposite. The record of wins after a European match was 1964-85: 52.4%; 1991-2001: 61.4%; and 2001-2011: 50.4%.

c) *Liverpool perform better in games after home European ties than in away European ties* – No, overall the Reds win 54.9% after away games, and only 50.7% after home games (losses are respectively 16.9% and 26.8%).

d) *Liverpool have only lost one game on neutral territory after playing a European fixture* – True, this was the Chelsea League Cup Final of 2005. Not surprisingly, neutral games after Europe are relatively rare, as neutral games will generally come at the end of a season, when there are probably no European games left. Altogether there have been 12 neutral games after Europe, six won, five drawn and only one lost. Where the preceding game was not in European competition, the corresponding record is won 22, drawn 15 and lost 17, so again Liverpool improve theit record on neutral grounds if the game follows on directly from a European match.

After Europe home matches, within 5 days

	Played	Win	Draw	Loss
1964-1985	60	31	18	11
1990-2001	21	10	4	7
2001-2010	57	29	9	19
Total	138	70	31	37

After Europe away matches, within 5 days

	Played	Win	Draw	Loss
1964-1985	62	33	21	8
1990-2001	22	16	4	2
2001-2010	58	29	15	14
Total	142	78	40	24

After Europe all matches, within 5 days

	Played	Win	Draw	Loss
1964-1985	124	65	40	19
1990-2001	44	27	8	9
2001-2010	115	58	24	33
Total	283	150	72	61

POSSESSION: 9/10THS OF LFC LAW?

By Paul Tomkins

November, 2010

One thing is undeniable: Liverpool have not passed the ball as well this season as in the recent past. But do you need possession in order to win games?

Comparing with last season is fraught with perils on a number of levels; not least because it was not a good season, and it was the reason – publicly at least – behind the dismissal of Rafa Benítez. If Benítez underachieved last season, the onus on the new man has to be to better that.

And yet comparing with the season before is equally dangerous, as that was a remarkably good one; 25 wins (66%) and just two defeats.

So I will compare with both, in the belief that somewhere in between those two extremes should be what Liverpool are aiming for, in terms of results.

Keep ball

Possession, of course, is all about what you do with the ball; you can win with little of the ball, and you can lose with loads of the ball.

But over the course of a number of games, a pattern should emerge. And in terms of being successful – as a big club should, relatively speaking – maintaining possession has to be the key, right?

Well, the answers are below.

Balls

In the games played so far this season, Liverpool have attempted 4,451 passes and been successful with 3,662.

This is down on last season, when 5,111 were attempted in the same fixtures (replacing teams with their equivalent if no longer in division), with 4,325 finding a red shirt.

In other words, last season saw almost as many successful passes as the total number the Reds have even attempted this time.

Last season, 84% were successful, as they were a year earlier. This season, it's down to 82% accuracy. Not a big drop, but a drop all the same.

However, the same fixtures in Liverpool's most successful season under Benítez (2008/09) saw a figure between these two totals: 4,910 passes with 4,148 successful.

Last season the Reds made a greater number of passes in 75% of the fixtures compared with this one: nine games out of 12.

It's hard to make sense of the fact that Roy Hodgson's best possession stats come from defeats at Old Trafford and Goodison: 461 and 510 attempted passes respectively. Last year, the Reds managed 351 in both games.

Even more bizarrely, the Reds won 4-1 at Old Trafford 18 months ago with just 295 passes. But if there's one game in which you want to be counter-attacking, it's probably this one.

To me, the problem comes with counter-attacking at home. It does not get the crowd behind the team; it makes them edgy. The cries of 'attack! attack! attack!' have been more pronounced this campaign.

In terms of this season and last, possession doesn't seem to make much difference to the result. However, compare this season against two years ago, and having more possession appears to have made a big difference.

Home Faults

At home, Liverpool just aren't making as many passes anymore. And this has been my major problem with Hodgson's approach.

Compared with last season, only 80% of the number of passes are being attempted: 335 to 415. To show how consistent Liverpool were at home in passing under Benítez, it was 420 in 2008/09 in the same six fixtures.

If it feels like the football isn't as good, there's a reason: because, quite simply, it isn't.

Allen Wade's Way

Perhaps surprisingly, given the way 'Wadian' sides seem to play, comes this observation from Jonathan Wilson, talking about coaching in English football 35 years ago, when things were really starting to head long-ball:

"On the side of possession was Allen Wade, the technical director of the FA, whose coaching course was such an influence on the likes of Roy Hodgson. Arguing against that was Charles Reep, whose ideas would become FA policy under Charles Hughes, Wade's successor as technical director."

So, compared with the long-ball advocates, Hodgson is on the side of possession. But this is possession in the old English way, not possession in the new world of Arsenal and Barcelona.

Wilson adds something interesting: "[Charles] *Hughes's figures, insubstantial as they are, tend to support the theory that the higher the level, the less effective direct football is (very briefly, if you separate goals scored in internationals in his sample, 63% resulted from moves of five passes or fewer, as opposed to an overall figure of 87%)."*

So, it seems that in higher quality football, possession becomes all the more important. But there's a caveat:

"Where the analysis of Reep and Hughes seems deficient is that they seem to have assumed teams should constantly be trying to score. Inter last week [against Barcelona] had little intention of doing so. Other sides in a similar position – Brazil against England in the 2002 World Cup, for instance, or Liverpool in the away leg of their Champions League quarter final against Juventus in 2005 – may have defended their advantage by holding possession; Inter preferred to surrender possession and hold a position just outside their own box. It worked, and while they may have had a touch of fortune, it is also the case that they frustrated Barça as well as anybody has done this season, so in that regard it must be regarded as having been a successful tactic."

But recent statistics seem to show that, if you had to choose possession-based football or purely counter-attacking, you'd be better off with the ball at your feet. As Wilson says:

"Opta statistics, produced in conjunction with Castrol, show that over the past two seasons in the Premier League in only around a third of games did one side have 60% of possession or more, and when they did they won 52% of the time, and lost 25%. If a side had 70% possession or over (which happened in 4.7% of games), they won 67% of the time and lost 17%. Only once in the past two seasons did one side have over 80 per cent possession – Liverpool, in their 3-2 win at Bolton last August [2009].

"In the closer games, having 50-59.9% possession meant a side won 43% of the time and lost 31%. So there is a clear correlation between dominating possession and winning matches. Intuitively, we know that there are sides that are successful at counter-attacking, which logically means accepting a lower percentage of possession."

So there you have it. Inter beat the best footballing side in the world with tactics similar to those used by Hodgson.

But most weeks, if you're Liverpool FC, you don't play the best sides in the world: you play sides inferior to yourself. And that result was at Barcelona's ground; at home, they approached the game very differently.

Houllier's Home Hang-ups

As I noted recently, Houllier – another Wadian – won an average of 10.8 home games per season, compared with Benítez's 13.

In other words, the Frenchman won only 83% as many home games as did the Spaniard.

I don't know the possession statistics for Houllier, but as we've seen, Hodgson's are only 80% of what we were seeing in Benítez's final two campaigns. And the similarities between the styles of Houllier and Hodgson are uncanny.

So far, despite it being just six home games, Hodgson's 50% win rate at Anfield is down on Benítez's 66% in the same fixtures last season, and 66% the season before. (Roughly in keeping with Rafa's 68% win record at Anfield during six years in the Premier League.)

Conclusions

With Roy's apparent distrust of Agger and Johnson – by a country mile the two most gifted footballers in deep areas of the pitch – and with the solid, unspectacular Konchesky replacing the raw but far more technically-gifted Insúa, it's no wonder that building from the back has proved more difficult. And it's not by accident, either.

Add Reina – himself a great passer from the back – being forced to hit more hopeful long passes, and you see a team squandering possession all too easily.

In midfield, the graceful Aquilani (who is now showing his brilliance again in Italy) has been replaced by the more robust but slightly less gifted Meireles, to complete a side being shorn of its passing skills.

As you will have seen, almost all of the stats laid out in the piece suggest that Liverpool do not have the right approach.

To conclude, I may be spotting patterns here that are not as relevant as they seem. But all the same, the patterns are definitely there.

LIVERPOOL'S PRESSING APPROACH

By Mihail Vladimirov

November, 2011

There are two ways to gain possession of the ball – steal it from an opponent or intercept it before it reaches an opponent. This can be done either by pressing or by standing off.

"Pressing" is the art of closing down the opponent, denying him space either to receive the ball or do anything once he does receive it. This is sometimes labelled as a "proactive" defensive tactic because the defending team takes the initiative in forcing the opposition to cede the ball. In modern football, nearly every big club does this, especially the ones playing with an attacking mentality, with Barcelona the archetype, famed not only for their superb passing and creativity but also for their ability to win the ball high up the field. They are the benchmark for everything that is "right" in football. (Well, according to some.)

"Standing off" is the antithesis. In this system the team will pull back to defensive positions as soon as it loses the ball. In basketball we might refer to this as the difference between the full-court and half-court press. Players sit back and protect their defensive zones, waiting for the opposition to come onto them before engaging in foot-to-foot combat. This is a much more passive form of defence (reactive as compared to the proactive pressing approach), forcing the opponent to try something special to break you down rather than making a pre-emptive strike.

Pressing denies time on the ball; standing off denies space in key areas. No team is capable of doing both (not even Barcelona), so the one you choose is dependent on the relative skill and tactical threat posed by the opposition.

More often than not, smaller clubs tend to adopt the passive approach. This means that the attacking team can enjoy a lot of possession, but it is hoped that possession will be in deep and wide areas where they will not pose much of a threat. Of course, this can be suicide against a really creative team who will patiently pass the ball around until they find a gap. On the other hand, over-enthusiastic pressing can be just as dangerous. For example, if the opposition has three central midfielders to your two, heavy pressing will pull your midfielders out of position, leaving at least one opponent completely free to wreak havoc in the centre of the field.

This is why I thought Liverpool were right to stand off Brighton, in the second half of their League Cup tie this season. Brighton could have all the ball they wanted in safe positions, because they lacked anyone of the calibre necessary to expose Liverpool at the back. Since the onus was on them to come at Liverpool and score a goal, the Reds were able to say "let's see what you've got" rather than opening themselves up by pressing too heavily and creating gaps all over the field. If you deny the opposition space in key areas, any team in the world will struggle (as Mourinho proved so brilliantly with Internazionale against Barcelona a couple of years ago). Conversely, if you give good space to players with even a modest skill set you are likely to be punished.

With all that said, my own theory is that the superior team should look to deny the lesser team space. Even if you concede a possession advantage, their lack of creativity (relative to your own) should mean that you can comfortably defend your goal. Sooner or later their lack of technique will lead to a poor pass or a poor attempt at controlling the ball, allowing you to regain the ball and take advantage on the counter.

But when teams are closer in ability, more proactivity is required. Teams with decent creativity and technique will eventually break you down, if given the time to manufacture enough space. You cannot rely on the bad pass or the ill-judged run. No team can keep 100% concentration throughout the entire match. Eventually they will pass the ball around, pull you out of position and find that small amount of space necessary to drive a wedge through the defence. Denying the opposition time on the ball gives them less opportunity to dictate the play.

Pressing with a three man midfield

As I said in a recent article, modern football is all about possession. Formations are selected to ensure that the team wins this battle, or at least to offset the effectiveness of the opposition's time on the ball. From a numerical point of view, the three-man midfield is the best way to achieve an advantage in the possession stakes. It has a spare man over the two-person midfield and can at the very least match a three-man midfield, player-for-player.

Rafa Benítez provides a good example of this. His 4-2-3-1 used a midfield trio in the centre not only to control that zone of the pitch in attack but also to assert dominance in defence. The 4-2-3-1 formation creates a 2-1 triangle in midfield. It is more defensive than the 4-1-2-3 (with a 1-2 triangle) because it utilises two deep-lying midfielders rather than just the one. By doing this, you can cover both wings at the same time, as one or both players can drift wide to cover any gaps. Doing so shuts down space and time for the opponent. With only one holding midfielder, only one flank can be covered at once, which means any team capable of quickly switching the ball from one flank to the other can play around your pressing patterns and break down a passive defence.

The 4-2-3-1 formation allows you to press with the front four because the deeper midfielders provide a covering base. It also allows the full-backs to come out of defence to close down the opposition because the midfielders can drift to plug the gap. In this way, the pitch is covered both vertically and horizontally because the four covering players (the deeper midfielders and the centre backs) defend the danger zone while the rest of the team chase down the player on the ball and reduce his passing options. No other formation is so balanced. With four covering and six pressing, I will refer to this system as 4×6 for the sake of clarity.

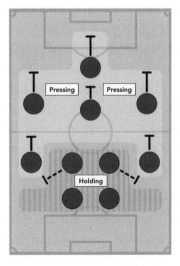

With the 4-1-2-3 you have to focus on the centre of the pitch because your full-backs are not able to push on as aggressively. Although it is a more attacking formation (the two advanced midfielders can both offer creativity and drive through the centre), it forces the opposition to drift wide where there is more space. In this zone the opposition will get more time on the ball because of the passivity of the full-backs in the defensive phase. So, the team has to utilise five covering defenders (the back four and the holding midfielder) while the other five press. Or, to continue with the same format as above, a 5×5 system.

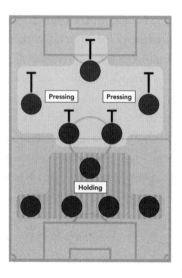

When used by a proactive attacking team, both of these formations focus on heavy pressing by the advanced players in order to deny the opposition time on the ball. They also use their deeper players to cover the dangerous areas in the centre of the pitch in front of the goal by using the extra men in the midfield. The effects of this can be magnified when they play against the 4-4-2. Passive sides, however, have a slightly different outlook. The midfield and defence will push close together in their own half, creating a very congested area in the centre which will be hard to penetrate. This will tend to "flatten" the triangles, but it will still be possible to send a deeper midfielder out to the wing or have one of the advanced midfielders step out of the line and close down the opposition. That is because there are enough bodies in the centre to cover if one leaves the line. As a result, both formations are equally suited to playing a "standing off" game.

Standing off with a two-man midfield
In theory, 4-4-2 is especially vulnerable to diagonal balls played into the channels. To prevent this, teams tend to defend by creating two banks of four which are tightly

packed together. This is, I have argued, the best defensive formation. But in order to pull this off, the team needs to be incredibly disciplined and it needs to play with a stand-off mentality. It also means the side tends to be rigid and static, which isn't always the best thing for a team looking to attack.

If a side playing 4-4-2 wants to press heavily, it will inevitably create fissures between the various pairings (the centre backs; the central midfielders; the forwards; and the winger and full-back). Sacchi's Milan managed it in the late 1980s, but that was under a different interpretation of the offside law. Today, a traditional 4-4-2 is rarely played with a heavy pressing mentality against a quality side, even one playing with the same formation. It needs to provide fluidity in attack as well as rigidity in defence. Without good movement, the team will be stagnant and lack creativity (see: Hodgson); so the best way to provide the platform for this is to have a passive defence which stays tight without the ball. The three-man midfield formations allow much greater flexibility when defending because there is a "spare" man available who can either cover a gap or press the player on the ball without exposing the team to danger.

This is a logical conclusion and a practical consideration. Fluid play requires a lot of physical effort as players run into new positions. To be fluid in both the attacking and defensive phases requires supreme fitness – something not all teams possess. And a tiring team makes mistakes, which in turn can leave the defence exposed.

In 4-4-2, defensive fluidity would require both central midfielders to press heavily and as a unit. But given that there are only two of them, that would tire them out quickly and leave them less useful on the attack. In a three-person midfield, the roles can be divided so that some press while others rest, rotating the physical burden and keeping the team alert in both phases.

So to compensate, the 4-4-2 stands off, giving the team time to recover, minimising the chance of making defensive mistakes, and giving the team the platform to attack once it regains possession.

The mixed approach

"Mixed pressing" is a term I've been using for a while now to describe how Liverpool defend.

In essence, it means that whichever formation is chosen, the different lines have different duties when defending. The attacking band (the front four – forwards and wingers – in a 4-4-2 or the lone striker and wingers in a 4-1-2-3) are generally the most active. They close down the opposition defenders in the final third, forcing them to get rid of the ball. The two midfielders (let's ignore the holding midfielder in the 4-1-2-3 for a moment) are generally the second wave of defence. If the opponent is attacking through the centre, they will tend to close them down. But if the opponent is attacking down the wing they will fall back to create a defensive unit with the back four. Against West Brom we saw a 4+2 situation; against Manchester United and Arsenal the addition of Lucas as the holding player meant it was more 4+3. That floods the danger zone in the centre of the pitch and denies the opposing team any space in which to play. The back four are less active, usually pulling back into their positions rather than pressing heavily. They will only engage once a player enters their zone of the pitch. This is also true of the holding midfielder, who tends to sit in front of the back four rather than pressing the man on the ball.

So the result is that the team is more active in the opposition's half and around the centre circle, but less active in the defensive third. They do not play with a high defensive line and often look vulnerable in the central zone (especially when playing 4-4-2 and one of the central midfielders has pushed on to join the attack). Gaps are created between the attacking band and those standing off in the defensive positions.

This division can be explained tactically, especially if we look at the squad Dalglish has available. First, it's clear that with 4-4-2 the team cannot press in every zone of the pitch. Second, the shape means that the team cannot play 6×4, even against other 4-4-2s or inferior players.

So, something needs to be done differently in the midfield zone. Currently the team is blessed with players with pace (Enrique; Johnson) and a good work ethic (Downing; Kuyt) in wide areas. In the centre, however, mobility is an issue. Although Agger and Škrtel have a bit more pace than Carragher, they are nowhere near as quick as Enrique or Johnson. They are probably closer to John Terry and Ivanović, and the Chelsea-Arsenal game showed how exposed they can be in a system that plays with a high line and aggressive pressing when playing against mobile forwards. Lucas and Spearing are the only two who possess a good balance between mobility and defensive stability. Therefore the most balanced tactical approach is the mixed approach. The front four (occasionally helped by the full-backs who have the pace to recover their positions) press while the others stand off and hold the fort. If the entire team presses, the central defenders will be heavily exposed, even if Lucas is covering in front of them.

Of course, the risk is that the opposition will bypass the first pressing wave and will be given a lot of space in between the attack and midfield. But we've already seen that, while they might be getting good ball possession here, they are finding it very difficult to get into dangerous positions and create chances. Liverpool are the fifth-best team in the Premier League in terms of shots conceded with 13, only three more than the best team, Chelsea. Plus, as Dan Kennett has already pointed out, the opposition have had a freakishly high conversion rate against the Reds (six goals from just eleven clear-cut chances). So, in other words, for every 1.1 chances (per game) Liverpool concede, the opposition scores; that doesn't necessarily indicate a poor defence, rather an unlucky one.

Plus, Liverpool are not just "parking the bus" or sitting deep doing nothing. The team averages 21 tackles per game, compared with Norwich, Newcastle and QPR who lead the league on 22. In interceptions the team is 16th with 13 per game, quite a way behind Blackburn on 20. This suggests that even though Liverpool are not pressing the opposition in defence, they are still engaging their men making a lot of tackles, rather than sitting back and hoping to pick up a loose pass.

There is another important thing to note here – a high defensive line in attack is not the same thing as a high defensive line in defence. There are pros and cons to both, but they don't necessarily have to be played at the same time.

High defensive lines when attacking compact the team and make it easier to play possession-oriented football. But as soon as the other team regains the ball, the defensive line can drop, leaving the front four to press the midfield, helping to reduce the chance of creating a rift between the attacking band and the midfield band. We have seen this approach taken by Liverpool all season, with the West Brom game the best example of how this should work in practice. This allows the team to play with a slower centre-back (Carragher), as you are not holding a high line when the opposition have the ball, so he shouldn't be so exposed. Of course, a quick counter attack and a long ball over the top could allow an opposition striker to get in behind the defence – but this is when you call upon those other skills in football such as anticipation, positioning, concentration and experience.

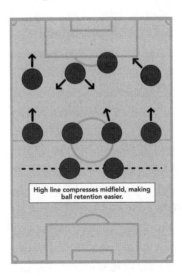

High line compresses midfield, making ball retention easier.

As ever, the key thing is how the team deals with the transitional phases from defence to attack and from attack to defence. When attacking, the aim is to push forward in a fluid way so that the opposition cannot track you; but when the team loses the ball, the players need to get back into their positions so that they do not leave gaps all over the pitch. This then allows the front four to press and the back four to retreat while the midfield duo find their optimal positions to cover everything. If the opposition is slow to react, you will have the chance to press with the forwards and drop back with the defenders with ease.

However, in the quicker-tempo Premier League the team needs to react with speed so that the time delay between being in attacking mode and defensive mode is as short as possible. In the last few matches, it has become clear that Liverpool are starting to gel as a unit and are completing this process far more smoothly than at the beginning of the year.

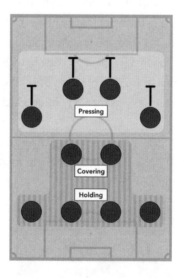

This approach has been adopted whenever Liverpool have played 4-4-2 this season, most of the time successfully. At the beginning of the season, Adam's lack of pace made the team look exposed at times. But now that he appears more disciplined, perhaps because he has been given more specific instructions, he is making better decisions about when to go forward and when to hold his position. The match against Everton and especially the WBA game were great successes in this respect. The Arsenal and Manchester United games also showed that it can work with the 4-1-2-3.

However, as the final months of last season showed, the team looks even better from a defensive and tactical point of view when Lucas and Spearing play as the central midfield duo. They allow the team to push forward in attack but also to protect the back four when the team lose the ball because they are natural ball-winning midfielders. The

League Cup tie against Stoke City showed how effective this approach can be.

Let's finish with a brief discussion about the high defensive line in defence. With this system the team can press the opposition all over the pitch because the team is more compact and will naturally limit the amount of space and time they have on the ball. This is more risky, however, because if your central defenders are not mobile enough they can be exposed to balls played into the channels and into the big space between the back four and the goal keeper (as I've already said, check out the Chelsea-Arsenal game). This risk exists even with a three-person midfield and is exacerbated in 4-4-2, as the defence has little-to-no cover.

Conclusions

It is perfectly logical that Dalglish and Clarke are not delivering the "get stuck in" approach that some of the fans are clamouring for. While it pleases English audiences to see aggressive defenders and midfielders, it is not necessarily the best way to play.

It is wrong to suggest that backing off is a sign of defensive weakness. It is also wrong to suggest that the reason for this system is the age and lack of mobility of Jamie Carragher. He is *a* reason why the team plays this way, but that pre-supposes that this form of defence is somehow defective. The team cannot play the Barcelona style of pressing for the entire match – few teams can. Especially if the coaches persist with the 4-4-2 formation.

Hopefully this article will begin to explain how teams defend and why Carragher doesn't deserve the stick he's getting. The bigger picture is that even if Carragher wasn't in the starting line-up, the team would still (more than likely) play with this passive sort of defence.

As the team gels more over the coming months and the coaches gather more experience and data on the way they play, the team should move in the right direction. The way they attack with such flamboyancy at the moment – alongside their defensive stability – suggests to me that they are well on their way.

And, lest we forget, Liverpool have only played ten league games this season. With the levels of improvement we've seen, the final three-quarters of the season are looking intriguing.

THE SECRET TO TRANSFER SUCCESS

By Paul Tomkins

June, 2012

The notion that players aged between 20 and 22 make the ideal signings has gathered weight in recent times. Anyone younger may just be a flash in the pan, while older players tend to command bigger wages (because they're used to being paid well) and have a diminishing sell-on value.

With this in mind, I thought it would be a good time to look back at Liverpool's Premier League signings – over 100 deals – to see how value for money relates to age. We can all think of great young buys and rubbish older purchases, just as we can all think of rubbish young buys and great older purchases.

But what's the general trend? Does the theory about buying players aged between 20 and 22 hold true? Which Liverpool managers have been most successful at buying players at the right age?

Also [teaser alert], it turns out that there is one age-range that is totally disastrous – but what is it?

My starting point was Graeme Riley's incredible TPI database, and also some of the work I'd done filtering the results in 2010 for our book, *Pay As You Play*.

First of all, for a basic overview, I split the transfers into five age groups: under 20; 20-22; 23-26; 27-28; and 29 and over. In the under 20s, I excluded the really young and inexpensive signings for the youth team, as only a small percentage of these can ever be expected to make the grade.

Due to the study spanning the entire Premier League period, TPI inflation simply had to be used; comparing fees from 1993, 2002 and 2011 is pointless without taking inflation into account. CTPP is the term we use in TPI for "current day money"; the *Current Transfer Purchase Price*; unless otherwise stated, all prices are CTPP. Obviously judging the relative success or failure of any player is open to subjective forces, but for this, I mostly looked at objective measures.

One clear sign of success with a transfer is the player starting a large number league games; it could be seen as a problem that the database doesn't cover cup matches of any kind, but poor signings are less likely to be risked in the league, and if they are, it won't be for long (whereas the duds can often end up in the Carling Cup squad). Graeme's data also only covers games started, so it works against subs, but on the whole, the best players get to start a high number of league games.

(NB: Although certain groups are filtered out for later results – free transfers, and players still at the club – this first section is all-inclusive, with the single exception of reserve goalkeepers, who can go years without even getting a game if there's an outstanding or reliable no.1; as such, they cannot be fairly judged, especially with David James and Pepe Reina both racking up several seasons in a row without missing a league game.)

It's only fair to say that some of the age groups have only a handful of players, which makes the sample size small.

The numbers are as follows: **U20s**: 9; **20-22s**: 23; **23-26s**: 43; **27-28**: 16; **29 or over**: 15.

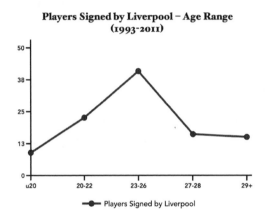

The age group that makes the highest number of starts, on average, during a player's time at Liverpool FC, is the fabled 20-22 range, at 63.4. The 23-26 group follow closely after, at 59.7, and a little way behind them come the 27/28 year olds, on 45.3. Then there's a big drop to the 29+ group – who obviously have a short shelf-life anyway – at 20.3. As if to prove that players below 20 can be hit and miss (and indeed, more miss than hit in Liverpool's case), the 16-19 range only made 16.7 starts on average, despite having the most years ahead of them.

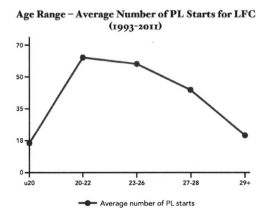

There's nothing wrong with buying an older player if the price is right. On average, the 29+ age group were the cheapest, at £2.3m, just behind the teenagers, at £3.0m. But none of the other three groups average out below £8m; proving that players in their 20s obviously cost a lot more money.

The most expensive group is the one aged 20-22 (prime targets) but despite costing on average roughly £3m more than the 23-26 and 27/28 groups, they perform better than both when it comes to limiting CTPP loss. In other words, they provide a sell-on value that more than makes up for the high initial fee. (Due to inflation, it's very hard to make a CTPP profit; if you buy at £5m, but sell at £8m – a profit in normal, non-accounting terms – you have made a CTPP *loss* if the average fee at the time of sale is £10m; and football inflation almost always rises. Therefore, while individual deals make CTPP profits – Fernando Torres being the most successful example – the averages of all five groups result in a CTPP loss. It's the nature, and extent, of that loss that is telling.)

The CTPP loss for the teens is just £92,843. For 29+, it's only £1.7m, given those relatively small fees (if not a Bosman) tend to be paid to start with. Mid-ranked of the five groups is '20-22', at £3.7m. The second worst group is 23-26, with an average £4.3m loss per deal. But the worst – and, for me, the moral of this entire story – are the 27- and 28-year olds, at £4.6m. As I noted in *Pay As You Play*, the average fee for a footballer drops sharply after the age of 28; clubs can sense 30-something looming like a bad smell. Occasionally it might make sense – United won titles thanks to the contributions of Dwight Yorke and Dimitar Berbatov (despite losing fortunes in sell-on value) – but the law of averages warns against it.

In recent times, Liverpool have paid £20m apiece for a 28 year-old Robbie Keane and Stewart Downing, a year younger at 27. The quick sale of Keane limited some of the damage – roughly 75% of the original outlay was recouped six months later – and it was left to Spurs, who had initially sold Keane to the Reds, to take the bigger hit; selling him to LA Galaxy for a massively reduced price (likely to be around just 25% of what they paid the Reds).

Now that Downing is 28, a decision looms – but as £20m was an inflated fee to start with, Liverpool would do well to get half of their money back. By the summer of 2013, Downing's value will most likely be no more than £7m at most, and probably as low as £5m.

How Good?

The one subjective measure I included was a rating for all of the players, out of 10. This was based on how well I thought they had done in a red shirt. I tried not to be too heavily swayed by the price-tag, but did take it into account to some degree.

It was only when I took the averages for each age range that some interesting results leapt out: yet again, 20-22 was the star bracket (containing the likes of Reina, Agger, Lucas, Alonso), with a mark out of 10 of 7.0; well above the overall average mark of 6.1. It's one thing having a healthy sell-on value, but – on the whole – players of this age played well. (Of course the likes of Diao and Cissé, proved costly mistakes, but they still didn't heavily damage the overall average.)

Next came the 23-26 year olds – buoyed by the inclusion of Torres, Hyypia and Hamann, but weighed down by Diomede, Dundee, Josemi and Cheyrou – with 6.2; slightly above average overall, but unremarkable. The worst two categories were the extremes: over 29s and under 20s, at 5.4 and 5.6 respectively.

That leaves one category. Dead-on average at 6.1, were the 27-28 year olds. Not only were they grossly overpriced, but they mostly failed to do much more than be 'okay'. Markus Babbel and Yossi Benayoun are the two standouts (I gave both an 8, although Babbel would probably have been higher but for his illness), with Raul Meireles joining Benayoun as the only two players to produce a CTPP profit, albeit marginal. (Andriy Voronin also produced a profit, but that's often easy on free transfers.)

The transfer policy of Roy Hodgson looks even more flawed, when you consider that none of his purchases was aged below 27. With 29-year-old Milan Jovanovic already set to join, he (and Christian Purslow) added Meireles, 27, Cole, 28, Konchesky, 29, Aurelio, 30, and Poulsen, 30 (excluding reserve keeper Brad Jones, 28). Clearly it's not easy hunting for bargains, but within a year, an overall loss was made on the three who cost fees, and two years – and hardly any football – later, Aurelio was released. Contrast this with the team Brendan Rodgers built at Swansea – the second-youngest in the league last year. When Hodgson left Fulham, he left behind the oldest XI in the league at 29.7, and they remain stuck with an average age of 30+.

(As an aside, I thought I'd take a quick look at Harry Redknapp's dealings at Spurs. Of his 20 main signings, six were in their 30s, *with another in his 40s.* The average age of purchases was 27.7 – akin to Hodgson's, but four years older than those of Houllier and Benítez – and even though Spurs did fairly well under 'appy 'Arry, he was only concerned with the here and now; there was no real building for the future. What is it with old school British managers?)

Transfer Price Index Coefficient v.2.0

Last year I created TPIC – the Transfer Price Index Coefficient. The aim was to judge the best and worst transfers in recent times based on:

• the number of games played;
• the fee paid;
• the fee recouped;

• and the percentage of games started.

While a lot of the study remains valid, the coefficient itself, while rewarding all the right things, seemed a little arbitrary in its scoring system; I worked hard to balance the average out at zero, but there was no one defining piece of logic that made those particular numbers *the only* numbers. With the emphasis now on the optimum age to buy players, I thought I'd go back and refine the system, with this new emphasis.

For TPIC, free transfers were excluded, and the date-range was 1994-2011. So the data used is a little different to that used in the first section of this article. On top of that, in a further edit, I removed all players still at their respective clubs, given that their data following the transfer in question is not definitive (with games still to be played, and/or transfer fees to be recouped; there's no way you can *conclusively* judge a transfer like Andy Carroll's in 18 months, when he has time to alter perceptions). That left around 1,500 deals.

So, the new coefficient was basically the average number of games played by each age group, multiplied by 100,000, plus (or minus) the CTPP profit (or loss). The higher the remaining number, the better value the age group. With the data set so much larger than that of just Liverpool, a more accurate picture should emerge; but, on top of that, it provides something to compare the Reds' business against.

To start with I'll look at *all* ages – 16 subsets, with only those under 19 and also those over 32 grouped together. After this I'll cluster them into just five bands – the ones used at the start of this piece.

TPIC (Value for Money) of PL Players by Age

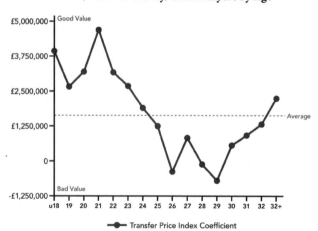

As you can see, 21 is the best-value age, 29 the worst. For some reason 26 is worse than 27, but, otherwise, there's a clear downward trend between 21 and 29; and then, a rise in value for money at 30+, as transfer fees drop to minimal amounts. The ages of 25 to 32 remain below the overall average, but nominal fees paid for those aged over 32 can often result in a couple of worthwhile seasons; although obviously this is the one area where goalkeepers are only entering their peak years, and doubtless they skew the figures somewhat (paying fees for outfield players aged 33 or higher is rare).

Average Age Bands
Now the data is grouped into the original bands: under 20, 20-22, 23-26, 27 and 28, and 29+.

Liverpool perform below par *in all areas*. In many ways this is no surprise; the Premier League is full of teams aiming to avoid relegation with cheap signings, who cost a couple of million pounds and can play 100+ games in the top flight.

The Reds are closer to the average across the middle of the spectrum, but with youngsters and those 29 and over, Liverpool have clearly suffered. The Reds have had precious little success signing teenagers – contrast this, with the £67m and £71m CTPP profits racked up by Arsenal and Man United on Anelka and Ronaldo respectively. And, although Liverpool have had success with free-transfers (albeit excluded in this study) such as McAllister and Maxi, the only four fees paid for players aged 29 or over – on Riedle (31), Xavier (29), Ince (29) and Ferri (29) – represent largely, money poured down the drain. (As the data runs up to 2011, it does not include the money wasted on Poulsen and Konchesky.)

The temptation to pay large fees for players of this age and experience seems to stem from a desire to find the final piece of the puzzle. Both Ince (£18m in 2011 money) at the age of 29, and Robbie Keane, a year younger, represent that desire. After a few years of building, that final push can be justified with one big deal. Only, in Liverpool's case, it hasn't really worked.

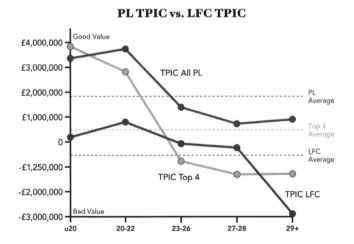

PL TPIC vs. LFC TPIC

A more pertinent comparison of average TPIC values would be against those teams to have qualified for the Champions League (or in Everton's case, the qualifying rounds) in recent times. Here, Liverpool performed worse at both ends of the spectrum, but actually do slightly better in the double-bracket encompassing ages 23-28. Perhaps this is because teams like Manchester United, Chelsea and Manchester City (although their most recent purchases are not included) paid premium prices, for established 'peak' years players, for an instant hit. By contrast, Liverpool's biggest CTPP fees have gone on players aged 23 or below: Heskey (22), Cissé (22), Torres (23), Alonso (22) and Mascherano. (And, though not included, as they haven't yet been sold, Carroll and Suárez.) Downing, at 27, is the only player over 25 with a CTPP at £20m or more.

Best Manager?

Well, we knew it wouldn't be Roy Hodgson, but his figures aren't quite as bad as expected. Whereas Roy Evans and Gérard Houllier had a negative TPIC average on their purchases, Hodgson's is just a fraction over neutral. This is due the fact that he only had three qualifying deals – players both bought and sold by Liverpool – and Meireles accounted for a small profit. Konchesky and Poulsen, while making losses of a few million, did start enough games to wipe out some of that damage.

Gérard Houllier fares worst, and this is something I've covered on a few occasions; but even with the new TPIC system, he still doesn't come out of it well. The reason is simply that his best purchases – Hyypia, Hamann, Finnan, Dudek, Henchoz and, based on Istanbul alone, Smicer (plus McAllister and Babbel, both excluded as free transfers) – were all 25 or over. This was great for a few years, but left nothing for his successors to sell. So the value ran out, and they recouped just pennies when combined. Still, Hyypia and Riise (his one young success) racked up over 500 league starts between them, and they rank in the top five (by contrast, Hamann's CTPP is £23m, and that needed a lot more games to "pay off").

The problem is that Houllier's younger signings were mostly very poor. In today's money, both Heskey and Cissé cost over £32m at the age of 22, while Diouf, aged 21, cost £20.5m. An astonishing £60m CTPP was lost on those three players alone, and only one of them – Heskey – started more than 40 games for the Reds. A further £26m was wasted on Kirkland, Le Tallec and Cheyrou. Alongside Riise, Baros was the one surprise success: just 45 starts, but a profit of £9.4m.

Which brings us to Benítez; whatever anyone says about his transfers, he *got it*. Numbers one and two on the TPIC chart are Torres and Alonso: bought young, over 200 starts between them, sold for a combined CTPP *profit* of £35m, and a non-CTPP profit of £50m.

Given that Dalglish's signings are all still at the club, he could not be included;

Hodgson's paid-for transfers, bar Jones, have all departed. Benítez, however, still has plenty of players who are still at Liverpool, and who, if they were included, would rank high on the TPIC chart.

Indeed, were Pepe Reina to never play another game for Liverpool, and never command a transfer fee, he'd rank 4th. Škrtel and Lucas would also be in the top 20 as things stand, should they simply vanish into the ether. However, if they were all sold tomorrow, at reasonable estimations of transfer value, then Reina would rank top, and Lucas and Škrtel would edge out Riise to leave Rafa with five of the top six, while Agger rises to 9th. Eleven of the top 20 would be Rafa signings, and six of the top ten.

Should Rafa's signings never be sold, and instead, double the number of league games started (distinctly possible for Reina, Agger, Škrtel and Lucas), they'd still all occupy the top 10, and Reina would stretch his lead at the top. (The only player to suffer would be Lucas; dropping down to 8th, but at 25, doubling his league starts to 200 underplays his future potential).

See the graph below for overall managerial performance, with Benítez's *projected* figures in brackets/shaded.

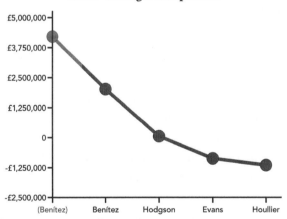

TPIC – Manager Comparison

Aside from Robbie Keane and Alberto Aquilani, Benítez bought big only with players aged 20-23, and in the case of Keane, minimised the hit by selling quickly (he was sacked before he had a chance to make a decision on Aquilani). In the overall TPIC chart – of all teams, 1994-2011 – only Torres and Reina are in the top 20 when it comes to Liverpool players (Hyypia narrowly misses out, ranked 26th), and barring injury or illness, Reina is a shoo-in for the top 20.

The question now is whether Liverpool cash in on one or two of these players when they're at their peak – in particular, Škrtel springs to mind, with Manchester City's interest – or keep them because of what they can offer, knowing that injury or loss of form could cost the Reds both an effective player and also the money to reinvest. If Liverpool could get £15m+ for Škrtel, who turns 28 in December, and find that Sebastián Coates, who cost half that amount, is just as reliable, then that, in essence, is Moneyball. But the skill is in knowing – or accurately guessing – that, in this example, Coates can fill the void (and trusting that Agger can stay fit), or that a youngster from the Academy is going to be even better. As we've seen with Lucas, sometimes it can take a young player a season of constant first team action to reach his potential, but that year comes at a price. Alternatively, Coates replaces Carragher as third choice centre-back, and a new 24-year-old centre-back is purchased for around £10m. So there's no great secret to transfer success; but hopefully this article helps prove just why FSG's approach is right.

Now, the question is, can they find the right players.

THE TRANSFER PRICE INDEX PREDICTIONS FOR 2012/13

By Zach Slaton.
September 2012

A flurry of activity at the end of this summer's transfer window punctuated what was the second most active window in recent memory (in terms of pounds spent at £498m/$778m), although net spend by clubs was a much tamer £224m/$350m according to *Forbes*' Bobby McMahon. Readers of the *The Tomkins Times* and Transfer Price Index (TPI) blog know that both numbers matter.

The gross spend of nearly £500M is indicative of just how much player movement is going on in the league, as well as how much it costs to purchase a good player in today's Premier League. Sure, there are a number of big ticket players like Robin Van Persie (£24m from Manchester United's kitty) and Eden Hazard (£32m paid by Chelsea) that drive a good bit of this spending, but there's also the rapid fire, smaller deals that get done on deadline day that help raise the total as well (see Manchester City's swap of six players and net spend of £38m on the final day of the window).

Expensive
The net spend is crucial because it's indicative of the relative talent being swapped in and out of clubs, which over time adds up from season to season in terms of

compounding advantages for these clubs. If the regression plots in *Soccernomics* and at the TPI blog have taught us anything, it's that the openness of the market for football players has made it ruthlessly efficient at allocating such talent to the clubs willing to spend the most money on their squad. It's not good enough to simply buy big in only one transfer window. A club must have a net positive spend year-over-year or a system to consistently find hidden talent that costs less, because today's Premier League is a big-money game.

At TPI we have introduced a fair number of models over the last few years to measure the impact such spending has on a club's odds of finishing in a certain table position. The latest metric, team total valuation (TTV), combines the TPI's transfer database with the publicly available wages data to estimate what it would cost to assemble and pay a team for a single season. Unfortunately, the audited club wage bills often come out up to a year after a club has completed a season, so while very useful the TTV metric is a lagging indicator.

The next quickest metric to generate is the starting XI cost in terms of transfers (£XI, which takes inflation into account), and a fair bit of retrospective analysis has been done with this metric to quantify match odds, as well as the best and worst performing managers against those odds. The challenge with any £XI analysis is that it requires confirmed starting lineups before any data can be generated for a match. It's a great tool for accurate post-mortem analysis of a match, but not very useful in up-front match predictions. The final metric, squad valuation on the basis of transfer fees paid after inflation is factored in (Sq£), may be more coarse than the £XI metric, but it has the added value of being a potential predictive tool. It only requires the confirmed overall squad members and their current transfer purchase price (CTPP) valuations. The closing of the transfer window on August 31st provides the former, while Graeme Riley's expertly maintained TPI database provides the later.

Last year the TPI team provided a prediction as to the final league table based upon the MSq£ model, which is a longer-term, simple regression model that takes into account the relative Sq£ of each club in relation to the average Sq£ for the season. It served a purpose at the time, but given the unexpected results last year (expensive Chelsea in sixth place, inexpensive Newcastle finishing fifth, all three promoted teams staying up, etc.) and the simplicity of the model meant the prediction's accuracy wasn't the best.

This season the TPI prediction returns with a far more sophisticated model and a likely far more accurate prediction, as well as a number of key observations of just how bifurcated the Premier League is getting in its third decade of existence.

But before we get to the model, a recap of where each club stands is in order.

Graeme Riley provided a superb write up as to where things stood prior to the start of the season, with a number of good statistics as to player value concentration in the top few clubs. There's no need to re-state those facts, as they stand on their own. This article will instead provide a simple update as to where each of the clubs stand as the transfer window closed, and thus their odds of finishing towards the top of the table. The table below provides a comparison of each club's 2011/12 and 2012/13 Sq£ values, with the three promoted/relegated clubs being averaged together as there is no direct way to compare them. All figures quoted in 2011-12 CTPP values.

EPL Sq£ Values (2011-12 & 2012-13)

Row Labels	2011-12	2012-13	Change
Chelsea	£445,326,377	£428,536,520	-£16,789,857
Manchester City	£326,807,282	£358,472,580	£31,665,298
Manchester United	£339,167,055	£349,608,518	£10,441,463
Liverpool	£200,809,943	£211,168,845	£10,359,352
Arsenal	£166,408,943	£182,716,985	£16,308,042
Tottenham	£133,783,998	£144,866,949	£11,082,950
Aston Villa	£99,808,220	£101,787,941	£1,979,722
Everton	£84,259,081	£86,983,309	£2,724,227
Sunderland	£97,631,615	£80,342,692	-£17,288,923
Newcastle United	£70,133,991	£68,892,999	-£1,240,992
Stoke City	£56,226,614	£68,033,760	£11,807,146
Fulham	£60,836,581	£49,173,250	-£11,663,331
QPR	£34,606,280	£47,421,946	£12,815,666
Wigan Athletic	£40,614,978	£41,128,968	£513,990
Norwich City	£20,951,623	£28,779,531	£7,827,907
West Brom	£23,224,416	£25,805,337	£2,580,921
Swansea City	£11,105,769	£25,379,871	£14,274,102
Pro/Rel Average	£46,707,787	£27,999,716	-£18,708,071

Transfer Price Index © Paul Tomkins and Graeme Riley

Chelsea remain at the top of the table given a number of expensive, older players (Frank Lampard = £18.8m, Peter Cech = £18.8m, Paulo Ferriera = £26.5m, Ashley Cole = £30.7m, Fernando Torres = £50m), and they added the expensive Eden Hazard (£32m), Oscar (£25m), and several others to round out their squad. The challenge for Chelsea is that their value is greatly inflated by the average length of time their transferred players have been at the club – 3.43 years, which is the highest in the league, and far higher than the average (2.33). A good bit of their transfer valuation is based upon inflation of the transfer fees paid during the free spending years of Jose Mourinho, when they often spent ten times the average fee of the time. The obvious conclusion is that while they do hold an advantage over most of the league, it's likely not as large as it looks and will make for a far closer competition with the two Manchester clubs for the league championship.

Also of note is Manchester City's second position in the table. This is the second time in three years that the club passed their city rivals in the Sq£ metric, while they also passed them in terms of wages for the first time during the 2011-12 season. City's flurry of activity at the end this summer's transfer window is what moved them past United (net spend of £38m on *August 31st alone,* for a £32m gain over last season and a £9m advantage over United). Last season Roberto Mancini continuously complained about a lack of resources that he felt he needed to compete on multiple fronts. He was a bit prescient, given City's inability to get into the knockout rounds of the Champions League, loss to Manchester United in the FA Cup third round, and loss to Liverpool in the League Cup semi-finals. All of that was forgotten when the club won its first title in more than 40 years. The spending over the summer may have been modest compared to years past, but it should provide some player rotation relief for a club looking to repeat as champions and progress deeper into the Champions League.

Outside of Robin Van Perise, United's spending was quite modest. They also let go of Park Ji-Sung and Dimitar Berbatov, a combined hit of £34.7m in Sq£. Therefore they only realised a net gain of £10m on a Sq£ basis. They have now finished third in the Sq£ rankings for the second time in three years, something that hasn't happened to them since the golden "free" generation of Butt-Scholes-Giggs-Beckham in the late 1990s. The difference this time is that there is no aberration of a second golden generation to offset the lower levels of spending, meaning that Manchester United may be falling further behind their two rivals for the championship.

After the top three clubs there is a nearly £140m drop off in value to a second clustering of teams between £150m and £200m in Sq£ valuations. First in that second list of clubs is Liverpool. Liverpool's Sq£ is inflated by Andy Carroll's transfer fee, as he was used in both of their first two matches before being loaned to West Ham. This may seem like a bit misleading, but these are the rules as to how the TPI calculates Sq£ values to make calculations consistent (after all, Liverpool didn't *have* to loan him out; he was their player, to play if they wanted). If Liverpool's Sq£ were reduced by his transfer fee they would have a Sq£ much more in line with Arsenal's (a point that will become more important when potential finishing position is discussed), and would actually represent a £25m decrease from 2011-12's Sq£. Needless to say, Liverpool's start to the season has been much worse than expected, but the season is young.

Arsenal's Sq£ goes up even in the face of losing Robin Van Persie. This is because CTTP values are calculated based upon the original transfer fee paid by the club and transfer inflation since then (£3m paid by Arsenal in 2003 for the Dutchman = £6.6m CTPP). Thus, even though United paid nearly four times as much on a CTPP basis for van Persie, the Arsenal Sq£ valuation from that one deal only decreases by £6.6m. A similar situation applies to Alex Song's transfer to Barcelona as well. Thus, while the Gunners are projected to have had another net positive transfer window by several million pounds, their SqE actually increases as they had originally bought a number of the outgoing players on the cheap. The jury is still out as to the net impact the player changes will have on the team, with the club relying a good bit on Wenger to work his magic yet again.

Tottenham, like Manchester City, had a flurry of activity the last week of the transfer window. Swooping in to get the want-away Clint Dempsey was the final act in a week of three transfers totaling £29m. This activity more than offset the sales of players like Rafael van der Vaart and Luka Modric. The net spend results in a modest gain in SqE and a stable of players that should have Tottenham Hotspur challenging for a top four spot if they can overcome their early missteps.

The third band of clubs in the table cluster between £80m and £100m in SqE valuations. It will be interesting to see if Aston Villa continues to underperform like they have the last few seasons, while Everton and Sunderland should outperform Villa and will likely finish close to what their SqE's suggest they should be able to achieve.

Just below them are two of the more interesting clubs when it comes to financial valuations. Newcastle United actually went down in SqE valuation this year, with a number of more junior players leaving on free transfers. Only two players were transferred out on fees, with four coming in on a fee. Newcastle are essentially hoping to repeat last season's magic where Alan Pardew delivered 15.6 points more than his transfer valuation would have suggested. Stoke, on the other hand, continue their steady upward march in SqE valuations (2009/10 = £35m, 2010/11 = £55m, 2011/12 = £56m, 2012/13 = £68m) via a number of departures on free transfers and modest incoming player purchases.

The twelfth to fourteenth positions are occupied by clubs with SqEs between £40m and £60m pounds. Last season's relegated teams reminded everyone that spending does not guarantee avoiding the drop (their average SqE was nearly £47m), so there are no guarantees for Fulham, QPR, and Wigan. Both QPR and Wigan barely avoided the drop last season, so they may be good candidates for relegation this season. However, the fact that the bottom six teams in this year all average around SqE's of £27m may bode well for these three teams.

The three promoted teams have much lower SqE valuations than the three clubs relegated at the end of last season. This makes for a very interesting situation where their average SqE values are within £1m of the next three clubs – Norwich, West Brom, and Swansea. The competition for relegation spots will be tight, perhaps providing for exciting moments similar to last season's run-in.

How do these SqE values translate to league title, Champions League, and relegation odds? At the core of such predictions is the mSqER model. Yes, this is yet another model, but its architecture and results are very similar to those found in the m£XIR model already written about for over a year now at the TPI blog. The mSq£R model uses the club's Sq£ values in evaluating the resources available to the club. Just like the m£XIR model, the mSq£R model uses the Sq£ values for the two clubs in a match (the "m" at beginning of the model name) to create the ratio of Sq£'s (hence the "R" at the end of each model name). It also uses the input of which team is home and which is away. Using this information for a match, and how both terms have historically impacted matches in the post-Abramovich era, the model calculates the win, draw, and loss percentages for each of the two clubs in the match.

A 10,000-run Monte Carlo simulation is completed with matches in the forthcoming season having outcome probabilities assigned to them. The simulation returns the odds of each team finishing in each finishing position. This model provides far more information than the MSq£ model as it predicts individual match outcomes that are then rolled up to a season total rather than the macro-level view that the MSq£ starts with. A top four finish in the table represents UEFA Champions League qualification barring another run like Chelsea's last year, while a top five finish represents European competition qualification (Champions or Europa League). The table below summarises the results of the league tables from the 10,000 season simulations. The order of the clubs is based upon their average finishing position in the simulation.

2012-13 EPL Table Predictions Based on mSq£R Model

Position	Row Labels	% Title	% Top 4	% Top 5	% Rel
1	Chelsea	30%	77%	84%	0%
2	Manchester City	22%	68%	77%	0%
3	Manchester United	22%	67%	77%	0%
4	Liverpool	8%	41%	53%	1%
5	Arsenal	6%	35%	45%	1%
6	Tottenham	4%	26%	35%	2%
7	Aston Villa	2%	17%	24%	4%
8	Everton	1%	13%	19%	6%
9	Sunderland	1%	12%	18%	7%
10	Newcastle United	1%	9%	14%	9%
11	Stoke City	1%	9%	13%	10%
12	Fulham	0%	6%	9%	15%
13	QPR	0%	5%	8%	16%
14	Wigan Athletic	0%	4%	6%	20%
15	Southampton	0%	3%	5%	23%
16	West Ham	0%	3%	5%	25%
17	Norwich City	0%	2%	3%	29%
18	Swansea City	0%	1%	2%	33%
19	West Brom	0%	1%	2%	34%
20	Reading	0%	0%	0%	65%

Transfer Price Index © Paul Tomkins and Graeme Riley
mSq£R model and resultant data © A Beautiful Numbers Game

What was clearly a separation of the top three in terms of Sq£ values translates to a similar separation for those clubs when it comes to table position. All three are more than 2/3 likely to qualify for the Champions League, while they split nearly 3/4 of the title odds between the three of them. They're also the only three clubs assured of not being relegated. It's a virtual toss-up amongst the three as to who will win the title, with the debate being whether or not Chelsea have bought enough to reverse last season's sixth place finish, whether or not United have spent enough to close the gap to their cross town rivals, and whether or not City can virtually stand on last year's squad to repeat their success. One can only hope that the title run-in this season is as exciting as the last one.

As previously mentioned, Liverpool's Sq£ is high given the inclusion of Andy Carroll. This also means their higher odds of winning the league and European competition are a bit inflated. If Carroll's fee is excluded, their Sq£ and likely finishing position are much closer to Arsenal's, making it a three way race for the fourth and final Champions League finishing position. No matter the valuation, all three clubs in the second tier – Liverpool, Arsenal, and Tottenham – have about a one-in-three shot in making it into next season's Champions League competition, and a less than 10% chance of winning the league. Stumbles out of the gate for all three have made those title odds even longer.

The remaining 14 clubs in the league combined have a less than 6% chance of winning the league, none of them more than a one-in-five chance of making it into the Champions League, and less than a one-in-four chance of making it into any European competition via league finishing position. Meanwhile, only one team – Reading – has a worse than even odds of being relegated. Positions 14 through 19 have between a one-in-five and one-in-three chance of being relegated, indicating how exciting the race to avoid the drop may be this year.

All of these predictions are based upon a model that predicts about three quarters of the variation in table position by club spending. The other 25% is left up to the players and managers who go out on the pitch every single match. That's what makes this game so exciting, even in the face of increasingly deterministic outcomes dependent upon the spending of sugar daddies and debt laden clubs. It will be interesting to see how the table ends up, and how closely it mimics the TPI predictions above.

A Review of the Predictions, June 2013

In retrospect, the mSq£R model fared relatively well compared to previous TPI forecasts, both in terms of accurately capturing the breadth of possible final table positions at the beginning of the season, and quickly converging to an accurate answer by mid-season.

The table below makes a comparison between key metrics and how the mSq£R and the MSq£ model mentioned in the original TTT piece each fared.

Results vs. Beginning of Season Forecast
Average Error in Table Position. MSq£: 4; mSq£R: 4
Standard Deviation in Table Position Error. MSq£: 4.92; mSq£R: 5.29
Number of Predictions Within 1 Table Position. MSq£: 6; mSq£R: 6
Number of Teams Within 50% prediction interval. MSq£: 4; mSq£R: 11

The two models are statistically similar in the first three metrics that convert the models' outputs into a single predicted table position for each club, but where the mSq£R's superiority stands out is in its ability to properly capture the variability in finishing position forecasts due to the role non-financial matters play in individual matches. This is reflected in the far higher number of clubs that fell within the mSq£R model's 50% prediction interval (the band centered on the single predicted table position and captures 50% of predicted table positions). Thus, the probabilistic outlook of the mSq£R model is superior to the deterministic, single point estimate of the longer-term MSq£ model.

The m£XIR model was updated on a weekly basis incorporating the latest results for clubs' goal differentials and resultant points into final table predictions, but forecasts run prior to the January transfer window close continued to use the same squad valuations as the forecasts at the beginning of the season. By the end of the first ten matches the mSq£R model had lowered its average error in final table predictions to 2.9, and properly placed nine teams within one position of the one they occupied in the final table. Adjustments were made to squad valuations in early February based upon January transfer window activity, and the results of the first post-window mSq£R forecast are compared in the table below to a similar one from the MSq£ model.

Forecast After January Transfer Window Close
Average Error in Table Position. MSq£: 4; mSq£R: 1.3
Standard Deviation in Table Position Error. MSq£: 4.98; mSq£R: 2.29
Number of Predictions Within one Table Position. MSq£: 3; mSq£R: 14

By this point in the season the mSq£R model predicted the top eight final table positions correctly, and held an average of 2.2 positions of absolute error for the remaining twelve.

What proved the most confounding to the financial models throughout the season was the success of West Brom, Swansea, West Ham and Norwich on limited squad valuations, and the struggles of Aston Villa, Newcastle and Sunderland on much larger ones. All of this translated into a season that had the second-lowest impact from player valuations from the last six campaigns. As an example, Chelsea's median of a six-fold player valuation advantage in the post-Abramovich era would have given them a 41% likelihood of winning any random home match in 2012/13. In 2011/12 it would have translated to a 59% likelihood, while in 2007/08 through 2009/10 seasons it would have led to a nearly 70% likelihood of winning. One season does not a trend make, but with future seasons of data we'll be able to understand whether or not the magnitude of "increased player spending = automatic success" may have peaked in the second half of the 2000s.

Zach is a freelance football writer and a Tomkins Times/Transfer Price Index contributor. He currently writes for Forbes.com, and his work has appeared in Howler Magazine and The Blizzard. He has run his own blog, A Beautiful Numbers Game, for more than three years.

A LOOK AT LIVERPOOL'S TRANSFER NEEDS

By Ted Knutson
June 2013

Ah, the silly season. A time when we all like to play *Football Manager* with our favourite team, shipping out the deadwood, and buying wunderkind replacements in return. Today, I'm going to do a lot of that sort of thing, with a small twist you don't usually get with real-world analysis.

A warning up front. This isn't a normal transfer shopping wish-list. Far from it. The point behind this exercise is to look for high statistical performers that meet the needs of Liverpool Football Club.

I can also promise you that the thinkers at Liverpool FC are already using some similar methodologies at this very minute. Just because Damien Comolli gave the methodology a bad name, doesn't mean that using stats lacks value. Coutinho, Borini, Aspas and Luis Alberto all trigger immediate attention flags in any football stats database, provided you know what to look for.

Today I'm going to focus on three areas of need for this coming season (as noted by Liverpool fans I polled on Twitter), and provide multiple player options at different prices to fill those needs.

Some rules:

• The players recruited can't be starters in Champions League teams. I don't have data from smaller countries, and it's reasonable to think Liverpool could recruit Champions League players from smaller countries via wages alone, but anyone playing Champions League football in Italy, Spain, Germany, and England are likely to stay put. On the other hand, someone like Henrikh Mkhitaryan is still within reach.

• The players we look at also need to be just entering their prime (26) or younger. This maximizes the useful years you will get from the player and maintains resale value. Or if they aren't young, they need to be a hugely undervalued superstar. Example: Dimitar Berbatov went to Fulham for only £4.4m last year at age 31. Given his undeniable talent, that is undervalued. Meanwhile, David Villa, who is also 31, is currently being offered around at £12.5m. That is not undervalued.

Before we get started, a quick question: What position in the Premier League is most likely to have the most tackles and interceptions combined?

No, it's not central defenders. It's not even full-backs, though the best of them can come pretty close. The correct answer is...

Defensive Midfielder

The reason why, for this piece, we're shopping at this position is because Dan Kennett told me he was unconvinced by the current options. Lucas hasn't been at his best for two years. The jury is still out on Joe Allen (playing with a bad shoulder injury definitely affected his game), and he's not a real defensive midfielder anyway, so this is an area that needs bolstering.

The important things we are looking for are tackles and interceptions, plus a high level of passing aptitude. You also want a guy who doesn't give away a ton of fouls (two or more per game is the red zone), and who rarely gets dribbled past even though he plays in the middle of the pitch. Though many see him as immortal, Steven Gerrard isn't getting any younger, and finding someone who could potentially assume his position in the centre should his performances eventually decline is paramount.

Option 1 – Morgan Schneiderlin

Age: 23

Team: Southampton

Schneiderlin stepped straight from the Championship into the Premier League and didn't miss a beat, becoming one of the best two defensive mids in the PL in his first season. (The other guy in contention was Sandro from Spurs.)

League	Apps	Tackle	Int	Fouls	Was Drib	KP	PassPG	PS%	Long
EPL	36	4.1	3.9	1.8	1	0.8	52.1	85.2%	2.9

Those numbers are outstanding in any league in the world. The foul totals aren't terrible, he doesn't get dribbled past that often, and the passing stats mean he'd fit in just fine at Liverpool. He's already been blooded and proven himself in the Premier League, and he's used to playing a similar pressing-plus-possession system that Mauricio Pochettino installed at Southampton upon his arrival. It's not listed here, but Schneiderlin even managed to get on the score sheet five times last season.

In short, Schneiderlin offers a lot to love without any real reservations. His age also means that if you sign him now, he could be part of a central midfield group for the next seven years without any expectation of decline.

Likely price: £12m. Southampton are usually very good at making sure they get the best possible price for their players, and they also understand how important he was to them last season. That said, this isn't normally a position that commands large transfer fees, even when the player is worth it, and the transfer fee could be less.

Option 2 - Milan Badelj

Age: 24

Team: Hamburg

Already a Croatian international, Badelj put up excellent numbers as a central midfielder last year in the Bundesliga.

League	Apps	Tackle	Int	Fouls	Was Drib	KP	PassPG	PS%	Long
Bundesliga*	30(1)	3.7	3.5	1.8	1.7	1.1	58.1	81.5%	5.9

Badelj has the ability to do just about anything as a midfielder, but those sorts of tackling and interception numbers are elite for the defensive midfielder role, and I'd be really happy having him there either as the holding role or part of a double pivot. Key Pass numbers are good for playing that deep as well, and his versatility means he can fill in wherever you need him in case of injuries or specific tactical needs.

Likely price: I'm guessing, but given that Hamburg bought him for £3.5m, I'd put Badelj in the £10-12m price range.

Option 3 - Sebastian Rode

Age: 22

Team: Eintracht Frankfurt

Assuming neither of our first two options pan out, you always want to have a backup plan, and preferably one that doesn't cost a fortune in case something goes awry. How about a young German who spent a lot of time in the centre of the park last season for the 6th-best team in Germany?

League	Apps	Tackle	Int	Fouls	Was Drib	KP	PassPG	PS%	Long
Bundesliga*	33	3.3	2.5	2	1.4	1	53.5	84.4%	5.4

Foul numbers here are slightly high, but considering Rode is only 22, you can expect those to improve. The passing percentage is already great, as are the 5.4 completed long balls per game, a useful trait when trying to start the counter-attack. Key passes are fine for the position, and Rode can even dribble out of trouble regularly. He might not have the highest stats of the three players listed here, but it's possible he's the most talented of the lot.

Likely price: £6m. Bayern Munich have been rumoured to be interested in this kid, but their midfield is stacked already. Given the level of play in the Bundesliga, at this point it's fair to say that the Premier League teams need to be recruiting more young Germans, especially if they can do it on the cheap.

Central Defender

I did a similar piece to this one with my friend Ben Pugsley over at BitterandBlue.com and ironically, my advice for Manchester City was to save their money and keep Kolo Touré for another season or two. Instead, Liverpool hopped in and signed the Ivorian to their own two-year deal. I think he's an excellent short-term solution in the centre of defence.

I'm assuming Škrtel is off (Napoli is the rumoured destination). Combined with Carragher's retirement, the club are still short a good central defender even after the Touré signing.

Unfortunately, at this point centre-back is the single hardest position to evaluate using publicly available statistics (Goalkeeper is a close second). Defender stats depend immensely on the system in place for their team, and have follow-on effects from how their teammates perform that are difficult to minimise. You can't just look at guys who post good numbers and say, "Aha! He must be great!" I have a methodology that I think works, but it needs stats and ratios that aren't available via places like WhoScored.com or TransferMarkt.

I can only say that I think Swansea's Chico was one of the best centre-backs in the Premier League last season and would fit in great at Liverpool. I also like what I've seen about Kyriakos Papadopoulos, but admit that at this time we don't have the correct data on the analytics side to make great suggestions for this area of need.

Right Attacking Midfielder/Wide Forward

Let's assume that Suárez eventually bids Liverpool a tearful, heartfelt adios, and we now need a replacement. What sort of player are you looking for to fill that slot? I'm going to figure that Daniel Sturridge will remain the primary option up top, with Fabio Borini to deputise for him.

(Aside: Disappointed with Borini's first season in the Premier League? I was too, until I looked at 2011/12 and realised he was one of the best statistical prospects according to my methodology. It's rare that young players perform as well as he did in Serie A and rarer still that their skills just completely desert them if they do. He's still very young, fought through injuries, and I have faith that he'll return to form.)

You aren't likely to replace Suárez's goal contribution directly, but you know that you need a fast, creative player who passes well, and who hopefully doesn't kill quite so many attacks by himself with poor shot selection or losing the ball. Mkhitaryan is the hot name on the list, and at 24 he kind of ticks all the boxes, but I don't have enough stats to do proper analysis of him (almost no one does), so let's go a different way.

Option 1 – Pizzi

Age: 23
Position: Left or Right Wide Forward
Team: Played for Deportivo la Coruña, but is owned by Braga.
We know Liverpool are heavily scouting Spain and Portugal, and they had to have seen this guy.

Year	Apps	G	A	ShPG	KP	Drib	Disp	Trn	PS%
2013	35	8	6	2.5	2.7	1.2	1.9	1.6	80.9%

He was third in La Liga for Key Passes behind Özil and Rakitić. He had a successful pass rate of 81% in an awful team. The turnover numbers are reasonable (3.5 per game is okay – once you get out past 4 I start to wince), he put 44% of his shots on target this season, uses both feet regularly, takes set pieces, and even crosses well.

And he did all of this for a team that was relegated. That is a massive accomplishment.

He's primarily left-footed, but it would be easy to invert him as Rodgers often does with Downing, and play him on the right. His right foot is actually pretty solid too, so he'd bring the added benefit of unpredictability in that he could go wide or cut into the centre whenever he wanted (unlike Stewart-I-Always-Get-My-Shots-Blocked Downing).

Watch one of his highlight videos and then picture his passing ability on the right, Coutinho in the hole, Aspas or Sterling cutting in from the left, and Sturridge up top.

That's an attack that might be as dangerous as what Manchester City fields this autumn, and for about the same price as they will pay for one single player.

Likely Price: £12m

Option 2 – Pierre-Emerick Aubameyang

Age: 23

Position: Forward

Team: Saint Etienne

Maybe you are unconvinced by Pizzi, and want to replace Suárez's goalscoring more directly. Aubameyang has been linked with a number of top clubs so far this summer, but not one has moved for him yet. Presumably for this exercise we have £40m in our pockets from the Suárez sale, which means we can afford Aubameyang and still have money left over to strengthen other areas. These are his stats for the last two seasons in Ligue Une.

Player	Apps	G	A	Pen	G/90	ShPG	KP	Drib	Disp	Trn	PS%
Aubameyang	36	16	7	-	0.46	3.4	1.3	0.4	1.6	1.9	68.5%
Aubameyang	34(1)	19	9	1	0.55	3.8	1	0.6	1.2	2.3	73.8%

The first line is from last year when he was 22, the second is from this season. He's young and improving, and man can he score. He has the same combined goals and assists total as Suárez, with better turnover stats, and is three years younger. He's not as creative as Suárez is in terms of key passes and dribbling, but that's because Aubameyang is very much a forward and less an attacking midfielder (though he can player there too), and somehow that hasn't affected his assists one bit.

Passing success improved considerably this year, and he's not anywhere close to his prime yet, so expect him to keep getting better. Aubameyang would be a great addition to the squad if Liverpool could sign him at a price they liked, and he was willing to come be part of the rebuilding project.

Likely price: £25-30m

Option 3 – Thomas Ince

Age: 21

Position: Wide Forward

Team: Blackpool

Been there, done that, right? I think it's pretty fair to say that whoever decided to sell Ince (for uh... £57,000? Seriously?!) got it wrong. There's no harm in going back and fixing that mistake, especially since Liverpool are the one team who will get a discount from buying him back from Blackpool.

Ince	Age	Apps	G	A
2012	20	25(10)	7	7
2013	21	42(2)	18	14

I did some research recently into how players that score in the Championship usually do when they move to the Premier League, and I was surprised that they usually keep about 80% of their stats after a move. If you take 80% of Ince's totals for last season, you'd wind up with 14 goals and 11 assists, which is basically what Theo Walcott produced. Except Ince is three years younger and has a good chance to be better than Walcott. Players that produce numbers like that at such an early age usually grow up into being superstars.

Likely price: ?

Conclusion

These are some of the best value players statistics can find. As someone who enjoys watching Liverpool play, I'd be pretty happy with all the players I mentioned above. That said, stats aren't everything. That's why teams employ small armies of scouts and video analysts to add to the collective knowledge of the team and find exactly the right fits at prices they can afford.

I can honestly say I think Liverpool have done an excellent job finding value targets in the last year, perhaps more so than any other club in the Premier League (except maybe Swansea). I look forward to seeing who else they sign this summer, and my professional opinion (I'm the lead Premier League trader for one of the world's biggest bookies) is that Liverpool have a very good chance of challenging for a Champions' League spot this coming season. We'll know in about six months or so whether or not that opinion was misguided optimism or not.

'HOW DID THEY DO 2012/13?' – THE HIGHLIGHTS

By Various TTT Writers, Contributors and Subscribers
June 2013

For the last few weeks we've been running a series of articles where our panel assess the performance and contribution of each player who's made 10+ appearances this season, and give a rating out of 10. Subscribers could also vote in a poll on the site.

The articles have been published each day over the past few weeks, finishing on Friday June 7th. One of our panel had the idea of compiling a 'Best of' article to showcase the best writing of the many who contributed to the series. And so here we are.

The numbers by the players' names refer to the order in which they appeared in the series, rather than squad numbers.

1 - Brad Jones

Andrew Beasley: The Aussie keeper has done exactly what is required of a back-up, and so deserves a decent rating as a result. Not least because he's outperformed Pepe Reina in some key statistics.

Whilst Liverpool's first choice goalie has saved 69% of the shots he's faced in all competitions this season, Jones has stopped 77%. In the league, Jones has also only made one on-the-ball error in 630 minutes, whilst his Spanish rival has averaged one every 435 minutes this season.

The passing stats illustrate why Jones couldn't ever be number one whilst Rodgers is in charge (with his accuracy of 54% being the lowest in the Reds' squad this season), but he has displayed his credentials to be second in command to Pepe.

2 - Sebastián Coates

Dan Kennett: The only question that's left in my mind about Coates is, is he a poor player or one who just looks poor because he's not suited to the system? Whichever, it's difficult to see how he has a future at Liverpool because if he has strengths, we're never going to play to them under Rodgers. The biggest concern is his chronic lack of pace, but even his pure defending ability has to be questioned following his inability to handle a League One target man in the FA Cup.

3 - Andre Wisom

Dave Cronin: Wisdom's emergence was an unexpected positive to come out of this season. It's always risky to make predictions about young players but Wisdom looks like someone with the potential to be a Liverpool player for many seasons to come. At times he has looked exposed, but taking into account his age and lack of experience, not to mention the complete lack of defensive cover ahead of him, that is forgivable. Overall, he's looked decent enough and gained some valuable playing experience, including away games at Goodison, Stamford Bridge, Old Trafford and the Emirates. Despite playing some tough fixtures, Liverpool won half and kept clean sheets in a third of the games he started, losing only three out of 18. That said, he has some way to develop before he can challenge for a regular starting place when his team-mates are fit.

4 - Martin Škrtel

Chris Rowland: The problem here is, there are two Martin Škrtels. There's the one that's ever-so prone to human frailties like self-doubt and insecurity. He's prone to mistakes, making him look hesitant, and spreading his jitters throughout the defence. He's a pussycat compared to how he looks, i.e. like he should have one on his lap stroking one – 'and now Mr Bond, I expect you to die! Huh-huh-huh ....'

Then there's his Cyborg twin – powerful, quick, decisive, and as hard as he looks. Brendan Rodgers seems to see the human version – and I think we should sell the human version for £10m+. If we can find the Cyborg again, I'd keep him.

5 - Joe Allen

Si Steers: I have a great deal of sympathy for Joe Allen. His signing is very similar to that of Jordan Henderson, where there is a big increase in expectation and a £15m price tag to try and live up to. All of this at 22 years of age. As well as that, Allen also became the easy target for fans disgruntled with the sacking of Kenny and failure to speak to Rafa. He is seen as a poster boy for the Rodgers tenure.

So putting all of that to one side, I think Allen started well; he was calm, composed, assured on the ball and looked a class act. The wheels came off at around the same time his shoulder went, and in hindsight he should have had that treated immediately.

He then went on to suffer a loss of confidence and his form dipped. But he only needs to look as far as Henderson to see how quickly he can turn it around. I expect to see the 'real' Joe Allen come to the fore next year. He is a quality, classy player and just needs time to adapt.

I think he has had a 'steady' start; some of the noise in the background on Allen has little to do with his ability or impact and more to do with a resistance to a new manager. I have every confidence he will prove any doubters wrong.

6 - Suso

Dave Cronin: If you're a footballer called Jesus, get hailed as a wonderkid and look like this lad, you're surely destined for great things. Maybe Suso's exposure this season has come a tad too early but this lad oozes class. In terms of his contribution to this campaign, I can't score him too highly but he has shown real potential for the future.

He perhaps lacks a bit of pace but he looks elegant and composed on the ball, has an eye for goal, skill in abundance and oozes confidence. I loved his performance against Stoke at Anfield when his reaction to the opposition's thuggish tactics was to take the fouls and force the ref to penalise them, rather than dodging the contact and whining about it as his more senior team-mates did.

He's been unlucky not to have scored on a couple of occasions and obviously the signings of Sturridge and Coutinho (not to mention Rodgers' non-rotation policy even when 4-0 up) have seen his chances limited since the turn of the year but he is one for the future, no doubt.

7 - Oussama Assaidi

Alun Evans: How can a player who arrived with absolutely no fanfare whatsoever be a disappointment? YouTube is how. There should be a ban on looking at videos of potential new signings on YouTube because they're often very misleading. I was excited about Assaidi. He looked awesome on YouTube. And it's not that he isn't awesome, he might be, but we've just not seen him. Clearly Rodgers doesn't think so otherwise he would've played him. Will he still be around next year? Will we even notice?

8 - Luis Suárez

Daniel Rhodes: A genius. A maverick. A player, with the ball at his feet, who encapsulates everything you loved about football as a kid. A drop of the shoulder. A nutmeg. He turns you one way, he turns you the other, he's gone. He regularly makes opposition defenders look foolish. He makes the crowd gasp. He makes the opposition fans squirm with fear, or red with rage. A pantomime villain, in a production he didn't choose to be involved in, but then, he still throws the creators a juicy script every now and again.

He blows any other player out of the water when it comes to stats. As a whole package, he's an all-round phenomenon. He dribbles, he threads through-balls, he creates chances, he wins free kicks, he assists, he shoots (more than anyone in Europe), he becomes the focal point for the whole team. And, that's the issue. You can have as many individual world-class talents as you want, but if they make the team worse, there's no point. Either Suárez adapts his game, plays for the team and stops trying to do it all himself (and, sorts out his disciplinary record) – or sell him, at the potential peak of his value. Anything over £50m would be very, very good business.

9 - Pepe Reina

Alun Evans: A few years ago there wasn't a single Liverpool fan who would've traded Pepe for all the tea in China, but Roy Hodgson really messed with Pepe's mind. Can I blame Hodgson? Is anyone going to stop me if I do? What we do know is that Hodgson didn't like the idea of a European-style dynamic sweeper-keeper and really just wanted Reina to "just fucking launch it". Whether it was this that caused the alarming drop in form or whether it was something else, we don't know, but the drop in form certainly happened and for the first time people were casting envious eyes at other teams' goalkeepers thinking, "Why have they got someone who can actually *save* the ball?".

In the second half of the season he seems to have started getting his mojo back. Better performances. More clean sheets. Fewer errors. More saves. These are the things we expect from Pepe and the talk of replacing the Spaniard seems to have died down, at least for now. Plus, according to his interview on the Liverpool website regarding the hideous new Liverpool kit, he likes it because it's comfortable. Expect Reina to take the field in an LFC-branded onesie and a cardigan in the near future.

10 - Glen Johnson

Shaul Mitelpunkt: While I still think this is not a position we need to worry about, and that in Johnson we have one of the best right-backs in the land, this season was a bit worrisome in that it exposed Johnson's limitations. To put it bluntly, I don't think he is aggressive enough to really change games for us. To be fair, I don't know that there are many right-backs who change games (other than by screwing up in defence). It just feels a bit like Johnson didn't have much fire in his belly this season, realised that this is a bit of a transitional one, and kept a low profile. The pessimistic in me fears that looking back at things in two years we would realise 'We should have sold him at that point, when his price and age were still at peak market value.' The optimistic in me thinks that with a confident defence around him, the attacking-minded Johnson can really help propel Liverpool to the Champions League spots next year. With other burning issues to solve in the squad, I'll stick to optimism when it comes to Johnson.

11 - José Enrique

Barry Meehan: I remember earlier in the season I heard a conversation where they discussed players' form and levels. The point was when someone has had a period of good form and a period of bad form how do you decide which is their true level? I believe the conversation was actually about Torres but I immediately thought of Enrique's Liverpool career. He had a whirlwind start to his Liverpool career but his form then dipped dramatically. There has been a gradual improvement until he has reached a decent level of consistency this season, and I think he is currently playing at his actual level. I appreciate that at times he can look a little brain-dead as he runs down blind alleys but there can be an impressive end product at times too. I think it's telling that the players he connects with best in our team are Suárez and Coutinho, who are our two best players. He has a very good knack of getting his body between man and ball when defending, meaning he doesn't often have to commit to risky last ditch tackles, and he is often the one who can commit intelligent fouls. I do think it would be possible to upgrade on him, but I don't think this needs to be a priority, we have other positions which need to be filled first.

12 - Daniel Agger

Alex Tate: A player that I've always admired and had faith in despite his fragile body. This season his injuries have been fewer, but he's still some way from being as tough as the death metal he listens to. His nuisance causing forays in to the box have given his game a goal-threat edge, creating chance for himself and others. Three league goals, three bookings and a solitary red card show a disciplined centre-back, and one we'll need for the coming season. With his back conditioning underway, Agger's peak years should build upon this season's success.

13 - Jordan Henderson

Paul Tomkins: I would probably have marked him higher, but for the fact he was a fringe player for so much of the season. When he's played he generally played well, especially later on in the season. He looks stronger physically and mentally, and has a goal and an assist in his locker. He's moved from a player Rodgers was looking to offload on the cheap (one of the reasons I was a little wary of the new manager earlier in the season) to a potential future captain, judging by the way he conducts himself on and off the pitch. I don't know why, but you can harbour a greater desire to see certain players succeed, and Henderson, for me, is one such example. I'm not sure if he'll ever be truly *outstanding*, but he has something about him.

14 - Lucas Leiva

Alun Evans: I love Lucas. There, I said it. I do. His attitude and work ethic are incredible. Now with Carragher retiring we may be dreaming of a team of Lucas Leivas instead. He may even be a front-runner for the vacant vice captain's "armband" next year. If everyone showed even a fraction of Lucas' attitude we'd be doing alright. Lucas will forever be the go-to example of how, just because a player starts poorly at a club, it doesn't mean that they're finished. Work-rate, determination and the ability to take your own fans booing you onto the pitch and still keep working. No Rooney-style swearing into the camera for Lucas, oh no. He just got his head down and worked... *hard*! Admittedly his performances haven't been up to his usual high standards, but they've been affected by two serious injuries, and there *has* seemed a marked improvement recently (the stattos will be able to correct me if I'm wrong here!). He's getting back to his best, and with a fully fit Lucas anchoring the midfield, Steven Gerrard alongside providing the forward thrust and Henderson tucked in behind the front three, our first choice midfield looks strong, and it's all because Lucas provides the foundation for the more flamboyant players to go and do their thing.

15 - Daniel Sturridge

Joe Pepper: Is it right that Sturridge has scored more goals in his first 12 starts for LFC than any other player in the club's history? And yet – according to some he "needs a slap", has a bad attitude, doesn't try, is greedy, and is lazy.

I think this is crazy confirmation bias at work. I thought Sturridge was a potential world beater before we signed him, and now I think he's much better than that. He is the sort of player we have been absolutely screaming for for a long time.

His performance away at Man City was the best, most complete, leading the line-type of performance I have seen form a Liverpool centre forward since Anelka vs Newcastle back in 2001-02 at Anfield. I never got over Houllier's decision to not sign Anelka permanently. Until now. Sturridge has scored goals everywhere he's played. He is technically incredible. Very, very strong. He is a link-up player, who holds the ball up exceptionally well. Except he is also ludicrously lightning fast. Like Mark Hughes combined with Usain Bolt.

Having Sturridge in the team means the opposition cannot push high up the pitch because he will kill them in the space left behind for pace. Usually this would just mean that the other team can sit deeper and close out that space. Problem with doing that against Sturridge is that his technical link-up play, passing and ability to hold the ball up are superb. Forcing the opposition defence to sit deeper means there is much more space in front of them for clever players to exploit. Any player/matches in particular come to mind that might have shown this?

I wouldn't swap him for any striker in the Premier League. He'll score 30-40 goals next season, and be widely regarded as the most complete out-and-out striker in the world in the next three or four years. I think he's brilliant. I'm only massively annoyed he wasn't signed last summer.

16 - Philippe Coutinho

Damien Parsonage: Ever since he joined in January, I have found myself pausing and rewinding three or four times every game to watch and rewatch unbelievable through balls Coutinho has played. It's like listening to four voices in perfect harmony or seeing a stone skim effortlessly across a lake eleven or twelve times.

He's *breathtaking*. Breathtakingly brilliant. Exactly the kind of intelligent player I love watching; his craftsmanship is incredible, his talent immense.

He's got strength, too, which is always a worry with tricksy little ball-players when they come to England – the home of hoofball. But he's settled in well – and although he's had one or two matches where he's struggled to impose himself, he's looked better and better as the games have gone by. He's contributed goals, too, and looks fearless when he gets a chance.

It's easy to forget he's only 20. In the number 10 role, he could be our lock-picker for years to come.

A superb January signing – for a snip – and augurs well for the transfer committee this summer. More of the same please.

17 - Jonjo Shelvey

Dan Kennett: After regular first team appearances over three seasons, it's still difficult to know what type of player Jonjo Shelvey is. He doesn't seem particularly good at anything but he's not especially bad at anything either. His passing is average, his creativity is average, his winning the ball back is average, his duels numbers are below average. Somewhat ironically, the numbers for his alleged strongest suit, that "he's got a goal in him", were diabolical last season. Just one goal from 19 shots in the box and one from eight clear chances, the worst in the squad for midfielders and forwards. Three of those clear chances came vs Newcastle (H) and Chelsea (H), drawn games that could've been turned into wins. Another two came vs WBA (H) and Stoke (A), other games where a positive result could've been achieved.

However, the most disappointing thing for me with Shelvey has been his attitude. For a young player, he doesn't put in anywhere near enough effort, in fact some of his performances this season have smacked of someone who thinks he's already "made it", which is unforgiveable. If any kind of decent offer comes him for him this summer (£2m-£3m+) then I'd sell.

18 – Stewart Downing

Matthew Young: It's a difficult one for me, this, because Stewart Downing is one of the most frustrating players I can remember watching. I think he has all the attributes to be a really potent weapon, except one – courage. Or maybe it's confidence, to be fair. He's fast, has good technique, can beat players, can cross a ball ... he can do everything you want in a wide player. He really can ... but he doesn't (or at least, very rarely). He constantly chooses the safe, easy option. He's almost the polar opposite of Suárez in that sense. Having said all of that, it's impossible not to have been impressed by his professionalism and determination this season. He looked certain to leave in January following Rodgers' public dressing down in late September, but responding by knuckling down, getting back in the team, and doing pretty well. For me, unless Dr Steve Peters gets into his head, Downing is a case of a talent wasted. Which is a real shame, because potentially, he's exactly what we need.

19 - Fabio Borini

Chris Rowland: Hard to know what to make of him yet. Unselfish running, tick. Good movement off the ball, tick. Good positional sense, tick. Impact on the game – ah, well that's where it starts to unravel a bit. I know about the disruption of injuries, first the one on international duty then the dislocated shoulder, but he just looks a bit – peripheral. And you want more than peripheral when you cross the £10m barrier. Liked how he adjusted his feet to score at Newcastle though, that gave me reason to think there may be more to come. There needs to be.

20 - Raheem Sterling

Joseph Curran: I vividly recall the confused excitement as news filtered through that Raheem Sterling would start against Manchester City. Unanimously those around me agreed that "he can't be worse than Downing was versus West Brom" and were genuinely encouraged by his performance in that 2-2 draw. Much will be made of the fact young Raheem played too much football, and with justification – he wasn't ready physically or mentally to play every week. I think the most valuable 90 minutes to his development was the 2-2 draw at Everton; he should have been sent off for two bookings and should have scored (or passed to Suárez) when in one-on-one. Ideally, I would want to see him coming off the bench and running at tired defences with the same fearlessness he had in September and October before fatigue got the better of him. In many ways his drop in form has taken him out the limelight and thus the pressure off and we should see a more effective footballer next season.

21- Steven Gerrard

Krishen Bhautoo: Gerrard has been the best player at Liverpool for a generation. The only players who come close in this time in my opinion have been Torres, Alonso and Suárez. His almost superhuman powers are on the wane, but after a shaky start to the season he has become an integral part of Rodgers' team. On October 31st, a TTT poll rated him as our ninth best player of the season up to that point with 2% of votes (Allen had 56%). What is up for debate is whether the role he has been given is the *right* position for him and the team. It would seem that most of us agree that a Gerrard/ Lucas pairing doesn't have enough legs. If we assume Gerrard will always play whilst still at the club, then he needs another central midfield partner. Is it wise to build your central midfield around a 33-year-old?

For me, he needs to be moved to the top of the triangle and a replacement for him placed next to Lucas (Henderson? Allen?). But ignoring all that, and just looking at how his season has been, he's allowed us to tick over, sprayed ball all over the park, looked more patient as the season has progressed (not forcing play) and has been directly involved in over 25% of our goals (nine goals & nine assists). All from a deep lying central midfield role.

22 - Jamie Carragher

Anthony Mckenna: His absence from the squad has not really begun to sink in; but I expect that during times, next season, his loss will be felt ever more keenly. Not just because of Jamie Carragher the Player, but because of Jamie Carragher the Leader, the Organiser, and the man who possesses that indomitable spirit that epitomises the optimum game state when needed most: witness Istanbul. Such talents are unquantifiable and immeasurable.

How would I appraise his performance in his swansong season? As it so happens, that is easy. First, the backdrop: Rodgers' arrival had many sneeringly dismissive – Carra will not be able to play tiki-taka; he will not fit the system. For a while it seemed like he would be reduced to cameo roles, and he consigned himself to the bench with manifest dignity, an air of resignation tipping the hat to the 'younger players having a chance' – even in the knowledge that the clock was ticking down on his career. Then a replacement was needed for the ailing Škrtel. Carragher was asked to step up to the plate. He did so with aplomb.

Looking at EPLindex he recorded 100% pass accuracy in six games; and an overall 92% score in that department. Who said he couldn't do tiki-taka?

What score should I credit Carragher with for the whole season? Well, forgive me this one time. I rarely go overboard but a career finale is a rare occasion; and, since he delivered a proverbial "two fingers" to the "tiki-taka doubting Thomases"; and since I have a nostalgic heart: (maximum score given!).

The Voting Summary, by Krishen Bhautoo

After the recent 'How Did They Do?' series I volunteered to put the data together and see who TTT's Player of The Season is.

There are two sections to the voting. The rating given to each of the players by the TTT Brains Trust – the Symposium Panel – and a second rating given by the TTT community in the voting. It's quite interesting (but far from surprising seeing as we all support the same team) to see how closely the two different groups correlated. Without giving away the name of the eventual winner, here is how the voting looked.

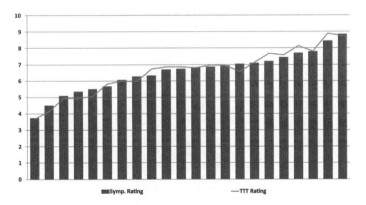

I don't think it takes a genius to work out which players ended up towards which end of the graph. What is also interesting is the average score given to the players by WhoScored.com was 6.92 which sits Liverpool sixth (0.02 ahead of Everton) when compared to the ratings they have given the other Premier League teams. Coming top was United with 7.01. Does a 0.1 improvement mean Liverpool would be challenging for the league? Conversely, Reading come bottom with 6.62.

Bearing in mind the 6.92 WhoScored score, the Symposium panel rated the team (on average) 6.69 and the TTT voters rated them at 6.70. Staggeringly close, but perhaps a touch too harsh?

So who wins the coveted TTT Player of The Season?

Player	Symp. Rating	Player	TTT Rating	Player	WhoScored Rating
Luis Suarez	8.85	Coutinho	8.90	Luis Suarez	7.89
Coutinho	8.44	Luis Suarez	8.75	Daniel Sturridge	7.62
Steven Gerrard	7.80	Daniel Sturridge	8.13	Steven Gerrard	7.52
Daniel Sturridge	7.70	Steven Gerrard	7.80	Coutinho	7.26
Jordan Henderson	7.44	Jamie Carragher	7.68	Glen Johnson	7.25
Jamie Carragher	7.21	Jordan Henderson	7.58	Lucas Leiva	7.15
Glen Johnson	7.09	Glen Johnson	7.12	Daniel Agger	7.03
Stewart Downing	7.05	Andre Wisdom	6.97	Stewart Downing	6.98
Daniel Agger	6.94	Daniel Agger	6.95	Jose Enrique	6.97
Andre Wisdom	6.86	Raheem Sterling	6.87	Raheem Sterling	6.96
Pepe Reina	6.83	Jose Enrique	6.86	Martin Skrtel	6.93
Raheem Sterling	6.75	Pepe Reina	6.81	Andre Wisdom	6.89
Jose Enrique	6.70	Lucas Leiva	6.74	Jordan Henderson	6.77
Lucas Leiva	6.33	Stewart Downing	6.58	Brad Jones	6.71
Joe Allen	6.27	Suso	6.00	Pepe Reina	6.66
Suso	6.06	Joe Allen	5.96	Joe Allen	6.58
Brad Jones	5.67	Brad Jones	5.81	Jamie Carragher	6.57
Jonjo Shelvey	5.50	Jonjo Shelvey	5.06	Suso	6.43
Martin Skrtel	5.36	Martin Skrtel	4.97	Jonjo Shelvey	6.42
Fabio Borini	5.09	Fabio Borini	4.94	Fabio Borini	6.34
Sebastian Coates	4.50	Sebastian Coates	4.14	Sebastian Coates	6.34
Oussama Assaidi	3.75	Oussama Assaidi	3.68	Oussama Assaidi	5.98

Well, there are two winners. Please stand up Mr Suárez and Mr Coutinho.

Looking at the list, I was quite surprised to see such a difference in opinion on some players, especially as we saw earlier that the overall rating was almost identical. So who caused the most conflict between the two voting groups?

Player	Rating Diff
Jamie Carragher	⇧ 0.46
Coutinho	⇧ 0.46
Daniel Sturridge	⇧ 0.43
Lucas Leiva	⇧ 0.41
Jose Enrique	⬈ 0.16
Brad Jones	⬈ 0.15
Jordan Henderson	⬈ 0.13
Raheem Sterling	⬈ 0.12
Andre Wisdom	⬈ 0.11
Glen Johnson	⇨ 0.03
Daniel Agger	⇨ 0.01
Steven Gerrard	⇨ 0.00
Pepe Reina	⇨ -0.02
Suso	⇨ -0.06
Assaidi	⇨ -0.07
Luis Suarez	⬊ -0.10
Fabio Borini	⬊ -0.15
Joe Allen	⇩ -0.31
Sebastian Coates	⇩ -0.36
Martin Skrtel	⇩ -0.40
Jonjo Shelvey	⇩ -0.44
Stewart Downing	⇩ -0.47

I hope the table is pretty self-explanatory and shows that the TTT community were harsher on Downing and more full of praise for Carragher when compared to the Symposium panel. We all agreed on the captain though.

I've combined both the Brains Trust and TTT votes to come up with the overall winner.

First up, the dreaded wooden spoon goes to Assaidi (3.72).

In third place with a score of 7.92: Daniel Sturridge.

In second place with 8.67: Philippe Coutinho.

Player	Rating
Luis Suarez	8.80
Coutinho	8.67
Daniel Sturridge	7.92
Steven Gerrard	7.80
Jordan Henderson	7.51
Jamie Carragher	7.45
Glen Johnson	7.10
Daniel Agger	6.95
Andre Wisdom	6.92
Pepe Reina	6.82
Stewart Downing	6.81
Raheem Sterling	6.81
Jose Enrique	6.78
Lucas Leiva	6.54
Joe Allen	6.12
Suso	6.03
Brad Jones	5.74
Jonjo Shelvey	5.28
Martin Skrtel	5.17
Fabio Borini	5.02
Sebastian Coates	4.32
Assaidi	3.72

And no prizes for guessing who came first, with a whopping scored of 8.80: Luis Suárez. A TTT chequebook and pen will be winging it's way to him. Let's just hope it's to an address in Liverpool and not Madrid or Munich.

RUSHIAN ROULETTE

By Paul Tomkins

June, 2012

It could have all been so different. Frustrated by a lack of opportunities, in 1981 Ian Rush strode into Bob Paisley's office and demanded a move. Eighteen months earlier, the young Welsh striker – then at Chester City – had turned down Liverpool's initial approach, believing that he wasn't good enough. Now it seemed that Paisley, having eventually secured the striker for a hefty £300,000 in May 1980, shared that opinion; or so it seemed to Rush, at least. Before having even really got started, a move to Crystal Palace beckoned. Paisley told Rush, who had yet to score a goal for Liverpool, that he was prepared to let him go.

It could also have been very different in a much more dramatic way. At the age of five, Ian was struck down with meningitis, and ended up in a coma. Two weeks were spent on the edge of life, in Cottage Hospital, Flint. But this is a story of comebacks, and of winning battles. Rush didn't just survive; he thrived.

Ian Rush made his first team debut against Ipswich in December 1980, but it was not going to be easy to break into one of the best sides in the world; it was, after all, a team destined to win its third European Cup in just five seasons. Despite only 12 goals in the reserves during his first season at the club, Rush was called up as an injury replacement to play in the League Cup Final replay against West Ham; he hit the bar with a powerful drive and then, after a smart turn, shot narrowly wide from a tight angle. He kept his place for the first leg of the European Cup semi-final against mighty Bayern Munich, but despite helping the Reds reach the final, and despite a promise from Paisley of a place in the squad even if David Johnson – for whom he was deputising – was fit again, he did not make the 18-man cut. His first season ended with seven league appearances, plus those two massive cup games. No goals were registered. Liverpool were European champions, but Rush found it hard to get into the celebratory mood.

The start of the 1981/82 season was when one of the club's greatest-ever love affairs almost ended before it began. Rush was deeply unhappy with Bob Paisley, first for the European Cup Final snub, and then for a paltry wage rise, despite having gained first-team experience. To compound matters, he was back in the reserves, as the new season got underway. Rush – a shy young man, wispy of body and moustache – admits in his autobiography that he hated life at Anfield, and that, during those awkward first steps, he was not fond of the Reds' legendary manager. Having burst into Paisley's office, he was put firmly in his place. "Your trouble is that you're frightened to think for yourself," the wily old boss told him. "As a centre-forward your main job in the team is to score goals. But you haven't scored a single goal yet. That's why you're not playing".

Rush responded angrily, and said that there was no point staying at the club. "Are you saying you want to go?" was the manager's response. "If that's what you want, you can leave." In reply, Rush said "you can stick your club!". But as the young man stormed out, the manager threw down the gauntlet, telling Rush that he'd been bought to score goals, and if he could do that, he'd have a future at the club. For his part, Rush, having signed up to the passing mantra of the club, resolved to be more selfish on the pitch.

Still in the reserves, the goals did indeed start flowing: six in five games. At the same time, the first team had started the season poorly, winning just two of the first seven matches, and were not scoring many goals. Having come on as a sub against Finnish minnows OPS Oulu, Rush finally broke his duck with a simple tap-in. Due to his simmering anger, he later admitted that it gave him no great joy. A run out in the

League Cup followed, against Exeter, and this time he bagged two; the second from 30 yards and, according to the man himself, as good as any of the 343 that followed. Much to his chagrin, Paisley never offered a word of praise, but the reward came in the form of a place in the starting XI against Leeds United in the league. Finally, with two Kop-end goals, he was up and running. He ended the campaign with 17 league goals from 32 appearances, and a further 13 strikes in the cups. The young Welshman was now officially a 30-goal-a-season striker. Only once in the next five seasons did he end with a total below that 30 mark, when injuries meant he missed a third of the league games. (Had he played more often, the 26 he did notch would almost certainly have become 30+.) In those first six years he scored 207 times in just 331 games. In other words, in every three games he started he was worth two goals.

Although he claimed that 1986/87 was the finest of his career – with 40 goals scored as a move to Juventus loomed – it was 1983/84 that broke records: 47 in one season, making him the only player to have won the European Golden Boot while at Liverpool.

Quite incredibly, going into the 1987 League Cup Final against Arsenal, Rush had bagged 201 goals for the Reds, but had never been on the losing side in games in which he scored. "It was incredible to go that long without losing when I'd scored," he told *the Guardian* in 2007. "In the previous year's FA Cup final against Everton they'd been 1-0 up at half-time and I equalised with about half an hour to go. Speaking to their players after the game some of them said they knew they were going to lose when I scored. We ended up winning 3-1." But with just a handful of games left at Liverpool, the record came to an end in April 1987. The week after, the Reds went to Norwich; Rush scored his 203rd goal for the club, but again Liverpool lost.

By the mid-'80s it was inevitable that the continent's best clubs would come calling. Here was a striker with an unbelievable goalscoring record in a major league, and whose goals had helped Liverpool reach two European Cup Finals. The deal to join Juventus was tied up in 1986, but due to the Italians already having the maximum of three overseas players, it was deferred for a year, at which point Michel Platini would retire. Of course, it didn't help that Rush would be joining a side losing its creative genius. But the no.9's departure could have taken place as early as 1984. Napoli offered a mind-boggling £4.5m for the striker – a 50% increase on the world record fee of the time – fresh from his 47-goal season and European Cup Final victory. It was two days before the transfer window closed in Italy, and Rush was eager to jump at the chance of a £1m signing-on fee and a lucrative wage. But the Reds' chairman John Smith was away in London, and refused to even discuss the matter. Napoli switched targets to Diego Maradona – a reasonable back-up plan! – and Liverpool got to keep Rush for another three years. At the time, however, the Reds' no.9 was livid, and having just lost a windfall beyond his wildest dreams, he was soon fearing for his career, due to a knee injury picked up in pre-season training. He recovered, but having missed the first couple of months of the season, he was limited to 'just' 26 goals. He returned in October, and any fears that the knee wouldn't be the same were swept aside with a hat-trick against Benfica in the European Cup. Three years later he joined Juventus for £3.2m.

In the end, his time in Italy was fairly torrid, scoring just seven league goals in 29 games, although Maradona was the top scorer with just 14, and Marco van Basten, also in his first season in Italy, scored just three times in eleven games. Rush, however, was homesick, and after just a year abroad, Kenny Dalglish paid a British record £2.7m to bring the striker home.

To help cement his hero status, Rush saved his best for Everton, the team he supported as a boy. His Welsh colleagues and close friends – Neville Southall and Kevin Ratcliffe – were routinely tormented, at a time when they would have got into the league's best XI. In total, Rush scored 25 derby goals. He equalled the previous record of 19 – held by Dixie Dean – in 1987, with virtually his last touch against the Toffees before leaving for Juventus; six more were to follow after his return. Three games stand out: a trip to Goodison in November 1982, where the 21-year-old bagged not one, not two, not three, but four goals against the blues; an achievement still sung about on the Kop today. (In total, Rush scored 13 at Goodison, almost twice as many as he managed against them at Anfield.) Next was the 1986 FA Cup Final, when the Reds came from a goal down to win 3-1, with the striker's second goal smashed into a camera placed in the back of the net. And the third occasion was the 1989 FA Cup Final, played in the aftermath of the Hillsborough disaster. Replacing John Aldridge on 73 minutes, he scored twice – his first goals as a substitute since his very first goal eight years earlier – which secured an extra-time victory.

Other memorable games include an encounter with Luton Town in 1983; before the game Rush had felt his boots were too stiff, so he threw them in the bath to loosen them up. Within five minutes of kick-off he already had two goals; three more followed. Having scored five goals in a game for the first time in his professional career, a new pre-match ritual was born. Later that season he scored four goals in just over 30 second-half minutes against Coventry. In between, he bagged a hat-trick at Villa Park on a frozen pitch, which included a thumping volley and, to complete the trio of strikes, a delicate lob. This was the first season of live televised league football, and people at home got a real treat. It was one of 16 Liverpool hat-tricks that Rush registered for the Reds.

But whereas Everton were Rush's favourite opponents – scoring 10 more against them than he managed against anyone else – his record against Manchester United provided stark contrast. By the time he had 24 goals against Everton, he'd yet to grab just one against the Reds' other main rivals. It took until late April 1992 – and 25 games – to finally put one past United; it just so happened to be the goal that ended the Manchester club's hopes of a first title in 25 years.

Overall, Ian Rush scored 346 times for the Reds – a club record. And it's fair to say that when you score that many goals, all manner of types of finish will be included; he wasn't a great header of the ball, a long-range blaster or a specialist volleyer, but he still got plenty of those types of goal. (In 1996, Dalglish noted that the heading ability of his former strike partner wasn't great, "and yet I can recall him scoring quite a lot of goals with his head".) But Rush did have his preferences, his hallmark finishes.

Primarily, his blistering pace often took him through on goal, particularly when Dalglish was supplying the pin-point passes. In latching onto the no.7's through-balls, the no.9 had the calmness of mind to find a finish. Although he frequently shot as a keeper narrowed the angle, he was particularly adroit at rounding them at speed. Rather than attempt to close-control dribble – which requires slowing down – he'd make a firm contact in pushing the ball wide. If the keeper didn't take him out – and plenty of penalties were won due to their fractional lateness – the ball would be yards clear. (One of the perils in close-control dribbling around a keeper is how they can often get a hand to the ball, even when it looks like they're beaten.) Rush was moving at speed, and the ball was moving at speed, but he frequently managed to catch it up, slide and slot it in from a tight angle. It was probably his trademark goal, although almost anything within the 18-yard box was in his armoury. (Anything, that is, with the exception of penalties.)

But if those one-on-ones were the most memorable Rush goals, then one- and two-touch finishes within the area were his stock-in-trade; his 'bread and butter'. So many times he was in the right place at the right time – having lost his marker – in order to slot a simple side-foot finish into the net. He had a way of getting his first touch out of his feet, sending it to one side to enable a swift finish. Also, he'd often receive the ball with his back to goal, take a touch and then, in one movement, swivel and swipe the ball home. It helped that he was two-footed; unlike many of his contemporaries, he didn't need to waste time trying to get the ball onto his preferred foot – he could hit it no matter on which side it fell.

That said, he wasn't a particularly 'sweet' striker of the ball like John Barnes or Robbie Fowler, who would caress curling shots into the inside of the far post, and he couldn't match Alan Shearer for power. With Rush, it was about committing the goalkeeper, and about finding angles.

The archetypal prolific forward is often referred to as a predator, and in Rush's case, it couldn't be more apt. There were the artful dodgers – inventive pickpockets – like Fowler; the creative geniuses – like Barnes and Thierry Henry; and bullish bullies like Shearer. But Rush – according to Barnes in a 2006 interview, the best British striker he'd ever seen – was a true predator. There was something almost animalistic about him: the constant movement, the narrowing eyes, and most of all, the brutal efficiency of a strike. He'd lurk, awaiting a slip; always on his toes, even if no opportunity seemed on the cards. The tiniest hint of miscontrol from a defender and the ball would be snatched. One touch, bang. Maybe it was the acceleration – allied to his lean physique – that made him seem especially predatory; the way he could switch from idle to full speed in the blink of an eye. His reactions were rapid. And just as predators prey on the weak and the tired, it's telling that almost 90 of his goals came in the final 15 minutes; that's a quarter of his goals in the final sixth of a game.

As noted earlier, penalties did not play a part in Rush's repertoire. He took – and scored – one absolutely vital one, in the shootout against Roma in the 1984 European Cup Final. But in actual games, he took just six, scoring only three. He once noted that had he been able to take them, he'd have scored 100 more goals. Out of the 89 players to have taken at least one penalty for Liverpool, he ranks 70th in terms of success rate. Contrast this with John Aldridge – the man who replaced him in 1987, and whom he eventually usurped in 1989. Out of any player to have taken more than 15 penalties for the Reds, Aldridge ranks as no.1, with a 94% conversion rate. But this leads to an interesting comparison, particularly as many fans and experts questioned Kenny Dalglish's decision to stick with Rush and sell Aldridge at the start of the Reds' last title-winning side.

In his two-and-a-half years at the club, Aldridge had seemed especially prolific, but those 17 successful penalties skewed his true value to the side. With penalties, Aldridge's strike rate was 0.61 goals per game; highly impressive, but below Rush's rate in four of the Welshman's initial six seasons with the Reds. However, take away Aldridge's penalties and his rate drops to 0.42 – as it so happens, absolutely identical to Rush's second spell at the club. With John Barnes, Peter Beardsley and, in particular, Jan Molby around to score the majority of the Reds' penalties, that side of Aldridge's game wasn't missed. (After all, a penalty is a free shot at goal that requires no positional instincts or tactical awareness.)

It's also worth noting that Aldridge played in an outstanding Liverpool side; but the latter part of Rush's career was spent in a relatively mediocre outfit, particularly between 1991 and 1995. By 1991, Barnes had lost his pace, Alan Hansen had retired, and the remainder of the spine of the 1980s side were now in their 30s. Graeme Souness came in and sold the evergreen Peter Beardsley – the nearest thing the club had to Kenny Dalglish – and filled the side with expensive flops. So for Rush to maintain a scoring rate that matched sans-penalties Aldridge's was doubly impressive. That Rush was also a far better footballer – and harder worker – highlights the wisdom of Dalglish's decision, as the reinstated no.9 went on to score 26 'open play' goals in helping the Reds land another title in 1990. In Dalglish's final season as manager, Rush yet again scored 26 goals but also, according to my calculations, registered at least 13 assists – an amount usually reserved for creative midfielders who take free-kicks and corners – and was voted into the PFA Team of the Year for the 5th time.

His scoring instincts came to the fore again in 1994/95 when, at the age of 34, he notched 19 goals in all competitions for the second season running, as a foil for the prodigious Fowler. Now captain, Rush never looked jealous of his protege; always happy to support him on and off the pitch. He lifted the League Cup in 1995, but it would be the last trophy of his career. Stan Collymore soon arrived, and proved to be a brilliant foil for Fowler; that was, when the new £7.5m man was interested and on his game. Rush had one season left at Liverpool, bagging five goals in 20 appearances, before his second – and final – farewell, which was a free transfer to Leeds United, the opponents against whom his top-level goalscoring career kicked off.

There's precious little doubt that those first six seasons were enough to see Rush selected into Liverpool's best-ever XI. But as with John Barnes, there's a before and after. Whereas Barnes' Liverpool career was split in two by the achilles tendon injury that saw a need to reinvent his game, Rush's was split by that year in Italy. Seven seasons at Anfield were broken by 12 months at Juventus, followed by a further eight years back on Merseyside. While the phenomenal goalscoring feats of the first stint were not matched upon his return, time in Serie A, plus a general maturing, meant that his game was more well-rounded. In time he would become the mentor and link-striker, passing on his wisdom to a young Robbie Fowler in the way that Dalglish had helped him more than a decade earlier.

As with Barnes, I can't help but wonder how Rush would be viewed had we only seen the second half of his career, with his electrifying early period erased from the records. If you take the best years away from any player, then obviously perceptions of their feats would suffer, but part of the problem was that between 1988 and 1996 Rush had to live up to that previous incarnation. He had set himself impossible standards to match. The Welshman still managed to get 139 goals, at a rate of 0.42 per game; a reasonable dip from the 0.63 of his prime, but still almost a goal every other game. But where would he rank in the Reds' pantheon had that second stage been all that we saw? Here was a player whose pace was still intact when Kenny Dalglish brought him back to the club, although it obviously waned as he moved towards his mid-30s. And the tail-end of anyone's career is bound to see a petering out, so it's not fair to be too harsh on his scoring record as the legs gave way. But the control, the hold-up play, the eye for a pass, these were all improved from first time around. Of the eight seasons, five saw him score between 19 and 26.

The first season after his return was blighted by injury and illness, and he missed more than half of Graeme Souness' first full season – although was on hand to score yet another vital FA Cup Final goal. And by his final campaign, in 1995/96, he was a mere bit-part player. Take away those three injury or age-blighted seasons, and what remains is a striker scoring virtually a goal every other game: 112 in 237 games. To contrast this with more recent examples, Michael Owen – at his best – scored 157 in 297 games. Remove Owen's 13 successful penalties, and his strike rate becomes 0.48, not that much higher than Rush 'at his worst' (0.42). Take away Fowler's 17 penalties from his first spell at Liverpool and his strike rate is 0.47. So even in his leaner years, and at an age far greater than the two aforementioned young bucks in their prime, Rush was still more-or-less as prolific from open play. The difference was that he didn't register any remarkable tallies second time around.

So there we have it. Some players cement themselves in folklore with a legendary act, but are not in themselves legends. But no matter how you poke, prod and dissect the word 'legend', which has grown shabby from rampant overuse, it still holds up when it comes to Ian Rush. In one hundred years' time, people will still know the name, and what it stood for. Ian Rush is a goalscoring legend.

FOOTBALL, FINANCE, LIVERPOOL AND THE TOP SIX

By Martin McLaughlin

September, 2012

It's been a few weeks now, but cast your mind back to 31st August. It all was a little bit slapstick, with Brendan Rodgers claiming he would be a sandwich short of a picnic to let Andy Carroll go without a replacement, only to embark on the season short of a substitute snack for the aforementioned pony-tailed sarnie.

It seemed like we suddenly couldn't afford a £6m 29-year old (Clint Dempsey) on a three-year contract at the higher end of the pay scale. Just how much of this money did we actually have? Where did the money we saved on wages go? Where did the money we saved from interest payments go? How can we compete without deficit spending?

This article endeavours to answer some of those questions by looking at the last six years' published accounts and how they compare to the "top six". Unfortunately, complete accounts have been published for all six clubs only up to the period 2010-2011, covering only the first six months of FSG's ownership. They do however give a very clear picture of what state the club was in and what is required to return the club to a stable and prosperous financial and footballing future.

First, a quick financial 101. In my simplified breakdown of footballing finances, income is composed of two items and expenditure is composed of six items.

Income:

Turnover

This is comprised of media, matchday and commercial revenue. This is a relatively fixed income which tends to rise in a steady and predictable fashion. As such, it provides a good reference for calculating percentages of other income and expenditure. This is why wages are often presented as a percentage of turnover.

Player Profit

Do not confuse paying cash for a player with how that is accounted for. You do not lose £50m when you buy a player; cash is converted to an asset, i.e. the player. However, if you sign him to a five-year contract, in five years he will be worth £0, as he will be able to leave for free. Therefore, you must reduce the value of the asset by £10m per year in a linear fashion until it is worth £0 at the end of the contract (otherwise known as transfer amortisation). If after three years, you have written off £30m in value, you are left with a player who you estimate to be valued, in accounting terms, at £20m. If you sell him for £25m, you make a "profit" of £5m on the sale of the asset. We will come to player profit and its importance later.

Expenditure:

Other Expenses

These are the general running costs of a football club. Items such as stadium operating expenses, land and building lease and audit costs are often grouped as other costs.

Depreciation

The value of "tangible" assets, i.e. stadiums or equipment must be reduced over the course of their usable life.

Transfer Amortisation

As described in player profit above, buying a player simply converts cash into an "asset" with the value of the asset reduced to zero over its expected lifetime each accounting year, i.e. contract length.

Wages

This includes players, management, executives, groundstaff, the tea lady, everyone.

Financing Cost

Interest payments and all costs directly linked to debt financing (even if they are one-off costs).

Exceptional Costs

Anything not included in parts 1-5 that is a one-off – the most common of which is manager contract termination fees, which Liverpool have paid a few times in recent years.

Before I begin, I will mention a very specific quote from the recent open letter from John W Henry , as it is a rather important point:

"The transfer policy was not about cutting costs. It was – and will be in the future – about getting maximum value for what is spent so that we can build quality and depth."

Part 1 – Where Did the Interest Money Go?

There has been something of an illusion which has built up around the Hicks and Gillett era that states Liverpool fell from competitive grace due to interest payments siphoning money from wages and transfers. I will put it bluntly, that is untrue. The figure below shows the income and expenditure breakdown for the years '05/06 to '10/11 with each area of income and expenditure expressed as a percentage of turnover:

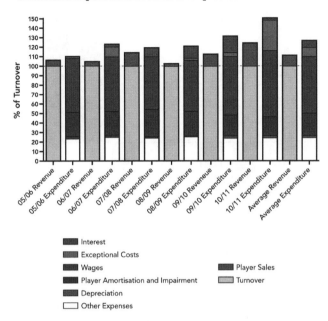

Liverpool 2005/06 – 2010/11
Income and Expenditure Breakdown Expressed as % of Turnover

Legend:
- Interest
- Exceptional Costs
- Wages
- Player Sales
- Player Amortisation and Impairment
- Turnover
- Depreciation
- Other Expenses

The average revenue and expenditure is shown as the final two columns. The interest payments have been placed at the top to indicate that in almost every year, the loss corresponds almost exactly to interest payments only*.

*It should be noted that the holding company used by Hicks and Gillett to purchase Liverpool had cumulative interest of £87m from 2007-2011. However, this was never paid by the club and after the purchase by NESV/FSG there is no risk of this ever being a cost the club will have to incur. Therefore it has been excluded.

This figure of all income and expenditure is a little overwhelming. To more closely look at the impact of interest and exceptional stadium expenditure, the graph below shows the six-year cumulative profit before tax (which I will occasionally refer to as simply profit) for Liverpool and Manchester United. Interest and stadium costs have been excluded to show their impact for each club.

(NB – the last expansion of Old Trafford occurred in 05/06 at a cost of £45m, but I have been unable to identify the year in which this was accounted for.)

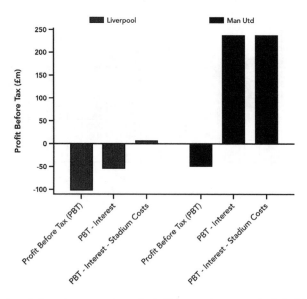

Cumulative Profit Before Tax Over 6 Years Excluding Interest and Stadium Costs

Notice how when interest payments and stadium costs are excluded, Liverpool would have broken even over six years, a £5.6m profit before tax actually. Manchester United is the perfect example of a club being drained by interest. They have made a cumulative loss of £47.8m over the period '05/06 – '10/11, but spent a mind-boggling £283.6m on interest and financing costs. Liverpool, on the other hand, were run with their fingers in their ears as to the accumulating cost of interest payments loaded onto the club (£46.8m) and stadium fees (£59.9m). We are talking about just interest payments here, not actually paying off the core debt. Manchester United are chipping away at their debt pile; Liverpool were adding to it. As for stadium payments, only £10.3m of stadium design fees in '06/07 had been accounted for. When FSG bought the club they found £49.6m which had been spent, but not written down in the books yet; £59.9m in total and no stadium, you have to wonder if they even bought a spade to put in the ground?

Part 2 – [It's] the Wages, Stupid!

FFP allows the exclusion of costs associated with stadium and other long-term developments such as academy and training facility investment. Therefore, while we made a thumping great accounting loss of £49.3m, we can exclude £49.6m. While it's nice that we can exclude this from FFP, FSG have said they will not run Liverpool at a loss. In that respect, FFP is somewhat irrelevant to Liverpool, they simply must break even, just as Arsenal, Manchester United and Tottenham do. FFP may rein in Chelsea and Man City, but Liverpool must still be run to break even, even if it doesn't.

We aren't going to write off £49.6m in stadium debt every year, so all is well – back to breaking even next year? Well, not quite. The next figure is player profit as a percentage of turnover; the grey dotted line representing an average percentage income over and above normal turnover for the top-six over six years.

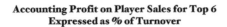

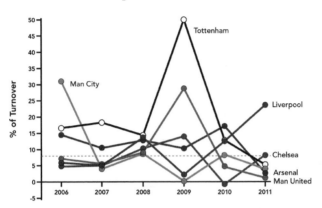

Accounting Profit on Player Sales for Top 6
Expressed as % of Turnover

In 2010/11, Liverpool recorded the third-highest player profit as a percentage of turnover among the now top six in the last five years. This is only bettered by 2008/09 when Manchester United sold Cristiano Ronaldo, and also '08/09 when Tottenham sold Dimitar Berbatov and Robbie Keane amongst others. This allowed Manchester United and Tottenham to pocket a cool profit before tax of £48.1m and £33.5m respectively. We must have pocketed a tidy profit as well then? Well, if you exclude the £49.6m stadium costs, we made a loss of £0.3m, so where the hell did it all go? Manager termination costs and wages, or Roy Hodgson and Joe Cole if you want an exact personification. Cue the dreaded wages to turnover figure.

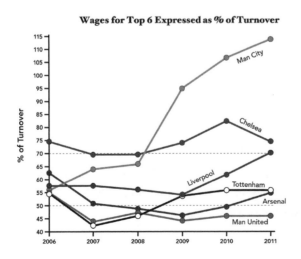

Wages for Top 6 Expressed as % of Turnover

Please try and ignore Manchester City and their bonkers wage bill for a moment. Instead look at the solid red Liverpool line. From 2006-2009 this was already undesirably high at around over 55% of turnover. It is in 2010 and 2011 that things take a horrible unsustainable turn for the worse. In 2010/11, Liverpool spent 70% of turnover on wages – Chelsea levels of unsustainability. What does this look like in real terms?

Look at the figures in real terms and ask yourself two things. Why can we spend as much as Arsenal and not match them in league position? Why can Tottenham spend so little and match Arsenal, Liverpool and Chelsea in league position? Clearly it's not how much you spend, but how you spend it that is the key. Remember when looking at this graph that in 2010 our wages were already at 62% of turnover. In 2011 turnover was stagnant (£184.9m dropped to £183.7m in 2011) yet wages were allowed to rise by a further £15m to 70% of turnover. This was not an increase due to dropping revenue, this was a further escalation in uncontrolled wage spending. Where did the money to pay this ballooning wage bill come from? The sale of Fernando Torres.

Part 3 – The "Exceptional" Manager Merry-go-round

Football clubs occasionally incur "exceptional" costs. For Liverpool recently, these have become much less exceptional. The figure below describes exceptional costs as a percentage of turnover for each of the top six.

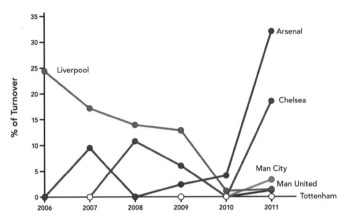

Exceptional Costs
(Contract Termination, Stadium Fees, Goodwill Amortisation)

For Chelsea, exceptional costs are terminating manager contracts as an almost annual occurrence. For Manchester United it is "goodwill" amortisation. This is because the Glazers paid more to take over the club than it was worth. They had been gradually writing off the difference, and this stopped in 2010.

Liverpool spent money on contract terminations in 2009, 2010 and 2011, in addition to stadium costs for a stadium that was never built; in total, £20.5m in termination fees and £59.9m in stadium costs. Man City, Tottenham and Arsenal barely register. That this is money we can ill afford to waste goes without saying. Combined, that's over two Andy Carrolls, or just over five Joe Allens in today's money. Added to an out-of-control wage bill, it paints a picture of a period of epic financial mismanagement. You could wipe away the interest payments, but Liverpool had been borrowing money to pay the interest anyway. All in all, £80m wasted on sacking managers and a phantom stadium, plus a wage bill so out of proportion to turnover that players had to be sold to break even. This is the legacy of Hicks, Gillett and Purslow, this was the mess which FSG found the club in when they arrived. In this context, someone needs to ask John W. Henry, why on earth did he decide to buy such a financial train wreck?

Part 4 –The Tottenham Model

Up until this point there are a few things in the financial narrative I haven't mentioned. Transfer fees (aka "Player Amortisation"), the impact of building a stadium ("Interest and Depreciation") and "other costs." "Other costs" is rather boring, although in order to move to the interesting part I will cover it briefly here.

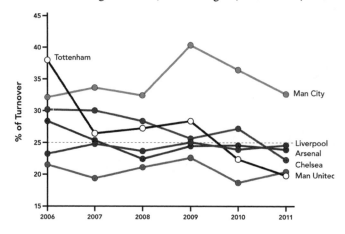

Other Costs
(Running a Stadium, Office Leagues, Audit Costs, etc.)

"Other costs" are actually relatively stable, except for Manchester City and Tottenham's 2005/06 value. The average "other costs" of the top-six over six years is about 25%. Liverpool are controlling these costs as well as other teams, though of course improvement in controlling expenditure would allow it to be directed elsewhere. Where would this elsewhere be? Back to the "Tottenham Model". To build a winning team it is fairly certain you will have to spend money on players. So let's look at transfer amortisation and the interesting financial story of the rise of Tottenham to Champions League contenders.

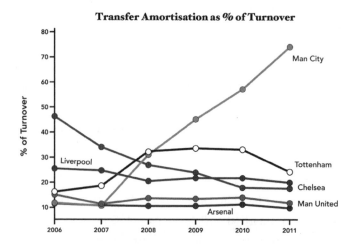

Transfer Amortisation as % of Turnover

We see two clear events: Man City spending astronomical amounts on transfer amortisation (the highest point on the right side of the graph) and the result of Chelsea (the hightest point on the left side of the graph) tightening the purse strings post-Mourinho. What is more surprising is a sustained spend of greater than 30% of turnover by Tottenham on transfers. Imagine the scale was not stretched by Man City and look at Tottenham again from 2008-2010. Let's look at those percentages in real monetary terms.

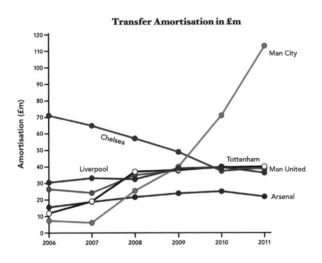

Transfer Amortisation in £m

From 2008-2011, Tottenham were amortising player values at an almost identical scale to Liverpool, Manchester United and Chelsea, while breaking even. How did they do this? The accounts say three ways, wage control, low exceptional expenditure and high player turnover.

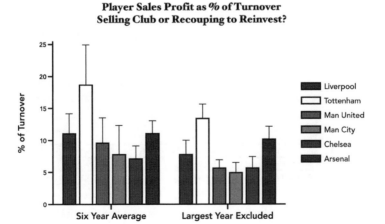

**Player Sales Profit as % of Turnover
Selling Club or Recouping to Reinvest?**

Why do I use the phrase "high player turnover" and not "selling club"? Above is the six-year average of the accounting player profit for the top six. I have excluded the single largest year in the right hand side to remove any exceptional selling events. The six year average for the top six is 8%. Arsenal are labelled a selling club to fund the Emirates debt, Liverpool in 2010 and 2011 became a selling club to counter wage inflation. Tottenham retain more of their revenue – over and above basic turnover (media, commercial, matchday) – than both Arsenal and Liverpool; significantly more. They don't use it to pay off stadium debt or wages though, they use it to sustain a highly abnormal transfer amortisation for a club which has had revenue half that of Chelsea, Arsenal and Liverpool for most of the last six years. What would it look like if Liverpool adopted the Tottenham split of income and expenditure and applied it to 2011 turnover? If we assume expenditure of 25% on other costs (the top six average), 50% of turnover spent on wages, no exceptional costs, depreciation of £2.9m (the six year Liverpool average), £3m interest (the 2011 figure) and a profit on player sales of 12.5% over and above turnover (our six year average is 11%).

	Actual 10/11	Hypothetical 10/11	Actual 6-Year %	Hypothetical 6-Year %
Match Day	£40.9m	£40.9m		
Media	£65.3m	£65.3m		
Commercial	£77.4m	£77.4m		
Other	£0.1m	£0.1m		
Total Revenue	**£183.7m**	**£183.7m**	**100.0%**	**100.0%**
Wages	(£128.9m)	(£91.9m)	[59.9%]	[50.0%]
Other Expenses	(£45.0m)	(£45.9m)	[24.2%]	[25.0%]
Expenses	**(£173.9m)**	**(£137.8m)**	**(84.1%)**	**(75.0%)**
EBITDA (aka Cash Left)	**£9.8m**	**£45.9m**	**15.9%**	**25.0%**
Termination Fees	(£8.4m)	0.0		
Stadium Fees	(£49.6m)	0.0		
Acquisition Fees	(£1.0m)	0.0		
Exceptional Total	**(£99.0m)**	**0.0**	**(8.7%)**	**0.0%**
Amortisation	(£36.3m)	(£63.0m)	[22.0%]	[34.3%]
Impairment		0.0		
Depreciation	(£4.2m)	(£2.9m)	[1.8%]	[1.6%]
Non Cash Flow Expenses	**(£59.0m)**	**(£65.9m)**	**(23.8%)**	**(35.9%)**
Operating Profit	**(£89.7m)**	**(£20.0m)**	**[16.6%]**	**[10.9%]**
Player Sale Profit (Loss)	£43.3m	£23.0m	11.0%	12.5%
Profit B/F Interest & Tax	**(£46.4m)**	**£3.0m**	**[5.6%]**	**1.6%**
Net Interest (Inc Holding Comp)	(£2.9m)	(£3.0m)	[4.9%]	[1.6%]
Profit (Loss) Before Tax	**(£49.3m)**	**0.0**	**[10.5%]**	**0.0%**

What I didn't mention was the figure left over if you put these entirely realistic values in. £63m in transfer amortisation. Refer back to the "Transfer Amortisation as £m" graph and look where £63m would position Liverpool. Wages of 50% gives a wage bill of £91.9m, which is ever so slightly smaller than the £96.1m wage bill from 2008/09 and is almost identical to Tottenham's £91.1m from 2010/11 when they entered the Champions League (and saw their wage bill rocket by 36% from the pre-Champions League level of £67.1m). To do this we have to sell players every year, I hear someone shout. Well, yes, but just the ones we don't need anymore. With the exception of Luka Modric and Dimitar Berbatov, Tottenham's player profit came from selling players they allowed to leave knowing they had replacements, or simply wanted to move on.

Part 5 – Liverpool, Millstone-Free Since 2012 (Joe Cole Excluded)

Thanks to FSG we are now entering new territory. Free from interest payments and, after some unpleasant surgery, in possession of a wage bill more in balance with other expenditure. There are two key points to think about at this juncture. Finding the best value in terms of investment for the 75% of turnover we have after other costs are covered. What does this look like? Well, a lot like walking away from Clint Dempsey.

Key to sensible investment will be wage control and investment in transfers where the probability of recouping and reinvesting from failed buys is high. Buying young and paying low wages initially means two things: a) should a player turn out to be worse than expected, he will still have a resale value (this may only be 50% of what you paid, but 50% of every failed transfer to reinvest is a lot more over the years than 0%); and b) lower wages mean prospective buying clubs can afford to match a failed player's wages instead of negotiating a knockdown fee just so we can remove someone from the wage bill (sound familiar?).

According to Deloitte and their football finance review covering the 2010/11 accounting period, the majority of the total commercial revenue increase of £83m in the Premier League was due to three teams, Manchester United, Manchester City and Liverpool. It is clear that Liverpool are pushing this aggressively. It is also clear that apart from Champions League qualification, it is difficult to gain an advantage in terms of media income.

This leaves matchday income. Total Premier League matchday income only increased by £20m in total to £551m (4% rise), indicating stagnation relative to the 13% and 18% increases in broadcasting and commercial revenue respectively across the entire league. You have to ask, if it's such a no-brainer to make money, why is it stagnant? Is it because it is a big investment for little return? Tottenham and Chelsea are also seeking to expand matchday revenue; even with a licence to print money, Chelsea are struggling. Looking at the next two graphs, we can see what Arsenal are dealing with due to the Emirates development: first, financing costs; second, depreciation.

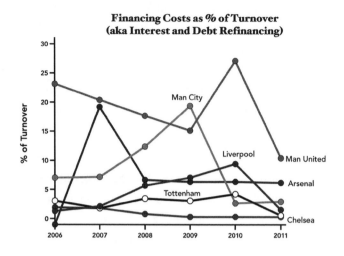

**Financing Costs as % of Turnover
(aka Interest and Debt Refinancing)**

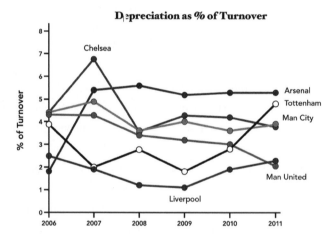

Depreciation as % of Turnover

Building a stadium gives you the twin Ds of the millstone world, debt and depreciation. Debt because you have to borrow to build it and depreciation because once it's built it becomes a £400m+ asset with a 50-year estimated lifespan, with a decreasing value which must be written off each year. Arsenal are now a self-sustaining business and as such have to break even; in fact, they have to make a profit to pay off the debt on top of the interest. Refer to the transfer amortisation graphs, and look at the flat-lining nature of Arsenal's transfer amortisation.

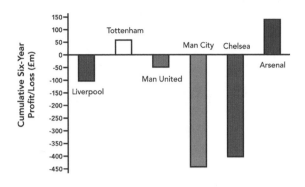

Accumulated Profit/Loss Before Tax 05/06 – 10/11

The figure above is the price of the Emirates, *after* £89.1m of financial costs and *after* £40m of depreciation you still have to add £138.9m of profit before tax over six years, which instead of being spent on players was squirreled away in a bank account to safeguard Arsenal's future against £250m of debt. Yes it's been a financial boom in terms of the turnover generated, but how much of that has actually trickled down into the team over and above what they would have earned at Highbury? Would Arsenal swap the Emirates for a redeveloped Highbury with its atmosphere and history? Matchday revenue is now an ever dwindling percentage of income; just how many extra percentage points does it need to be before the soulless bowl with the big brand for a name is really worth it.

In Conclusion

I hope I have been able to show a number of things, including just how catastrophically wrong things went in the years '09/10 – '10/11. Liverpool had turned into a club who changed managers on a yearly basis, wasted vast sums on a phantom stadium which couldn't possibly be financed, had begun the trend of decreased transfer spending and swapped it for vast ineffective wage inflation, relying on player sales to break even.

The actions of the last few years have suggested wages will go down, but they need to stay down. With that, transfer spending should begin to go up and stay up. Exceptional costs should now become an actual exception. A refusal to deficit spend should also signal high levels of interest are a thing of the past. That includes not loading vast amounts of debt on the club for the vanity project of a new stadium in a world where commercial and media revenue rises inexorably. To quote John Henry:

"We will build and grow from within, buy prudently and cleverly and never again waste resources on inflated transfer fees and unrealistic wages. We have no fear of spending and competing with the very best but we will not overpay for players. We

will never place this club in the precarious position that we found it in when we took over at Anfield. This club should never again run up debts that threaten its existence."

It all seems rather obvious; you wonder why everyone doesn't do it?

THE COSTS AND BENEFITS OF BUILDING NEW ANFIELD

By Ben Stoneman

November, 2011

The stadium is without doubt the biggest decision facing Fenway Sports Group. TTT subscriber and financial expert Ben Stoneman performs an in-depth cost/benefit analysis on New Anfield.

With groundshare well and truly off the agenda and FSG's stated preferred option of redeveloping Anfield far from certain, "New Anfield" seems a possibility, if a stadium naming rights partner can be secured.

When it comes to the value of a naming rights deal, Liverpool will be looking at the following benchmarks:

Arsenal made just £90m from selling shirt and stadium rights over 15 years in 2004 and have since acknowledged that they settled for less than £3m a season in naming rights to ensure 50% of the cash up front.

Manchester City, irrespective of how fair the value is and all of the controversy it has created, received £400m for a 10-year deal with Etihad this summer. This £40m-a-season covered shirt sponsorship, naming rights and the "Etihad Campus".

The current global market leader for naming rights is the recent $400m, 20-year MetLife sponsorship of New Meadowlands, home of the NY Giants and NY Jets NFL teams.

On the face of it, it seems like a terrible time to invest in such a large project. Countries around the world are currently in the midst of austerity programmes that are designed to rein in what is perceived to be excessive spending. Governments around the world are reducing outlay to balance their books, all in the hope that this will also somehow spur growth. Several disturbing parallels to these conditions, and how countries choose to react to them, can be made with events in the 1920s. Regardless, one of the industries hardest hit by the decreases in spending is construction. Investment in infrastructure has largely been put on hold until economic conditions improve. However, under UEFA Financial Fair Play, costs related to investment in infrastructure are excluded from the break-even calculation rules. The cost of finance (i.e. the interest on any loans required to build the stadium) is also excluded from the break-even calculation. Yet once the stadium is built, any extra revenues will count in our favour towards the break-even calculation. It's not really a surprise that so many have referred to the new stadium as "the game changer".

In this article I will make the case that it makes great sense (from financial, marketing and entertainment perspectives) to build a new stadium. I will then detail one of the largest problems that faces the owners now and in the future (and give a quick economics lesson to demonstrate how to solve this problem). Finally, I will offer a few ideas about how the club could maximise these revenues while remaining as sensitive as possible to the current economic conditions in the city.

Current economic climate

The problem with the logic that now is a poor time to invest in any sort of infrastructure, is that those very conditions are extremely favourable right now. That may sound counter-intuitive if one listens to the news – or mistakenly equates a household's spending with a government's or corporation's – but there are three main reasons behind this statement:

1) Interest rates are at historically low standards.

I know the mere mention of the word debt will send a chill down any supporter's spine after the past few years, but it is highly unlikely that the owners will have £300 million to spend out of their own wallets. It is important to note that debt financing for something like a stadium is fundamentally different to the leveraged buyout the old regime used to buy the club.

The current rate for a 10-year Treasury note from the Central Bank of England is around 2%. The owners will not be able to borrow at the same rate as a federal government, but they will surely have access to lines of credit far beyond that of the average person. For a £250m loan, borrowing at a rate of 5% would yield annual interest payments of £12.5m. This may seem like a lot of money, but with the large increase in revenues that a new stadium would bring, they are certainly not unmanageable.

2) The price of labour is comparatively cheap.

Basic economic theory states there is an inverse relationship between unemployment and wages. As the unemployment rate rises, the wages needed to pay employees fall. The unemployment rate in Liverpool in 2010 was 12.2%. To compare, the rate in the North West was 8.0%; the national rate was 7.7%. For males aged 16-64 in Liverpool, the unemployment rate was a staggering 15%.

As I noted above, if decreases in infrastructure spending are a primary result of austerity, construction is one of the first industries that is affected. There are many skilled and well-trained architects, labourers, foremen and other workers who would be ready and willing to build the new stadium. Plus, from a fan's perspective, how cool would it be to tell your grandchildren you helped build the new Anfield?

3) The price of building materials is cheap.

This is probably the largest competitive advantage the club would have in building a new stadium now. Below is a graph showing the price of the Dow Jones Steel Index over the past five years:

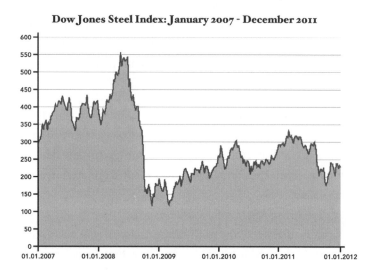

I don't want to suggest that Hicks and Gillett were right on anything – especially regarding their numerous broken promises on the stadium issue – but you can see that steel is much cheaper now than from 2007, due to the collapse in late 2008. Growth in countries like China, India, Brazil, and throughout the Middle East, over the next few years will lead to an increasing demand for building materials. The price for steel and other goods will increase as well. Also, it is worth noting that Henry made his fortune as a commodity trader. There is no doubt that redeveloping Anfield would be cheaper now. However, there are two underlying costs to factor in should the club decide against building a new stadium. The lifespan of a stadium that is currently over 120 years old will eventually reach, and perhaps is already approaching, its limit. At that point, a new stadium would be built at a significantly higher cost. Additionally, closing down a stand or a portion of the stadium during the season to increase capacity could lower revenues. It is these two issues – match-day revenues and attendance versus capacity – that I will discuss next.

Match-day revenue

In March 2011, The Swiss Ramble blog meticulously detailed the finances of the top six clubs in the Premier League. Its author shows how Man United and Arsenal both generate £2m more than Liverpool for every single home game, with Chelsea £800k more. It should also be noted that his article uses data from 2009/10, the last season Liverpool were in the Champions League.

It is this Revenue Per Match (RPM) that Liverpool need to significantly increase to better compete with United, Chelsea and Arsenal. Their advantages lie in a combination of larger stadiums and, due to the cities they play in, the ability to charge much higher prices per ticket.

Knowing that the markets the London and Manchester clubs operate in are very different from Liverpool's, I decided to divide RPM by stadium capacity (the attendance and capacity figures were taken directly from the Premier League stats page). It is here you can begin to see the different playing field that the London and Manchester clubs are on.

Unfortunately, the money generated per seat is not the only issue facing the club as they look to increase match-day revenue. Liverpool, especially in comparison to other English clubs, simply does not fill up Anfield.

Team	Matchday Revenue	Revenue/ Match	% Capacity	RPM/ Capacity	RPM/ Attendance	Spread- Attendance v Capacity
Man United	£100.2m	£3.58m	98.81%	£47.23	£47.80	£0.57
Arsenal	£93.9m	£3.48m	99.16%	£57.55	£58.03	£0.48
Chelsea	£67.2m	£2.40m	97.58%	£56.54	£57.94	£1.40
Liverpool	£42.9m	£1.59m	94.49%	£35.03	£37.07	£2.04
Tottenham	£36.8m	£1.53m	98.80%	£42.32	£42.84	£0.52
Man City	£24.4m	£1.02m	96.01%	£21.45	£22.34	£0.89

Attendance vs. Capacity

Anfield has been renowned for decades as a fortress, one of the most intimidating places to play for visiting clubs in all of Europe. It often seems that the fans in the stadium give the players an extra shot of energy on the big occasions, and our club is famous for the atmosphere on a European night.

Despite this reputation, Liverpool has not maximised the number of tickets sold for home games for many years. This is true not just for last season, during the Hodgson era, nor is it for Europa League or Carling Cup games. Even during the peak years of the past decade, winning the Champions League and ranked as the top club in Europe, Liverpool fell short of reaching capacity over a full season:

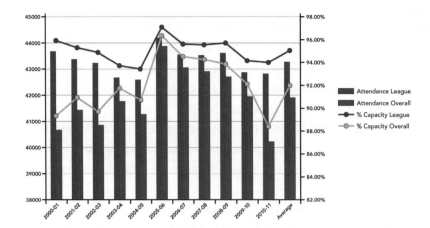

The left-hand bars show the average attendance for the nineteen home league games each season; the right-hand bars include any European, FA and Carling Cup games as well. For those who find it easier to think in percentages, the two lines indicate the percent capacity of Anfield for league games and total games, respectively, each season. (Note that for the Champions League, UEFA mandates a certain number of rows around the perimeter are kept vacant so there is always a reduced capacity for these games.)

During the best year – 2005-06 – in terms of attendance over the past decade, Liverpool could not sell an average of 1,286 tickets for our league games (remember, the team were fresh from being crowned European champions). In 2009-10, the season used for all of the financial figures in this piece, Liverpool were short an average of 2,633 tickets for league games and a surprising 3,560 seats for the total 27 home games played that season. It is easy to see why the club stated in the annual financial report that attendance versus capacity is one of the most critical drivers for financial performance. The problem is only magnified in comparison to the other top English clubs:

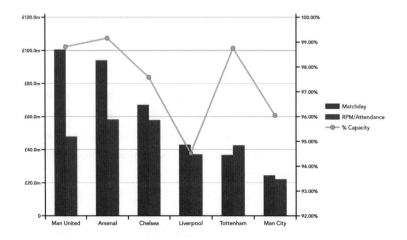

The blue/right-hand bar (RPM/Attendance), which should be counted in £millions, is total match-day revenue for the full 09-10 season; the red/left-hand bar indicates the revenue per match for every ticket sold. Note that this figure is different from RPM/Capacity to highlight the difference for clubs that more closely sell out their matches (only league games to provide more accurate figures):

Team	Matchday Revenue	Revenue/ Match	% Capacity	RPM/ Capacity	RPM/ Attendance	Spread-Attendance v Capacity
Man United	£100.2m	£3.58m	98.81%	£47.23	£47.80	£0.57
Arsenal	£93.9m	£3.48m	99.16%	£57.55	£58.03	£0.48
Chelsea	£67.2m	£2.40m	97.58%	£56.54	£57.94	£1.40
Liverpool	£42.9m	£1.59m	94.49%	£35.03	£37.07	£2.04
Tottenham	£36.8m	£1.53m	98.80%	£42.32	£42.84	£0.52
Man City	£24.4m	£1.02m	96.01%	£21.45	£22.34	£0.89

The UK clubs that maximize the capacity of their stadiums have the lowest spread in that final column. To think of it another way, Liverpool must charge a premium of over £2 per ticket to make the same amount of money as they would if all seats were sold. Or, with that £2 premium and selling out all seats, the club could make an extra £2.46m per year. Compared to the other five teams listed, a lot of work has to be done.

Current revenues

In the inaugural meeting of the Liverpool Supporters Committee, Ian Ayre revealed that roughly half of the club's total match-day revenues was generated from the 6% of total capacity that is allocated to corporate hospitality tickets. Using the numbers above, the breakdown for the 09-10 season follows:

Team	Matchday Revenue	Stadium Capacity	# of Matches	Revenue per Match	RPM/ Capacity
LFC (now)	£42.90m	45,400	27	£1.59m	£35.00
Hosp (now)	£21.45m	2,724	27	£0.79m	£291.65
Gen (now)	£21.45m	42,676	27	£0.79m	£18.62

Clearly, the prices charged to the hospitality tickets far exceed those for the rest of the stadium. As Ian Ayre correctly pointed out, we would all be paying far more to watch a match without these hospitality tickets. The club only makes 23% of its annual money through match-day revenue. Building a new stadium would raise this amount – this is of course important for the Financial Fair Play rules, but for sustainability purposes a club should, in theory, get one-third of its total money from each of matchday, broadcasting and commercial sources.

Potential revenues

When I first began crunching these figures, I used the assumption that we would want to increase that RPM/Capacity figure only to £40. Not only would it be terrible PR to drastically raise the prices, but as the American company Netflix recently found out, there is a chance that customers will opt out of paying for the service *en masse* (or in this case, not attend games – although football fans are not like normal consumers). Therefore, £40 seemed like a sensible amount to balance the need to pay for the stadium while minding current economic conditions.

First, as a baseline example, if the club were to keep the hospitality portion of total capacity at 6% and split the revenues between that and the general attendance, the figures would look like this:

Team (6%)	Matchday Revenue	Stadium Capacity	# of Matches	Revenue per Match	RPM/ Capacity
LFC (60k)	£64.80m	60,000	27	£2.40m	£40.00
Hosp (60k)	£32.40m	3,600	27	£1.20m	£333.33
Gen (60k)	£32.40m	56,400	27	£1.20m	£21.28

For simplicity, I assumed Liverpool would play 27 home matches per season. Moving the proportion of hospitality tickets to the rumoured 7,500, while keeping the 50/50 split, equates to:

Team (12.5%)	Matchday Revenue	Stadium Capacity	# of Matches	Revenue per Match	RPM/ Capacity
LFC (60k)	£64.80m	60,000	27	£2.40m	£40.00
Hosp (60k)	£32.40m	7,500	27	£1.20m	£160.00
Gen (60k)	£32.40m	52,500	27	£1.20m	£22.86

A few key points stand out here. First, the total revenue would increase by about £22m under these two scenarios. The RPM/capacity increases under both cases for the general tickets, but it is severely slashed when the hospitality seating proportion increases to 12.5%. What would happen if the aforementioned 50/50 split went away, and the RPM/capacity for the two segments remained at the levels it is now?

RPM/Cap Constant	Matchday Revenue	Stadium Capacity	# of Matches	Revenue per Match	RPM/ Capacity
LFC (60k)	£85.45m	60,000	27	£3.16m	£52.74
Hosp (60k)	£59.06m	7,500	27	£2.19m	£291.65
Gen (60k)	£26.39m	52,500	27	£0.89m	£18.62

Assuming the same ticket prices, increasing the hospitality capacity to 7,500 almost doubles the current match-day revenue! The club would make far more per match from the 7,500 hospitality seats in the new stadium than we currently do with 45,000+ seats in Anfield. This illustrates the importance that new stadiums, and particularly the need to cater for the wealthier fan base, hold for boosting a club's returns. It also gives an insight into how Arsenal, Chelsea, and Man United make so much more than Liverpool for each match.

Team	Matchday Revenue	Home Games	Stadium Capacity	Revenue/ Match	RPM/ Capacity
Man United	£100.2m	28	75,769	£3.58m	£47.23
Arsenal	£93.9m	27	60,432	£3.48m	£57.55
Liverpool (new)	£85.5m	27	60,000	£3.16m	£52.75
Chelsea	£67.2m	28	42,449	£2.40m	£56.54
Liverpool	£42.9m	27	45,362	£1.59m	£35.03
Tottenham	£36.8m	24	36,230	£1.53m	£42.32
Man City	£24.4m	24	47,405	£1.02m	£21.45

Of course, this assumes perhaps the best-case scenario we can hope for, and is probably too optimistic for what we should ultimately expect. Most likely, if Liverpool increase the quantity of the hospitality seats from 2,700 to 7,500, they will not be able to fill them all at the current prices. This is simple supply and demand. The club will have enough sales data to know what to charge for these tickets, but regardless it is clear that one of the primary goals is to maximise revenue from these seats. If the club cannot fill a 45,000-seat stadium throughout the year, it stands to reason that there may be problems filling a 60,000-seat stadium at the same prices. Liverpool must determine the optimal price to charge for each ticket in order to meet the twin goals of fully filling the stadium and maximising revenue. While this task may seem daunting, there is an entire field of study devoted to this that several industries have been using for decades.

Yield Management

Yield management is defined as "the process of understanding, anticipating and influencing consumer behaviour in order to maximise yield or profits from a perishable source (such as airline seats or hotel room reservations)." In order for the process to apply to this situation, three conditions must be met:

• There is a fixed quantity of resources for sale (a limited number of tickets).

• The resources sold are perishable (once the game ends, the tickets are essentially worthless)

• Different customers are willing to pay different prices for the same resource

(hence second hand markets for tickets)

Yield management is used far more often than most people realise. From children and senior citizens receiving discounts at a cinema to the passenger next to you on an airplane paying perhaps double or half the amount you paid for the same flight, companies use this concept to make more money than they would by charging a single price to everyone. In fact, to an extent football clubs already do this. Many will note that Liverpool already use this to set their ticket prices, and the price paid depends much on which section the seat is in, the age of the supporter, and who we are playing. At this point, the reader may think I am advocating raising tickets as much as possible. On the contrary, by giving a quick economics lesson I want to show how the club may even offer some tickets at lower prices than are currently available.

Liverpool FC: The Monopolist

Think of Liverpool for a minute as a monopoly. Football is a unique business in this aspect. Once most fans attach themselves to a club, whether it is Liverpool or any other team, there is no substitute emotionally to support another team. Irrespective of results, players, owners, or managers, a typical supporter will not move from one club to another. When a firm has no direct competition, it can act as a monopoly.

In economics, a monopolist typically will charge a single price for its product. Economic theory states that profit is maximised when marginal revenue (the extra money made for one more unit) equals marginal cost (the extra money spent for one more unit). Once the MR=MC figure is determined, the monopolist does not, and will not, charge at this price. Because there are no competitors for the product, the price charged to customers can be significantly higher – up to the demand curve. A graph would look like this:

– *The total revenue made by the monopolist would be the area inside the red box.*
– *The total cost is the rectangle with "MR=MC" and the black arrow inside of it.*

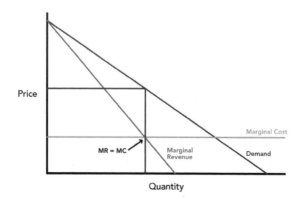

Total Profit is shown in the solid rectangle '1' below:

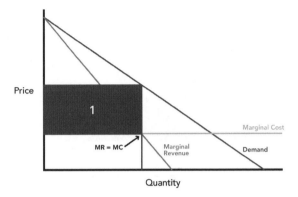

If football clubs all charged one price – for example, the RPM/capacity figure I used in the previous tables – for every ticket in the stadium, this determines how much profit is made. However, we have seen how much more money can be charged for a small percentage of hospitality seats. The profit made from these higher-priced tickets is shown in the yellow triangle '2' below:

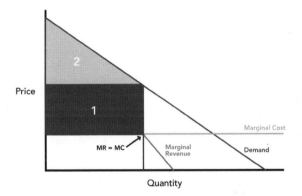

By recognizing that some fans can and will pay far more than the general admission price for the same product, a football club can make lots more money by utilising yield management. Liverpool currently doubles its match-day revenues, and will far exceed them with a larger stadium, by doing exactly this. Even if a firm can sell every unit of its product at this point, there are still customers who would be eager to purchase the goods at a lower price. Likewise, there are many football fans who would love to go to a match, but cannot due to the price of a ticket. If the yellow triangle (2) can produce profit at an extremely high price, more money can also be made by offering the same goods at a lower price. This is shown in the blue triangle '3' below:

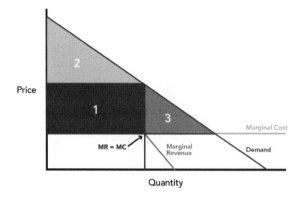

Quantity

This blue triangle (3) is where Liverpool can set itself apart from the other Premier League clubs they are competing with. Empty, unsold seats do not benefit the club at all. Reading the attendance vs. capacity section above, one may think the club could reduce the prices of those unsold tickets; indeed, some money must be better than none at all. Especially for the Premier League matches against weaker competition and the FA/Carling Cup games, the club should lower the prices of any unsold tickets in order to fill the stadium. Some ticket holders who pay full price for their seat will presumably be against this idea. However, it offers several benefits:

• The atmosphere in the stadium will be louder and probably more enjoyable for all involved.

• Fans who cannot afford tickets at current prices could attend a match and take in the experience of watching the team.

• More people in attendance will encourage more concessions and merchandise to be purchased.

• As the frequency of sellouts increases, no matter what fans are paying for individual tickets, there may be an effect where people, unsure if the cheaper seats will be available as the match approaches, will purchase them early at a normal (or at least higher) price.

• Finally, and perhaps most importantly from a public relations standpoint, the owners would receive a lot of positive attention for taking actions to offer a limited number of tickets at a price that more fans can afford. With almost every team in the league hiking prices, Liverpool would stand out by taking a small stance against pricing out some of their most loyal supporters.

The beauty of this plan is that the marginal cost for an extra ticket in a stadium is incredibly low. Almost every cost associated with a match – the total amount for the stadium, lighting for evening games, the wages paid to the squad – is exactly the same for that match whether one person is in attendance or 60,000. The only significant variable costs would be the cost of extra police and the part-time employees working at a match (for reference, the financial account stated that the club employed on average 895 people for match days. If roughly 42,000 people watched each game, an extra employee was hired for every 47 supporters. If capacity increases by 15,000, 300-350 new employees would be hired).

Final thoughts

I hope by now it's clear that the benefits of a new stadium, along with selling it out for each game, will more than offset the costs of building it. If a new stadium can generate an extra £30m or more of revenue per year with ticket sales, and the naming rights can bring another £10m, the cost would most likely be paid off within ten years. Additionally, the hopeful return of Champions League football could bring another £30m to the club (and help attract some of the world's best talent to the club). Moving away from Anfield, or alternatively redeveloping it, is a decision that will shape the future of our club. Compelling arguments can be made for each side, but from a financial perspective the possibility of New Anfield may be too tempting to pass up.

THE UNWRITTEN LAW OF MANAGERIAL SUITABILITY

By Paul Tomkins

December, 2010

This we know: that there are good managers, and that there are not-so-good managers. But it's equally true that the quality of the manager doesn't always dictate the results a team gets. The truth is that, even if a manager is gifted enough, he relies on so many other factors, many of which are beyond his control.

It's fair to say that players are largely responsible for much of their own form. Yes, they also rely on their team-mates for structure and support – even Lionel Messi needs the Barcelona set-up to flourish to such incredible degrees (in the way that he hasn't quite for Argentina); and if the ten other players are all performing like hungover park players, then it's hard for one individual (goalkeeper excepted) to excel. However, when a player takes a shot at goal, it is no-one else taking a shot at goal; they may be closed down or see a tackle coming in, but they are the ones who draw back their foot and let fly. Managers can't run out onto the pitch and do it for them (although it would be a nice novelty if one ever tried). Players experience bad fortune, suffer injury and encounter confidence crises, but when they make a decision on the pitch, they get to act it out. By contrast, a coach is like a chess player whose pieces have minds of their own.

Managers are always one or two steps removed from the action. They construct the team (albeit to varying degrees, depending on the time they've had in the job), they devise the tactics and they supply the words of instruction and motivation. Once the eleven cross the white line, they can shout and gesticulate from the sidelines (often like winos in late-night bus stations), and make substitutions, but the players – and the vagaries of cause and effect – take control.

Rarely do the world's very best players fail; wherever they go, they tend to shine. Of course, plenty of *very good* players fail to adapt to new surroundings, but the true geniuses of the game tend to be entirely transposable. But is the same true of managers? For all the difficulties of adapting to a new club, a player can still run out onto the pitch and showcase his own abilities. But a manager is judged by the abilities of others.

My current obsession – borne from a detailed study of the last two decades of top-flight football in England – relates to why good managers don't seem to be interchangeable; why an individual can succeed at one club but then, at times against all logic, fail miserably at another. How can Avram Grant come within a whisker – literally – of winning the Champions League with Chelsea, yet World Cup winner Phil Scolari found himself unable to impress his ideas upon the same personnel? Is it that managers, with their unique skill sets, are as different from one another as players, and need to be selected accordingly?

You wouldn't buy Messi to play him in goal, or Cristiano Ronaldo to deploy at centre-back. And yet when discussing an appointment to a certain club, the general notion seems to be that a manager is either 'good' or 'bad', often based on the results at his previous club; his suitability to the club he is joining is less-well scrutinised. And yet how many managers are so adaptable that they can alter their style to suit the expectations of *any* club, and so successfully unite men and minds that they will find *every* player is subservient and every chief executive compliant?

Factors

Obviously there are many factors to take into account when assessing why managers cannot take their success from club to club in the way players like Johan Cruyff or Diego Maradona looked a class apart wherever they played. Before a manager even gets the chance to make his own decisions, there is the quality of the squad he inherits – and every manager is bequeathed their own unique starting point. (They never begin from scratch, do they?). You can measure certain facets of his inheritance, like the age of the players, but what about the *quality*? – that's hugely subjective. Then there is the issue of who is fit and who is injured, and those great intangibles, such as the players' mental states, including their desire. Success can breed confidence, but also complacency; failure can kill confidence, but also breed hunger.

In my most recent book, '*Pay As You Play*' (co-written with Graeme Riley and Gary Fulcher), I attempt to judge the managerial performances of every Premier League manager since 1992, based on the cost of their personnel (with all figures adjusted to modern day prices using the Transfer Price Index – our own 'football inflation'). For each season, as well as the overall squad cost, we looked at how much of that talent was able to make it onto the pitch. Such an exercise can never be 100% conclusive – numbers can never explain every last detail of such a complex set of circumstances – but it did throw up some interesting results and, perhaps more surprisingly, some revealing trends.

(Stefan Szymanski, Professor of Economics at Cass Business School, City University, and co-author of "*Soccernomics*", has long been using wage bills to show a very strong correlation between spending and league position. Having reviewed our research into transfers and the cost of teams, Stefan devised a graph that, in his words, "shows quite strikingly how similar the measures are" in terms of predicting Premier League success. So we feel that our findings are suitably robust to be used to assess managerial performance, in relation to expected levels.)

While the context of each manager's performance must to a large degree be taken on an individual case study basis – no two situations are ever the same – there does seem to be a definite trend whereby those who achieve success at mid-ranking clubs consistently fail to transfer that to higher profile jobs. In some ways that makes sense – logically, it should be harder the further up the table you travel, where the best are already congregated, with their money, talent and experience. Yet conventional wisdom also tells us that if a manager can surpass expectations with a limited collection of players, 'imagine what he could do with those from a higher bracket'. In the book I call this the 'Newcastle Effect', because of how many successful managers at smaller clubs failed under the obsessive scrutiny of Tyneside. (Although as the otherwise successful Kenny Dalglish also failed there, and Sir Bobby Robson didn't quite deliver what such an expensive team *arguably* should have, there's also the notion that some clubs are just too difficult to manage, perhaps due to too many short-term decisions.)

The problem also seems to relate more to British managers. Perhaps this is because overseas managers rarely come in at the lower or middle level of our top division, and as such, a comparison cannot be made as to how they do when they get the biggest jobs.

Arsène Wenger, Claudio Ranieri, Gérard Houllier, Gianluca Vialli, Martin Jol, Rafael Benítez, Jose Mourinho, Guus Hiddink, Phil Scolari, Juande Ramos, Carlo Ancelotti and Roberto Mancini all took their first jobs in English football at 'top six' clubs, having first achieved notable success in other countries. Outside of this elite (where, of course, an understanding of European football is usually a prerequisite) the aims are much more parochial. These tend to be the most traditionally 'British' of clubs, where the emphasis is usually on striving to make headway in the league table or, increasingly, to simply avoid the financial implosion that comes with relegation.

The success rate of the Premier League's foreign managers is decidedly mixed, but Sir Alex Ferguson aside, they do account for pretty much every trophy won in English football over the past 15 years, as well as all of those won by Premier League clubs in Europe (and in three instances, close-fought runners-up in the Champions League). Since the end of the 1994/95 season, the only British manager other than Ferguson to win either the league title, FA Cup or Champions League is Harry Redknapp, with Portsmouth landing the main domestic cup in 2008. Perhaps as examples of the exceptions that prove the rule, British bosses have only prospered in the second-rate League Cup, for which most big clubs send out their reserve (or even youth) side; six successes since 1995.

Based on the cost of their squads and the XIs they fielded, there was definite success at smaller (or at the time of their appointments, struggling) clubs for Martin O'Neill (Leicester), Graeme Souness (Blackburn), Roy Hodgson (Fulham), Mark Hughes (Blackburn), Alan Curblishley (Charlton), Joe Kinnear (Wimbledon), Sam Allardyce (Bolton), Mike Walker (Norwich) and Gerry Francis (QPR). These represent some of the most notable cases of over-performance in the first 18 seasons of the Premier League. On the back of this relative success, each of these men went on to manage what, at the time of their appointment, would be deemed 'top six' clubs. Based on the finances of these clubs, and the expectations that surrounded them, the best the bunch achieved were the merely acceptable performances from O'Neill at Aston Villa and Curblishley at West Ham, when compared against spending. Though the rest might not have been given sufficient time to get their ideas across, each on the list is perceived to have been a failure in their biggest jobs to date.

The only British manager who seems to have risen from the middle of the pack is Harry Redknapp, who, on top of that FA Cup success with Portsmouth and the general good work at West Ham, has taken Spurs into the Champions League – although even this is only in keeping with the resources at his disposal (but at least he's matching expectations at the sharp end, unlike so many of his over-promoted compatriots). Again, Redknapp may be the exception that proves the rule, and even he isn't without blots to his copybook (relegation with Southampton, and poor performance the following season).

Why is this? Is there a lack of intelligence and mistrust of elite coaching methods in this country? – after all, countries like Italy, Germany and Spain have roughly ten times as many Grade A, B and Pro licensed coaches. (According to a report in *The Guardian*, England has just 2,679, while Spain has 23,995, Italy 29,420 and Germany 34,970. France has over six times as many as England, at 17,588.) Could it also be a problem in terms of the tactical malaise at the grass roots of English football, long bemoaned by the likes of Trevor Brooking? This remains the one 'developed' football nation that, below the top division, still relies heavily (for the most part) on brute force and route-one tactics ahead of skill, technique and intelligence. In England, it seems that you can work your way up by having bigger, stronger, fitter players who can bully their way out of the lower leagues. Skill is not essential.

Indeed, while the Premier League has developed massively in the past 15 years, to provide a wide variety of styles in the top flight, English footballers still remain a peculiarly insular breed; few travel abroad to play, and as most coaches still come from the ranks of the game, it leads to a very narrow outlook.

Writing for *The Independent* during the World Cup, Ian Holloway – himself once seen as the archetypal Brit boss – summed up the cultural lag:

"My favourite TV pundits are Clarence Seedorf and Edgar Davids. I can't get over how educated they are. They know exactly what they are talking about. They understand football, the formations and the problems teams face. But that just sums up the Dutch for me, and we have to try and educate our lads to the same standard ... I don't think our English lads are as football-educated as some of the others in the world."

At the lower levels on the continent, it appears that there is much more emphasis on the kind of approach that will also be required at the highest level; therefore, when successful second- and third- tier managers get promoted to more prominent positions in their domestic leagues, they can continue with similar ideas. But in the Premier League, rudimentary tactics seem to have a very definite glass ceiling; it's hard to recall anyone getting more than 60 points with an almost-exclusive long-ball approach since the 1980s. And the more sophisticated the elite teams become – as more top continental players are lured to the league by the riches on offer and the Champions League participation – the harder it is to bridge the gap with more agricultural approaches. Kick and rush will get you *into* the top division, and maybe a brief flirtation with the upper echelons, but it lacks the necessary sophistication and variety to endure.

Going to Stoke might be a nightmare for the aesthetes (although Andy Gray's notion that Barcelona might suffer there on a wet Wednesday in winter assumes that the home team would actually get a kick of the ball). But overall – due largely to limited resources – a club like Stoke are never going to work their way into the top four with such an approach. They cannot be blamed for their approach; they cut their cloth accordingly, and presumably have no delusions of ever reaching such giddy heights. Should they prosper long enough to buy better players, those players are going to want to get the ball down and play.

Perhaps one of football's great unseen experiments is how pure long-ball methods would work with the most technically gifted players. Imagine the likes of Lionel Messi and Cristiano Ronaldo playing off a target man, with midfielders backing up play in search of the second ball. Getting the ball into the 'mixer' – essentially playing the percentages – may give impoverished sides a fighting chance, but if you are lucky enough to have someone like Messi, delivering accurate passes into his feet in and around the area will surely increase his chances of doing damage; even if he happened to be 6ft 1 (but somehow retained that same delicate grace and balance) you'd surely still want to pass and move, rather than hit and hope. For the sake of argument, it would be fascinating to see someone like John Carew transposed to the Barcelona attack at the expense of Pedro, and insist that, rather than collect the ball in deep areas, David Villa, Andrés Iniesta, Xabi and Messi all look to feed off knock-downs and scraps from great booming balls upfield. With their finishing skills, you'd still expect them to make a good percentage of chances count, whenever the ball ran loose. But only a madman would ask those very players to change from such an incredibly effective way of playing to one that relies more on the lucky bounce of a ball in the area.

A Case Study

As a writer who, until 2010, wrote exclusively about Liverpool FC, this season has proved a minefield in terms of making sense of what's been going on at 'my' club. Why was Roy Hodgson so good at Fulham (relatively speaking), and yet so mediocre on Merseyside? And why was Rafael Benítez so good at Liverpool (relatively speaking) after incredible success at Valencia, and yet, despite two pieces of 'showpiece' silverware, endured a fairly torrid six months at Internazionale?

For 12 years Liverpool had been a 'continental' club in terms of management and player recruitment. While Gérard Houllier and Rafa Benítez didn't bring back the league title, they did perform better than the two Brits they succeeded (Graeme Souness and Roy Evans) in terms of winning trophies. Houllier and Benítez were in charge at a time when the club fell increasingly adrift of the rich elite (in Souness' time, the Reds had the costliest squad in England; since then, the squad has ranked between 3rd and 10th). Rivals were bought by rich benefactors, at a time when money was more limited on Merseyside.

Of the four men, Benítez won the best trophy (the European Cup) and attained the two highest points totals in a season: 86 and 82. Until his final season, he had over-performed in four of his five attempts in the Champions League, and won Premier League points at a cheaper cost than the average for such tallies. But there was suddenly a very conscious decision from the hierarchy that the club must 'go English'. Why? A couple more home-grown players were needed to meet new quota rulings, but that aside, it was seen as a case of getting back to good old British basics, and doing away with fancy foreign methods. It made little sense at the time, and it makes even less now.

Admittedly, Benítez's replacement, the nomadic Roy Hodgson, is not your typical English manager. That said, he had toured the world bringing the 4-4-2 teachings of 1970s FA coaching guru Allen Wade to countries steeped in the tradition of the sweeper system and open-play man marking. So rather than bring continental expertise to the Premier League, he essentially imported the very thing he had been exporting in the first place. That said, it clearly worked well at Fulham. But his time at Blackburn – at the time very much a 'big six' club with the league title won just two years before he arrived – was undeniably disastrous. This was quite a long time ago now – 14 years – and therefore it could be argued that he has hitherto learned some valuable lessons. But despite a fairly promising first year at Ewood Park, he spent £75m (in current money) ahead of the 1998/99 season, including large sums for Kevin Davies (£17m), Christian Daily (£13m), Nathan Blake (£10m) and Callum Davidson (£6m), plus £10m combined on Anders Andersson and Martin Dahlin.

But it went horribly wrong. When Hodgson was sacked in November, Blackburn were 20th, with just nine points from 14 games. By contrast, Brian Kidd, who was in charge at the actual time of relegation – and who therefore gets a lot of the blame – won a far better 26 points from 24 games (which is actually slightly better than relegation form). Hodgson's cost per point that season was £3.16m – which, if sustained for a whole campaign, would have been the *highest ever* (just ahead of Chelsea's, from when they finished 2nd in 2007 with their *über*squad). Kidd's was £1.44m, which in itself is terrible for a relegated side, but more than twice as good as Hodgson's. With the club already marooned at the bottom, and with the squad now built strongly in Hodgson's image, Kidd's task was all the harder. Put Hodgson and Kidd's figures together and it remains the costliest squad and the costliest £XI (the average cost of the XI over 38 games, adjusted with TPI inflation) ever relegated in Premier League history.

Despite this, Hodgson went on his travels again, winning a league and cup double with Copenhagen in 2001. Six years later he returned to steer Fulham to 7th in 2009 and to the Europa League Final in 2010. Top work. But maybe – just maybe – he remains someone who cannot transfer his backs-to-the-wall methods to clubs that, in a competitive league, have to win more than 50% of their games to be seen as sufficiently successful. In a bizarre quirk that suggests his approach will reap the same rewards no matter the quality of the players, in Hodgson's first 16 games of the past three seasons (two with Fulham, one with Liverpool), he racked up either five or six wins each time: always five at home, and on two occasions, one away (the other season saw no away wins). How's that for eerie symmetry? At Fulham in 2009/10, those first 16 league games saw just 20 goals scored; identical to his first 16 league games with the Reds. Hodgson's overall Premier League win record with Fulham was 34%; at Liverpool (at the time of writing) it's 35%. His overall career record in management has seen him win 43% of his league games since the mid-'70s; boosted by wins in the relatively uncompetitive Europa League this season, his overall Liverpool record reads 43%.

Perhaps this is all just coincidental, and, if given time and money to spend, he could get Liverpool back to where they were between 2004 and 2009 – winning more than 55% of games in all competitions. But he was given the money to spend at Blackburn, and at a time when the top teams were investing in talented continental schemers, Hodgson bought mostly bog-standard Brits. On the evidence so far across three Premier League clubs, Hodgson seems a prime example of an excellent smaller club manager whose mentality is not in keeping with one where simply avoiding defeat is not enough.

"You can be a very good manager of a corner shop," former Manchester City player and director Dennis Tueart famously said, "but that doesn't mean you can run a multinational. It's a different skill set." Sam Allardyce overperformed to incredible levels with Bolton, but when it came to managing a relative multinational at Newcastle, he fell short; the fans hated his tactics, and he was hounded out.

Despite all this, perhaps we're seeing a shift in thinking from some smaller clubs. In an exciting development, all three of the promoted clubs have attempted to play a passing style of football: particularly West Bromwich Albion (under Italian Roberto Di Matteo) and Blackpool, whose boss, Ian Holloway, took a year out to study the game under Wigan's Roberto Martinez, before returning with with fresh ideas; even promising, somewhat ambitiously, to try and replicate Barcelona's tiki-taka style. Martinez himself has turned an unfashionable club into one with a more progressive approach, although like Di Matteo, he is a young European who also played in England.

Can they translate this to bigger clubs, if given the chance? Maybe, but it's hard to know for sure until they're tested. But at least they seem to have transferable theories on how the game should be played.

FERNANDO TORRES – LIVERPOOL FC TOP 20 PLAYERS

By Krishen Bhautoo

July, 2012

When contributors to TTT were asked to write a piece about one of the best 20 post-war Liverpool players (as voted for by the readers), for some reason I was instantaneously drawn to our former no.9: Fernando José Torres Sanz.

I think I chose El Niño as it still felt like I hadn't got over an ex who had dumped me. Even though I've got a new girlfriend (Suárez) and a bit on the side (Carroll), I can't but help the occasional fleeting glance at what could have been with my earlier love. And I have to say, I did love Fernando. I hoped that by writing this piece, I would somehow gain closure on a relationship that could have been the sweetest ever.

Usually, I write pieces on statistics and compare metrics, but it doesn't feel right in this instance.

Atlético Madrid

In 1994 and at ten years old, Torres played for his first eleven-a-side team, Rayo 13. The three best players of the season were given the opportunity to try out with Atlético. Thankfully, he had scored 55 goals that season and was one of the chosen three. He signed with Atlético when aged eleven, which was the lowest age group. He states that playing under coach Manolo Rangel was the part of his life when he most enjoyed playing football.

At sixteen he began the season playing in the Honour Division and he finished it in the first team. From the way it started, nobody would have guessed how well it would end. Thanks to a cracked shinbone, and after an operation to put it right, he didn't start playing until December. Things started to pick up in February when he won the Algarve Tournament with the National under-16s. Playing in that summer's under-16s European Championship in England was his target, but it wasn't going to be easy, having been injured and not having taken part in the qualifiers.

Not only was he selected to play in the tournament, Spain went on to win it with the young forward top scorer and chosen as Player of the Tournament (sound familiar?). Not a bad trophy cabinet so far for a 16 year old.

After the under-16s championship, he played a match with the under-18s, and also played in the final of the Youth Champions Cup. A few days later he was called by a senior squad member to tell him that he was going to train with the first team, as he was going to be involved in the pre-season preparation and he might as well get integrated into the set-up. That was a Tuesday; the Wednesday he went to training, the Saturday he was in the squad and on Sunday he made his debut in El Calderon against Leganes – on the 27th May, 2001.

The following week he scored his first goal, against Albacete, and a few weeks later he suffered his first great professional disappointment when his team missed out on promotion to the First Division, on goal difference, after the game against Getafe. He'd been in the first team for a month and had already been through things that some footballers might not experience in their whole career. And his career had only just begun.

It's fair to say that 2002 wasn't a fantastic year for the young Spaniard – just six goals in 36 appearances. But the team reached its goal: promotion. In his own words:

"Two years previous the club had incurred a great debt to the fans, and we'd paid it back by getting back to the place we never should have left in the first place, the First Division."

Things got better for him that summer. In July, now 18, he played in the under-19s European Championship in Norway. They beat the Germans in the final, and he was sharp enough and lucky enough to score the winning goal in a game in which both teams played exceptionally (that sounds familiar too!). They were champions again, and once again he was both top scorer and Player of the Tournament. He enjoyed a good season in the First Division and scored thirteen goals, playing well all year – especially in the home games against Barcelona and Deportivo La Coruña. Those two games marked his footballing career in a way, because after those games the fans really started to believe in him and his ability, stopping him in the street to ask for photos and autographs.

"I'm an accessible person. I think signing autographs after a training session is almost a duty, a moral obligation. I'm aware of the enthusiasm and excitement that the fans feel towards me, the respect and affection they have for me. In fact, not long ago I was one of them. Being important to the fans is a source of pride and satisfaction for me."

His second season in the First Division was even better than the first. At nineteen years old, he made his debut with the national team, and at twenty he was playing in the European Championship. On top of that he had scored 19 league goals. Despite the personal achievements, Spain failed to do as well as expected in the tournament and Atlético lost out on a European spot on the last day of the season, despite winning at Athletic Bilbao. In the seven years spent at Atléti, Torres never achieved the aim he coveted most; European football (apart from losing the Intertoto Cup final on penalties to Villarreal in 2004). Finally, in 2006/07 season, they finished in the proper European places. But he still wouldn't get to play in Europe with his beloved Atléti because he would be playing his football in England. He may one day still get his chance. He said he would be interested in returning to former club Atlético eventually:

"I don't know if I will retire there, but I would like to go back and finish some things that are left to do."

Liverpool

After the 2006 World Cup, Torres stated that he turned down the chance to join Chelsea. Instead, he extended his contract with Atlético for another year, taking it to 2009.

However, in 2007:

"Summer began as normal with time to rest and look back, but a phone call changed everything. Liverpool manager Rafa Benítez wanted me to form part of his new project. It was late afternoon and he caught me out walking the dogs! When the phone rang, I saw that it was a number from abroad. I didn't answer. The next day I received another call, this time I picked up the phone. When I heard Rafa's voice, I froze. I was not expecting a call from him. He explained to me his plans and ideas, and I replied that he should speak to the owner of Atlético Madrid, Miguel Angel Gil. There wouldn't be any problems as long as the clubs could reach an agreement. From that moment on, I felt that this was not just any offer. A great club, the most successful in English football, was asking for me, when they could have gone after any world class striker."

We all have our memories of Fernando in a red shirt. His first goal against his current employers. His half volley vs Blackburn. The winner vs Inter Milan at the San Siro. Taking the ball from Vidic and slotting past Van der Sar. Hat-trick vs Reading after having lumps kicked out of him all game. There are almost too many of his 81 Liverpool goals to mention. Some of the happiest moments of my footballing life have been down to this one man.

Torres made his competitive debut for Liverpool against Villa in a 2–1 win on 11th August, 2007. He made his first appearance in the Champions League four days later. His first Premier League goal came on his Anfield debut on 19th August, in the 16th minute of a 1–1 draw against Chelsea. His first hat trick came in a 4–2 victory over Reading in the League Cup in September, with all of his goals coming in the second half. His first goals in the Champions League came on his third appearance in the competition as Liverpool beat Porto 4–1. He scored twice.

He was named Premier League Player of the Month for February 2008, during which he scored four goals in four appearances, including a hat-trick against Middlesbrough. This hat-trick, and another in a 4–0 victory over West Ham in March 2008, meant he became the first Liverpool player since Jack Balmer in 1946 to score a hat-trick in successive matches. Later in March, after he scored a header against Reading at Anfield, he became the first Liverpool player since Robbie Fowler to score 20 league goals in a season. In April, he scored another Champions League goal, this time against Arsenal in the quarter-final second leg. This goal took him onto 29 goals for the 2007–08 season in all competitions, eclipsing Michael Owen's personal record for goals in a season. In April 2008, it was announced that Torres had made a six-man shortlist for the PFA Players' Player of the Year award, which was eventually won by Cristiano Ronaldo. The Spanish international was also nominated for the PFA Young Player of the Year Award, which was won by Cesc Fàbregas and was named in the PFA Team of the Year. In May, he finished second to Ronaldo for the FWA Footballer of the Year award.

He was named in the FIFPro World XI team for the 2007–08 season, on 27th October. He was named on the shortlist for the FIFA World Player of the Year award in December 2008, and eventually came in third place behind Ronaldo and Lionel Messi. He was named in the PFA Team of the Year for the second season running in April 2009. Torres was named in the FIFPro World XI for the second successive season in December 2009. His stoppage-time winning goal against Aston Villa on 29th December 2009 made him the fastest Liverpool player ever to score 50 league goals.

In total, he scored 81 goals in 142 appearances.

He had a fantastic three and a half years at Liverpool. Whilst no trophies were won, he managed to play the best football of his career with (as he says) the best footballer he has ever played with, Steven Gerrard: high praise from a Spanish international.

But as we know, the honeymoon and relationship ended with a bad taste left in the mouth. With the club in turmoil, I'm certain Torres would have left the previous summer if he had had the chance. Liverpool were on a slippery slope and he wanted out. In a way, I don't blame him. He made the huge step of leaving his home country and boyhood club to join Liverpool in the hope of winning trophies. Something that even after a fantastic 2008/09 season, we looked to be moving further away from.

What I (and I suspect most Liverpool fans) found difficult to stomach was the way he left. On 9th January 2011, after Kenny was appointed, he was interviewed in *The People*:

"My head is in Liverpool and on helping to save our season."

As we know, what footballers say and what happens aren't always the same. On the 31st he moved to Chelsea. The deal was shrouded in a certain degree of mystery. We know from John W Henry that the cost of Torres' move to Chelsea was dependent upon what Newcastle wanted for Carroll, but a few murmurs and rumours emerged that he made a massive u-turn at the 11th hour, stating that he was furious that his agent had handed in the transfer request after we had a deal in principle to sign Suárez. If true, one can only imagine the partnership that these two could have developed if the agent had got it right. It could have been beautiful. If he had moved abroad in summer, I think he would have left with much more good will from the Anfield faithful.

NUMBERS THAT NUMB: THE AMAZING MAZE

By Anthony McKenna
June, 2013

Take a dice, or countless die, and place in a washing machine; hit fast spin. Watch the swirl of tumbling complexity. Sit down, or at least stand back. Try to make sense of the bombardment. Seek sequences, see patterns. Analyse, rationalise, seek truth and fathom falsehoods. Think logarithmically, think linearly, err greatly. Assess, appraise, be aghast. Be amazed.

It gets worse: the faces of the die are not conventionally dotted from one to six, but different number formats, sometimes of several digits, catching your eye. Fractions, percentages, decimals, integers, odds and evens, round numbers, square roots – a numerical plague of biblical proportion. Amidst the maelstrom, fail to make sense; defer to emotions; make nonsensical conclusions.

Numbers are, in short, mind-numbing – an invitation to embark on a tortuous traverse through a maze. Successful orientation is compounded by the sheer volume of numerical data, and the volume is exploding. It's like opening the door to your back garden to be greeted by the Savannah: mowing the lawn will take an eternity.

And if the task is epic, it is further compounded by our limitations in terms of understanding numbers and utilising them to understand The Beautiful Game. Emotions do get in the way of our willingness to embrace numbers. Even if you possess a Black Belt in Sudoku, there are still problems ... it's all in the mind.

The Tortoise & The Hare

The statistician's biggest challenge is the strangled bias of human emotion; opinion takes centre stage long before statistics accrue to the point of reasonable sample sizes. Emotions are the Hare, Statistics the tortoise. The tortoise may outpace in the longer term, but emotions, and the expression of such, have the advantage of immediacy and social visibility. Numbers, conversely, are garnered incrementally: slow burn undercurrents that must, by definition, concede the floor to the swifter impact of subjective gut debate ... at least for some time. Then something breaks.

On January 3rd and June 3rd respectively, esteemed TTT statisticians Andrew Beasley and Dan Kennett became active, once more carpet bombing the Social Media. Twitter was on red emotional alert.

Tweets by Andrew Beasley (3.1.13):

"Joe Cole... 2 Goals 1 Assist... Total 3... Mins Played 794... Mins per Goal or Assist 264.97"

"Bale... 7 Goals, 1 Assist ... Total 8... Mins Played 2451 ... Mins per Goal or Assist ... 306.28"

Tweets by Dan Kennett (3.6.13):

"Downing Chances Created: 14 in 633 mins vs teams above (2 per game), 51 in 1561 mins vs teams below (2.9 per game)"

"Downing Chances Created: 57 in 1721 mins (3 per game) since Fulham (end of LB experiment brought back into team), 8 in 473 mins before"

You go to buy a jacket. You see one you like. You happen to be in a rush and, in your haste, your reliance on a guestimate will do. You choose a jacket that seems approximate to your size. Later, you will try it on.

But for now, re-read the tweets by two of TTT's finest. If you have not seen them before, or the reaction to them, absorb and assess. Do the tweets fit? One set of tweets addresses numbers contrasting Goals and Assists for two different players; the other set indicates the creativity output of a third player. What unites each set is that they depict Liverpool players in a positive light; players whom populist opinion had already condemned.

Bridging The Gap

Dyscalculia is the overlooked twin of the more mentioned dyslexia, though not an identical twin so to speak. Where the latter denotes a problem with words, the former is about problems with numbers – and it may surprise some that there is such a word. I'm not a statistician or an analyst, nor do I have a gifted mathematical mind. There was a time when I thought I may be affected by dyscalculia, such was my struggle with numbers. Fortunately, this is not the case.

As we shall see, however, even without such a diagnosis, the mind's grasp of statistics and numbers is still challengingly obfuscated by its own limitations. Emotion becomes King; it is easier. A refusal to abdicate is premised on strength of feeling and preference for a short cut – why take a longer route?

But perception is altered, disturbingly so. Emotions are the spectacles through which we look at mirrors, the type of mirrors in fairground Fun Halls. What we see, judge and assess can be filtered as a distortion of reality. Someone put hallucinogenic illusions in your coffee, even if it tastes good.

As I am neither a statistician nor an analyst but a mere 'thinker', I realise that I must wrestle with the numbers. Football has changed in terms of how the game is being interpreted and understood. I must explore the literature; how my mind works in reaction (or may not work appropriately), and why the numbers can be so confusing at times. Here, I share that journey, and what I have learnt; maybe inaccurately so. But how I used to watch football will no longer suffice. I need to run with the revolution before it turns too fast.

That revolution has served me well so far; discovering many of Donald Rumsfield's 'Unknown Unknowns' has been attained. All those years ago, how incredible would be the idea that shots outside the box hardly lead to goals or that corners are over-rated and that Final Third Regains really matter. But there is much more to be discovered. For this, we need to bridge the gap between those who are accomplished 'Numbers' guys and those who are not. Lay people like me need to understand that we enter a maze where obstacles abound.

Reasons To Be Careful: Parts One, Two and Three

Part One

Numbers, in evolutionary terms, are quite new. Possibly about 10,000 years old, writes Alex Bellos. (*Alex's Adventures In NumberLand*). But the author points to a more fascinating and quite astonishing fact. The way we appraise numbers, or quantity, is not entirely reflective of our intuitive equipment; an influence of culture has overwritten our natural inclination. Over 10,000 years ago, before numbers, we utilised our logarithmic instinct to appraise quantity. This is our more natural propensity, yet education systems teach us to understand numbers in more linear fashion; as evenly spaced numbers on a ruler for instance.

This has been demonstrated experimentally. Pre-school children in Western Cultures, before formal education intervenes, share the trait of cultures where no number words or symbols exist: they appraise ratios between amounts. For example, shown a series of pictures depicting dots one to ten, they:

"...see that five dots are five times bigger than one dot, but ten dots are only twice as big as five dots." – Alex's Adventures In NumberLand.

Conversely, we, as adults, have been westernised to place the numbers sequentially as 1, 2, 3, 4, 5, etc.. They become evenly spaced. That said, apparently we do still apply the more intuitive logarithmic approach, particularly when we digest huge numbers (or try to digest as the case may be). We think of them as closer together. We can, for example, tend to equate all Premier League players as being paid 'huge amounts of money'. But there are significant differences in individual cases; 'huge amounts of money' implies the same thing. Here, we are quantifying amounts with approximations. Something we would not do to reflect the amount of goals in a football match; a 3-1 final score, for instance, is easily understood and untainted by the need for approximation.

This was news. Whilst we have a Language Instinct – born into the world with innate faculties that predispose us towards the way we use and understand the language of words – our minds are not inherently equipped for dealing with amounts the way we do; rather that cultural influences have bent the mind to work in this direction. Worse still, and specifically addressing statistics, our minds do not deal with such entities too easily.

Part Two

"Why is it so difficult for us to think statistically? We easily think associatively, we think metaphorically, we think causally, but statistics requires thinking about many things at once, which is something that System One is not designed to do." – Daniel Kahneman, *Thinking Fast and Slow.*

Kahneman depicts System One and System Two as personality traits of two distinctively different protagonists in our minds; they are fictional metaphors to help illustrate the different mental tasks we need to perform. System One is effortless, reactive and fast-thinking, intuitive by design. System Two deals with much slower types of thought processes; this approach, being more deliberate, is damn hard work!

Unfortunately, System One bears more influence on our judgement than we bargain for; snap assessments may be useful in many areas of our lives, but not when absorbing statistics it seems.

Preferably, we would like to see our own assessments as indicative of the methodological, slow and careful thinking of System Two; it makes us appear more clever and thoughtful. But this is not always the case; emotions get obstructively in the way. Most times, we will not even see our own transgressions, believing that we are, in fact, prudent and wise.

If in a maze you hit a brick wall, you will turn back; eliminate this blind alley to avoid future calamity. Think; but think slowly. That means take time to listen to System Two. It's that easy. Or is it? Often System Two will take its lead from System One; there is a tension between the two. We all possess the Yin and Yang of a Janus face; one is outwardly looking in an instant; its swiftness obstructs the other that needs to look in, more methodically. But this is not all.

Part Three

We possess yet another regrettable biological trait. It is an inclination for the truth of sorts, but not a wholesome one. We talk about a hindsight bias; but bias can look anywhere, by any means necessary – because self-validation will always commit the vanity sin to which it is biologically driven.

"It seems we have an innate tendency to seek out and overvalue evidence that confirms a given hypothesis." – Ben Goldacre, *Bad Science.*

Any scheme will do? Personally, I would add the following: we also may seem motivated to disregard – or deliberately not seek out – evidence that is contrary to the belief system we hold dear.

We can also be selective with evidence that offers comfort in justifying losing a player. I wonder: is this why we embrace the Stats that tell us Liverpool win more frequently when Luis Suárez is not playing? This sanctions the notion that his departure will not hurt us greatly. Yet we do not apply the opposite analysis.

We won more frequently when Andy Carroll played; he is leaving, without too much protest from the fan base. But of course, Liverpool paid over the odds for him, and we are prejudiced by that number: £35 million. So, 'he will not fit into Rodgers' system', we say; there, it's done; sorted, rationalised. Ditto for Jamie Carragher and tiki-taka? However, go and seek out his passing stats for last season.

How do we know a component will not fit a system until we try it? Too late – emotional assessment has already suffocated attention to the irrational outcome of the Carroll solution. Take a loss, take a mighty loss; get stung, again.

Hearts & Minds

"Downing is crap, shits out of tackles, and is just shit ... and shit sticks". This is analysis; to some people anyway. Laughingly bereft of an 'assist' for such a long time in the early part of his Liverpool career, the jokes came thick and fast. But people ignored the other stats; emotions became the isolated tools of analysis, and imperfect tools at that.

This was also the season when Liverpool not only hit the woodwork a record number of times, but were sorely struggling to convert chances in general. Downing, however, had met his own remit; tackling was not one of those requirements, that's just a red herring. Or else, go and judge Reina on how many goals he scores.

Ultimately, Downing delivered the goods his role demanded: creating chances. If the Chef prepares a good meal on a plate, is it his fault if the diners drop the dish? It's a team game, remember?

These things matter. Do we want to sell 'bad' players who are actually contributing to the cause? We want our club to progress; our emotional apparatus may thwart progress if we allow it to bully our assessments. The soul-search for every fan is the truth; but we are not biologically cut out for the task of impartiality. Our opinions are already cloaked in the emotional and psychological uniform we choose to wear; the constraints of the strait jacket are difficult to remove.

Recognition of this weakness should be an almighty strength, the acknowledgement that our navigation equipment is faulty will enable us not to trust it implicitly and foster caution. We need to take a slower amble through the maze and via other means. Advice from others holds value; other people have already taken a slower, deeper consideration of the route. Those people are statisticians and analysts; embrace them.

Shock & Awe

A closed mind becomes an empty mind. But the dial has been set. Assessments have been made without realisation that the evidence is flawed; now the world is once again flat. Should anyone try to talk a different walk? Should anyone tweet anything that remotely depicts Joe Cole and Stewart Downing in a positive light? The car crash of cognitive dissonance looms. It's shock and awe.

What? That can't be right; Joe Cole and Stewart Downing? A flurry of tweets in response and the debates are launched; counter-attacks of consternation rail for the truth. People are trapped on the stickiness of emotional flypaper, unable to wriggle free. Rejoinders to the tweets, usually beginning with 'but', reach a general consensus: this is not what they see!

But I understand why. As Goldacre warns: *we place an over-confidence in our own assessments*. Remember that jacket you bought in a rush? You now try it on, bewildered to find that it actually doesn't fit. How could your judgement be so wrong? So close, so upfront, so easy really – or, at least, it should have been.

Your judgement, using no guide other than the human brain, was fallible. If your cranial apparatus failed to measure, accurately, with regard to the mundane task of buying a jacket, how will it fare in the evaluation of more complex undertakings? With an imperfect view, at such a distance, the odds are never in your favour.

A Room With A View

So what do people actually see when watching football? The Armchair Supporter, a much-maligned figure of the past, is now the most important consumer of the game; otherwise why would Sky pay so much for TV rights? Obviously, more people watch the game at home, or in a pub, than those housed in the stadia, and there is nothing wrong with that.

But think about the view all scenarios entail, even in a stadium: the singular angle at your disposal, the obstructions, and the distractions. It is a limited view, obscured and corrupted, beyond perfect reach. Furthermore, you absorb emotionally, not rationally, and your human mind, without question, is unable to count the frequency of passing percentages, chances created, clear-cut chances, etc..

Opinions take root without counting the things that might count. Yet the collation of such metrics requires the painstakingly slow process of detection; the work that statisticians and analysts do; the stuff of Kahneman's System Two. We watch football using System One, our emotional hard drive. It lets us down constantly. You could be wrong! Is it wise to run amok in the Maze?

Where application of considerable thought, time, study and diligence has taken place, how is it feasible to question this with – on the spot – emotional knee jerk reaction? If your doctor makes a diagnosis, would you tell that professional: "hey, this isn't right?" Or put it another way, as Dan Kennett tweets with captive aptness, humour and ironic twist:

"If Stewart Downing creates a high-quality chance in front of 45,000 people does it actually exist? #zen" – Dan Kennett, 3.6.13.

Stats Not All

Neither Andrew Beasley nor Dan Kennett arrived at their respective stats as defences of Cole or Downing; in fact, if I recall rightly, they both expressed surprise at their findings. I am not trying to defend Cole or Downing either; rather the core principle involved – that if numbers ever run at a tangent to your emotional expectation, then we must learn to question our emotions first, then the numbers, then everything else. Stats alone are not enough – good statisticians acknowledge that. Debating them is also fine, but it is the immediate emotional assumption of their wrongfulness that is not, just because they do not sanction the belief system you have formulated.

I mentioned 'everything else'. That 'everything else' includes the role of chance, randomness and luck. Those whose mantra is 'nah, don't do stats' will surely have a more difficult job accepting the incidence of chance and luck in The Beautiful Game. But those entities are now taking a serious hold within the football debate.

Recall our season of record woodwork hits; that, and our failure to convert more chances, was rationalised by some as the players not 'being clinical enough'; or simply, 'not good enough'. Try, at least, to broaden your assessments to incorporate this:

"And so, after all those hours and hours of watching goals, how many did Lames and his team qualify as fortunate, as owing more than a little to luck? The answer is 44.4 per cent, though that varied a little from league to league and competition to competition." – Anderson/Sally, *The Numbers Game.*

How blasphemous. That's practically half! How terrible for those to have to relinquish control when the need is to be in control. Yet, luck is a deity which even the atheists crave: "hope I get lucky"; "I need a bit of luck"; "wish me luck". It is buried deep in our psyche, and it takes place on a football field. Take time, also, to reflect on how Liverpool have fared in the Debatable Decisions Tables over the last couple or so seasons (most harshly treated in 2011/12 and 2012/13).

Again, as with stats, the presence of luck is not to throw all hope at it. Anderson and Sally point firmly to budget, training and optimising the use of players at your disposal etc. Black Swans and randomness, however, do warrant consideration in the whole scheme of things; a significant part in fact. But as with stats, wise people know these entities are not the only things where to dip your brush – on football's gigantic palette – to paint a picture. Refusal to engage with any one of these, however, may render your picture incomplete.

Luck, incidentally, takes place off the field too. If it makes you feel better, call it Sturridge: a player tossed between two billionaire Football Club owners, now he is ours. Call it Coutinho – what were Milan thinking of? But, thank you ... always.

Journey's End (for now)

If you're in a Maze and you hit a brick wall, turn back; eliminate this blind alley. I'm still in the Maze, but slowly finding my way around the terrain. It's the Savannah after all. My grasp of numbers, no doubt, will continue to err; but knowing that the human mind is an imperfect tool – regarding comprehension and use – is a start at least. I can resist the temptation for my emotions to paint the picture single-handedly. I can take numbers, and all the other variables, inherent in The Beautiful Game, including Black Swans, and maybe get closer to the truth.

Mind you, it is exhausting; sometimes you need to take a break from the journey. Time to hit the 'Stop' button on that washing machine – let the die settle until the numbers disappear. Close the door to your back garden; mow a bit more of the lawn later. It's been emotional.

"To be "at sixes and sevens" is a British English idiom used to describe a state of confusion or disarray." – Wikipedia.

BACK TO LFC'S FUTURE

By Dave Cronin
December, 2012

Just before Christmas 2012, we ran a competition to see which subscriber could come up with the best summation of the fortunes of Liverpool FC since the launch of TTT. This light-hearted take by Dave Cronin received the most votes.

It was the 14th March, 2009. Liverpool had just beaten Manchester United 4-1 at Old Trafford to revive a title race that had looked over. Just days earlier, the Reds had routed Real Madrid 4-0 in the Champions League. I was on cloud nine.

I sat down feeling a sense of contentment I had rarely known. Mentally I reeled off the names of our players – the heroes that had vanquished our mortal enemy in such style. Reina, Carragher, Hyypia, Škrtel, Aurelio, Mascherano, Lucas, Riera, Kuyt, Gerrard, Torres. And then we had Alonso, Agger, Babel and Arbeloa who hadn't even started today. Just the names of some of these players filled me with excitement. "We have a great team and a great manager," I thought to myself.

Suddenly there was a loud noise accompanied by a white flash. I ran to my door to see a silver DeLorean in my driveway. As I stepped outside, its door lifted open and an old man with zany white hair climbed out. It was the Doc.

"Marty, you gotta come back with me!" he called.

Just to clarify, my name isn't Marty but that's the Doc for you. Some days he thinks I'm his brother, others his aunt. He's addressed me as worse names than Marty so I decided to indulge him on this occasion.

"Where?" I asked him.

"Back to the future!" he exclaimed.

"No, no, no, Doc," I replied. "We've just beaten Man U 4-1! I just want to reflect, bask in the glory and thank God for Rafa Benítez."

"Well, bring him along. This concerns him too," said the Doc.

"Wait a minute, Doc," said I. "What are you talking about? What happens in the future? What, do we become assholes or something?"

"No, no, no, Marty," answered the Doc. "Both you and Rafa turn out fine. It's Liverpool FC, Marty something has got to be done about Liverpool FC!"

"Okay," I said. "You're going to have to elaborate. What happens to Liverpool in the future?"

Reluctantly, the Doc sat down on the front of the DeLorean, accepting he would need to divulge more of what he knew in order to convince me to go with him.

"Rafa is going to be sacked as manager after next season," he said.

"Sacked?" I exclaimed. "Bastards! Why would they sack him?"

"Liverpool will finish 7th behind Spurs and Man City."

"Spurs? Spurs are crap! They've had to bring 'Harry Houdini' just to keep them up this season! How can they finish above us? I don't believe it. We've got a great team here. We're so close to landing the title. We've got the money from the Robbie Keane sale to reinvest in the summer. All we need to do is keep this group together and add a couple of quality players and we can take that final step to being Champions."

"Forget the Keane money," said the Doc. "You'll never see that again. And forget keeping the group together. Alonso will be off in the summer. The club won't strengthen in the summer and you'll still only have Torres and N'Gog as forward options next season."

"No way! That's ridiculous!" I shouted. "They sack Rafa? Who will they bring in to replace him?"

The Doc shifted uncomfortably and looked down at his feet avoiding my gaze. "Roy

Hodgson," he said.

"Roy Hodgson? Roy Hodgson? Is this a joke? Roy *Hodgson*? The Fulham manager? Why? How could anyone possibly think he was a better manager for Liverpool than Rafa Benítez?"

"And he'll sign Paul Konchesky for Liverpool too."

"What? Konchesky is crap!"

"I know."

"This is a nightmare," I said.

"It gets worse," said the Doc.

"How?"

"Liverpool will sell Mascherano to Barcelona where he will win the Champions League and La Liga playing as a centre-half."

"What? Are you sure?"

"Hodgson will replace him with an utterly useless washed up Danish footballer and will try to get the team playing for nil-nils with two solid banks of four lined up in front of the goalkeeper. Stoke will dominate possession against Liverpool ... while beating them 2-0. Liverpool will lose 2-0 to Everton and Hodgson will describe it as the best performance under his leadership. Hodgson will insult the Liverpool supporters and lose League games at home to Blackpool and Wolves and get knocked out of the League Cup by bottom-tier Northampton at Anfield."

"Who else will we sign in the future?" I asked.

"Joe Cole," he said.

"Joe Cole?" I said. "Oh well that's encouraging. Joe Cole is a quality player!"

"Not in the future," said the Doc. "He's actually going to be chronically useless for the Reds and his £100K a week wages are going to prove a terrible burden for the club."

"Is there nothing good you can tell me?" I asked.

"We will finally get shot of Hicks and Gillett. They will dramatically lose a high court battle – which fans will celebrate like a cup final – leaving the dud duo powerless to prevent the sale of the club just days before it would otherwise have been put into administration."

"Well that at least is positive," I said. "We finally get the Yanks out? So who was the club sold to? Mega-rich Arabs? Sheikhs? A Russian billionaire?"

"No," said the Doc. "It will be sold to some other Americans."

"Oh," I said feeling a tad disappointed. "Are they mega-rich Americans who invest significant amounts of their own money in our team?"

"No, they are practical guys who want to run the club within its own means and won't deficit-spend to finance improvement on the pitch."

"But they will build the new stadium won't they?"

"No. You'll stay at Anfield."

"So what else happens in the future?" I asked.

"Well," he said. "What are your thoughts on Lucas Leiva?"

"Lucas Leiva? He's shit. I can't understand why Rafa plays him. I just don't know what he sees in him. He's *supposed* to Brazilian! He's the least Brazilian footballer I've ever seen."

"Well, in the season after next, Lucas Leiva will win the Fans' Player of the Season Award," said the Doc.

"This is messed up!" I said.

"And just after that we will sign Stewart Downing."

"Stewart Downing?" I said. "He's rubbish. We shouldn't be lowering our standards to the point where we're signing players like Downing. Are we really that short of cash that we have to sign garbage like Downing?"

"Actually you pay £20 million for him."

"£20 million!? For Stewart Downing?! How can that be? Does he suddenly become brilliant in the future?"

"No, he's still average at best and an utter coward," said the Doc. "The Reds are just throwing cash around wastefully at that point. Liverpool also sign Andy Carroll from Newcastle for £35 million then loan him to West Ham for £1m, and sign Jordan Henderson from Sunderland for £16m and offer him to Fulham in exchange for Clint Dempsey."

"That's crazy!" I said. "There's no way Clint Dempsey is worth £16m!"

"Neither is Jordan Henderson," replied the Doc.

"None of this makes sense." I said. "Is this all Hodgson's doing?"

"No, by this time he's been sacked and appointed England manager."

"You're kidding?"

"Liverpool reappoint Kenny Dalglish as manager."

"King Kenny?" I said. "Wow! And how does that work out?"

"Initially it's great, as he takes over from Hodgson with the Reds languishing 12th. The Reds surge up the table, beating Manchester United 3-1 and Manchester City 3-0. He gets given the job on a permanent basis for the following season. He wins a League Cup and gets to the FA Cup Final, but overall it's a bit of a mess. He only manages to win five home games in the league all season, and loses at Anfield to West Brom, Wigan and Fulham. As a consequence, he gets sacked after only a season and a half."

"So wait a minute," I said, "Are you saying we'll sack three managers in just two years?"

"That's right," confirmed the Doc.

"So, who comes in to replace Kenny?" I asked.

"Brendan Rodgers," replied the Doc.

"*Who?*" I asked.

"Brendan Rodgers," the Doc repeated. "Oh, of course! I forgot no-one has heard of Brendan Rodgers yet."

"So who is he?" I asked. "His name doesn't sound too exotic. I take it he's English?"

"Irish actually," replied the Doc. "Liverpool poach him from Swansea City."

"Swansea City?" I exclaimed, struggling to comprehend. "We're going to let a proven world-class manager go and start nicking managers from Swansea City? What happens to Rafa?"

"Oh, he ends up managing Chelsea who, by the way, sign Fernando Torres and win the Champions League. Although ironically Torres isn't very good in the future."

"I've got to tell you, Doc," I said, "I'm having a hard time taking all this in? It's as though the future has been written by a Man United fan?"

"I doubt it," answered the Doc.

"Why's that?" I asked.

"Because Man City win the League," he replied.

"Now you're just being silly, Doc," I said.

"No, Marty, it's all true," he insisted. "It is what will come to pass. That's why we need to take the time machine, go into the future and try to put things right."

"Or..." I suggested, "we could just go back in time and relive the glory days."

"Ooh, that's a much better idea," he said. "Screw the future, let's go back to the past!"

I climbed into the DeLorean along with the Doc.

"Hey, Doc," I said. "We better back up, we don't have enough road to get up to 88."

"Road?" he replied. "Where we're going we don't need roads."

* * *